THE KING

THE KING

The Life of Charles III

Christopher Andersen

G

Gallery Books

New York   London   Toronto   Sydney   New Delhi

Gallery Books
An Imprint of Simon & Schuster, Inc.
1230 Avenue of the Americas
New York, NY 10020

First Gallery Books hardcover edition November 2022

GALLERY BOOKS and colophon are registered trademarks of Simon & Schuster, Inc.

For information about special discounts for bulk purchases, please contact Simon &
Schuster Special Sales at 1-866-506-1949 or business@simonandschuster.com.

The Simon & Schuster Speakers Bureau can bring authors to your live event. For
more information or to book an event, contact the Simon & Schuster Speakers
Bureau at 1-866-248-3049 or visit our website at www.simonspeakers.com.

Interior design by Davina Mock-Maniscalco

3   5   7   9   10   8   6   4   2

Library of Congress Cataloging-in-Publication Data is available.

ISBN 978-1-6680-3031-8
ISBN 978-1-5011-8161-0 (ebook)

Insert Photo Credits: Alpha-Globe Photos, Inc.: 25, 32, 38; Rex/Shutterstock: 1, 2, 3, 4, 5,
6, 7, 8, 9, 10, 11, 12, 13, 14, 15, 16, 17, 18, 19, 20, 21, 22, 23, 24, 26, 27, 28, 29, 30, 31,
33, 34, 35, 36, 37, 39, 40, 41, 42, 43, 44, 45, 46, 47, 48, 49, 50, 51, 52, 53, 54, and 55.

Printed and Bound in the UK using 100% Renewable
Electricity at CPI Group (UK) Ltd

For Graham, Charlotte, and Teddy

Uneasy lies the head that wears a crown.
—The king in *Henry IV* by William Shakespeare

CONTENTS

The Queen died peacefully
at Balmoral this afternoon.

The King and the Queen Consort
will remain at Balmoral this evening
and will return to London tomorrow.

Thursday, 8th September 2022

—Buckingham Palace

PREFACE

She's gone. A colossus clutching a purse, standing astride eight decades and five generations, she was arguably the most famous person of the modern age. Her reign—by far the longest of any British monarch—spanned fifteen prime ministers, fourteen US presidents, and seven popes. By one estimate, fully 98 percent of the Earth's population had known only a world with Queen Elizabeth II in it.

For her entire time on the throne, a son and heir waited in the wings. From the first moment he drew breath, his fate was preordained. Like only a handful of people on the planet—those others destined to inherit a crown—he was born to do one job and one job only. There was no way of knowing that he would have to wait a lifetime to actually do it.

In the meantime, the world watched as Charles, Prince of Wales, grew from gilded infancy to dignified middle age and beyond—caught up along the way, as the unfaithful husband of the idolized Princess Diana and father to princes William and Harry, in scandal, tragedy, and heartbreak.

Yet for all the pomp and pageantry and spectacle and palace intrigue and history in the making—not to mention the millions of words written about him and his celebrated family—King Charles III remains an enigma. This is his story.

Prince Charles is the loneliest human being on earth.
—Charles's friend Patti Palmer-Tomkinson

ONE

PHANTOMS, BULLIES, AND A TUNNEL OF GRIEF

Westminster Abbey is filled with ghosts. Little wonder. More than three thousand people are interred here, in elaborately carved tombs or beneath the cold marble floor. Charles Dickens, Rudyard Kipling, Charles Darwin, George Frideric Handel, Laurence Olivier, and Sir Isaac Newton are among those buried at Westminster Abbey. Knights and their ladies also rest in peace within the abbey's hallowed walls, along with adventurers and poets and prime ministers and military heroes. They all share the honor with no fewer than seventeen British monarchs, including Edward V (who as a boy was smothered to death in 1483, along with his younger brother the Duke of York, on orders of their uncle Richard III), the headless (or at least not attached) Mary, Queen of Scots—whose body lies within feet of the cousin who had her executed, Queen Elizabeth I—and Elizabeth's tormented and terrifying half sister "Bloody Mary" Tudor.

The ghosts Charles might sense on the day that he prepares for his own coronation are of a more recent vintage. It was in this spot that in 1953, as a boy of only four, he sat squirming between his granny the Queen Mother and his aunt Margaret while Mummy was being crowned queen—the climax of history's first televised coronation. It was in this spot in 1997 that Earl Spencer, delivering the moving eulogy at his sister Diana's funeral, blamed the press for killing the Princess of Wales while at the same time chastising her in-laws, the royal family, for their lack of

1

compassion. It was in this spot that five years later, after donning his naval uniform as part of the "Vigil of Princes" watching over the Queen Mother's coffin as she lay in state in nearby Westminster Hall, Charles bade a final farewell to his beloved Granny, dead at the age of 101. And it was on this spot in 2011 that his son and heir Prince William wed the beautiful, stylish, and infinitely patient Kate Middleton—who had waited a full decade for a marriage proposal—in a ceremony watched by two billion people around the world.

It is now the spot where Elizabeth II's eldest child and heir will at last be crowned King of England—the job he was promised from birth, and has grown old waiting to do. Charles has known all along that when it came, this moment would be bittersweet if for no other reason than his mother would either have died or become too frail to continue in the role she had played on the world stage longer than any of her predecessors. "It is better not to have to think too much about it," he once said, struggling to find just the right words to describe his peculiar dilemma. "I think about it a bit, but it's much better not to. This is something that, you know, if it comes to it, and regrettably it comes as the result of the death of your parent, which is, you know, not so nice, to say the least."

For all the spectacle, ritual, and pomp, for all the prayers and planning, most coronations have not gone smoothly. Amid rumors that her uncle was planning to kill her and grumbling in Parliament over the cost, Victoria's 1838 coronation was interrupted briefly when eighty-two-year-old Lord Rolle tripped while attempting to greet the new queen and, to Her Majesty's horror, rolled backward down the steps.

Just two days before his scheduled coronation in 1902, the famously libidinous Edward VII, Victoria's eldest son, was stricken with appendicitis, an illness that at the time had a high mortality rate. The new king might well have died had his physician not performed what was then a radical new surgical procedure, allowing him to be crowned six weeks later than originally planned.

George V, Edward's son, was coronated in 1911 amid murmurs of alcoholism and rumors of bigamy that ended in a sensational libel trial; the French journalist who alleged in print that King George had secretly married an admiral's daughter in Malta wound up going to prison for a year.

Edward VIII's accession to the throne on January 20, 1936, proved so thorny that he had no coronation at all. His insistence on marrying the American divorcée Wallis Simpson precipitated a full-blown constitutional crisis that ended only with his abdication "for the woman I love" after just eleven months, on December 11. Edward was supposed to be crowned on May 12, 1937, so it was decided to keep the date for the coronation of his younger brother Bertie as George VI. "S-s-s-s . . . same date," Charles's painfully shy, stuttering grandfather said. "D-d-d-d . . . different king." This time it was the Dean of Westminster who fell down the steps while carrying St. Edward's crown—which the Archbishop of Canterbury then fumbled as he tried to place it on the sovereign's head. With his wife, Elizabeth Bowes-Lyon, crowned the Queen Consort beside him, the accidental king was convinced that he was not up to the job; as it turned out, he was wrong. Elizabeth worried that the burden of leading a nation through the Great Depression and World War II would take too great a toll on her husband's health. Sadly, she was right. After a reign of fifteen years, one month, and twenty-five days, George VI died on February 6, 1952, at the age of fifty-six.

Just hours before he died in his sleep, George VI played with his grandchildren, Charles and Anne, on the grounds of Sandringham, the royal residence in the county of Norfolk. Charles, who was only three at the time, does not remember his grandfather the King. But he vividly recalls what happened the following year when his mother was crowned queen. The night before the big event, Charles recounted later, he and Anne could not suppress their giggles as Mummy tentatively walked from one end of her bedroom to the other, wincing as the four-pound crown wobbled on her head. Her husband, standing in a corner, was dubious. "It can't be that bad," Prince Philip said.

"Well, it is," the Queen shot back. "Very unwieldy. Honestly, Philip, I feel as if I could break my neck if I don't do this right." Decades later, the Queen would concede with a wry smile that "there are some disadvantages to crowns, but otherwise they're quite important things."

Behind the scenes, there were those who wondered at first if the twenty-five-year-old Queen wouldn't soon be crushed under the weight of her royal duties. Prime Minister Winston Churchill had wept when he learned that George VI had died and worried that Elizabeth was too young and naïve to cope. "But I don't even *know* her!" he blurted. "She's only a child!" The new queen's own mother had her doubts as well. "I cannot bear to think of Lilibet," she said, using the Queen's childhood nickname, "so young to bear such a burden."

The public felt otherwise. Rationing was still the norm in a country that had yet to regain its economic footing. Britain, which had literally not yet dug itself out of the postwar rubble, was in many ways still merely a cold, dreary, dispirited place; its people needed something to celebrate, and the crowning of a glamorous young mother offered just the right combination of spectacle, pride—and hope for a brighter future.

The outpouring of love for the new sovereign was palpable. Charles remembered waiting inside Westminster for his mother to arrive, the roar from the crowds outside so deafening that it seemed to crash like a wave against the walls of the abbey. Riding through the streets of London in the twenty-four-foot-long Gold State Coach pulled by eight gray geldings—Cunningham, Tovey, Noah, Tedder, Eisenhower, Snow White, Tipperary, and McCreery—the Queen smiled and waved gamely even though she was in pain. "Horrible," she said decades later, describing the five-mile ride, which left both her and Philip jostled and bruised. "It's only sprung on leather," she said of the fairy-tale coach's eighteenth-century design. "Not very comfortable."

The Queen's younger sister, Princess Margaret, would later describe this as a "phoenix time" for Britain. "Everything was being raised from the ashes," she said. "There was this gorgeous-looking, lovely young lady, and nothing to stop anything getting better and better." Even the normally irascible Philip was impressed with the changed mood of the nation. "The adulation was extraordinary," he marveled. "You couldn't believe it."

On the occasion of his own coronation, Charles will walk to the spot where he stood that day as a child of four. Wearing navy blue shorts and a ruffled white satin shirt pinned with a medal, his dark hair plastered down with pomade, the little boy (two-and-a-half-year-old Anne was deemed too young to attend) spent most of the time either bored or fidgeting next to his grandmother. No longer Britain's queen but its Queen Mother, she patiently leafed through the large program while placing an affectionate and reassuring hand on her grandson's back. The Queen Mother was, in fact, the one family member Charles could turn to for hugs, kisses, or any of the physical displays of familial warmth considered the norm in most households. Philip was a notoriously brusque father—the result of his own wildly dysfunctional childhood in exile—and while Elizabeth had a warm and loving relationship with her parents, she threw herself into her new role with such ferocity that she had little time to tend to the emotional needs of her own children.

In truth, even as a princess, Elizabeth rarely had time to speak with her son. Charles and Anne were given a fifteen-minute audience with their parents after breakfast and at teatime before being handed back to their nannies. Even those brief encounters, with the exception of Mummy's memorable crown-balancing act, were cut short during the frantic weeks leading up to what Elizabeth would view as the single most important day of her life. Charles hadn't any idea what all the fuss was about—until, like all the other offspring of royals, aristocrats, and dignitaries deemed worthy of the honor, a footman handed him a special hand-painted children's invitation to his own mother's coronation.

In an apparent nod to his station as the heir apparent, television cameras zeroed in on Charles's face the moment the Archbishop of Canterbury placed the crown on the new queen's head. This act made Charles think of the "most appalling gunge [slime]" on his own head, which he wiped off with an open hand and disdainfully held up to his grandmother's nose for inspection. But aside from the foul-smelling brilliantine and a vague memory of royal robes and trumpets sounding, Charles could not distinguish between what he actually remembered about his mother's coronation and what he learned from watching newsreels.

What happened later, however, remained indelibly etched in his mind. Once the royal family returned to Buckingham Palace, they were rushed to the Centre Room, just inside the twelve-foot-high glass doors leading to the balcony. Every child who stepped into this garishly decorated room was beguiled by the colorful dragons, Chinese murals, and lotus-shaped chandeliers—all examples of the exotic chinoiserie brought to the palace from the Royal Pavilion in Brighton. Outside, more than a million Britons who had waited in the cold and rain chanted, "We want the Queen! We want the Queen!" Two footmen threw open the balcony doors, a fanfare of trumpets sounded, and Charles winced visibly as the throng roared its approval. The Queen, still bedecked in full royal regalia, stepped out first, trailed by seven maids of honor who fussed with the ermine-rimmed train of her robe. As the heir apparent, Charles appeared next—ahead of his sister, Anne; his father, the Duke of Edinburgh; the Queen Mother; and Princess Margaret. Suddenly energized, the little Prince stepped up to the balcony railing in front of his mother and began waving to the hysterical throng below. Within moments, Charles heard a thunderous roar from above and, with the other royals, looked up to see the traditional "flypast" of Royal Air Force aircraft streak across the sky in salute to the new sovereign.

Within minutes, Charles and Anne were whisked off the balcony by their handlers, eventually leaving the Queen alone—with the exception of her dashing consort—to wave awkwardly to her besotted subjects. It had lasted only a few minutes, but Charles's stint on the balcony alongside his mother marked the first time that he truly realized that he was not like every other little boy in England. It was also the moment that Charles comprehended that his mother was truly beloved by her people, and that, for reasons he would learn over time, this bond held the monarchy and the country together.

Sitting down in the exact spot where he had fidgeted alongside his aunt Margaret and his grandmother seven decades earlier, Charles may be haunted by the question that he has been asking his entire life: Will they love me like they loved her? How can they, he answers with a rhetorical question of his own, after all I've done? To my first wife. To my people. To my own boys . . .

London
September 6, 1997, 10:00 a.m.

He cannot bear to look at his sons. Not now, not as they stand with him in the blazing late-summer sun in front of Kensington Palace, waiting for her coffin to pass before them. No matter that they are only a few feet from him, clearly craving tender words of encouragement or at least a comforting touch. Prince Harry, who, at just twelve years of age, barely comes up to his father's shoulders, is positioned to Charles's immediate right—so close that all his father has to do is reach out and place a hand on the boy's shoulder. But Charles does not. So Harry stands in solitary silence, ramrod straight, his small fists clenched at his sides so tightly that his fingernails dig into his palms. The youngest prince is dwarfed by the Prince of Wales and the three other men walking behind his mother's coffin: his grandfather Prince Philip, his brother, William, and his uncle, the six-foot-four-inch-tall Earl Spencer. Were Charles to turn and look at Harry and fifteen-year-old William, he would see the fixed expression on his boys' stricken faces—a look blending their mother's famous upward "shy Di" glance with undertones of dismay, grief, and no small amount of molten fury.

So much had happened and would happen in the years to come, but for the men destined to carry the monarchy into the twenty-first century, the thirty-minute march behind Diana's coffin would be the most indelibly painful memory of all—one that, they would reveal two decades later, shaped them not only as men but also as torchbearers of the monarchy. At the very moment when they so desperately needed to share their feelings, they were commanded to walk in stony silence while the rest of the world wept over the loss of the "People's Princess."

For all the undeniable heartache they were experiencing, William and

Harry were not the only men in the Windsor family being tested that day. In truth, the young princes were in some ways better equipped than their father to handle the grenade of sorrow, shock, and rage that had been tossed in their direction. It was a sad commentary on the strangulated psyches of the Windsors that, precisely because Diana had infused her now-motherless boys with a measure of humanity, they could at least *sense* that it was wrong to suppress their feelings.

Charles, like every other male and female member of the royal family who preceded him, was raised to regard any outward expression of emotion as conduct unbecoming a member of the ruling class. Yet the last five days had put that famous stiff-upper-lip resolve to the test, forcing him to cope with more mental anguish and inner turmoil than he had faced in his lifetime. At times, even for the preternaturally passive Charles, it was simply too much.

The Keep Calm and Carry On approach personified by Charles and his mother the Queen had, in fact, begun to soften in recent years—thanks almost entirely to Diana's humanizing influence. After fifteen tempestuous years spent trying to force his strong-minded wife to fit the royal mold, Charles now harbored a new respect—even affection—for the Princess of Wales. She felt the same. They had been divorced for only a year, but, during that short time, they had finally, miraculously, made peace with each other. Gone was the jealousy, deep resentment, and anger that had defined their lives as a married couple both in public and in private. Charles and Diana saw each other in a new, more sympathetic light, and both finally realized that they were inextricably bound together by one thing: the profound love they shared for their two young sons.

Sadly, it was too little, too late. Charles's life—and the history of the British monarchy—was changed forever on August 31, when the black phone next to his carved-mahogany four-poster bed jangled him awake shortly after one o'clock in the morning. The phone rang a half dozen times while the Prince of Wales, a notoriously heavy sleeper, clung to Teddy, the stuffed bear of his childhood. At forty-eight, Charles still traveled everywhere with Teddy, insisting that when the toy animal lost a button or began to fray, the Prince's childhood nanny, Mabel Anderson, be called in to sew Teddy back to health.

When he finally did pick up the phone, Charles heard the Balmoral Castle switchboard operator announce in her thick Scottish brogue that Robert Janvrin, the Queen's deputy private secretary, was on the line. "I'm sorry to awaken you, Sir," Janvrin said, quickly explaining that he had been called only minutes earlier by the Court of St. James's ambassador in Paris with news that Princess Diana had been injured in a car accident there.

"An accident in Paris?" Charles answered groggily. "Diana?"

"The facts are still coming in, Sir," Janvrin said. "But it appears it was a very serious accident. The Princess's friend Dodi Fayed was killed, as well as their driver."

Once he had finished hearing what few details Janvrin could supply, Charles called the one person he relied on most in the world: his longtime mistress, Camilla Parker Bowles. Camilla, unflappable to her core, did what she always did when she detected genuine worry in her lover's voice: offered soothing words of reassurance. Diana always wore her seatbelt. She was young and fit, and likely to bounce back quickly if she was injured at all. The press, Camilla reminded him, had a way of grossly exaggerating things. It remained to be seen if there had really been an accident at all.

Charles's next call was to the Queen's bedroom, on the far side of the castle. She had already been briefed by Janvrin, and told her son that she had decided there was no point in waking William and Harry until they knew more about Diana's condition. In the meantime, Charles went into the sitting room adjacent to his sleeping quarters and turned on the radio. As of three thirty in the morning, London time, BBC Radio 5 Live was reporting that an eyewitness to the crash in Paris's Alma tunnel saw Diana walk away from the accident scene. Sources at Pitié-Salpêtrière Hospital, where she had been taken, were being quoted as saying the Princess had suffered nothing more than a fractured arm, a concussion, and some cuts and abrasions to her legs.

When he heard these reassuring reports, Charles had no way of knowing that Diana had, in fact, been pronounced dead thirty minutes earlier. Neither did the Queen's private secretary, Sir Robert Fellowes, who also happened to be married to Diana's sister Jane. Sir Robert picked up the phone moments later and was told the devastating truth. The Princess had bled to death, a British embassy official at the hospital told him, on the operating table. Ashen and trembling, his hand clutching the telephone, Fellowes repeated the news to Charles.

What happened then shocked Fellowes and the Paris embassy official still on the line. The Prince of Wales let out a "cry of pain that was so spontaneous and came from the heart," said the embassy official. "The howl of anguish," as one witness described it, was heard down the hall, loud and stressed enough to bring Balmoral staff scurrying to Charles's room to find the Prince collapsed in an armchair, weeping uncontrollably.

Charles was not alone. The same switchboard operators whose impenetrable Scottish brogue Diana had affectionately mimicked were so upset that they had to be replaced at their posts. Footmen, maids, and uniformed members of the Queen's Scots Guard sobbed openly or choked back tears. The same could not be said for Charles's parents. As shaken as they undoubtedly were by the news, the Queen and Prince Philip were not about to be overcome by the emotion of the moment. They calmly addressed the most pressing matter at hand: how to break the terrible news to William and Harry.

Charles's initial impulse was to wake them up immediately. The Queen, however, convinced him that it would do no good to deprive the boys of one last good night of sleep. "I just don't see the point," she said almost matter-of-factly. But one of the children wasn't sleeping at all. William said later that he had tossed and turned incessantly, unable to shake the inexplicable feeling that "something was wrong. I kept waking up all night."

As the moment when he would have to break the news to his sons approached—unquestionably the hardest thing he would ever have to do—Charles went for a stroll on the Balmoral grounds. On his return to the castle an hour later, he made no effort to conceal his feelings; as one staffer recalled later, "the Prince's eyes were red and swollen from weeping."

At seven o'clock, Charles knocked on William's door, sat down on the edge of the boy's bed, and, within minutes, the two princes were sobbing in each other's arms. Once they had pulled themselves together, they went to the adjoining room, where Harry was sound asleep, and the heartbreaking process—"Harry, I'm afraid there's been a terrible accident in Paris"—was repeated.

Sad as the moment was, this ability to share their deepest feelings of grief—previously unheard of among members of the royal family—came naturally to Charles and his sons. Although the world was well aware of Diana's undying devotion to "mah boys," as she jokingly called them, it was less familiar with the fact that Charles had always been the sort of dad who had pillow fights with his sons on the living room floor, read them bedtime stories, and, despite the fact that they were now adolescents, still kissed them good night.

The father-son bond seemed that much stronger at Balmoral, where the three Windsor men wiled away the long summer days fishing, hunting, and hiking along the moors. Once the Princes had all regained their composure, they joined Elizabeth and Philip in the Queen's drawing room. With its tartan carpets, corgi figurines, and well-worn, chintz-covered armchairs, this was Her Majesty's inner sanctum at Balmoral.

If Charles had hoped that the Queen would sweep up his sons in her arms and envelop them in her grandmotherly embrace, he was sadly mistaken. Granny, as they had always known her, told William and Harry how deeply sorry she and Prince Philip were, then listened in silence as Charles filled them in on the sketchy details provided by the Queen's private secretary.

Charles was wholly unaware that his mother had already done some investigating of her own. Concerned that Diana might have been traveling with jewelry that belonged to the Crown—something that the Princess had often done over the years—the Queen instructed the British embassy in Paris to make sure they didn't fall into the wrong hands. Along with the other staff members at Pitié-Salpêtrière Hospital, head nurse Beatrice Humbert was shocked when a British embassy official burst into the room where Diana's naked body lay beneath a sheet and demanded, "Madam, we must find the jewelry, quickly! The Queen wants to know, '*Where are the jewels?*'" Diana, it turned out, had not taken any royal jewelry with her to Paris.

Even the Princess's friends would acknowledge later that the Queen, who had stripped Diana of her royal status after her divorce from Charles the previous year, wanted to shield the boys from what Diana's confidant Lady Elsa Bowker referred to as "unpleasantness." Her Majesty methodically ordered that all televisions, radios, and other electronic devices be disconnected, and that newspapers be hidden away from the young princes. Charles was taken aback, however, when his mother insisted that everyone—William and Harry included—attend services at the local parish, Crathie Kirk, as they did every Sunday when in residence at Balmoral. Was it wise to make them face other people only three hours after learning of their mother's death? Charles asked. "Yes," the Queen replied without hesitation. "I have learned that one always finds solace in routine." Besides, she continued, it was simply better for her grandsons not to "dwell on things."

Charles conceded later that he was in too much of a daze to fully appreciate how much of a strain it was for his sons to attend church that morning. Just across the River Dee from Balmoral Castle, the worshippers who gathered every Sunday to catch a glimpse of the royal family now stared silently as Charles and his sons emerged from one of three black Rolls-Royce limousines. The Prince of Wales watched helplessly as William and Harry made their way up the stone walkway to the church, looking "shocked and pale, but calm," in the words of one parishioner.

Inside, Diana's name was never uttered by the minister—not even during the prayers that mentioned, as they did every Sunday, each member of the royal family by name. "What could her boys have been thinking?" asked one congregant, who said she expected both princes to "jump and scream, 'What is going on?'"

Charles felt like doing the same thing. Occasionally glancing over at his sons with a pained expression, he knew that they were, like the rest of the congregation, confused by the lack of any mention of Diana. Harry finally blurted out to his father, "Are you sure Mummy is dead?"

Certainly no explanation would be forthcoming from the Queen or the Duke of Edinburgh, neither of whom seemed the least bit disturbed by the failure of anyone to acknowledge the sudden and tragic passing of the Princess of Wales. It did not take long for Charles to figure what was going on. The minister, at Her Majesty's request, would not be "upsetting" the boys by mentioning their mother's name during the service.

Be hard. Be detached. Be, in every conceivable way, simply above it all. This was the very definition of being a member of the royal family. Emotion was the enemy. When, as a young naval officer, Charles became upset while telling his mother about the death of one of the teenage sailors under his command, the Queen reacted with disdain. "Charles," she told her first cousin Margaret Rhodes at the time, "really must toughen up." Of course, her son would never have dared to display the slightest hint of such sensitivity in the presence of Prince Philip. *Harsh* and *hectoring* were just two of the many pejorative words Charles used to describe his father. Throughout Charles's life, he was made keenly aware that the Duke of Edinburgh was repulsed by what he often derisively called his eldest son's "delicate" nature.

The Queen Mother was scarcely a fan of Philip's, and Charles's father found in his mother-in-law a formidable foe. After her husband's death, the Queen Mother built her own power base, finagling an appointment as Counselor of State. Wielding whatever influence she had, Charles's grandmother opposed Philip's ambitious plans to reform and modernize the monarchy.

At the same time, Philip's nemesis was wary of pushing too hard or too far. While she occasionally told the Queen that Philip was unduly harsh with his son, the Queen Mother was reluctant to force the issue—

particularly since she had seen to it that Philip's children would bear the royal family's adopted English surname of Windsor and not Mountbatten, the Anglicized version of the too-German-sounding Battenberg. (Technically, Philip's real surname was even more Teutonic: Schleswig-Holstein-Sonderburg-Glücksburg.) "I am nothing but a bloody amoeba," Philip protested. "I am the only man in the country not allowed to give his name to his own children!"

As for the Queen's own parenting skills, "It's not that she was distant or even cold," explained her former private secretary, Martin Charteris. "But she was very detached. And she believed Philip was in charge. She would never have interfered with his authority. Even if he was being very tough on Charles."

William and Harry had been raised differently, protected by their mother from the more toxic influences of the Windsors. The product of a truly painful upbringing, Diana was only six and her brother Charles three when their mother deserted the family for another man, leaving her children to be raised by a succession of nannies—one of whom reacted to the slightest infraction by smacking them on the head with a wooden spoon. As a result, Diana invariably sided with the underdog in any situation and possessed a degree of empathy never before seen in a member of the royal family. Determined to make that the rule rather than the exception at Buckingham Palace, Diana exposed her sons to the pain and suffering of those less fortunate—AIDS patients, terminally ill children, the homeless, and the abused—and encouraged William and Harry to not be afraid to show their feelings.

Diana had been gone for less than twenty-four hours, and already it had become disturbingly clear what their lives were going to be like without her. Still, Charles was ill-equipped to provide all the comforting they needed. Numb with shock, he now found himself locked in a battle royal with his own mother over how the monarchy should pay its respects to Britain's beloved People's Princess. The Queen felt that a royal jet should not be sent to Paris to retrieve Diana's body, that the Princess did not warrant lowering the flag over Buckingham Palace to half-mast, and that she did not merit a royal funeral—all things Charles felt the mother of his children deserved, and that the public demanded.

The Prince of Wales was trying to rescue the monarchy from itself, and in that undertaking his staunchest ally was the new Prime Minister, Tony Blair. "Public anger," Blair said of that pivotal moment, "was turning toward the Queen." The Prime Minister's own popularity soared as he praised Diana as the People's Princess while at the same time defending the royal family from Fleet Street's stinging accusations. "I really felt for the Queen," he recalled later, acknowledging that, as a new Prime Minister he "respected the Queen and was a little in awe of her. I didn't know her or how she would take the very direct advice I know I felt I had to give her. So I went to Charles."

The Prince of Wales insisted on flying to Paris and accompanying his ex-wife's body back to London aboard one of Her Majesty's royal aircraft. He was not prepared for what he saw once he stepped inside the room at Pitié-Salpêtrière Hospital where Diana lay. Because Paris was in the midst of a heat wave, the air conditioning was turned on high, and fans had been brought into the room. The force of the air ruffled Diana's hair and caused her eyelashes to flutter. "Just for that moment," said Colin Tebbutt, a member of Diana's staff who had arrived hours earlier, "I thought, 'My God, she is alive!' I was in shock."

So, too, was the Prince of Wales. Once he stepped into the room and saw the Princess, Charles reeled back "as if he had actually been stricken by some unseen force," nurse Humbert recalled. "He was absolutely white, as if he could not believe what he was seeing. It was too much, too much." The Prince of Wales was "crushed," said another nurse on the scene, Jeanne Lecorcher. "Like everyone else, I knew that he really loved Camilla. So I was very impressed by how emotional the Prince became. Very impressed."

In the meantime, the Queen made the unwise decision not to return to London but, instead, to continue her holiday at Balmoral. Although Her Majesty would later try to explain that she felt she could better concentrate on comforting her grandsons at Balmoral, to most of her subjects it looked merely as if she were unwilling to cut short her summer vacation.

"Where Is Our Queen? Where Is Her Flag?," the *Sun* asked on its front page. The *Mirror* pleaded, "Speak to Us, Ma'am—Your People Are Suffering," while the *Express* demanded, "Show Us You Care."

Once Prince Charles returned to England, he finally persuaded his mother to leave Balmoral for London, where the flag would now fly at half-mast over the palace. She also agreed grudgingly to a televised public funeral inside Westminster Abbey—technically not a royal funeral or a state funeral, but a service uniquely suited to the beautiful, passionate, complicated, and embattled young woman who had seized the world's attention and held it for seventeen years.

The Queen had incurred the wrath of her people by remaining silent, and it was left to Charles to warn her that she might be booed at the funeral—or worse. If she wanted the monarchy to survive this crisis, he argued, the Queen would also have to speak to the people directly. "If you do not do this," Charles told his mother bluntly, "I will go on television and apologize myself." The Queen, recalled one Palace staffer, "looked stricken, as if the fog had lifted, and she saw for the first time what she had done. Or more to the point, what she had failed to do."

As it turned out, there was ample reason for concern. Three days after Diana's death, polls showed that fully two-thirds of the British people believed the monarchy was doomed. Fifty-eight percent stated flatly that they now wanted William, not Charles, as the next monarch. Those numbers might have been more dire if the public had been aware that the Queen personally vetoed plans to have Diana buried alongside other royals at Windsor Castle, as the coroner to the Queen, Dr. John Burton, had initially been led to believe.

The next day, Charles, surrounded by his tight circle of advisors, sat glued to the television in a second-floor study at St. James's Palace while his mother gave the speech of her life. With her back to Buckingham Palace's famous balcony and thousands of mourners visibly milling behind her, the Queen took a deep breath and gazed straight into the camera. "What I say to you now as your Queen and as a grandmother, I say from my heart," she began. "First, I want to pay tribute to Diana myself. She was an exceptional and gifted human being. . . . I admired and respected her for her energy and commitment to others, especially for her devotion to her two boys."

The Queen had delivered a masterful performance, but Charles remained doubtful that it was enough to tip the scales back in favor of the royal family. With key members of his staff still in the room, the Prince of Wales picked up the phone and called his most trusted advisor: his mistress. The Queen's speech, Camilla Parker Bowles told Charles, "seemed heartfelt."

Nevertheless, the heir to the throne was not entirely convinced that this was enough to do the trick. "The Firm," as the royals called themselves, had only reluctantly agreed to show Diana the respect she warranted—and then only because of the screaming headlines, angry crowds, and sinking poll numbers.

Even after delivering her landmark speech praising Diana, the Queen viewed much of the public's reaction to her daughter-in-law's death as "irrational." Yet looking out the window of her study at the tsunami of flowers lapping up against the palace gates, she could not deny that this was an outpouring of raw emotion unlike anything she had seen during her reign. "Hundreds of thousands of people jammed the streets to pay their respects to the Queen's father and Winston Churchill," Lord Charteris said. "But the mood then was very different, much more sober and subdued. The mood in London during that first week after Diana's death was a kind of mass hysteria, to put it bluntly."

———

The night before Diana's funeral, Charles led William and Harry to the Chapel Royal in St. James's Palace, where Diana's body lay in state. There they tentatively approached their mother's coffin, draped with the gold, red, and blue lions and harps of the *ancien regime* royal standard. An aide pulled back the flag and carefully opened the lid to reveal a serenely beautiful Diana. Clasped in her hands were photos of her sons and her late father, Earl Spencer, along with a rosary that had been given to her only weeks before by her friend Mother Teresa. (In a strange twist of fate, Mother Teresa would die the day after Diana was laid to rest.)

Harry did not dare look, but William wiped away tears before Charles instructed that the lid be closed. A spray of white lilies—Diana's favorite flower—was then placed at the head of the coffin, and Harry arranged a wreath of white roses at the opposite end. The young prince then took a square white card out of his pocket and set it atop the wreath. He had written "Mummy" on the card boldly, and in capital letters—the one word that defined what Diana had meant to her boys could be easily seen at a distance.

According to an attendant inside the chapel, "the Prince of Wales appeared surprised when Harry reached over and placed the card on his mother's coffin. Prince Charles reached up and brushed a tear from the corner of his eye. It was a very emotional moment."

With Charles continuing to take the lead—aided by Blair and Sir Robert Fellowes—the funeral itself was mapped out with military precision. Given that more than a million people were expected to clog the streets of central London hoping to catch a glimpse of Diana's coffin as it made its way from Diana's official residence, Kensington Palace, to Westminster Abbey, a comparatively low-profile hearse was abandoned in favor of a horse-drawn carriage on which the flag-draped coffin would be borne in plain sight. Ever since the horses at Queen Victoria's 1901 funeral bolted and sailors had to step in to pull her coffin along the procession route, it was customary for servicemen to do the job. Now six black geldings from King's Troop, Royal Horse Artillery, were giving the cavalry a chance to redeem itself in what would be the most-watched funeral of all time.

The idea that the Windsor and Spencer men—Charles; William; Harry; Diana's brother, the 9th Earl Spencer; and Prince Philip—would walk behind the coffin was hatched by the mysterious Palace plutocrats Diana called the "Men in Gray." Yet Charles—and particularly his father, whose celebrated feud with Diana made it necessary for him to literally go the extra mile in paying tribute to his daughter-in-law, went along with-

out reservation. Diana's brother had his doubts. From the outset, the notion of subjecting William and Harry to such a soul-wrenching experience
seemed callous if not sadistic. "I genuinely felt," Spencer recalled, "that
Diana would not have wanted them to have done it. Tiny Harry should
not have made the grueling walk. I was just so worried—what a trauma
for a little chap to walk behind his mum's body. It's just awful. And, actually, I tried to stop that happening, to be honest. It was a very bizarre and
cruel thing for them to be asked to do. I still have nightmares about it. It
was horrifying."

Harry felt he was in no position to object. "Before I knew it," he remembered, "I found myself with a suit on with a black tie and a white
shirt . . . and I was part of it." Even as he joined the Windsor men, Earl
Spencer continued to protest the boys' inclusion, but was told—falsely—
that William and Harry had asked to walk behind their mother's coffin. In
truth, it was Philip who stepped in to persuade the boys. "If I do it," asked
the boys' grandfather, "will you?"

Charles, at first strangely unaware of his sons' reluctance, chimed in to
convince them that they should acquiesce to the wishes of the powers that
be. "Both our parents brought us up to understand that there is this ele-
ment of duty; that you have to do things you don't want to do," William
said later of that painful moment. "When it becomes that personal, walking behind your mother's funeral cortege, it goes to another level of duty.
But I just kept thinking about what she would want and that she'd be
proud of Harry and I, and, effectively, she was there with us. It felt like she
was walking alongside us to get us through it."

William tried but failed to get his father's attention. Charles conceded
later that he was lost in his own thoughts—"in a terrible kind of daze"—and
so confused by the "sea of humanity" around him that he probably "did not
fully comprehend" the lasting impact this forced march would have on his
sons. William, meanwhile, employed several tricks to maintain his composure once the "long and lonely walk," as he called it, began. Gazing down
at the pavement before him, he hid behind the Shy Di fringe of blond hair
he had as a teenager—"my safety blanket," he said. All the while, he was

balancing "me being Prince William and having to do my bit versus the private William, who just wanted to go into a room and cry because he'd lost his mother." His little brother would spend years grappling with the intermingled grief and resentment he felt that September morning. Although he would eventually claim that he was glad to have taken part, Harry also marveled at the insensitivity of the adults around him that day. "My mother had just died, and I had to walk a long way behind her coffin, surrounded by thousands of people watching me while millions more did on television," Harry recalled decades later. "I don't think any child should be asked to do that, under any circumstances. I don't think it would happen today."

Describing the walk behind his sister's coffin as "the most harrowing experience of my life," Earl Spencer, positioned between his nephews, described a "clear feeling of high emotion around you of the most sad and confused sort, all hammering in on you. It was a tunnel of grief."

The streets were clogged with an estimated one and a half million people, creating what William called "an alien environment." Just how alien became clear the minute Diana's coffin arrived at Kensington Palace, where Charles, Philip, Earl Spencer, William, and Harry joined the cortege. On either side of them stood a dozen Welsh guards wearing tall, black bearskin hats. "Mummy, Mummy, look!" cried out a little girl standing with her mother. She pointed to the flag-draped casket. "It's the box with the Princess!"

Charles suddenly glanced at his sons, a look of alarm on his face. Only now had it occurred to him that Philip and the others might be wrong—that it was too much for any child to bear. But it was too late. "Prince Charles seemed so sad as he gazed over at William and Harry," said one of the spectators standing behind police barricades at Kensington Palace. "You got the feeling he was thinking to himself, 'Oh, no. What have we done to these boys?'"

For most of the procession, the crowds remained silent—eerily so. But, as with the little girl who announced the arrival of "the box with the Princess," every block or so "there were people in the crowd just unable to contain their emotion," Harry said, recalling how with each outburst, he nearly broke down himself. William, remembering "the horrible screams" coming from the crowd, was confused and upset by the "hysterics" of strangers. "I couldn't understand why everyone wanted to cry as loud as they did and show such emotion as they did," he said, "when they didn't really know our mother. I did feel a bit protective at times—I thought, 'You didn't even know her; why and how are you so upset?'"

"All you could hear was the clip-clop of hooves and sobbing people," agreed royal photographer Arthur Edwards, a palace favorite for decades. "One woman called out, 'Harry, God bless you!' and he just kept walking with his head down." At one point, Edwards, who worked for the *Sun*, "saw his face break apart. I couldn't take the picture because he was so hurt."

It was all William and Harry could do to survive the walk behind their mother's coffin—"the hardest thing we've ever done"—and the other historic events that followed that day. The Queen waited outside Buckingham Palace for Diana's funeral cortege to pass by, and just as it did, she bowed her head in tribute—an unprecedented gesture of contrition and respect that Charles had pleaded for his mother to make.

Across the globe, an audience of two and a half billion people—one of the largest ever to witness a live event on television—continued to watch the royal drama unfold at Westminster Abbey. After Elton John sang his haunting musical tribute to the Princess, "Candle in the Wind 1997," which instantly became the biggest-selling single in history, Earl Spencer delivered his moving and incendiary eulogy. Following a blistering attack on the press, which he accused of hounding Diana to her death, the Princess's brother took aim at the House of Windsor itself. With the Queen, Philip, and Charles seated just a few yards away, Spencer noted that Diana was "the very essence of compassion, of duty, of style, of beauty. . . . Someone with a natural nobility who was classless and who proved in the last year that she needed no royal title to continue to generate her particular brand of magic."

The Queen Mother's eyes widened with surprise as Diana's brother then went on to promise in the name of the Spencers that "we, your blood family, will do all we can to continue the imaginative way in which you were steering these two exceptional young men so that their souls are not simply immersed by duty and tradition but can sing openly as you planned."

Spencer's voice trembled as he concluded, thanking God "for the life of the unique, the complex, the extraordinary and irreplaceable Diana—whose beauty, both internal and external, will never be extinguished from our minds." Hundreds of thousands of people watching the service on jumbo television screens outside the abbey signaled their approval with thunderous applause. Nearly all those inside, including William and Harry, joined in—but not the Queen and her four children, including Charles. Instead, the monarch reacted not at all, pointedly staring straight ahead at Diana's coffin, expressionless. Her eldest son could not conceal his simmering rage over Earl Spencer's full-frontal attack on the royal family. Seething, at one point he could clearly be seen pounding his knee with a clenched fist—stopping only when he looked over to see tears streaming down his sons' faces.

There would be more heartbreaking moments on this Saturday in September. After the historic funeral service at Westminster Abbey, a motorcade accompanied the hearse carrying Diana's coffin the seventy-six miles from London to Althorp, the Spencers' spectacular five-hundred-year-old country estate in Northamptonshire. There Charles, William, Harry, and Diana's Spencer kin stood with heads bowed as the Princess of Wales was laid to rest on a secluded 75-foot-by-180-foot island in the middle of what was called the Round Oval, a small ornamental lake on the grounds of the estate. Again the tears flowed, and this time, away from his parents and other members of the royal family who'd chosen instead to remain behind in London, Charles broke down.

"Prince Charles is the most introspective of all the men in the royal family, but that's not saying much," the Queen's cousin and close confidant Margaret Rhodes said. "He was thinking of his sons and the pain they were experiencing. They were now suddenly motherless, after all."

But later, Charles would confide to one of his few close friends that he was crying for himself as much as he was for Diana and their sons. Her Majesty's cousin allowed that neither the Queen nor Prince Philip ever really expressed "what might be called parental affection" toward Charles. "It is not a cozy relationship and never has been," said Rhodes. "The family is not set up to be cozy."

For Charles, it was more than that. In that moment, caught up in the maelstrom of emotions triggered by Diana's death, the Prince of Wales was overwhelmed with a sense of guilt. It was one thing for him to suffer under the influence of a domineering father, but quite another to allow Prince Philip and the Palace to inflict pain on his own children. Had Charles become the sort of person he despised above all others—a bully?

May 1962

"Get him!" Before he could react, Charles was plowed face-first into the mud, then furiously pummeled and kicked before his fellow rugby players were satisfied he'd had enough—for now. "We did him over," Charles later recalled one of them boasting before giving him one final cuff to the back of the head. "We just punched the future king of England!"

Such was life for the sensitive, jug-eared newcomer at Gordonstoun, the spartan boarding school on Scotland's northeast coast, where Charles was dispatched at the age of thirteen. A year earlier, the Queen Mother had pleaded with her daughter to send Charles to Eton College, Britain's most revered private school and an institution of learning that was conveniently located within walking distance of Windsor Castle. Indeed, the general assumption was that Charles would, like nineteen British prime ministers and generations of aristocrats before him, become an Etonian.

"I suppose he will be taking his entrance exam for Eton soon," she wrote blithely to the Queen. "I do hope he passes because it might be the ideal school for one of his character and temperament. All your friends' sons are at Eton," the Queen Mother added, "and it is so important to be able to grow up with people you will be with later in life. And so nice and so important when boys are growing up that you and Philip can see him during school days and keep in touch with what is happening. He would be terribly cut off and lonely in the far north."

Knowing Charles better than any other senior member of the royal family, the Queen Mother had every reason to be concerned. Unfortunately, Elizabeth II stated flatly that she had no particular desire to be near her eldest child and wondered aloud if the boy wouldn't become too "soft" if he knew that he could always "run home to Mother." Besides, to compensate for forcing her husband to accept the humiliation of naming their offspring Windsor instead of Mountbatten, the Queen agreed that Philip would have the last word in all matters relating to the children.

Charles's enrollment at Gordonstoun was, in fact, a fait accompli. Twenty-eight years earlier, the rootless young Prince Philip of Greece arrived seeking some sort of direction in his life and a sense of stability denied him in early childhood. Born into the Greek and Danish royal families on June 10, 1921 (albeit on the kitchen table of the somewhat shabby Greek royal residence on the island of Corfu) and christened Philippos, the Prince was related to his future bride in a number of ways: great-great-grandson of Queen Victoria, distant cousin of King George III, and direct descendant of Czar Nicholas I of Russia. Unfortunately, he was scarcely eighteen months old when a revolutionary court sentenced his father Prince Andrew to death by firing squad in 1922, forcing the family to flee into exile. Philip was smuggled out of town in an orange crate, and the family made its way to a waiting British warship dispatched by King George V.

From that point on, Philip's newly impoverished family relied almost exclusively on the generosity of their royal relations in Britain, although they chose to settle in the Paris suburb of Saint-Cloud. Andrew's deep sense of humiliation over having essentially lost everything was keenly felt by his only son. "Philip really loved his father," a family friend said, "but his father was lost in his own world. Andrew had little time for his son."

When Philip was nine, his father left his family to live with his mistress in the South of France. The next year, his mother Princess Alice of

Battenberg, who had been born deaf, nonetheless began "hearing voices"—and not just any voices. She became convinced that God was speaking directly to her, and to further complicate matters, that she was having sexual relations with Jesus and other religious figures. Diagnosed with schizophrenia, Charles's paternal grandmother underwent a radical new procedure advocated by Sigmund Freud that involved bombarding her genitals with x-rays. This bizarre "treatment" triggered a complete nervous breakdown, and Princess Alice was drugged and spirited away against her will by men in white coats to a mental institution in Switzerland.

Abandoned by his parents, Philip could hardly turn to his elder sisters, three of whom—Sophie, Margarita, and Cecile—were married to German princes who became powerful figures in the Nazi Party. One, Philip's brother-in-law (and Charles's uncle) Prince Christoph of Hesse, not only was a colonel on the staff of SS chief Heinrich Himmler and a director in the Third Reich Air Ministry, but also headed Luftwaffe commander Hermann Göring's dreaded secret intelligence service. Prince Christoph and Charles's aunt Sophie were so enamored of Adolf Hitler that they named their son—Charles's first cousin—Karl Adolf in der Führer's honor.

"There was a confusion: uncertainty, neglect, and nevertheless the feeling of being special mixed together," observed British historian Ben Pimlott. Philip was, after all, a prince in his own right. Certainly he was known to Britain's royal family even as a small child; following tea with Philip at Buckingham Palace, Queen Mary (the wife of King George V and Charles's great-grandmother) declared the ostensibly Greek prince without a trace of Greek blood to be "a nice little boy with very blue eyes."

After spending most of his early childhood in Paris, Philip was abruptly shipped off across the English Channel to Cheam, a boarding school forty-eight miles southwest of London in Hampshire. Founded in 1645, Cheam was the oldest private school in Britain, so famous for catering to England's elite that by the midnineteenth century it was dubbed "the Little House of Lords." For Philip, the school not only gave his life much-needed structure but also enabled him to become fluent in what was loosely referred to as the King's English. Although Philip of Greece and Denmark did not speak Greek or Danish, up until this point he communicated primarily in French and German. When he did speak English, it was usually at the MacJannet American primary school he attended in Paris, and he spoke with a pronounced American accent.

That was, of course, all taken care of quickly at Cheam. According to a classmate, within a short time Philip "was sounding very posh, like everyone else." Determined to fit in, Charles's father downplayed his royal connections. Philip kept his framed photograph of King George V—signed "From Uncle George"—hidden beneath a pile of clothes in his footlocker.

A perennial outsider who was accustomed to making himself instantly at home in strange surroundings, Philip quickly won over the other boys at school. Due to his natural athleticism and his innate sense of confidence, there was never a question of the newcomer being bullied. "Nobody would ever have had a poke at him," said his classmate John Wynne, "because they'd have got one back!"

Three times in the space of one year, Philip flew to Germany for the weddings of his sisters. For a short time, he was enrolled in a German school that was already in the process of being taken over by the Nazis. Most of the students were being enlisted in the Hitler Youth movement, and Philip, like the other students, was pressured to give the "Heil Hitler" salute several times a day.

"The Nazis had more or less taken over," Philip remembered, "and life was getting a bit tricky." The thirteen-year-old may have felt uncomfortable having to deal with the Nazi influence at the German school he attended, but that paled in comparison with what the school's founder was going through. Kurt Hahn was a respected educator, but he was also an outspoken critic of Adolf Hitler—and he was Jewish. In 1933 he fled Germany and settled in Moray, Scotland. There he established Gordonstoun, a school that, following principles outlined in Plato's *The Republic* and born out of Germany's humiliating economic collapse following its World War I defeat, sought to build a new generation of "philosopher-kings"—political leaders with both "the willpower of the dreamer" and "the nerve to lead."

The future father of England's king became the tenth student to enroll at Gordonstoun. As he had at Cheam, the highly adaptive, Viking-handsome Philip flourished in his new surroundings. With the exception of letters he received from his sisters—for the next five years, neither of his parents even bothered to send him a birthday card—Philip had little contact with his family. Headmaster Hahn, the teaching staff, and his fellow students filled the void, serving as Philip's emotional anchor. "The family broke up," he recalled later of this period. "I just had to get on with it. You do. One does."

Even for someone who was accustomed to turmoil, the events of November 16, 1937, dealt Philip a devastating blow. The plane carrying Philip's favorite sister Cecile, her husband, and two of their three children crashed on the way to a family wedding in London, killing all aboard. Cecile, who was eight months pregnant, had given birth moments before the crash; the body of a newborn infant was found in the charred wreckage.

Kurt Hahn summoned sixteen-year-old Philip to his office, sat him down, and delivered the sad news. "He did not break down," the headmaster recalled. "He had had too much practice dealing with tragedy and shocks of all kinds in his young life."

Philip flew alone to Darmstadt, Germany, for the funeral of his sister, brother-in-law, and two nephews aged four and six. Flags and banners bearing swastikas fluttered. and spectators gave the Nazi salute as a somber Philip walked behind the coffins alongside family members in their SS uniforms. Göring was among the mourners, and messages of condolence from Propaganda Minister Joseph Goebbels and the Führer himself were read aloud.

Tellingly, there was another figure marching in the funeral procession: Princess Alice's brother Lord Louis Mountbatten, conspicuous among the mourners in his British naval uniform. "Dickie," as Philip's fatally charming and eternally scheming uncle was known to friends and family members, had been one of the first to spot Philip's potential. Without hesitation, he stepped into the breach as a sort of surrogate father—a role that he would come to assume in Charles's life as well. It was hard to imagine a more suitable or impressive mentor. George VI's favorite cousin and a towering presence at court, Lord Mountbatten was destined for greatness in his own right—as a World War II military hero, Supreme Allied Commander of Southeast Asia, Admiral of the Fleet, First Sea Lord, and the last Viceroy of India. After famously overseeing the retaking of Burma from the Japanese in 1945, Charles's great-uncle Dickie was given the title Earl Mountbatten of Burma.

Early on, Mountbatten began grooming Philip and lobbying with members of the royal family on his nephew's behalf. "I don't think anybody thinks I had a father," Philip once remarked. "Most people think that Dickie's my father anyway."

Philip returned from the funeral to Gordonstoun and resumed his studies, a classmate said, "as if nothing had happened." Childhood friend Gina Wernher knew otherwise. "He didn't talk much about it," she said, but at one point he reached into his pocket and pulled out a small fragment of wood. He explained that it came from inside the passenger cabin of the doomed plane. Philip would carry the fragment with him for decades.

Graduating from Gordonstoun at eighteen in 1939, Philip dutifully followed Uncle Dickie's advice and promptly enrolled at the Royal Naval College in Dartmouth. He also began seriously playing the field. "The fascination with Philip," observed Queen Alexandra of Yugoslavia, "had spread like influenza through a whole string of girls. Blondes, brunettes, and red-headed charmers, Philip gallantly and I think quite impartially squired them all." In this, Philip was following in his uncle's footsteps—not to mention the example also set by Mountbatten's promiscuous wife, Lady Edwina, who counted among her many lovers Prime Minister Jawaharlal Nehru of India. "Edwina and I spent all our married lives," Lord Louis once admitted, "getting into other people's beds."

In July 1939, less than three months after he entered Dartmouth, the young cadet was asked to entertain George VI's daughter Elizabeth, then thirteen, and her nine-year-old sister Margaret while the King toured the college. Philip took his distant cousins outdoors to play croquet on the lawn and, observed one of the other cadets, "show off by jumping over the tennis nets." Uncle Dickie already had his eye on a royal match between Philip and the future queen—a match that would fortify the Mountbattens' ties to the Crown. "Philip was a great success with the children," Lord Louis wrote in his diary that day. One of the children's governesses, Marion "Crawfie" Crawford, noted that while Philip spent most of the afternoon teasing little Margaret and ignoring her older sister, Elizabeth "never took her eyes off him the whole time."

For Charles's mother, it was indeed love at first sight. Philip, however, had weightier matters on his mind. Shipping off as a lieutenant the following year, he saw plenty of action during World War II—first escorting convoys threatened by German submarines along the stretch of English coastline known as U-Boat Alley, and, later, in the Mediterranean Sea. All the while, royal circles were abuzz with gossip that kept the names Philip and Elizabeth linked throughout the war.

Meanwhile, Princess Elizabeth and the rest of the Windsors were making their own, unique contributions to the war effort. Rather than flee Britain for Canada, or, at the very least, exit London before German bombs fell on the nation's capital, George VI made the courageous decision to keep his family right where they were in an effort to boost morale. "The children will not leave unless I do," his wife said. "I shall not leave unless their father does, and the King will not leave the country in any circumstances."

A turning point of sorts came in September 1940 when Buckingham Palace suffered two direct hits that crashed through a glass ceiling, obliterated the royal chapel, and injured several servants. At the time, Charles's grandmother was in the process of trying to remove a wayward lash from the King's eye. "We heard the unmistakable *whirr-whirr* of a German plane," she told her grandson later, "and then the scream of a bomb. It all happened so quickly that we had only time to look foolishly at each other when the scream hurtled past us and exploded with a tremendous crash in the quadrangle."

Hours later, the royal couple visited bombed-out areas of the East

End. Having themselves nearly been killed by German bombs, George VI and his queen consort felt they had earned the admiration of their subjects. "I'm glad we have been bombed," Charles's grandmother said famously at the time. "Now I can look the East End in the face." During the blitz, from September 1940 to May 1941, Buckingham Palace would be hit no fewer than sixteen times.

It was hardly the first time Princess Elizabeth had seen her parents handle themselves valiantly under duress. Only four years earlier, young Elizabeth's playboy Uncle David told the nation he could not rule as king "without the love and support of the woman I love" and abdicated to marry the twice-divorced American Wallis Simpson. That momentous decision brought an end to a constitutional crisis, but it also meant that the full weight of the monarchy fell on the shoulders of Charles's highly sensitive, stammering, chain-smoking grandfather. George VI rose to the occasion, essentially teaming with Prime Minister Winston Churchill to stand tall in the face of German aggression. But the burden of kingship was ruinous to the King's health, and the woman who later became Queen Mother would never forgive her brother-in-law and Wallis Simpson for, as she would say frequently, "killing my husband."

While Princesses Elizabeth and Margaret spent most of the war in relative safety at Windsor Castle, twenty-four miles west of London, the presumptive heir to the throne made her own distinctive contribution to the war effort. At fourteen, Elizabeth made the first of several radio broadcasts aimed at bolstering the spirits of her fellow Britons. Later, she signed up to undergo training as a driver and truck mechanic with the women's Auxiliary Territorial Service. Her service number: 230873.

All the while, Philip and Elizabeth exchanged letters and saw each other whenever he was in England on leave. "She was completely besotted with him," said nanny Crawfie Crawford, who, like a handful of close family members, never stopped calling Elizabeth by her nickname, Lilibet. "There was no question from quite an early time in her mind that they were going to marry." As the war drew to a close, Philip always carried with him a small photograph of Elizabeth in a battered leather frame; she proudly displayed a photograph of a bearded Philip on the desk of her room at Buckingham Palace. Princess Margaret revealed later that her sister kissed the photograph each night before going to bed. Yet there were very few outward displays of affection between them. No hugs, certainly no kisses. Very seldom did they hold hands, and then only furtively. From childhood, the future Queen was, said her cousin Margaret Rhodes, "aloof, I guess you could say. Very much in control of her emotions. She loathed the gushy stuff. Besides, they both think all that sort of thing is phony."

Unfortunately for Elizabeth, she was not the only woman who fell hard for the dashing prince. Usually in the company of Mike Parker, a first lieutenant in the Royal Australian Navy who over the next two decades would become his closest friend, Philip made a point of sampling the local nightclubs, bars, and brothels whenever they pulled in to port. Since they both sported beards at this point, Philip was fond of exchanging identities with Parker—if only to prove to himself that women were willing to go to bed with him not just because he was a prince. "He needn't have worried," said a shipmate. "He always got the girl, whether she knew he was a prince or not." At dozens of ports of call, including India, Egypt, North Africa, Australia, Gibraltar, the Far East, and the South Pacific, Philip would return to his ship and sign back in. If he put an exclamation point next to his name, said his fellow officers, it was to signify that he had bedded someone there. Most of the time, he signed back in with an exclamation point.

After much behind-the-scenes maneuvering, much of it on the part of Philip's ubiquitous Uncle Dickie, Philip proposed to Elizabeth in August 1946. In truth, Philip would say later that he did not propose in any formal or traditional way. Princess Elizabeth had made it clear she wanted to marry him, and, at that point, it was being treated as a foregone conclusion. "I suppose one thing led to another," Philip confessed later. "It was sort of fixed up. That's the way it really happened."

Elizabeth's father the King was fond of Philip, but he was not particularly enthusiastic about marrying off his beloved Lilibet to a man she had fallen in love with when she was thirteen. Nor was George VI or anyone who knew Philip convinced that the impetuous prince would refrain from cheating on his bride. No one feared for Elizabeth more than her father's private secretary, Sir Tommy Lascelles. Philip was, Lascelles stated flatly, "rough, ill mannered, uneducated, and would probably not be faithful."

It was only natural that the Queen Mother—whose own husband, a shy and uncertain figure, never had a wandering eye—should write to her new son-in-law, seeking assurance that he would "cherish" her daughter. Twenty-six-year-old Philip, perhaps sensing that his plans for a royal marriage were beginning to founder, wrote back, "Cherish Lilibet? I wonder if that word is enough to express what is in me." He went on to say he had "fallen in love completely and unreservedly. The only thing in this world which is absolutely real to me, and my ambition, is to weld the two of us into a new combined existence that will not only be able to withstand the shocks directed at us but will also have a positive existence for the good."

Such high-mindedness notwithstanding, the King insisted they not formally announce their engagement until she turned twenty-one the following year—enough time, His Majesty reasoned, for Philip to solve another pesky problem by renouncing his Greek citizenship and becoming a naturalized citizen of Great Britain.

Princess Elizabeth was on tour with the rest of the royal family in South Africa when, on her twenty-first birthday, she made a "dedication" radio broadcast that would have profound implications for her as-yet-unborn son and heir, not to mention the institution of the monarchy itself. "I should like to make that dedication now," she said in a strong and unwavering voice. "It is very simple. I declare before you all that *my whole life*, whether it be long or short, shall be devoted to your service and the service of our great imperial family to which we all belong." That pledge would be Queen Elizabeth II's guiding principle, and one that would keep Charles waiting in the wings far longer than any of his predecessors.

From the beginning, the relationship between Charles's parents was rooted in mutual respect and the understanding that, in many significant ways, they complemented each other. He was outspoken, impulsive, adventurous, at times rude and even bullying—yet he brought elements of excitement and spontaneity into Her Highness's otherwise well-ordered and largely preordained existence. She was disciplined, calm, restrained—a paragon of self-control who might persuade her mate to hold back and ponder the consequences rather than do or say something he might profoundly regret later.

Still coping with severe economic hardships just two years after the end of the war, most of George VI's subjects were eager for a reason to celebrate. Toward that end, the royal wedding of England's young and attractive heiress presumptive to the newly minted Duke of Edinburgh was conceived as both a lavish spectacle and global event—a party the likes of which Britain had not seen since the coronation of George VI a full decade earlier.

Three decades before the world had ever heard of Lady Diana Spencer, much less William and Kate, the Wedding of the Century took place on November 20, 1947, in Westminster Abbey. Elizabeth's wedding gown, created by royal dressmaker Norman Hartnell, was a fairy-tale concoction of ivory silk satin garlanded with white roses, embroidered with orange blossoms and encrusted with crystals and—by Hartnell's own count—"ten thousand pearls."

Even though the German relations were pointedly excluded from the festivities, the list of royals in attendance (many of them Windsor relatives) included the King and Queen of Denmark, the Kings of Romania, Norway, and Iraq, the Queen of Greece, and the future Queen of the Netherlands. Another guest observed that when Winston Churchill, at this point leader of the Conservative opposition, walked into the abbey late, "everyone stood—all the kings and queens."

One of the most important wedding gifts Elizabeth received was intangible: on that day, the groom, who had been a chain-smoker since the age of sixteen, made good on the promise he'd made to his nonsmoking wife to give up cigarettes. The gesture was historic. Smoking contributed to the death of Edward VII at age sixty-eight, and to George V's lifelong battle against chronic obstructive pulmonary disease and pleurisy. Elizabeth's grandmother Queen Mary was a compulsive smoker, as was her father the King. The Princess "was grateful that Philip was giving up smoking for her," Margaret Rhodes said. "One less thing to worry about."

The newlyweds divided their honeymoon between Broadlands, the Mountbattens' stately Palladian manor in Hampshire, and Elizabeth's favorite place in all the world, Balmoral. The newlyweds' main London residence was to be Clarence House, overlooking the Mall and adjacent to Saint James's Palace. Boasting dozens of rooms spread out over four floors, Clarence House had been built in 1824 for the Duke of Clarence—later King William IV—and had been unoccupied since its last occupant, the Duke of Connaught, died in 1924. When Elizabeth and Philip looked the place over, they were shocked to see that it was a veritable shambles; not only had the elderly Duke of Connaught failed to keep up the place, but also large sections of Clarence House that had been hit by German bombs had yet to be repaired. It would take eighteen months and the then-sobering sum of $200,000 (roughly the equivalent of $2.8 million today) to make the place habitable.

In the meantime, the couple was forced to move back into the Princess's old rooms at Buckingham Palace, just down the hall from her parents the King and Queen. Still, now that she was married and considered to have her own "household" within the royal household, Elizabeth was treated more seriously by Palace operatives. To prepare her for what her private secretary Jock Colville called "the Big Job," it was generally understood that the Princess should keep up-to-date on affairs of state. Toward that end, she was given her own gold-embossed red leather royal boxes—the famous red boxes of state supplied by the luxury leather goods firm of Barrow Hepburn & Gale—filled with copies of the important state papers that required her father's attention for hours each day: intelligence reports, cabinet minutes, confidential cables, documents requiring the monarch's signature, and dispatches that were intended to keep the King apprised of what was transpiring in his realm and the world beyond.

Even though she had no power to act on her own, Princess Elizabeth was already keenly aware of the responsibilities that would one day fall on her slender shoulders. When Colville's old boss Winston Churchill learned the King's daughter was now being required to plow through mountains of paperwork each day just to keep up with her father the King, he took a puff on his ever-present cigar and shook his head. "Poor girl," Sir Winston muttered. "Poor little Princess Elizabeth."

In fact, at this stage in her life Elizabeth seemed, in the words of one of her ladies-in-waiting, to be "all bliss"—particularly when it came to Philip. The Duke of Edinburgh, who now spent his days as an operations officer at the Admiralty, was blunt-spoken to the point of rudeness ("He's in the navy, you know," Elizabeth would say by way of apology) and at times brazenly uninhibited. While Elizabeth always wore a nightgown to bed, Prince Philip insisted on sleeping in the nude. On one occasion, the King's valet, James MacDonald, knocked on Philip's door and entered to find him naked in bed with the Princess. MacDonald was mortified, as were the maids and other household staff members who would later watch the Duke of Edinburgh give his children swimming lessons in the buff. "Of course, we were all shocked and embarrassed," MacDonald said, but the Prince "didn't care at all."

At times, it seemed the only appearances Philip was interested in keeping up were his own. Elizabeth enjoyed long walks in the Buckingham Palace gardens and was an accomplished horsewoman who rode whenever she could at Sandringham, Windsor, and Balmoral, but she had no exercise regimen per se. She kept her hairstyle simple and wore little makeup. There was no need: Elizabeth's skin was routinely described in the press as "porcelain," and her cornflower-blue eyes startled most people meeting her for the first time. The Princess also had little interest in fashion at the time, usually allowing her dresser to pick out her wardrobe for the day. "She's not a clothes person," her longtime designer Hardy Amies would later complain. "She doesn't care."

Philip was the narcissist in the royal family. In the beginning, he may have cared even less about his wardrobe than Elizabeth did about hers. "He is not interested in clothes and simply cannot tie a tie," grumbled his valet at the time, John Dean. Philip was vain, however, about his looks. He worried that his hair was thinning prematurely; while still in his midtwenties, the Duke used a special lotion from his barber, Topper's of Bond Street, and began combing his hair to hide a bald spot at the back. Obsessive about his weight, he carefully monitored what he ate. His exercise routine—a game of squash or tennis, followed by laps in the pool and a five-mile run on weekends—often proved so taxing that he would go to his room and collapse. "I think," his wife would say to anyone within earshot, "Prince Philip is mad. Yes, quite mad."

To offset the obvious imbalance of wealth, fame, influence, and power in their lives, Elizabeth was more than willing to defer to her husband in the manner of most housewives in the postwar era. In this very limited sense, theirs was a traditional marriage. Although the Princess's wartime service behind the wheel of an army truck made her an expert driver, Philip always drove whenever they decided to strike off on their own— something they did quite often as young marrieds. Philip was a notorious speed demon, but Elizabeth was careful never to criticize.

One weekend, as Philip negotiated a hairpin turn while hurtling through the countryside at breakneck speed, his wife braced herself and gasped. "Do that once more," he shouted at her, "and I'll put you out!" Lord Mountbatten, sitting in the backseat, was alarmed at the way his nephew spoke to the future Queen but also concerned that Elizabeth did not speak up about her husband's recklessness. "But didn't you hear him?" she protested. "He said he'd put me out!"

Mountbatten would soon learn that Philip had no qualms about barking at his wife the way he did to everyone else, occasionally in front of shocked members of the public. "That was a bloody idiotic thing to say," he might blurt out, cutting off Elizabeth midsentence. "Don't be a stupid clot" was another favorite put-down that Philip used on household servants and the heir to the throne of England alike.

Yet the Princess "never took it to heart," said a longtime courtier. "She understood that it was just his way. Prince Philip was cantankerous, but as far as she was concerned, that was part of his charm. Her father could be the same way: very abrupt or upset with people. But she worshipped the King, and, in a way, she worshipped Philip."

The Duke of Edinburgh was not always churlish with his wife—far from it. "They were newlyweds and acted like it," his valet said. "They could be very frisky, very flirtatious." Not only at this early stage in their marriage but well into their fifties, Philip would occasionally be caught (when he thought no one was looking) pinching his wife's derriere as she preceded him up a staircase, or suddenly reaching out to tickle her when she least expected it. Elizabeth would invariably act incensed and slap away his hand ("Now, Philip, stop! Now, *really*!") as if he were "a naughty little boy," said one of her ladies-in-waiting. "But she clearly loved it."

This playful side of their relationship occasionally meshed with royal responsibilities. Within three months of exchanging vows in Westminster Abbey, Her Royal Highness the Princess Elizabeth was pregnant. Even those at court who had been among Philip's harshest critics were impressed. "Such a sense of duty," Tommy Lascelles said, "to put the heir to the throne in a family way—all according to plan."

*Our thoughts go out to the mother and father and,
in a special way today, to the little prince,
now born into this world of strife and storm.*
—Winston Churchill, speaking in the House of Commons

The Queen is not good at showing affection.
—Martin Charteris, longtime advisor and private secretary to Elizabeth II

*He is a very gentle boy with a very kind heart—
which I think is the essence of everything.*
—the Queen Mother

TWO

THE LITTLE PRINCE

Mummy was a remote and glamorous figure
who came to kiss you smelling of lavender and dressed for dinner.
—Charles

Buckingham Palace
November 14, 1948, shortly after 9 p.m.

S ir!" Tommy Lascelles shouted as he rushed into the column-lined
North-West Pavilion, designed by architect John Nash, and toward the
two naked men standing by the royal swimming pool. Philip and Mike
Parker, who now served as the Prince's private secretary, had spent much
of the day on the adjacent squash court—far more in keeping with Philip's
man-of-action ethos than simply pacing the floor like most expectant fathers of the time. They had followed their squash match with a swim and
were toweling off when the King's famously straightlaced private secretary,
trying hard to look the Prince squarely in the eyes, paused to catch his
breath. In the days before ultrasound, this was the moment when Philip
would learn the sex of his firstborn child.

"And?" the Prince asked impatiently.

"It's a boy, Your Royal Highness," Lascelles replied with uncharacteris-
tic enthusiasm. "A boy!" Philip pulled on his pants and then, fumbling
with the buttons on his shirt, strode up one flight of stairs and down a series of hallways to the Palace's Belgian Suite, located directly below Elizabeth's bedroom and overlooking the Mall. The aquiline-nosed royal

midwife, Sister Helen Rowe, had already taken the baby to the nursery when Philip burst in, his hair still wet. Elizabeth lay motionless, still unconscious from the anesthetic she had been given to, it was explained, "ease the birth pangs."

Standing by the bed were two other visitors: the King and Queen, who had arrived ten minutes after the baby's delivery and expressed relief that, as His Majesty put it, "everything seems to have gone smoothly, thank God." The four doctors in attendance explained that, while the Princess had begun experiencing mild labor pains thirty hours earlier, only the last two hours were intense. There was, in fact, a legitimate concern that this would not be a routine birth. The Princess Elizabeth herself, who may have been conceived through artificial insemination, was delivered via emergency Caesarean section—a risky operation in 1926, made all the more so by the fact that it took place in the Mayfair home of her maternal grandparents. Since at the time of her birth no one seriously expected the Princess to become heir to the throne—she was ten years old when her Uncle David made his shocking decision to abdicate—this marked the first time since the Middle Ages that a monarch was born in a house, and not in a castle or a palace.

The new baby's birth inside the walls of Buckingham Palace was, at least medically speaking, unremarkable. Much like other fathers of the time, Philip visited the nursery to get his first glimpse of his newborn son, then returned to the Princess's room. When his wife came to, Philip was standing there with a bottle of champagne and a large bouquet of red roses, lilies, camellias, and carnations—all of Elizabeth's favorite flowers—courtesy of Mike Parker, who had the foresight to have them at the ready.

The arrival of the new princeling broke tradition in one way: for the first time since the eighteenth century, there was no Home Secretary or other high government official on hand to witness the birth—an ancient practice designed to prevent an imposter from being slipped into the line of succession.

It would have been hard to find anyone whose blood ran more royal. The baby was a direct descendant of Alfred the Great, William the Con-

queror, and of course, Queen Victoria, his great-great-great-grandmother—
all of which made him the most English prince in four hundred years.
Counting Robert the Bruce and Mary, Queen of Scots, among his ancestors,
the baby was also the most Scottish prince since Charles I. Through his maternal grandmother, he was also descended from the storied high kings of
Ireland and the medieval figure Owen Glendower, the last Welsh native to
hold the title Prince of Wales. On both sides, he was also a direct descendant
of the Electress Sophia, mother of England's first Hanoverian monarch,
George I.

For the moment, however, the future Queen was enthralled with her
new baby, marveling at, among other things, the size of his hands. "They
are rather large," Elizabeth commented, "but fine with long fingers—quite
unlike mine and certainly unlike his father's. It will be interesting to see
what they will become." When someone asked the Duke of Edinburgh
what his son the future King of England looked like, he replied tersely: "A
plum pudding."

He was not yet three hours old when, shortly before midnight, the
seven-pound, six-ounce "plum pudding" was carefully swaddled in white
blankets and taken by Sister Helen to the cavernous gilt-and-red-velvet ballroom, by far the largest and most ostentatious space in the Palace. There, beneath the four-story-high ceilings and Brobdingnagian crystal chandeliers,
the baby was placed on display in a small cradle at the center of the room—
directly in front of the twin imperial thrones and massive domed canopy
with its royal coat of arms embroidered in gold silk thread on draped red velvet. Every member of the Palace staff—numbering in the hundreds—was
invited by the King to file by and catch an in-the-flesh glimpse of the royal
family's newest arrival. "The child was beautiful, with big blue eyes," reported one of the backstairs staff who had dropped by still in her kitchen
maid's uniform. "He seemed perfectly happy even with all the strange faces
coming up and staring. But you couldn't help feeling sorry for him. So tiny
there in that room, and, of course, he has no idea what's in store for him."

While Elizabeth was upstairs in her rooms, reveling in the joys of new motherhood ("I still find it difficult to believe that I have a baby of my own," she wrote in a letter to her cousin), a sign was posted on the wrought iron railings outside Buckingham Palace just before midnight proclaiming that the Princess Elizabeth had given birth to a son. News of the little Prince's birth was instantly trumpeted at home and around the world. Still coping with fuel shortages and food rationing, Britons viewed the heir's arrival as a welcome distraction well worth celebrating. Thousands who had waited for hours outside Buckingham Palace began clamoring, "We want Philip! We want Philip!" and "We want Grandad!" When neither the Duke nor the King materialized, they began singing lullabies.

Church bells rang for three hours, and, across the nation, bonfires were lit. The King's Troop Royal Horse Artillery discharged a forty-one-round salute next to Buckingham Palace, while at the Tower of London, cannons boomed sixty-two times. The fountains in Trafalgar Square were awash in blue light—for a boy—and His Majesty's warships fired off royal salutes at sea. *The Times* of London proclaimed Charles's birth nothing less than a "national and imperial event. . . . All can be united as the guns salute and the bells peal."

Prince Philip was determined to keep his son's name secret—and that he should be the one to spring it on the world at the child's christening. One of the few let in on the secret was the court's favorite photographer, Cecil Beaton, called in less than a week after the baby's birth to snap the first official pictures of mother and child. Beaton, who among other things would later win an Academy Award for designing the costumes Audrey Hepburn wore in *My Fair Lady*, wrote in his diary that "Prince Charles, as he is to be named, is an obedient sitter. He interrupted a long, contented sleep to do my bidding and open his blue eyes to stare long and wonderingly into the camera lens, the beginning in a lifetime in the glare of publicity."

Considering how earlier kings named Charles had fared, this was not a particularly popular choice among royals, courtiers, and students of British history. Charles I was deposed and decapitated in 1649. His son Charles II managed to regain the throne after years of exile, only to rule during two of the seventeenth century's worst disasters: the Great Plague and the Great Fire of London. "Charles—bad news," said the man put in charge of running the Princess's household, Sir Frederick "Boy" Browning. "Definitely bad news."

With eight godparents looking on—including his grandparents King George and Queen Elizabeth, his maternal great-grandmother Queen Mary, Prince Philip's grandmother the Dowager Marchioness of Milford Haven, the King of Norway, and Philip's paternal uncle Prince George of Greece and Denmark—the newest royal was cradled next to the elaborate, cherub-festooned silver gilt lily font designed by Prince Albert and used to baptize all nine of his children with Queen Victoria. Using holy water from the River Jordan, the Archbishop of Canterbury christened the newborn Charles Philip Arthur George. For the time being, he would be addressed simply as His Royal Highness Prince Charles of Edinburgh.

Elizabeth was doing her best to identify with other mothers in her realm. Intent on further spreading the joy among what the royal family routinely referred to as "common folk," she also instructed that the mothers of all children born on Charles's birthday be sent a gift: carefully wrapped slices of cake like the one served to her guests at the royal christening.

Determined, as her nanny Crawfie put it, to "give him as good a foundation as possible," Elizabeth breast-fed Charles for two months—until she contracted measles. Her doctors, concerned that the infection could be passed along to the baby, ordered her not only to stop nursing but also to stay away from the infant until the measles had run their course. Baby Charles was separated from his mother for the next month—a harbinger of the physical and emotional distance that would come to define their relationship.

Princess Elizabeth and Prince Philip placed their infant son in the capable hands of nannies Helen Lightbody and Mabel Anderson and promptly plunged into London's rebounding postwar social scene. When

Charles was five months old, they celebrated Elizabeth's twenty-third birthday by attending a performance of Richard Brinsley Sheridan's eighteenth-century farce *The School for Scandal* at the New Theatre, then inviting the play's husband-and-wife stars, Laurence Olivier and Vivien Leigh, to join them at London's chic Café de Paris nightclub. There, according to Churchill's private secretary, Sir John Colville, Charles's parents "tangoed and sambaed, waltzed and quick-stepped" until everyone decided to head to another venue.

In the coming months, there would be countless galas, banquets, and balls packed with aristocrats, movie stars, and foreign dignitaries all waiting to catch a glimpse of the golden couple. At a costume party thrown at the American embassy by US ambassador to the Court of St. James's Lewis Douglas, the Princess wore a maid's uniform and Philip came dressed as a waiter, complete with a long white apron and a towel draped over one arm.

For most of their nights on the town, however, Elizabeth wore "one of those spectacular gowns that usually matched her incredible blue eyes and a glittering tiara," recalled Douglas's daughter Sharman, who became a close friend of Princess Margaret. Philip "often wore his naval uniform with all that braid and those medals. They really were like a fairy-tale prince and princess. They took your breath away."

During this period of frenetic social activity—before she assumed the heavy burden of the monarchy—Elizabeth differed from other mothers in that she expressed little desire to be around her baby. "She was never maternal in that way," Margaret Rhodes said. "Neither was Philip. For whatever reasons, it just wasn't the way either of them were built psychologically."

Thus from the age of two months, Charles saw his parents only twice a day—for fifteen minutes starting at nine in the morning and again for a fifteen-minute session at around six o'clock, right before dinner. When time was up, he was abruptly whisked away by one of his nannies. Over the years, Elizabeth and Philip seldom made physical contact with their children. "Somehow even those contacts," Martin Charteris observed, "were lacking in warmth."

The chasm between Charles and his parents grew even wider when, in

October 1949, Philip was made second in command of a destroyer stationed in Malta, headquarters of Britain's Mediterranean fleet. A month later, less than a week after Charles's first birthday, Elizabeth joined her husband for the first of several lengthy stays. Although she had to leave her infant son behind with the nursery staff for months on end, the Princess reveled in her life abroad as "just another navy officer's wife."

Not quite, of course. Although she lived in a hilltop villa owned by Philip's Uncle Dickie instead of in a palace, she did rush down to greet her husband's ship and socialized freely with the other navy wives. Her large retinue of staff and servants aside, it was the closest Elizabeth would ever come to experiencing what ordinary wives and mothers experienced. It was also, she would say revealingly—and often—"the happiest time of my life."

More accurately, for Charles's parents these six weeks were something of a second honeymoon. They went to parties, danced in the moonlight, sunbathed, and swam in the Mediterranean. On one occasion, Philip, whose practical jokes had livened up their courtship, chased his wife around the room wearing a pair of giant false teeth. On another, he left her with a booby-trapped can of nuts to open that contained a giant and unnervingly realistic rubber snake.

Back at the newly renovated Clarence House—finally the official London residence of the Edinburghs—Charles spent the first two years of his life having virtually no contact with his father and precious little with his mother. When he contracted a case of tonsillitis—at the time rather serious for a one-year-old—neither Elizabeth nor Philip returned to London to check in on their son. Charles also spent that Christmas of 1949 without his parents; they chose instead to remain in Malta, where they also rang in the New Year with the Mountbattens and Philip's navy friends.

Princess Elizabeth, now pregnant for a second time, returned to Clarence House only after her husband's ship put to sea. Charles's sister Anne was born on August 15, 1950—the same day Philip finally achieved his dream of being given command of his own ship. This time Elizabeth took three months to recover—during which she concentrated not on her young children but on the deteriorating state of her father's health. "The King was going downhill very fast, and it was terribly obvious to everyone," Margaret Rhodes said. "Elizabeth loved her father dearly. She worshipped him, really. But she wasn't at all emotional about it. She just stepped up and filled in wherever she was needed." Years later, Elizabeth offered a simple explanation about what it was that gave her the confidence to take charge. "I am," she said firmly, "an executive person."

Princess Elizabeth stayed at Clarence House to celebrate Charles's second birthday, but after just a few days, she left him and Anne behind to join Philip in Malta for the Christmas holidays. It soon became obvious, however, that the couple's idyllic sojourn in Malta would soon be coming to an end. When word came from Buckingham Palace that Princess Elizabeth was needed in London, Lord Mountbatten's wife Edwina remarked, "They're putting the bird back in its cage."

———————

Philip followed his wife back to Clarence House in the summer of 1951—just as King George VI was diagnosed with lung cancer. Bitter over being forced to give up his navy command, the Duke of Edinburgh was now prone to dark moods and petulant outbursts. "Prince Philip was extremely unhappy and impatient," a Clarence House staffer observed. "He was torn from the life he loved at sea and was now under the thumb of Buckingham Palace. He resented that he had no control over his own life, and he took it out on everyone around him."

It didn't help that his wife was now called upon to substitute for the King even more frequently. She hosted a banquet for her uncle King Haakon VII of Norway, and even filled in for her father on horseback during the Trooping the Colour ceremony that marked the monarch's official birthday each June.

In September George VI underwent surgery to have his left lung removed. While he recovered, Elizabeth and Philip embarked on a whirlwind tour of Canada and the United States. They were still abroad when Charles, who now frequently asked his nannies where Mummy and Papa had gone, celebrated his third birthday. This time the King and Queen were on hand to watch their grandson valiantly attempt to blow out the three candles on his cake. At one point in the proceedings, King George, looking natty in a double-breasted suit, posed for official Palace photographs of the event with his wife and two grandchildren on a silk brocade sofa. The Queen wore pearls and a long foxtail stole, while Charles, hair neatly combed, was appropriately dressed by nanny Mabel Anderson in shorts, ankle socks, and a short-sleeved shirt. While Granny beamed from ear to ear as she dandled Anne on her knee, Charles tried earnestly to communicate with his grandfather, who appeared to listen intently.

The touching photograph, which would occupy an important place in Elizabeth II's study throughout her long reign, nonetheless belied the fact that it was staged primarily to reassure the British people that their seriously ill sovereign was well on the road to recovery. It also captured the only real memory Charles would ever have of his grandfather. "I think of it as a tragedy, really," the Prince of Wales would say a half century later, "that I never really knew my grandfather."

Granny was a different matter entirely. While Charles had already been instructed to bow in the presence of the King and Queen, he was also encouraged to hop into Her Majesty's lap and listen to her read fairy tales and nursery rhymes. His grandmother also shared stories of her girlhood in the early part of the twentieth century, when horses still pulled carriages through the streets of London, and of a royal court turned upside down by a weak-willed king and an American interloper named Mrs. Simpson.

More than any other member of the royal family, Charles's grandmother nurtured and defended him, taking the time to look out for his interests and make him feel wanted even when his own parents persisted in ignoring him. In the process, the Queen Mother, who often spent time with him at Royal Lodge, her thirty-room Gothic Revival residence at Great Windsor Park, shaped Charles's character and personality. Most important, she provided him with the love that was so willfully withheld by Elizabeth and Philip. It was a responsibility she would not relinquish until her death in 2002 at the age of 101.

Charles would later describe her as "the most magical grandmother you could possibly have," and for the little boy she was precisely that: a plump, apple-cheeked, perpetually cheerful storyteller and teacher who lavished him with hugs, kisses, and praise. Granny introduced him to the wonders of art, history, books, music, and dance, and was touched by what she recognized as the boy's inherent "kind heart" and "sweetness of nature."

During his parents' long absences, toddler Charles routinely clambered onto his grandmother's bed and went through her jewelry and cosmetics cases, wrapping himself in strands of pearls and trying on lipstick. As early as the age of four, he would comment admiringly on the dresses and hats of ladies of the court, using words such as "lovely" and "beautiful." Periodically, he would be taken to visit his great-grandmother Queen Mary, the sour-faced, steel-willed widow of George V and mother of the King. But she, too, was charmed by the little boy, who showed none of his sister Anne's rambunctious qualities but rather what Queen Mary called "a thoughtful, almost delicate sensibility." Gan-Gan, as Charles called her, allowed him to touch her spectacular collection of jade objects—something no other children (and, for that matter, very few adults) were permitted to do.

Over the years, Charles's grandmother delighted in taking him to concerts—Mozart was her favorite composer—museums, West End shows, the opera, and the ballet. "My grandmother took me to all sorts of performances," he recalled on a BBC special celebrating his sixtieth birthday. "I've never forgotten the sheer excitement of going to see the Bolshoi Ballet at Covent Garden when I was seven. I was hooked for life."

Perhaps because of his own diffident nature, Charles was noticeably kinder than his peers. Unlike his high-spirited, rather bossy sister, the Prince never teased other children and was eager to share his toys—even Jumbo, the blue elephant on wheels that helped him learn to take his first tentative steps. "Prince Charles never took the last piece of cake," recalled Countess Patricia Mountbatten, the elder daughter of Lord Mountbatten, and Philip's first cousin. "He just handed over his favorite toys without thinking twice. He was just that kind of child—very aware of other people's feelings."

Only one other person was as great an influence on Charles during these formative early years. Gradually Miss Lightbody, whom Palace insider Martin Charteris branded a "bitch who was rough on Anne and spoilt Charles," took a backseat to Mabel Anderson, a no-nonsense but warmhearted Scot. (The headstrong Miss Lightbody would abruptly depart Buckingham Palace in 1956, fired by the Queen when Her Majesty added a pudding to Charles's dessert menu and Lightbody refused to serve it.)

Prince Philip, who agreed with Charteris that Lightbody clearly favored Charles over Anne, was delighted with the change. He had far more in common with his boisterous, daredevil daughter than he did with his son, who even as a toddler seemed timid and whiny. The Duke could shout at Anne if she misbehaved, and "it had practically no effect," a close friend said. "Anne just went on doing whatever it was she was doing, and often Philip would just laugh it off or walk away, exasperated." Charles was another matter. "If Philip said a cross word to Charles, the poor boy would dissolve in tears. Philip was trying to bring up a son who would be able to take over as King in a tough world. Certainly Charles wasn't a crybaby, but he was terribly sensitive. Charles used to curl up. He just shrank."

Philip was right about Mabel Anderson in one respect: she could be strict to the point of administering a spanking when it came to exhibiting bad manners and disobeying the rules. But he misread the depth of compassion she had for both her charges, Charles in particular. Anderson proved to be as kind, comforting, and reassuring as the Queen Mother—the center of his daily life from the moment she woke him in the morning until she tucked him back into bed at night. Far more influential on Charles than either of his parents, Anderson was a surrogate mother, and, as the Prince of Wales put it later, "a haven of security, the great haven." The child of a senior courtier who played with the little prince and princess saw even then that, for all intents and purposes, "the nanny was the real mother figure. Charles must have been baffled about what a natural mother-son relationship was meant to be like." It was not hard to figure out why Charles would forge such a deep personal attachment to his nanny. "At least," he observed, "she was there for me."

February 6, 1952

He is young to think so much.
—Winston Churchill, on Charles at age three

Even at such a tender age, Charles was sensitive enough to realize that, on this particular winter morning, something was wrong. There were hurried footsteps in the hallway outside his room at Kensington Palace, and the sound of more adult voices than usual echoing up from the marble-floored galleries below. When Mabel Anderson came into his room to begin Charles's morning routine, he saw tears streaming down his twenty-four-year-old nanny's face. What she couldn't tell him was that, at seven thirty that morning, the King's valet found George VI lying dead in his bed.

The little boy would soon learn, though by no means comprehend, that his grandfather had "joined the angels in heaven" and that his mother was now queen. No one bothered to tell him that his status had also changed. No longer His Royal Highness Prince Charles of Edinburgh, he was now Prince Charles of the House of Windsor, Duke of Cornwall, Duke of Rothesay, Earl of Carrick, Baron Renfrew, Lord of the Isles, and Prince and Great Steward of Scotland. The most important honorific—Prince of Wales—would come later. Still, one of these new titles—Duke of Cornwall—carried with it an income-producing trust fund, instantly making the royal toddler with the plastered-down hair and blue toy elephant extraordinarily rich.

The news of the King's death, only now being broadcast over the BBC, stunned everyone—Welsh coal miners and aristocrats alike. It had been presumed that His Majesty's treatment for lung cancer had been successful and his recovery assured. The King had actually spent an enjoyable day at

Sandringham shooting pheasant, and dined with his wife and Princess Margaret. "There were jolly jokes," Margaret recalled, "and he went to bed early because he was convalescing. Then he wasn't there anymore." In the early-morning hours, King George suffered a fatal coronary embolism. He was fifty-six.

At that moment, Charles's mother, wearing jeans and a safari jacket, was high up in a fig tree in Kenya, taking pictures of the equatorial sunrise. She was substituting for her father on a royal tour of the Commonwealth, which had turned into yet another honeymoon for the Edinburghs. Charles would later hear from his mother that, at the precise moment the King died, a white eagle darted out of the sky and hovered overhead. "It was," she told her wide-eyed son, "very, very strange."

Four hours later—long after the rest of the world already knew—word finally reached Kenya. Philip broke the news to his wife, who looked "pale and worried" but did not shed a tear. Instead, she apologized to her staff and ladies-in-waiting for "ruining everybody's plans" by cutting the trip short. Later, on the twenty-four-hour plane trip home, she excused herself several times to go to the bathroom, where members of the royal party could hear her weeping.

Since her father had been christened Albert (Bertie to his family) but chose to reign as George VI, Martin Charteris asked his boss what name she preferred to be known by as sovereign. "My own, of course," she shot back, incredulous. "What else?" Twenty-six-year-old Elizabeth then returned to sitting ramrod straight at her desk on the plane, writing letters in her loopy script, firing off cables—"seizing her destiny," Charteris said, "with both hands."

Royal favorite Winston Churchill, who had only recently been voted back into office as prime minister after a six-year absence from government, was among the dignitaries in mourning dress standing in the wind and driving rain to greet their new queen at London's Heathrow Airport. Behind them was a line of black leviathans: the Daimler limousines then favored by the royal family. "Oh," she said, pausing momentarily at the top of the stairs to survey the scene, "I see they've brought the hearses."

There would be few such glimpses of gallows humor, or for that matter any humor over the next several days. Less than twenty-four hours after Elizabeth set foot back on English soil, the Earl Marshal formally declared from four separate locations in London that Charles's mother had ascended to the throne:

"The High and Mighty Princess Elizabeth Alexandra Mary is now, by the death of our late sovereign of happy memory, become Queen Elizabeth the Second, by the grace of God Queen of this realm and all her other realms and territories, head of the Commonwealth, defender of the faith, to whom her lieges do acknowledge all faith and constant obedience."

Charles saw nothing of the somber pomp and pageantry surrounding his grandfather's funeral. It was decided by the nursery staff that the whole grim tableau—more than three hundred thousand grief-stricken mourners filing past the King's flag-draped casket as he lay in state in the candlelit Westminster Hall, the diamond-encrusted imperial crown sitting atop the coffin, the massive funeral procession through the streets of London, the outpouring of emotion from average Britons, and the interment in St. George's Chapel at Windsor Castle—was simply too overwhelming for someone so young. Charles spent this trying period for the nation cosseted with Mabel Anderson and his toys at Sandringham, protected from what at times looked like a national nervous breakdown.

The court was still officially mourning the death of the King when Elizabeth and her family moved into Buckingham Palace that April. The Queen and her consort took second- and third-floor rooms on the north side of the building. Above them was a six-room suite for Charles, Anne, and their nannies, and what soon became a separate classroom for Charles. In a royal switch, the Queen Mother—a title Charles's grandmother invented for herself in part to avoid confusion with the new Queen Elizabeth—moved out of Buckingham Palace with twenty-one-year-old Princess Margaret and into Clarence House. The Queen Mother was accustomed to being at the center of power and had wanted to stay at Buckingham Palace, but Philip had other ideas. Still harboring a grudge over the role she'd played in forcing his children to give up his Mountbatten surname, he ordered the central heating cut off in her rooms, and, within a week, she capitulated.

"If his mother was a mystery to Prince Charles before," Charteris observed, "she was much more of a mystery after she became Queen and could spend even less time with her children." For those who knew the new queen, the distance she maintained between herself and her children had less to do with her growing duties than it did her psychological makeup. "She's one of those people who is deeply unemotional," said veteran BBC documentary producer Sir Antony Jay, who claimed Elizabeth was part of an old-school ruling class whose members "had to develop a shell" that "gave them balance, detachment, and a very profound coolness."

Jay claimed that "emotionally detached people like the Queen" came to see "institutions as more important than families. The Queen's children were handed over to nannies, and a kind of emotional cauterization took place. Something was sealed off very early." For the Queen, Jay continued, "that is a strength." Charteris agreed, saying, "As children, I don't think they felt they could talk to her. She's so strong, so stiff-upper-lip, so afraid of her emotions."

There was one concession Charles's mother made to her young son and daughter: a change in the sort of royal protocol that governed the way royal children had acted toward their parents for centuries. Although her own mother and sister were required to bow or curtsy in the Queen's presence whenever they were in public, Charles and Anne were no longer obligated to do so. "It's silly," she told Charteris. "They're too young to understand what's going on."

Charles seldom knew what was going on, only that his parents were extremely busy people doing very important things. Still, as the Prince would recall years later, he had hoped they would be with him in London to celebrate his fourth birthday. Instead, the Queen and Prince Philip chose to spend their son's birthday in Sandringham—a two-and-a-half-hour drive away—while Charles stayed behind in the city. The following week, Charles's parents stopped back in London just long enough to embark on a six-month tour of the Commonwealth—without their children.

When the Queen finally did conclude her tour, Charles eagerly rushed up to greet her. Instead of scooping him up in her arms the way Princess Diana would do with her sons nearly forty years later, the Queen brushed the boy aside. "No, not you, dear," she told the crestfallen prince, turning instead to greet the waiting line of dignitaries. After twenty frustrating minutes, Charles reached toward his mother for a hug, only to have her bend over, shake his hand robotically, and—without uttering a word—return to chatting with the grown-ups.

Charles's father was, if anything, worse. The heir to the throne later described Prince Philip as "undemonstrative—incapable of sensitivity or tenderness." These were, in fact, qualities that the Duke of Edinburgh abhorred. Unfortunately, these were also qualities that he recognized in his son. "To be blunt," a longtime courtier said, "Prince Philip was desperately afraid that Charles was going to be a sissy, or, even worse to a man like him, a nancy [gay]."

Another, more sympathetic character stepped into Charles's life when he turned five: his new governess, Glasgow-born Miss Catherine Peebles—Miss P, or Misspy for short. Instructed by the Queen not to push her son, Misspy spent two hours each morning teaching her royal charge how to read, write his name, draw—all in his own time. She knew if she didn't behave toward him with patience and understanding, or corrected him too abruptly—"He was not terribly good at arithmetic, to say the very least"—her pupil would look stricken and mope for the rest of the day. "He was very responsive to kindness," Miss Peebles remembered, "but if you raised your voice to him, he would draw back into his shell."

Over the next three years, Misspy used the magnificent sculptures, paintings, tapestries, suits of armor, and illustrated books at Buckingham Palace, Sandringham, and Windsor Castle to bring history to life—and, according to court historian Dermot Morrah, to make Charles "see the story of England through the eyes of boys his own age." When Charles was seven, she began to teach him French. Most of the time, however, the Prince seemed distracted, unfocused, preoccupied, anxious—all the words one would use to describe, as Morah put it, "a lonely child abandoned by his parents."

During one of her daughter's long absences, the Queen Mother sat down and penned a letter to her. "You may find Charles much older in a very endearing way," she wrote, as if it were understood that Elizabeth had become a stranger to her own son. "He is intensely affectionate. And loves you and Philip most tenderly."

Despite the physical and emotional distance between Charles and his parents, the boy was not entirely immune to the royal family soap opera dominating the headlines during this period. His aunt Princess Margaret had always treated him with warmth, kindness, and encouragement, sharing the Queen Mother's view that Charles's more thoughtful nature was "something to be admired, not ridiculed."

When Charles was six, the Queen began grappling with how to handle her sister's headline-making plans to marry dashing World War II flying ace Peter Townsend. At the time, Margaret was third in the line of succession behind Charles and Anne—"Just a car crash away from the throne," Churchill observed darkly. Unfortunately for Margaret, Townsend was the divorced father of two sons, as well as a commoner. Both Parliament and the Church of England strongly opposed the marriage. Churchill pointed out to Elizabeth that if her sister and Townsend insisted on going ahead with their plans, she would have to renounce her title—and perhaps more important to the high-living Margaret—her royal income.

The crisis dragged on for two years. On several occasions, and despite his nanny's best efforts, Charles heard his Aunt Margaret shouting angrily at the Queen from behind closed doors. More than once, he asked Mabel Anderson if something was wrong with the usually ebullient Princess, who now stood silent and unsmiling behind the Queen at formal events, eyes red and swollen from crying. In the end, Princess Margaret yielded to pressure and gave up the fight to marry Townsend.

Although he obviously had no concept about the nature of the scandal that dominated the news in Britain for so long, young Charles sensed that the aunt who had paid more attention to him than his mother ever did had been hurt deeply, and that the relationship between Margaret and her sister the Queen had changed. Deftly maneuvering behind the scenes to try to make it appear to Margaret that she was blameless, Charles's mother had actually been the prime force in blocking her own sister from marrying the man she truly loved. Margaret came to view this as an outright betrayal, creating a rift between sisters that would never be entirely repaired.

At the age of eight, Charles—whose predecessors had all been taught within palace walls by governesses and tutors—became the first heir to the throne to attend a primary school. He had no idea what to expect. "Mummy," Charles asked the Queen when he was told of plans for his early education, "what *are* schoolboys?" On the morning of January 28, 1957, Charles was driven in a royal limousine to Hill House, a redbrick private school tucked behind Harrods department store in West London's Knightsbridge district. Prince Philip had decided that, if his eldest son was ever to build the strength of character to be king, he would have to learn something about his subjects. "The Queen and I want Charles to go to school with other boys of his generation," Philip explained to an American reporter at the time, "and learn to live with other children, and to absorb from childhood the discipline imposed by education with others."

Unfortunately, Charles's experience was anything but typical. Once Fleet Street got word of the secret plan to send the heir to the throne to a primary school outside palace walls, photographers lay in wait for his arrival. The press backed off once the Palace asked them to respect the boy's privacy, but the fact remained that Charles was hardly being treated like his fellow students. The headmaster's wife greeted him at the door when he arrived by limousine each morning, and the headmaster bid the Prince good-bye at the end of the day.

Sometimes, having a royal in their midst paid off for the other children. Since it was deemed inappropriate for the future king to swim in a public pool, each week Charles and his classmates were driven to Buckingham Palace to swim in the Windsor family pool. Conversely, Charles got his own small taste of real life when he boarded a bus and rode with the other children to the soccer field used by Hill House. But even then it was impossible to escape who he was; the fields were located on King's Road.

For the most part, Charles adjusted well to student life—as long as he could be certain that each day he'd return to the familiar comforts of his Buckingham Palace home and the warm hugs he could always count on from Mabel Anderson and the Queen Mother. "It was all too comfy for Philip," said Eileen Parker, the wife of Philip's private secretary and friend, Mike Parker. "He wanted his son to have an experience that would build character, but I suppose he thought Charles was still soft—not like his sister at all."

To be sure, Anne was her father's daughter—loud, rowdy, and fearless. When the Queen put Charles on a horse for the first time at the age of four, he was terrified—so frightened ("Scared me stiff," Charles recalled) that he begged to be let down. At the same age, Anne did not hesitate to be deposited on her mount and, confident that she needed no assistance from others, tried to wrestle the reins from the stable hand.

From the very beginning, the heir would never feel wholly at ease around—or wholly accepted by—his parents and siblings. The age gap between Charles and his brothers—Andrew, born in 1960, and Edward (in 1961)—was simply too great for them to ever form a close bond. Besides, from the age of nine on, Charles was away at school. Prince Philip, determined to see his son "toughened up," as the Queen later put it, sent Charles to his old boarding school in Hampshire, Cheam, in September 1957. The Duke of Edinburgh would write later that the school's "Spartan and disciplined" approach made him stronger, more resilient. Ironically, Philip enrolled in Cheam after he had been abandoned by his parents—an obvious parallel to Charles's situation.

Charles, however, was not Philip. At that age, the Duke of Edinburgh already had Nordic good looks, athletic ability, and a personality that was both forceful and outgoing. His son was shy, anxious, chunky, and clumsy at sports such as cricket and rugby. It was also suggested that something might be done about his ears. A simple and common operation to make them less protruding might spare him added embarrassment, Charles's parents were told. According to one of the Queen's cousins, both Elizabeth and Philip offered the same one-word response to such a suggestion: "nonsense."

From his very first day, when a Pathé News film crew dutifully recorded his arrival at Cheam, Charles was a boy apart. After the newsreel showed the other students happily unpacking their model sailboats and planes, its narrator proclaimed breathlessly, "The boats and airplanes are forgotten as a sports car drives up to the door, for it contains a new boy making history: Prince Charles, heir to the throne." Pulling up the school's gravel drive in a Jaguar driven by Prince Philip, the Queen climbs out of the front passenger seat, followed by Charles in his school uniform. But even in this respect, he is different from the others; rather than the school's blue necktie, his is black. The royal family, it is explained, is still in mourning for Charles's recently deceased great-uncle, King Haakon VII of Norway.

"He will be the first king of England to be educated as a boy among other boys—admittedly, a boy with a rather special destiny," the narrator continued. "But his rank will count for little in the rough-and-tumble democracy of playground and dormitory, which is exactly how his parents and his future subjects would wish it."

Within minutes, Charles's parents sped off, leaving their son on his own. A math instructor at the school remembered looking out and seeing Charles standing by himself, a "solitary and utterly wretched figure" who kept his distance from the other boys.

"Charles himself had no experience at all of forcing his way into a group of strangers," British journalist Anthony Holden wrote, "and winning the acceptance of his peers." The other children quickly decided on a nickname for the awkward, chubby newcomer—no matter that he was heir to the throne: "Fatty! Run faster, Fatty!" The sting of those words would still be felt more than sixty years later.

Fully aware that her little prince would be desperately homesick, Mabel Anderson made sure Charles took his beloved teddy bear with him to school for company. But at Cheam, Teddy was simply not enough. When he wasn't crying into his pillow—Charles slept on an iron-framed bed in a dormitory room shared with seven other students—he was writing letters to the Queen and his grandmother begging to come home.

Foreseeing that his son might be teased, Prince Philip had two of his military aides give Charles some self-defense tips—boxing and wrestling moves that would come in handy. Twice during his five years at Cheam, the Prince would end up in a scrap with a classmate so severe that both boys wound up being spanked with a wooden paddle. There were two faculty members at the school who seemed to enjoy it when they "took turns at beating us," Charles said. After the second brawl, "I didn't do it again," the Prince recalled later. "I am one of the people for whom corporal punishment actually worked."

Convinced that her son was a "slow developer," the Queen was determined that he stick it out despite his pleas to leave Cheam. "Charles is just beginning to dread the return to school next week," she wrote in a letter to Prime Minister Anthony Eden during a break in the school year. "So much worse for the second term."

So much worse indeed. One afternoon in July 1958, Charles and his schoolmates were called into the headmaster's sitting room for a special treat: to watch the closing ceremony of the British Empire and Commonwealth Games in Cardiff, Wales. The young Prince sat on the floor with the other boys, eyes riveted to the fuzzy black-and-white images on the small screen, when suddenly Prince Philip appeared. His wife had been expected to preside over the closing ceremonies but was sidelined at home after undergoing an operation on her sinuses. Elizabeth did, however, have an important tape-recorded message for the crowd in the stadium and the millions watching at home.

Charles began to squirm with embarrassment. "To my total horror," he said later, "I heard my mama's voice." The British Empire and Commonwealth Games, said the Queen, "have made this a memorable year for the principality [of Wales]. I have therefore decided to mark it further by an act which will, I hope, give as much pleasure to all Welshmen as it does to me. I intend to create my son Charles Prince of Wales today. When he is grown up, I will present him to you at Caernarfon . . ."

Charles was painfully aware that all eyes were upon him. "All the other boys turned around and looked at me," His Royal Highness would recall in a speech more than a half century later, "and I remember thinking, 'What on earth have I been let in for?' That is my overriding memory."

———

The crowd in the stadium cheered wildly at the news, and the other students congratulated their royal classmate. But Charles, mortified at once again being singled out from his peers, felt an acute sense of betrayal. "It was supposed to be a wonderful surprise," a faculty member said, "but understandably he felt ambushed. No one that age wants to be fawned over. They want to belong. Prince Charles never really belonged."

As predicted, the teasing ramped up. His book bag may have been monogrammed "HRH," but to the rest of the student body, he continued to be known as Fatty. Even the school newspaper got in on the act, blasting him for not being hard-driving enough on the playing field and letting down his fellow players as captain of the Cheam soccer team.

There is no doubt that the Queen knew full well that, as she told her cousin, Charles's years at Cheam "had been a misery for him." Yet nothing could persuade her to overrule her husband or even to make small allowances that would have made the experience more tolerable. Even when it came to her son's health, Her Majesty took a decidedly hands-off approach. Charles suffered from sinus and throat infections, a marked susceptibility to the common cold, and those recurring bouts of tonsillitis that had plagued him since infancy. At the age of eight, he finally underwent a tonsillectomy. Although he was hospitalized for several days, neither the Queen nor Prince Philip stayed by his side at the hospital. One visitor to the Palace that day, former First Lady of the United States Eleanor Roosevelt, was surprised her host was as "calm and composed as if she did not have a very unhappy little boy on her mind."

At Cheam, Charles came down with a particularly virulent strain of the flu, and again, neither the Queen nor Philip looked in on their son. Nor did they when he contracted chicken pox or when he broke his ankle falling down the stairs. While no members of the royal family visited him when he contracted a severe case of measles at Cheam, the Queen Mother did finally step in, insisting that her grandson be transported to her residence on the grounds of Great Windsor Park to recover.

Years later, after thirteen-year-old Charles had been writhing in pain for hours, he was finally rushed to London's Great Ormond Street Hospital in the middle of the night for an emergency appendectomy. The Queen remained in bed, checking on his progress over the phone.

In the end, the only memorably rewarding experience for Charles at Cheam occurred onstage. Cast to understudy the lead role of Richard III in a school production of David Munir's *The Last Baron*, Charles stepped into the spotlight at the last minute when the star transferred to another school. The young prince prepared for the role by listening repeatedly to a recording of Laurence Olivier's iconic performance in Shakespeare's *Richard III*. Since the Queen and Prince Philip were, as was so often the case, out of the country, Princess Anne and the Queen Mother made it a point to be in the audience.

This time the school paper had kind words for Charles. "Prince Charles," wrote the *Cheam School Chronicle*'s drama critic, "very well conveyed the ambition and bitterness of the twisted hunchback." The Queen Mother concurred, writing in a letter to her daughter that "he acted his part very well, in fact he made the part quite revolting!" The irony that Charles would only truly be comfortable playing another misfit monarch—one who was bent both physically from scoliosis and emotionally—sailed over the heads of his relatives.

With the exception of this and a handful of other moments that would fade into the recesses of his memory, Charles was blunt about his first five years at boarding school. "Did I enjoy it?" he would say, pausing for effect. "I *loathed* it."

As he was about to find out, things could get worse—and did.

I can never remember my father ever telling me he loved me. I can never remember him praising me for anything. I can never remember him putting his arms around me or giving me a hug. It was all very sad.
—Prince Charles

He's a romantic, and I'm a pragmatist.
—Prince Philip

THREE

DAYLIGHT UPON MAGIC

They stood silently in the shadows, waiting as the solitary figure finished showering and began to dry himself off. Then they pounced. One older boy, a senior, tied up their unsuspecting target in a sheet, another shoved him into a large empty wicker laundry basket, and yet another secured the latch that locked their victim inside. Together they hoisted the basket up to the wall and hung it from a hook that stuck out from the tiled shower wall.

"Ready?" the ringleader shouted. They could see their thirteen-year-old victim's widening eyes plainly through the gaps in the wicker, and the look of terror on his face.

"Ready!" replied one of the attackers, his hand firmly gripping the shower handle.

The ringleader gave the command, and a blast of freezing water—there was no other kind at Gordonstoun—hit the basket full force. Whooping with delight, the attackers fled, leaving their future king naked, drenched, and shivering. It would be a half hour before a faculty member, hearing Charles's cries for help, came running.

If nothing else, Gordonstoun, Philip's alma mater on the remote, windswept north coast of Scotland, taught the Prince of Wales to endure freezing temperatures. Each day began with a regimen designed to "shake the sleep out of them": a predawn shirtless run through the countryside—

even when it snowed—followed by an icy shower. Classrooms were un-heated, and, in keeping with the school's antediluvian philosophy that "fresh night air" was good for you, dormitory windows were left wide open while the boys slept, regardless of the season. Charles was assigned to Windmill Lodge, a long, narrow, stone-and-timber building with a green asbestos roof and bare wooden floors. There were fourteen beds to a room and bare lightbulbs dangling from the ceiling. Throughout the winter, Charles, whose wooden bed was located beneath a window, often woke to find his bedcovers encrusted with frost or even snow. On those occasions when it rained, he was forced to gather up his blankets and sleep on the floor in the center of the room.

After Charles emerged from five dismal years at Cheam, the Duke of Edinburgh was still worried that his son was "too soft" for the job he was born to do. The Queen, bowing to her husband's authority in all matters related to Charles's upbringing, agreed that four years at Gordonstoun would undoubtedly do the trick. "Charles was a very polite, sweet boy—always incredibly thoughtful and kind, interested in art and music," Elizabeth's cousin and confidant Margaret Rhodes said. "But his father interpreted this as weakness, and the Queen believed he knew what was best." Gordonstoun was supposed to " 'make a man out of him,' although I never really understood what that meant."

From what Charles had heard, life at Gordonstoun was, as he put it, "pretty gruesome." He was leaning toward another school, Charterhouse, where some of the more palatable students from Cheam were going. But he had little to say in the matter. According to court historian Dermot Morrah, a close friend of the Queen Mother who had chronicled Charles's early life with the royal family's blessing, Philip believed his son was "of a shy and reticent disposition" and that "something that would draw him out and develop a little more self-assertiveness in him seemed to be required." Moreover, "Philip himself had been very happy there."

Unfortunately for Charles, he had to overcome one major obstacle not faced by Philip. Anyone who attempted to befriend the future sovereign was immediately branded a bootlicking sycophant, a "suck-up." Whenever Charles walked down a hall on the way to class, he invariably did it to a chorus of boys making a loud sucking noise. At times, according to classmate Ross Benson, they "followed him in packs making that dreadful slurping sound."

If he wasn't being piled on by his rugby teammates or hung up in the shower, the Prince of the realm had to contend with being battered in bed. "The people in my dormitory are foul," he wrote in a letter home. "Goodness, they are horrid. I don't see how anybody could be so foul." It didn't help that Charles snored. According to the Prince, most nights he was pummeled with shoes, pillows, and fists. "I simply dread going to bed," he complained, "because I get hit all night long."

There were other indignities to be suffered. On a school trip to the village of Stornoway Harbour on the Isle of Lewis, Charles was suddenly swept up in a crowd of onlookers. Seeking refuge in a bar, he was asked what he wanted to drink. "My God! What do I do?" Charles thought. "Everybody is looking at me." The fourteen-year-old hesitated a moment before answering. "Cherry brandy," replied Charles, who explained later that he'd had it before while shooting at Sandringham, and it was "the first drink that came into my head." A reporter ("That dreadful woman," Charles would call her) happened to be standing nearby, and the next day, the press had a field day with the tale of the Prince's underage drinking. "The impression grew," recalled Dermot Morrah on behalf of the Queen, "that the heir to the British throne must have been discovered in a drunken orgy." Charles was mortified. "I thought," he said, "that it was the end of the world." Deeply upset over having embarrassed his family, he called his mother and tearfully apologized.

The Prince of Wales needn't have worried about his mother. The incident, she told Morrah at the time, "will do him good. He learnt the hard way" that, given his position, even "the smallest thing" would be blown out of proportion in the press.

But the unfortunate episode did have other, even more hurtful ramifications for Charles. During his first two terms at Gordonstoun, his six-foot-five-inch-tall royal protection officer, Don Green, had become a confidant and father figure to the beleaguered boy. When Green was discharged after the cherry brandy incident, the young Prince was crushed. "I have never been able to forgive them for doing that," Charles said decades later, "because he defended me in the most marvelous way, and he was the most wonderful, loyal, splendid man. . . . It was atrocious what they did."

Charles called home to apologize again after someone pilfered his book of essays and sold it to the German magazine *Der Stern*. "I suppose," he told Mabel Anderson, searching for a reason to blame himself, "I could have been more careful and locked them up."

Referring to Colditz Castle, the infamous medieval stronghold in Germany that served as a Nazi prisoner of war camp, Charles called Gordonstoun "Colditz in kilts." It was "a prison, the worst place on earth, pure torture. I hated every minute of it." Many alumni, none of whom faced the kind of ostracism and cruelty meted out to Charles, agreed. The novelist William Boyd described his nine years there as a kind of "penal servitude."

Bullying at Gordonstoun was, in fact, institutionalized. And nowhere was it worse than in Windmill Lodge, where a sadistic headmaster—"a nasty piece of work . . . vicious, a classic bully," said a classmate of Charles's—oversaw the persecution of younger boys at the hands of older ones. "Prince Charles got the worst of it, and I mean the *worst* you can imagine, simply because of who he was." Karate and boxing lessons aside, Charles did not resist. "Maybe once or twice he made the effort," a former teacher said, "but I never really saw him fight back."

Because of Charles's special circumstances, the chairman of Gordonstoun, Sir Iain Tennant, invited the Prince to spend weekends at Innes House, his nearby estate. Tennant and his wife, Lady Margaret, had close ties to the royal family; Sir Iain had, among other royal duties, been an usher at Elizabeth's coronation. At Innes House, a weepy Charles spent hours holed up in his room, pouring his heart out in long, melancholy letters to relatives and friends.

Intermittently, the Prince of Wales, who had fallen in love with the cello and was now taking lessons at Gordonstoun, would be carted out to give recitals for the Tennants' bemused guests. "He was fairly awful," one said, "but I'm certain he knew that. It was extremely awkward, and I'm sure I wasn't the only one who felt sorry for him."

Once he had finished sawing his way through one of these impromptu weekend cello recitals, Charles invariably made some polite conversation— "It is rude not to make the effort," he observed later—before excusing himself and retreating to his room. "Charles was crushingly lonely for most of his time there," Ross Benson said of his schoolmate's time at Gordonstoun. "The wonder is that he survived with his sanity intact."

Charles's mental health wasn't the only thing that seemed to be deteriorating during this period. The strain, not to mention the primitive living conditions, took a toll on his already fragile health. At one point in his second year, the Prince contracted pneumonia and spent ten days at the Walson-Frazer Nursing Home in Aberdeen.

The arrival of two new siblings only made Charles feel that much more isolated and, in the words of the Queen's cousin, "unwanted. The Queen treated Andrew and Edward very differently than she did Charles and Anne. She was very affectionate toward the two younger ones, especially Edward. Perhaps by that time she felt more comfortable in her role as Queen." Another visitor to Buckingham Palace, shortly after the birth of Edward, said it "was as if a switch had gone off, and suddenly there she was, a loving, caring mum. Too late for Charles and Anne, sadly."

Rather than voicing any resentment toward his mother for blatantly favoring her younger children, Charles saw his little brothers as just something more to miss while he was away from home. Whenever there was a break in the school year, he rushed back to the palace and straight to the nursery floor to spend time with Andrew and Edward and his beloved

Mabel. Once it was time to fly back to Scotland and his dreaded boarding school, Charles fought back tears and dug in. Much of the time, he would simply vanish, forcing Philip to dispatch footmen to track him down inside the palace. "The car would be running in the drive," one recalled, "and you'd finally find him upstairs reading a bedtime story to Andrew or crying in his room." Leaving Mabel was "a big part of it. He said good-bye to his mother as a courtesy—if she gave him the time and wasn't busy doing something more important. But he loved Mabel, and when he said good-bye to her, he was genuinely sad."

"Papa rushed me so much on Monday when I had to go," Charles complained in a letter to his grandmother. "He kept hurrying me up all the time." Hell-bent on stiffening up his son's spine, Philip, a trained pilot, sometimes flew Charles up to an RAF air base just a mile from school and drove him the rest of the way. For the Duke of Edinburgh, part of the trip was invariably spent listening to Charles's anguished pleas to be transferred out of Gordonstoun—followed by Philip's oft-repeated defense of the school and his rationale for sticking it out. As soon as he returned to London, Philip, pale and shaking, would down a pint of Boddingtons—the Duke's favorite brand of beer—to calm his nerves.

Once he returned to Gordonstoun, Charles knew there was always one other person he could go to besides the Tennants. While her grandson attended school in Scotland, the Queen Mother made a point of spending even more time than usual at Birkhall, her estate on the grounds of Balmoral—a two-hour drive due south of Gordonstoun. This was all for the express purpose of providing her grandson another escape hatch when needed.

Victoria and Albert lost their hearts to what she called "this dear Paradise" when they first visited Balmoral, and bought the old castle on the banks of the River Dee in 1852 for $50,000—the equivalent of at least $1.5 million today. The existing structure proved too cramped for the royal household, so Albert replaced it with a baronial granite castle of his own design the following year. Balmoral and Sandringham are technically the only two royal residences privately owned by the Queen and therefore not held in trust for future sovereigns; in other words, she can leave them to whomever she wishes.

The castle itself remained essentially unchanged since Victoria and Albert built it. Antlers jutted out everywhere—over stairways and fireplaces, in bedrooms, dining rooms, and hallways, even in bathrooms—reminders of the royal family's centuries-old passion for what animal rights activists decried as blood sport. Massive paintings of Highland scenes hung throughout the castle, and nearly everything seemed to be covered in tartan plaid: carpets, curtains, linens, furniture—even the china and the kitchen linoleum.

The River Dee Valley seemed no less a magical place to its current inhabitants than it did to Charles's great-great-great-grandmother Victoria. With its endless purple vistas of heather, broad swaths of emerald lawn, dark pine forests, and glistening groves of silver birches, Balmoral struck a special chord with the aesthete prince. Charles was besotted with the "lichen-covered, gnarled grandeur" of Victoria's "dear Paradise." Riverside Walk, a pathway along the banks of the Dee punctuated by a series of miniature white suspension bridges, added to Balmoral's storybook appeal.

Looming in the distance was Lochnagar Mountain, with its eleven peaks rising more than three thousand feet—sentinels mirrored in the dark waters of Loch Muick to the south. When Charles dreamt of running away, which was often, it was to Lochnagar, where he imagined himself living out his life in a secret moss-covered cave.

For the Prince of Wales, who inherited his grandmother's love of fishing, Balmoral was a kind of Nirvana. Its lochs, rivers, and streams teamed with salmon, trout, and pike; when given the chance, Charles would gladly give visitors a tour of the secret pools and river bends where serious fishermen were most likely to get lucky.

It was difficult to imagine any place in the kingdom where wildlife was more plentiful. A handful of species, including the golden eagle and peregrine falcon, were protected. But pretty much everything else was literally fair game, including pine martens, polecats, deer, rabbits, and wildcats—not to mention game birds such as grouse, pheasant, mallard, and pigeon.

Balmoral held special memories for the Queen. It was here that she was "blooded," shooting her first stag at the age of seventeen. With Lord Mountbatten as his guide and mentor, Charles was only ten when he went on his first foxhunt and began tagging along with the adults on weekend shooting parties at Broadlands, Sandringham, and Balmoral. "I have been having great fun shooting lately," he wrote to his great-uncle when he was eleven. "Yesterday I got 23 pheasants, and today I got ten and a partridge, a moorhen and a hare." On a good day, the royal party could expect to bag more than three hundred birds.

Hoping to make his father proud, Charles was just thirteen when he killed his first stag. Instead, Philip embarrassed his guests by hammering away at his son over some perceived misstep—a spilled drink, perhaps, or the unsatisfactory answer to a question. By making his son the object of relentless ridicule, Philip reduced the boy to a stuttering, sputtering puddle of insecurity and self-doubt. Clearly, Philip "thought Charles a bit of a wimp," one guest said, "and Charles realized what his father thought, and it hurt him deeply."

"I thought, 'How could he do that?'" another told historian Jonathan Dimbleby after witnessing a particularly withering dressing down that reduced Charles to tears. Virtually everyone who knew the royals used words such as *rough* and *bullying* to describe the way the Duke treated his eldest child. Eileen Parker, the wife of Philip's private secretary, described Philip's remarks to his son as "incredibly cutting." How did this make Charles feel about his father? "Simply put," a senior courtier confided to the *Times*, "Charles was frightened of him."

Balmoral gave Charles a chance to get away from the toxic influence of his father and immerse himself in nature. Long walks along the moors, fishing and bird-watching expeditions, hours spent identifying the trees, plants, and wildflowers that thrived on the estate—these were the solitary pursuits that, he would say years later, "restored my soul."

Balmoral was used by the royal family only about ten weeks a year, from the "glorious twelfth"—August 12, the official start of grouse season—until early October. Because of Queen Victoria's intense love of Balmoral, for more than 150 years it has marked the beginning and the end of the court calendar. Charles's relatives may have enjoyed their time at Balmoral every bit as much as he did, but that had little to do with a pure love of nature. Most of the royal schedule there was devoted to hunting—specifically, shooting grouse from dawn until dusk.

Decades later, Charles's wife Diana would be no fan of court life at Balmoral. Although she'd been blooded at fourteen—three years earlier than the Queen—the Princess described the time spent there as "days and days spent killing things." Indeed, these all-male shooting parties often came to resemble military maneuvers, with convoys of Land Rovers streaming across the countryside, pausing at various points where they were met by "beaters," who flushed out their quarry, and by "loaders" who made sure they never ran out of ammunition.

Queen Elizabeth would often join the men for lunch, barbecues, and picnics in the field. She always nursed a gin and tonic, whether dining indoors or al fresco, and it was not unusual to see her set the table, serve the food (out of Tupperware containers), and then clear the plates. One guest at Balmoral, Tony Blair, described the whole scene as "intriguing, surreal, and utterly freaky. You'll think I'm kidding, but I'm not. The Queen asks if you've finished, she stacks the plates up, and goes off to the sink. Then she pulls on a pair of yellow rubber kitchen gloves and gets to work."

Longtime Palace spokesman Dickie Arbiter recalled standing at the sink and saying to the Queen, "I'll wash, you dry." Making perfectly clear who was in charge, she replied with a quiet but firm voice: "No, I'll wash, you dry."

All the royals—especially Charles and his mother—were never more content than they were tromping through muddy fields in their Wellington boots, trailed by Irish setters, golden retrievers, Labradors, and, of course, corgis. A common sight was to see Her Majesty, wearing a kerchief tied over her head and a buttoned-up mackinaw, standing at a butcher block chopping up meat for her dogs.

Charles felt most comfortable here, and it was at Balmoral that he felt closest to the rest of the family—despite Philip's ongoing assault on his confidence. So whenever it came time to return to Gordonstoun, Charles would be even more distraught than usual. "I cannot tell you how much I miss Balmoral and the hills and the air," Charles wrote in another mournful letter home. "I feel very empty and incomplete without it all." Emptier still when compared with his life at Gordonstoun. "I hate coming back here," he wrote, "and leaving everyone at home." In another letter, he reminded his mother that the attacks from other students had never really abated. "I hardly get any sleep in the House," he wrote, "because I snore and I get hit on the head all the time. It's absolute hell."

Yet for all Charles's "whinging" (a Briticism for *whining*), the unvarnished truth about what actually went on at Gordonstoun when he was there and for decades afterward only began to surface more than a half century later. In 2015 Gordonstoun was among the more than 160 UK boarding schools hit by a wave of sexual abuse allegations dating back to the 1950s. During a five-year period in Scotland alone, 116 sexual crimes were reported at boarding schools, leading to more than one hundred arrests and convictions.

As late as 2018, when police files on abuse allegations at Gordonstoun disappeared, horror stories emerged about students who had been abused twenty, thirty, fifty years earlier. One former student testified to being drugged by a teacher, photographed naked, and then sexually assaulted in his dormitory bed. That same teacher similarly "groomed"—a term for the seduction, exploitation, and sexual abuse of children—at least a dozen other boys. The man was killed in a car crash before he could be brought to justice.

Another Gordonstoun faculty member, this one a respected physics instructor, was sent to jail for giving naked "swimming lessons" to students and then groping them underwater. Yet another made a habit of passing by a student's desk, bending over him as if to check his work, and suddenly thrusting his hand down the boy's pants. Edinburgh journalist Alex Renton, who attended a different but equally posh boarding school, was victimized in a similar way in 1970. "A math teacher pulled me—an eight-year-old pupil—to his chest while he pushed his hand down the front of my corduroy shorts," he recalled. "It wasn't wholly a surprise. I knew this could happen with [this teacher], and that it was best to submit. He was violent: he liked to grab ears as well as penises, and would occasionally throw children who had annoyed him down the short flight of stairs that led from his classroom to the next." Once the teacher "finished his fumbling in your shorts," Renton went on, he "would give you a reward": candy.

Not all of the abusers were faculty and staff. For many of the younger students, not just Charles, the hulking upperclassmen also posed a threat. Encouraged to be tough on underlings when enforcing the rules, many older boys subjugated and humiliated younger students in what amounted to one protracted hazing ritual.

He probably would have faced a similar situation at any top British boarding school. Old Etonian Danny Danziger, who became a prolific author and newspaper columnist, described an atmosphere of "adolescent eroticism" at his school that often resulted in "homosexual liaisons—sometimes lustful, sometimes innocent."

By today's standards, much of what went on at these elite boarding schools would be considered serious crimes. Assault, rape, underage drinking, drug dealing, and drug abuse—not to mention grooming, in its most abhorrent sense—were rampant. "Particularly in the nineteen sixties," said a classmate of Charles's, "because you had this clash of the Old World aristocracy and the sex, drugs, and rock and roll counterculture." For some emotionally vulnerable students, the stress was too much. "Back then, they tried to sweep it under the rug," said the classmate, "but suicide was a problem."

Charles has never claimed he was the victim of any kind of sexual assault, but classmates recounted that he was taunted, threatened, physically attacked, and belittled constantly.

More than one Gordonstoun alumnus of the time said that older students sometimes urinated on underclassmen to establish dominance by humiliating them. But at the time, "None of these things were considered crimes, if you can believe it. It fell under the heading of horseplay."

"Neglect was a part of the magic of the British boarding school system," Renton said, "admired and copied across the world. . . . It is now abundantly clear that the system left the children of the privileged just as vulnerable to sadists and predatory pedophiles as were the occupants of Britain's worst care homes and young offenders' prisons."

Authorities looking into the allegations stretching over more than fifty years often still find that their hands are tied. Alumni and current students alike are reluctant to break the code of silence that Renton likens to the Mafia's omertà. At Gordonstoun, "the rule is don't snitch, don't tell, don't talk outside the class." Even in an age of zero tolerance, victims of past abuse would find it almost impossible to overcome these obstacles. In 2018 one former student from another boarding school who had been assaulted told the *New York Times* that his search for justice was "like knocking my head against a brick wall."

Charles may have complained ceaselessly in his letters home, but he, too, obeyed the code of silence when it came to the more degrading aspects of life at Gordonstoun. "The things that went on there," he once confided to an American friend. "Unspeakable."

It didn't help matters that every time Charles seemed to be making some headway with his peers, he would be called back to London to take part in a ceremony that served to again remind the others that he was not—and could really never be—one of them. In January 1965 Charles stood alongside his parents at the spectacular state funeral for Winston Churchill. Once again Gordonstoun students gathered around the headmaster's television set to watch their classmate lead more than 110 world leaders in paying tribute to one of history's titans—someone Charles regarded as a friend of the family. When he returned, said one member of the teaching staff, "Prince Charles was given the cold shoulder. How are you supposed to behave toward someone who is from such a different, rarified world—particularly if you don't want to appear to be sucking up?"

Nevertheless, by the time he turned seventeen later that year, the Prince of Wales was settling into his upperclassman status and managed a few small victories. Although he was by and large a mediocre student and scarcely setting the world on fire with his cello playing, Charles surprised everyone with his portrayal of the doomed Scottish king in a school production of *Macbeth*. He had hoped to at last impress the Duke, but instead Charles heard Prince Philip laughing in the audience. "All I could hear was my father and 'Ha, ha, ha.'" After the curtain went down, Charles asked his father why he was laughing. "It sounds like the Goons," replied Philip, referring to Peter Sellers and the other over-the-top, slapstick comedy stars of British radio's *The Goon Show*.

It was scarcely the first time Philip went out of his way at a public event to make known his thinly veiled contempt for his eldest son. In addition to his artistic pursuits, Charles found some consolation and reassurance in religion. He was keenly aware that he was destined to become the head of the Church of England, and when it came time for his confirmation in 1964, the sixteen-year-old prince regarded the matter seriously.

Prince Philip, apparently, did not. Throughout the confirmation ceremony, which was presided over by Archbishop of Canterbury Michael Ramsey in the private chapel at Windsor, Charles's father sat quietly but very visibly reading a book on naval tactics. The Duke, whose own religious affiliation over the years had drifted from Greek Orthodox to German Protestantism to the Windsors' Anglican faith, was sending a message that managed to offend both the clergy and his son. Furious, the Archbishop told the Dean of Windsor that Prince Philip was being "bloody rude." Charles, who simultaneously idolized, feared, and resented his father, chalked it up to just one more incident of parental callousness.

Charles's love of the arts, coupled with his decided lack of interest in science and team sports, convinced Philip all the more that his son was a weakling. Even Gordonstoun, with its draconian methods and history of systematic bullying, hadn't turned Charles into the man Philip wanted him to be. Australia, the Duke decided, would test his son's mettle in ways it had never been tested before.

To make certain that this time the job got done, Charles was going to Timbertop, the wilderness survival program run by Geelong Church of England Grammar School near Melbourne. "It will put some steel in him," Philip said, "or I simply give up."

The Prince of Wales, who had no say in the matter, was excited by the prospect of making the ten-thousand-mile journey more or less on his own. He was also understandably apprehensive when, with his father's trusted equerry David Checketts at his side, he arrived in Australia in February 1966. Landing in Sydney, Charles nervously watched out the window of his plane as dignitaries—including the Prime Minister and the Governor-general—lined up at the foot of the steps to greet him. He wrote to his great-uncle Dickie Mountbatten that he was glad he "did nothing as foolish as to fall down the steps and land on my face at the bottom," and that the Australians who turned out to cheer him "all seemed to be happy and kind."

In the absence of the abuse and sadistic bullying that so poisoned the atmosphere at Gordonstoun, Charles flourished in the Australian Outback, even under the harshest conditions. Days were spent chopping wood, clearing brush, feeding pigs, and setting out on fifty-mile hikes through the wilderness. Along the way, he encountered giant huntsman spiders with twelve-inch-long legs, venomous tiger snakes and lowland copperheads, poisonous bearded dragon lizards, and "flying foxes"—huge fruit bats with a wingspan of up to five feet. "You have to inspect every inch of the ground you hope to put your tent on," Charles wrote, "in case there are ants or other ghastly creatures." He was referring to bull ants, "which are three-quarters of an inch and bite like mad!"

Charles's exposure to Australia and its people had a "profound, very spiritual" effect on the Prince. He visited missionary outposts where natives newly converted to Christianity "were eager to take part in the services, and the singing was almost deafening. . . . It is rather wonderful to go somewhere where this strikes you." One of these converts was Davey Douglas, an aborigine who was convicted of murder and cannibalism after a tribal fight in the 1920s. Douglas assured the future King that, at age seventy, he no longer "ate people."

Charles's Australian sojourn had some unexpected side benefits. In the course of making more than fifty public appearances Down Under, he managed to conquer his paralyzing fear of crowds. "I took the plunge," he told the *Daily Mail*, "that suddenly unlocked a completely different feeling." Now convinced that the people who waited for hours to catch a glimpse of him were not his enemies, he was "able to communicate and talk to people so much more." For a public figure destined to make thousands and thousands of public appearances in his lifetime, this was a major breakthrough, and one that was facilitated by what Charles called "the natural warmth and kindness—the goodness—of the Australian people."

Not all of Charles's six months in Australia was spent battling giant spiders and working the rope line at staged events. The Prince was also feted as the guest of honor at dozens of dinners, galas, and parties attended by people his own age. At a school dance in Melbourne, he met Dale Harper, the spirited blonde daughter of wealthy printing magnate Barry Harper. Nicknamed Kanga by Charles because of her bouncy personality, Dale—later Lady Tryon—eventually became his mistress and confidante.

When Charles departed Australia, he was scarcely recognizable—tanned, fit, and confident. Much to Philip's surprise, his son had returned home a far more formidable foe on the polo field. Although Philip had taken up the sport relatively late in life, he was, as with all things athletic, a fierce and skilled competitor. Even before Charles entered Gordonstoun, the Duke gave him his first polo pony and oversaw his son's first attempts at wielding a polo stick on Smith's Lawn at Great Windsor Park. At fifteen, Charles played his first match on a team captained by his father. Predictably, Philip was never satisfied with the novice's performance, offering up hefty portions of profanity-laced criticism and virtually no praise. "He was just brutal," a teammate said, "singling Prince Charles out at every turn." Now Charles, having practiced under the blazing Australian sun with some of that country's leading players, was competing against his father—and winning. "Was Prince Philip finally proud?" their teammate asked. "Hard to tell. Never heard him say it if he was."

Philip was aware that his influence over his son was diminishing. Having never attended college, he now turned to others to decide the proper course. On December 22, 1965, the Queen hosted a dinner at Buckingham Palace for the sole purpose of deciding which university the heir to the throne should attend. Among the guests were Prime Minister Harold Wilson, the Archbishop of Canterbury, Lord Mountbatten (technically representing the heads of all the armed services), and Philip—but not, of course, Charles himself.

Mountbatten, mentor to Philip and now mentor to Charles, took charge. The choices were quickly narrowed down to the predictable two: Oxford and Cambridge. The teenager's great-uncle Edward VIII, now the all-but-exiled Duke of Windsor, living in France with his wife, the former Wallis Simpson, had attended Oxford, as had Prime Minister Wilson. However, the last king—Charles's grandfather George VI—had attended Cambridge. No monarch, however, had actually stayed long enough to earn a degree. By the end of the dinner, Charles's immediate future had been mapped out: he would attend Trinity College at Cambridge University with the intention of becoming the first heir to the throne to actually graduate, followed by the Royal Naval College in Dartmouth and a stint in the Royal Navy.

The final decision was, theoretically at least, entirely up to Charles. "He was at an age when many boys tend to either fall in love with tradition or rebel violently against it," said Morrah, again speaking for the Queen. "He was among the lovers. To him, tradition appeared to be the foundation of all our lives." Charles was smitten with the ancient architecture of both Oxford and Cambridge, but he was also looking for a campus with the requisite escape hatch—a place to seek refuge if the strain was too much, as it had been at Cheam and Gordonstoun. Since Cambridge was only an hour's drive from Sandringham, that seemed the logical choice. For those visits with the family, Charles would stay at Wood Farm, a five-bedroom brick farmhouse on the grounds of the estate.

While he finished up his final term at Gordonstoun, Charles celebrated his eighteenth birthday with a party at Windsor Castle attended by 150 guests—mostly the teenage and twentysomething sons and daughters of the aristocracy. The hosts of the bash, Queen Elizabeth and Prince Philip, remained discreetly on the sidelines. Not long after, Charles was back at Gordonstoun watching the news on television when he learned that he had been officially appointed a Counselor of State. Having reached the age of eighteen, he was now empowered to step in as regent if for some reason the Queen became mentally or physically incapacitated. He also joined a select few—the Queen Mother, Princess Margaret, and George VI's brother Prince Henry, Charles's great-uncle the Duke of Gloucester—who were authorized to act on the monarch's behalf whenever she was abroad.

Turning eighteen also meant that Charles would receive a bump in pay. Income from the Duchy of Cornwall was to go directly to the heir apparent, but in steps. Now Charles was entitled to $80,000 a year—the equivalent of more than $600,000 today. At the age of twenty-one, he would begin collecting six times that amount.

Once again the press and onlookers swarmed Charles's two-passenger Mini as it pulled up to the gates of Trinity College, Cambridge University in October 1967. Charles glanced up at the looming figure of his ancestor Henry VIII, who founded Trinity in 1546. Grinning from oversized ear to ear, the Prince of Wales shook hands with a visibly edgy Lord Richard Austen Butler, former chancellor of the exchequer and now master of Trinity, and then went on an abbreviated tour as newsreel cameras dutifully recorded the scene for posterity.

Although "Rab" Butler promised that Charles would be treated like every other student, that was clearly impossible from the start—a fact of life painfully obvious even to the Prince. As the huge wooden gates of the college were closed behind him, preventing the crowd from pouring in, Charles likened it to "a scene from the French Revolution."

That first day, the new student was ceremoniously presented with a key to his own second-floor rooms—quarters that included a bedroom, a sitting room, a kitchen, and, most important, a private bathroom installed especially for Charles by Buckingham Palace workmen. All other freshmen made do with sharing cramped dormitory rooms and communal toilet facilities in the basement. The Queen had, in fact, paid a secret visit to Trinity to inspect her son's accommodations in advance of his arrival. Finding them wanting, she instructed her interior decorators to install draperies, rugs, and a tartan plaid comforter from Balmoral for the Prince's narrow iron bed. In addition to the maid assigned to every Trinity College student, Charles was attended to by his equerry David Checketts and a bodyguard, both of whom had been given their own rooms adjacent to the Prince's suite.

In the event that Charles began to feel the walls of his still relatively modest quarters close in, Lord Butler slipped him a separate key to the luxuriously appointed Master's Lodge, giving the teenager even more space in which to unwind. With the understanding that His Royal Highness would be zipping off to Sandringham for shooting parties and polo matches, Butler gave special dispensation for Charles to park his MGB at the college. All other first-year students, meanwhile, were expressly forbidden to have cars on campus.

In their zeal to provide a future king with the proper training, Uncle Dickie Mountbatten and Prime Minister Harold Wilson had drawn up a list of courses that included history, constitutional law, economics, and foreign affairs—all the obvious areas of study for someone destined to occupy a place on the world stage. Charles would have none of it. Inspired by his contact with aboriginal peoples in Australia and New Guinea, as well as archaeological digs he had been a part of in northeastern Scotland—specifically inside the caves of Covesea and Kinneddar—Charles instead decided to study anthropology and archaeology. He argued that these subjects were equally valuable, especially if he were to rule a multiracial society. "To get on with people of other races and countries," he said, "you've got to know how they live, eat, work, what makes them laugh—and their history."

Yet Charles remained cut off from others, even in the rarified atmosphere of Trinity College, Cambridge University. Although the student body at the time approached one thousand, Charles spent most of his time in the company of four or five students whose families had some connection to the Palace. The Dean of Windsor's son Edward Woods and his cousin James Buxton, both urged by their families to help Charles adjust to his new situation, walked with him to his lectures, dined with him in his suite of rooms, and asked him to go with them to concerts and movies.

Aside from Woods, Buxton, and a handful of others he felt comfortable inviting to the royal family's Saturday shooting parties at Sandringham, Charles had little interest in consorting with any of Trinity's remaining nine hundred–plus students. Checketts told journalist Graham Turner that Charles "didn't really mix with anybody. He lived for the weekends." To be sure, from the standpoint of someone raised to appreciate such Edwardian era pursuits as weekend shooting parties, nothing about college social life could compare with what Sandringham had to offer. "You really had the crème de la crème of wild birds," Charles once tried to explain. "They are beautifully driven. Everything is perfect."

Such statements only buttressed the negative opinion most young people had of His Royal Highness. While the counterculture took hold on British campuses and students took to the streets en masse to protest the Vietnam War, Charles looked like he had just stepped out of a 1940s issue of *Town & Country*. Even those he allowed into his tight inner circle conceded that Charles—who always wore corduroys, tweed jackets, immaculately polished dress shoes, button-down shirts, and a tie—"was unbelievably straightlaced. He never let down his guard."

Charles, dismissed as "stuffy" and "a snob" by most on the Trinity campus, did not hesitate to return the favor. He was openly contemptuous of his long-haired contemporaries, repeatedly dismissing them as "dirty," "smelly," "noisy," "sadly misguided," and "pathetic." He defended tradition—"tradition is really the basis of everything"—over "change for the sake of change, which from my point of view is pointless."

If Charles's resolute pomposity offended most, he did have admirers on the faculty. Theologian Harry Williams, who combined Church of England teachings with Carl Jung and Sigmund Freud in his thought-provoking lectures on "finding the inner self," saw in Charles "grace, humility, and the desire to help other people. It may sound absurd, but I always thought that he had the makings of a saint when he was young." Ironically, the word *saint* would never again be seriously applied to the Prince, although it would be frequently used to describe his spurned wife.

Charles, whose academic career had thus far been lackluster, managed to do well in his final exams at the end of his first year at Trinity. The Prince, who felt that the press was determined to make all members of the royal family "look rather dim," was thrilled that this achievement was "applauded in the national press. . . . I have achieved my desire anyway, and shown them in some small way, at least, that I am not totally ignorant or incompetent! The tables will now be turned, and I will be envisaged as a princely swot!"

It would be another fifty years before Charles revealed that he was nearly killed during his first year on campus. While he was riding his bicycle just outside the Trinity library, he was "run over by a bus. Quite how I survived, I don't know." Had Charles not recovered—incredibly, he escaped with scrapes and bruises—his brother Prince Andrew would have become first in line for the throne, followed later by his daughters Beatrice and Eugenie.

Starting his second year in 1968, Charles—against the advice of his less-than-sympathetic father—decided to return to the stage. He auditioned for the college's drama group, the Dryden Society, and was instantly cast in a Joe Orton comedy called *The Erpingham Camp*, playing a doddering minister who takes a pie in the face while trying to deliver a sermon. The Prince of Wales discovered that he had a knack for slapstick, and was soon portraying "an expert on 'Bong' Dynasty Chinese bidets," an angler who catches a fish so large that it pulls him off the stage, and a weatherman clad in gas mask and flippers forecasting "a manic depression over Ireland" and "a warm front followed by a cold back."

The comedy was dreadful, and meant to be so. By making fun of himself in such an outlandish way, Charles hoped that he might break down the invisible barriers between himself and other people his age. But the strategy didn't work. "When I try to go around with people, it is a pretense," he said, "and the awful thing is that I feel *they* can feel it." The Prince acknowledged that he was simply "a single person that prefers to be alone. I'm happy just with hills or trees as companions."

Not for long. At the age of twenty, Charles had never been seriously involved with anybody romantically. In fact, to the best of anyone's knowledge, he had never been on a date. Rab Butler and his wife, Mollie, were determined to change that. When the Prince attended a dinner party at the Butlers' in May 1969, he was introduced to Rab's twenty-five-year-old research assistant, Lucia Santa Cruz. She was, Mollie Butler said, "a most charming and accomplished girl. I am confident she will find favor with Prince Charles."

The daughter of Chile's ambassador to the Court of St. James's, Santa Cruz had degrees from Oxford and King's College London, spoke four languages, and was as stunning as any model gracing the cover of British *Vogue*. With her fashionably short skirts, wide-set brown eyes, lush lips, and long, sable-colored hair, Santa Cruz invariably captured all the male attention in the room—and the Prince of Wales was no exception.

"Prince Charles was totally smitten with Lucia," Mollie Butler said, "and she with him." Santa Cruz was a Roman Catholic, and, by law, that precluded Charles from ever marrying her and becoming king. Since their affair could never result in matrimony, Mollie reasoned that Santa Cruz was "a happy example of someone on whom he could safely cut his teeth, if I may put it thus."

In what would become a decades-long pattern in his dealings with women, Charles did not hesitate to use all the tricks at his disposal—including the services of Palace officials—to arrange his trysts. At this point in his sexual career, Charles leaned heavily on the Queen's deputy master of the royal household, Patrick Plunket, to ensure the couple's privacy.

Privacy in matters of the heart was one thing. But when it came to the ongoing success of the monarchy, Charles was one of the first in the family for whom a carefully mapped-out publicity campaign was essential. For years, the Queen's press secretary, the dyspeptic Richard Colville, had essentially waged war on Fleet Street, controlling what little access the press was allowed with an iron fist. Now he had retired and been replaced by William Heseltine, an easygoing Australian with new ideas about how best to use the news media to the monarchy's best advantage.

"The essence of the Queen's role was communication," Heseltine said, "and it needed improvement." When the BBC approached the Palace to film a documentary on Charles's life, the Queen and Prince Philip nixed the idea. They were concerned that he would somehow embarrass them. When Heseltine suggested a more wide-ranging television documentary on the royal family pegged to the upcoming investiture, famed broadcaster and anthropologist David Attenborough was among the many who tried to shoot it down.

"You're killing the monarchy, you know, with this film you're making," Attenborough wrote to the producer-director of the controversial and groundbreaking BBC television documentary *Royal Family*. "The whole institution depends on mystique and the tribal chief in his hut. If any member of the tribe ever sees inside the hut, then the whole system of the tribal chiefdom is damaged, and the tribe eventually disintegrates." Even Bryan Forbes, a shrewd commercial filmmaker, had his doubts. "If you let the genie out of the bottle," he said, "you can never put the cork back again." All echoed the verdict of Victorian constitutional historian Walter Bagehot when it came to monarchical mystique: "We must not let in the daylight upon magic."

But let it in they did. For seventy-five days, the Queen allowed cameras to shadow her and members of her family in an effort to sell the Windsors as just regular folks—sort of. The film began by describing Charles as heir to the "thirteen thrones" of the Commonwealth, and then showing the Queen's piper, wearing full Royal Stewart tartan regalia, play his bagpipes just outside Her Majesty's bedroom window at precisely nine a.m.—a tradition that has endured since Queen Victoria decreed that every sovereign should awake to the sound of Scottish bagpipes.

Over the next ninety minutes, viewers were treated to, among other things, the Queen chatting on the phone with US President Richard Nixon, working the room at Palace receptions, accepting diplomatic credentials, riding sidesaddle during her official birthday parade, feeding carrots to her horses, decorating a Christmas tree, moving among the guests at garden parties, presiding over a family barbecue at Balmoral, tending to the ever-present red boxes of state, fishing for change in her purse to buy four-year-old Edward some candy at a Balmoral sweets shop ("This is all I've got," she tells the bemused clerk), and laughing with her children at a sitcom.

Some moments were cringe inducing: "How do you keep a regally straight face when a footman tells you, 'Your Majesty, your next audience is with a gorilla'?" the Queen asks. "It was an official visitor, but he looked just like a gorilla." In another scene, Prince Philip reveals that his father-in-law, George VI, "had very odd habits"—like wearing a huge bearskin hat while he hacked away savagely with a pruning knife in the royal gardens. More than once, Philip heard the King shouting obscenities from inside a rhododendron bush. "Sometimes I thought he was mad."

Charles, as it happened, was shown in the best possible light—as an action man on water skis, riding a bicycle, and studying for his finals in history, which he added to his major as a college sophomore. Eventually, as Attenborough and others predicted, the film would be viewed as an enormous mistake. The public had not simply been given a peek behind the imperial curtain. The curtain had been yanked open and pulled down, revealing the royals to be anything but superhuman. The Queen felt that, by essentially stooping to the level of her subjects, she had lost no small amount of their respect; much of the sense of mystery that had always surrounded royalty had been eroded. This was the first breach in the wall, which would now be chipped away with every new misstep and scandal. Elizabeth II was convinced that the institution of the monarchy had been seriously damaged by *Royal Family*—so much so that she would eventually order that it be locked away for good.

In the short run, however, *Royal Family* was an enormous success. Beginning on June 21, 1969, it aired five times and was seen by an estimated four hundred million people in 130 countries. Sir Peregrine Worsthorne warned at the time: "Initially the public will love seeing the royal family as not essentially different from anybody else and in the short term letting in the cameras will enhance the monarchy's popularity. But," Worsthorne went on, "in the not-so-long run, familiarity will breed, if not contempt, familiarity."

Although his grandmother was adamantly opposed to doing the documentary—"It is the most terrible idea," she had told the Queen—Charles was happy for the goodwill it created in the weeks leading up to his investiture. By way of preparing himself for his role as Prince of Wales, Charles had already spent nine weeks at the University College of Wales at Aberystwyth immersing himself in the region's history, culture, and language. Now confined to a tiny room in a granite-walled residence hall, Charles once again largely shunned his fellow students, labeling them "the same long-haired, bare-footed, and perspiring variety" that he had come across at Trinity College. Two days a week, he drove the twelve miles north to Towyn Royal Air Force base, where, on the advice of Prince Philip, he donned an RAF flight suit and took flying lessons.

When Charles finally did make his maiden speech in Welsh at an arts festival, he was booed and heckled by protestors calling for Welsh independence. Police subdued the demonstrators, and the Prince, looking slightly bemused, persevered. "I was grateful," he said later, "because they were distracting people in the audience from my terrible pronunciation. The Welsh language is impossible—I felt as if I had a mouth full of marbles!"

In the years leading up to the investiture, there had been a surge in Welsh nationalism that created some serious security issues. Now bombs were being detonated in northern parts of the principality, and there were terrorist threats aimed at disrupting the ceremony at historic Caernarfon Castle. The Queen worried about her son's safety. To assuage Her Majesty's concerns, 250 extra police officers were brought in to man roadblocks, guard bridges, and search every nook and cranny where an explosive device might be planted. Another seventy undercover agents mingled with spectators.

The first English Prince of Wales was born in 1284 at Caernarfon Castle, so the turreted medieval fortress seemed the logical setting for Charles's investiture. The ceremony itself, however, had occurred only once before in modern times—when Charles's Great-Uncle David, later Edward VIII, was forced to don white satin britches and purple satin robes trimmed in ermine and be crowned by his father, George V, in 1911. The whole spectacle was concocted by then Prime Minister David Lloyd George, a Welsh native, to glamourize the monarchy and further cement Welsh ties to Britain.

Under the direction of Princess Margaret's husband, Lord Snowdon, whom she married in 1960 when he was just the photographer Antony Armstrong-Jones, Charles's investiture offered plenty of spectacle for the thousands gathered at Caernarfon and the tens of millions more watching around the world. Aimed at evoking Arthurian themes, Snowdon's set was located in the castle courtyard and featured three medieval slate thrones beneath an enormous Plexiglas canopy (to allow a multitude of camera angles). Charles, spared from having to wear white satin breeches, wore instead the uniform of the chief in command of the Royal Regiment of Wales beneath his princely robes.

Trying not to be distracted by the muffled sound of bombs going off in the distance, the Prince rode through the streets of Caernarfon in an open carriage to the castle. Choirs sang, military bands played, and three thousand ceremonial troops paraded beneath battlements draped with banners bearing Welsh red dragons and the royal coats of arms. The Queen, wearing a pale yellow dress and Tudor-inspired hat, took her place on one of the three slate thrones. Philip, in full military garb, sat to her immediate left. Despite the carefully crafted medieval atmosphere, the Queen kept her handbag and a matching yellow umbrella propped up at her side.

Once escorted into the courtyard by the elaborately outfitted Garter King of Arms, Charles knelt and glanced about absentmindedly as speeches were read in both English and Welsh. Then the Queen bestowed upon him the symbols of office—a ceremonial sword, gold rod, and gold ring symbolizing his "marriage" to Wales. When the moment came for the Queen to place the heavy gold crown on Charles's head, both stifled giggles. During rehearsals at Buckingham Palace a few days before, the crown was, Her Majesty recalled, "too big and extinguished him like a candle-snuffer!" The crown still proved unwieldy; after the Queen placed it on his head, a straight-faced Charles struggled to readjust it.

Once the Prince of Wales was finally swathed in purple and ermine robes, the ceremony reached its climax. "For me," he wrote later in his diary, "by far the most moving and meaningful moment came when I put my hands between Mummy's and swore to be her liege man of life and limb and to live and die against all manner of folks—such magnificent medieval, appropriate words, even if they were never adhered to in those old days."

Charles's official debut as Prince of Wales drew a global TV audience estimated at a half billion and won high marks for the seemingly calm and collected prince. For the next several days, he toured Wales in a bubble-topped Rolls-Royce ("It was July, and I was boiled!" he wrote), drawing huge, enthusiastic crowds wherever he went. As expected, neither the Queen nor Prince Philip offered words of praise to their son, and made sure they were busy doing other things when he returned home to London.

One of those few people whose opinion he valued did write, however, and gave him a nine out of ten for his performance. "I'm sure you'll keep your head," his great-uncle Lord Mountbatten wrote. "Your Uncle David had such popularity that he thought he could flout the Government and the Church and make a twice-divorced woman Queen. His popularity disappeared overnight." Mountbatten reassured Charles that his place in the people's hearts was secure, "provided you keep your feet firmly on the ground."

Possessing not the slightest inkling of what pitfalls lay ahead for him, the newly invested Prince of Wales replied to his great-uncle with confidence. "As long as I do not take myself too seriously," he wrote to the man he now called Grandpapa, then "I should not be too badly off."

Certainly not financially. On his twenty-first birthday, Charles came into full control of all revenue generated by the Duchy of Cornwall, a vast real estate empire set up by Edward III in 1337 to provide a steady income for future kings. The duchy is composed of 135,000 acres spread out over Cornwall, Herefordshire, Somerset, Dorset, Wiltshire, and Gloucestershire, and almost all of the Isles of Scilly. It includes farmland, forests, waterfront property, London real estate, Dartmoor Prison, tin mines, and even a cricket stadium. In 1968 Charles would collect the equivalent of $3.6 million in 2018 dollars. Ultimately, the Duchy of Cornwall would be valued at more than $1.2 billion, providing Prince Charles—who, incidentally, also has other sources of income—with an annual take well in excess of $35 million.

To celebrate Charles's coming of age, the Queen threw a black-tie party for four hundred at Buckingham Palace. The Prince of Wales, whose musical tastes were the most refined in the family, asked for a classical concert to kick off his twenty-first birthday celebration—specifically, an all-Mozart program performed by legendary violinist Yehudi Menuhin. There was a banquet, followed by fireworks over the Palace, and dancing to a rock band. Charles took time to take a quick spin in the gift his mother had given him to mark the occasion: a Seychelles-blue Aston Martin Volante DB6 MKII convertible. (The car, which Charles would convert to run on sustainable fuel in 2008, was famously driven by Prince William on his wedding day.)

Charles graduated from Cambridge on June 23, 1970, having studied history, anthropology, and archaeology—and earning a less-than-stellar C average. He was the first heir to the throne ever to earn a college degree, but he also knew that, despite his mediocre grades, the general assumption would be that he had been, as he himself put it, "treated with kid gloves." He was, of course—from his accommodations (he was moved into an even more spacious suite of wood-paneled rooms in his final year), to his private staff, to his frequent absences to perform royal duties on behalf of the Crown.

On one of those missions that took him away from his studies—a monthlong tour of Australia, New Zealand, Hong Kong, and Japan—he made stopovers in New York and Los Angeles. It marked the first time Charles set foot on US soil, and the impression it left on him was scarcely a positive one. "A bevy of microphones, pushy photographers and reporters, a host of bulging-bodied cops with itching fingers," he wrote in his diaries, describing the scene in LA. "Much back-slapping, hand-clutching and endless speechifying." One official in particular irked him: "Pretty insufferable, rather pompous . . . wouldn't let me get a word in edgeways."

Charles got more than a word in edgeways when, as his Cambridge days came to a close, he took part in the famous Cambridge Union debates. The question posed:

"This house believes that technological advance threatens the individuality of man and is becoming its master." Not surprisingly, the Prince, whose few public utterances had already weighed in on the side of nature, environmental protection, and tradition, argued in the affirmative. Unfortunately, in what was a harbinger of things to come, he took a swing at the Concorde supersonic aircraft being built jointly by the British and French.

Although he admitted that the new aircraft was "exciting" and that "sometimes I think I would like to go on it," he concluded that "if it is going to pollute us with noise, if it is going to knock down churches or shatter priceless windows when it tests its sonic booms. . . . Is this what we really want?" Even though the novelist C. P. Snow and Charles's Uncle

Dickie, Lord Mountbatten, argued against his position and in favor of technology, the Prince's side won the day, 214 to 184.

It was something of a Pyrrhic victory, however. The aircraft industry shot back almost immediately, charging that the Prince of Wales was ill-informed and that the development of the Concorde was critical to the British economy. Besides, they argued, sonic booms would occur out over open water, not over populated areas.

Buckingham Palace scrambled to contain the damage, and Charles was cautioned by his handlers to talk to the experts before making potentially incendiary public remarks. Getting him to listen was easier said than done. "Are we all so frightened and cowed," Charles said, "by the shadowy 'experts'?" The Prince insisted he had the right to an opinion "like anybody else. It seems strange to me that I, of all people—someone who might actually be in a position to make a difference—should have no opinions and should shut up. Well, I do—and I won't."

In the end, Charles and other members of the royal family would fly the Concorde more than a dozen times.

*In a case like yours, a man should sow his wild oats
and have as many affairs as he can before settling down.*
—Lord Mountbatten to Charles

I learned the way a monkey learns: by watching its parents.
—Charles

*If he were anyone else, we would have thought,
"What a nice man. What's he going to do for a living?"*
—a fellow RAF officer in training, on Charles

FOUR

"I'M HOLDING OUT FOR A KING"

Uncle Dickie was adamant. "You must," he said firmly, "have a 'mother service' that you really belong to and where you can have a career. Your father, grandfather, and both your great-grandfathers had a distinguished career in the Royal Navy. If you follow in their footsteps," he went on, "that would be very popular with the people." Philip, standing just a few feet away, scotch in hand, nodded in agreement.

In the coming weeks, the Duke of Edinburgh, whose own career in the Royal Navy had been cut short by his marriage to the sovereign, would send his son letters and memos outlining in cold and precise detail the trajectory of Charles's time in the military. In the fall of 1971, eighteen months from now, he would begin his navy training at Dartmouth. Prior to that, he would train with the Royal Air Force to be a jet fighter pilot.

Charles agreed to it all, but the detached tone of Philip's letters only underscored the widening rift between father and son. Although their palace apartments were just down the hall from each other, they never spoke. Philip had no expressed interest in connecting with his eldest child, and Charles admitted later that he was "reluctant to face the paternal rebuke that hovered in the atmosphere between them." When it came to his father, Charles observed, "criticism sprang much more easily to the lips than praise."

Nevertheless, the Prince of Wales hurled himself into his training at Cranwell, the RAF College 135 miles north of London. For the first time, he clicked immediately with the other officer trainees—several of whom shared his love of *The Goon Show* and a new and equally ridiculous BBC comedy series, *Monty Python's Flying Circus.* "Immediate compatibility!" he cheered in his diary. That said, it was difficult adjusting to military life. "I ought to be calling senior officers 'Sir,'" he wrote, but "I haven't called anyone 'Sir' for a long time. . . . They seem more nervous of me than I do of them."

Toward the end of his RAF training, Charles narrowly cheated death yet again. This time he was making his first parachute jump over water when his chute opened, and he realized he was upside down, his legs tangled in the lines. Somehow he managed to free his feet and had just enough time to right himself before landing. Charles felt "exhilarated and happy beyond belief" once he was safely on the ground—but also proud that he acted with such calm in the face of danger. "I've done it," he said, "and nobody can take that away from me."

———

One year after setting up his daughter Tricia on a disastrous date with a young George W. Bush, Richard Nixon was at it again. This time the President of the United States had the heir to the British throne in his sights and dreamt of his daughter one day becoming Queen. In July 1970 Prince Charles and his sister Anne, who had forgone college for a career as an equestrienne, were accompanying their parents on a state visit to Canada when they took a detour to Washington, DC. It was not an official visit, but Nixon pulled out the stops anyway: Charles and Anne were given a formal welcome on the South Lawn of the White House, and after the President said a few words, it was the Prince's turn to step up to the podium. Now comfortable addressing large crowds, Charles seemed more articulate and in command than his host. He called the United States "a very fascinating and intriguing country" and allowed that he and Anne had "always longed to come."

For years polls would rank Charles as the world's most eligible bachelor and Tricia Nixon, like millions of young women around the world, had a serious crush on the callow prince. The American President arranged a whirlwind of events both big and small, and saw to it that Tricia was Charles's date at every one. Among other things, over three days, they: picnicked, swam, and went skeet shooting with Tricia's young friends at Camp David, the presidential retreat in Maryland's Catoctin Mountains; had lunch at Mount Vernon; cheered the home team at a Washington Senators baseball game; were given a tour of the Smithsonian Air and Space Museum by astronauts Neil Armstrong, who a year earlier had become the first man to walk on the moon, and Frank Borman; cruised the Potomac River aboard the presidential yacht *Sequoia*; had tea at the British embassy; visited the Washington Monument, the Lincoln Memorial, and the US House and Senate; and danced on the White House lawn to the music of hit makers the Guess Who and Gary Puckett and the Union Gap.

President Nixon was not exactly subtle in his approach. Both royals were staying at the White House in the private second-floor East Wing living quarters known as the Residence—Anne in the Queen's Bedroom, named after her mother, and Charles in the Lincoln Bedroom. Several times during the visit, it was arranged for Charles and Tricia to suddenly find themselves alone. "My wife and I will keep out of the way," Nixon told Charles with a wink, "so you can feel at home."

It was Tricia's father who most fascinated Charles. They were originally scheduled to have a fifteen-minute-long chat about "what young people want," but instead were engaged in a wide-ranging conversation that touched on Russia, China, Southeast Asia, India, and the Middle East. Nixon also urged the heir to the throne to walk a fine line when it came to expressing his opinions—to always be "a presence" and not shy away from controversy, but also to pick and choose his battles.

Ultimately, it was the President's clumsy attempt at matchmaking—which Tricia would later describe as "embarrassing"—that would stick in the Prince's memory. He ungraciously described Tricia to a friend as "plastic and artificial," but what most irked him was the fact that he was being treated as a child and not the heir to the throne of England—that he was not, in terms of protocol, being given the deference he deserved. "Protocol and decorum mean a great deal to Prince Charles," a former equerry said. "He asks himself if his mother or his father would stand for this sort of treatment, and then his blood starts to boil."

Thirty-five years later, Charles was asked to describe his first trip to the White House. "That," he said with more than a trace of disdain, "was the time they were busy trying to marry me off to Tricia Nixon."

The Prince of Wales was not disappointed with his treatment in Paris when he represented the Queen at the funeral of French president Charles de Gaulle that November. Heading up a delegation that included then Prime Minister Edward Heath and three former PMs—Anthony Eden, Harold Macmillan, and Harold Wilson—Charles took his place with the other crown princes, directly behind the Shah of Iran and Emperor Haile Selassie of Ethiopia. It was a far cry from making polite conversation with the daughter of an American president. In this scrum of emperors, potentates, and assorted dignitaries, the Prince was entirely at ease. "I feel," he said with a shrug, "I belong."

———

Essentially giving up on ever forging a loving bond with his mother and father, Charles turned increasingly to Grandpapa—Lord Mountbatten—for advice on every aspect of his future, including his sex life. Mountbatten was more than willing to oblige. He urged the Prince of Wales to have as many sexual adventures as possible now, before he was forced to choose the woman who, presumably, would one day be his queen. Even then, Mountbatten told Charles, as Prince of Wales it would be expected for him to have a mistress—as long as everyone was reasonably discreet about the arrangement.

Discretion notwithstanding, in the years following the Princess Margaret–Peter Townsend brouhaha, the Crown had been periodically buffeted by scandal. At the height of the Profumo spy case and sex scandal in 1963, there was intense speculation that Prince Philip was the notorious "naked waiter" who, wearing nothing but a hood over his head and a pink ribbon tied to his genitals, served drinks at a sex party. (Ultimately, it was revealed that a member of Prime Minister Harold Macmillan's cabinet was the naked waiter.)

Back in those days, when Charles was still at Gordonstoun and too busy fending off attacks to be aware of the tensions in his parents' marriage, rumors swirled constantly about Philip's extramarital activities. In the late 1950s, the Queen dispatched her husband on an overseas tour after it was reported that he had been whooping it up at a Soho men's club every Thursday afternoon with a crowd that included British intelligence officer Kim Philby (who turned out to be a Russian spy) and actors David Niven and Peter Ustinov. While Charles was away at school, his father was linked to, among others, British author Daphne du Maurier, dancer Pat Kirkwood, singer Helene Cordet, television personality Katie Boyle, actress Merle Oberon, the Duchess of Abercorn ("We had a passionate friendship, but I did not go to bed with him"), and even the Queen's cousin Princess Alexandra of Kent. "You can take it from me," Philip once conceded, "the Queen has the quality of tolerance in abundance."

Now that he was a grown man, Charles weighed Lord Mountbatten's words carefully. But for the moment, he focused on his officer's training at Dartmouth and the planned seven-year Royal Navy career that was to begin with a tour of duty aboard the guided missile destroyer HMS *Norfolk*. Until he was piped aboard his ship, the Prince of Wales set out to amuse himself with the usual royal pursuits: polo, and blasting hundreds of pheasants at Sandringham and Broadlands. "You are the most astonishing Great Uncle ever," he wrote to Mountbatten after one such shooting party. "Thank you for the most exciting, indescribable, memorable, exhausting, record-breaking, finger-burning, shattering 'day of days.' . . . I shall never forget it."

Charles's dear "Grandpapa" had his own reasons, of course, for keeping the Prince close to his side and urging him not to get tied down and to play the field for the time being. To infuse even more Mountbatten blood into the royal family, he was now hoping to arrange a match between the Prince of Wales and his teenage granddaughter—and Charles's cousin— Lady Amanda Knatchbull. That would have to wait, however, since Lady

Amanda was nine years younger than the Prince—only fourteen at the time.

To make sure his protégé was suitably occupied, Uncle Dickie drew up a list of appropriate young ladies and made Broadlands available to Charles for trysting "at any time of your choosing." But before Charles could take Mountbatten up on his offer, fate intervened.

It was at an August 1971 polo match at Smith's Lawn, Windsor, that he first laid eyes on her. Charles had just climbed off his mount and was wiping the sweat from his face with a monogrammed towel when he heard someone shouting. Standing off to the side, away from the other girls who pressed up against the fence hoping to catch a glimpse of the Prince, she wanted more—to catch his attention. "That's a fine animal, Sir!" the slim young blonde called out, brushing her hair from her eyes. "I thought you played wonderfully well."

Charles did not recognize her. Her uniform was much like the others—tight jeans, boots, a green Barbour jacket buttoned up against a light drizzle—but she was neither as pretty nor as well put together. Still, there was a direct, unaffected quality about her that appealed to him. Before he headed back to the palace, Charles stopped to chat with the mysterious young woman about horses and polo. Her name, she said, was Camilla Shand. If Charles hadn't seen her before, his Argentine polo-playing pal Luis Basualdo certainly had. "She was of the girls," Basualdo said, "who we called the 'Windsor groupies.'"

———

At a dinner party several weeks later, Charles's old flame—the Chilean woman to whom he allegedly lost his virginity—cornered the Prince and purred, "I have found the perfect girl for you!" Lucia Santa Cruz then disappeared and returned moments later with Camilla in hand.

"I believe we've already met," Charles said, gazing into Camilla's cobalt-blue eyes.

Perhaps it was because she was sixteen months older than Charles, or maybe she, like Prince Philip, was accustomed to blurting out whatever happened to be on her mind. "My great-grandmother and your great-great-grandfather were lovers," she declared. "So how about it?"

Candor and the ability to flirt with ease were obviously qualities that ran in the family. Camilla's great-grandmother Alice Keppel was the celebrated mistress of King Edward VII, who succeeded Queen Victoria to the throne in 1901 when he was almost sixty. "My job is to curtsy first," she once explained, "and then jump into bed." Keppel's position as the King's more or less official mistress was so widely accepted that Queen Alexandra summoned Keppel to her husband's bedside as he lay dying in 1910.

Camilla ignored the ancestors who built a massive fortune by wisely developing real estate in London's pricey Mayfair and Belgravia districts. Instead, she identified with the scandalous Mrs. Keppel even as a child, oddly enough. At the appropriately named Queen's Gate, a boarding school not far from Kensington Palace, ten-year-old "Milla" bragged incessantly about her great-grandmother. "We're practically royalty," she'd tell the other girls. Actress Lynn Redgrave remembered her classmate well. In a school where "landing a rich husband was at the top of the agenda," Redgrave said, Camilla "wanted to have fun, but she also wanted to marry well because, in her mind, that would be the most fun of all."

A mussy-haired tomboy who like Charles was most at home in the country, Camilla spent every weekend at the Laines, the Shand family estate fifty miles south of London in rural East Sussex. Joined there by her younger sister Annabel and brother Mark, Camilla rode horses, mucked out the stalls, planted vegetables, and engaged in the one upper-class pastime that spurred animal rights activists to violence: foxhunting.

After the requisite year spent at finishing schools in Paris and Geneva, Camilla returned to London to become a debutante, and to collect the $1.5 million (the equivalent of $12 million in 2019) bequeathed to her by a distant relation. Working briefly as a receptionist at the Colefax & Fowler decorating firm, she watched as her first roommate and then her second roommate married lords. Why hadn't she? Camilla was asked by a friend. Her totally serious reply: "I'm holding out for a king."

Camilla's icebreaking "How about it?" line had Charles in stitches, but he did not have the whole backstory. In 1966 she'd met and fallen in love not with a member of the royal family or even a high-ranking aristocrat, but with a soldier: dashing twenty-seven-year-old Sandhurst graduate Andrew Parker Bowles. Nevertheless, the blond, matinee-idol-handsome lieutenant in the Blues and Royals Regiment of the Royal Horse Guards had royal connections that ran deep and wide. He was the great-great-grandson of an earl, his parents were close friends of the Queen Mother, and the family seat was Donnington Castle in Berkshire County. At the age of thirteen, Parker Bowles was a page at the coronation of Elizabeth II. Now he was a star player on the Prince of Wales's polo team.

By the time he met Camilla, Parker Bowles had already carved out a reputation for himself in royal circles as a highly polished lothario. "Camilla did not fit the mold," a friend of the Shands said. "He was dating all of these gorgeous models and the daughters of lords. Camilla was certainly ragged around the edges in comparison, but she was always great fun and loved to flirt. She would say *anything*. Everyone liked her, women as well as men."

Their on-again, off-again courtship would last seven years—hitting a particularly nasty snag in 1970 when Parker Bowles began dating Charles's sister. "I think this was the first real love for her," the Queen's longtime private secretary, Martin Charteris, said of Princess Anne, who went on to numerous affairs and two marriages. The author Sarah Bradford, who was known to her aristocratic friends as the Viscountess Bangor, understood why the Princess Royal enjoyed such an active and varied romantic life. "Despite her rather horse-faced looks," the Viscountess observed, "Anne, with her powerful, direct personality and her healthy interest in sex, was attractive to men."

Now Camilla wanted to make Parker Bowles jealous, and the best way to accomplish that was by dating an even bigger prize than the Princess Royal: the heir himself. "I don't know how much of her going after Charles at that point had to do with trying to relive her great-grandmother's role," a Parker Bowles cousin said, "or how much had to do with just getting revenge on Andrew."

In the meantime, Camilla was beginning to wonder if indeed she was the reincarnation of Edward VII's mistress. "Strange, but I never felt intimidated in his presence, never," she said. "I felt from the beginning that we were two peas in a pod. We talked as if we'd always known each other."

Stranger still that they would be drawn together at all, since they were so fundamentally different in so many ways. Charles hewed to tradition and formality in his dress; His Royal Highness's impeccable wardrobe of Savile Row suits, blazers, and custom-made shirts was immaculately tailored, reflecting a level of taste rarely seen in someone so young. He was passionate about the old masters, Mozart, and classic architectural styles, and demanded that his surroundings reflect his refined personal style. He was subdued and reserved, and generally dismissed as gauche anyone who wasn't. He detested smoking, calling the habit "nasty."

Camilla was none of these things. Her taste in fashion ran to boxy tweeds worn with scuffed boots and a loose blouse. Her hair was usually mussed and tangled; she bit her fingernails to the quick, had little use for cosmetics, and chain-smoked three packs a day. She was so unmindful of her surroundings that her roommate Virginia Carrington described her flat as looking like "a bomb had gone off in it"—with dirty dishes piled in the sink, and soiled laundry and papers covering every square inch of the floor. She never made her bed or picked up her clothes. "As soon as she walked in the door," said Carrington, "her coat and shoes and everything else hit the floor—and that's where they stayed until someone else came to pick them up."

Camilla had no interest in art or classical music—her taste ran to the Beatles, the Rolling Stones, and Tom Jones—and was as open, uncensored, and outgoing as Charles was quiet and diffident. What trumped all their differences was a shared love of country pursuits that for centuries have defined England's landed gentry: farming, riding, hunting, fishing, and gardening. That, and the undeniable fact that earthy, plainspoken, overtly sexual Camilla was quite unlike anyone he had known. In Charles's eyes, Camilla was "pretty, bubbly, and she smiled with her eyes as well as her mouth."

The Prince of Wales later confessed that he "lost his heart" to Camilla "almost at once." There was clearly physical chemistry between them and, perhaps even more important, she provided a young and sympathetic ear when for years the only two people he could turn to were the Queen Mother and his great-uncle Louis Mountbatten. "For the Prince, real life began with Camilla," said Luis Basualdo, one of Charles's buddies at the time. "He was just down from Cambridge, and if he wasn't precisely a virgin, he was certainly wet behind the ears."

Soon Camilla, with Uncle Dickie's all-important blessing—for now— was joining Charles on his weekend excursions to Broadlands. "He knew that Camilla would make a perfect mistress for Charles," Mountbatten's longtime private secretary John Barratt said, "until his granddaughter was of marriageable age." At Broadlands, Mountbatten made certain that his great-nephew and Camilla be given the Portico Room, where Charles's parents spent their wedding night in 1947.

Charles had not been particularly discreet with Lucia Santa Cruz, and he seemed even less so with Camilla. For months, the couple was seen at polo matches during the day and out on the town in London at night. Newspapers were filled with photos of Charles and Camilla through the windows of limousines, or trying to slip into trendy clubs of the time, such as the Saddle Room, the Garrison, and Annabel's.

Camilla shared Charles's love for *The Goon Show*, and soon they were calling each other by pet names based on two of the program's Peter Sellers–voiced characters, Gladys and Fred. By the end of 1972, it seemed to Fleet Street and even to Charles's parents—much to Lord Mountbatten's chagrin—that Camilla was more than just a passing fancy for the future King. It was only a matter of time, courtiers whispered, before Charles popped the question.

But there were forces working against them. Mountbatten was still angling to have Charles marry his granddaughter Amanda, and worried that Charles might jump the gun and marry Camilla. He plotted feverishly to speed up the Prince's navy orders and ship him out to sea. The Queen Mother also weighed in against Camilla—she wanted Charles to marry one of the Spencer family granddaughters of her lady-in-waiting and close friend, Lady Fermoy. The Queen, Prince Philip, and Palace operatives all agreed that Camilla, while the granddaughter of a baron, was an unsuitable bride for the Prince of Wales. "With hindsight, you can say that Charles should have married Camilla when he first had the chance," said Mountbatten's daughter Patricia Knatchbull, Amanda's mother. "They were ideally suited; we know that now. But it wasn't possible. . . . It wouldn't have been possible, at that time."

Right before Christmas 1972, Camilla joined Charles at Broadlands for "one last weekend" before he shipped out for an eight-month tour of duty in the Caribbean Sea aboard the frigate HMS *Minerva*. At least the Prince had someone other than his grandmother and great-uncle to write to; now, in scores of letters addressed to "Gladys," he shared his deepest feelings and innermost thoughts. He was cautious, however, never to mention matrimony; Lord Mountbatten had convinced him to wait until thirty before "even considering" marriage.

Charles was halfway through his tour of duty and still at sea when he learned that the woman he loved—and who, he thought, loved him equally in return—had instead accepted Andrew Parker Bowles's proposal of marriage. The Prince was, understandably, heartbroken. Theirs had been, he thought, "a blissful, peaceful, and mutually happy relationship," Charles wrote to Uncle Dickie. "I suppose the feeling of emptiness will pass eventually." But, he added woefully, "Now there is no one to go back to" in England. The Prince confessed later that, for weeks, he "brooded alone" in his cabin, hiding his pain from the rest of the crew.

By way of rubbing salt in the wound, Charles had to read in the press that when the happy couple married at the Guards Chapel, Wellington Barracks, on July 4, 1973, his sister and the Queen Mother were given places of honor in the front row. The Prince had forgotten that his grandmother's family, the Bowes-Lyons, were cousins of the Parker Bowleses.

Camilla's betrayal triggered a frenzy of bed-hopping on Charles's part. During frequent breaks in his schedule, when he was called upon to represent the Crown at various official functions, the Prince of Wales squired dozens of eligible young women. The standouts included Georgiana Russell, daughter of Great Britain's Ambassador to Spain; brewery heiress Sabrina Guinness (who, by this time, had already been involved with Rod Stewart, David Bowie, Mick Jagger, and others), and his old Australian flame "Kanga" Tryon.

The Prince was dealt another emotional blow—a "spasm of shock and amazement"—when in 1973 he learned that his twenty-three-year-old sister was marrying Mark Phillips, a captain in the Queen's Dragoon Guards and, like Princess Anne, a champion equestrian. Charles did not believe Phillips was a suitable match for Anne, but, more important, he was not ready to take a backseat to another man—an outsider, no less. Brother and sister had grown close in their early twenties, and, next to the Queen Mother, Anne was now the only woman in the family he felt he could truly confide in. News of her impending nuptials sent Charles into what he described as a "state of near panic." After several weeks of "abject despair," Charles confessed to a friend that he recognized "the writing on the wall. I can see I shall have to find myself a wife pretty rapidly; otherwise I shall get left behind and feel very miserable!"

Charles had managed to pull himself together by the time he flew to Singapore to take on his new duties as the communications officer aboard another frigate, the HMS *Jupiter*. The *Jupiter* toured Australia, New Zealand, and the South Pacific before proceeding toward the North American coast. In Hawaii, Charles wrote, he met "two spectacular blonde ladies . . . who purred that they would give me an evening I would never forget." They proceeded to a small apartment, where they presented the Prince with "the rarest, most expensive form of marijuana from Thailand." Charles, sensing immediately the potential for scandalous, monarchy-shaking headlines, made a hasty retreat. In Acapulco, the Prince and a group of fellow *Jupiter* officers made their way to a disco, where Charles summoned the courage to walk up to a young woman and invite her to join his table. "No thanks," she replied to the Prince of Wales, in what he described as a "terrifying American accent."

The reception was considerably warmer in San Diego. There Charles was whisked off to Sunnylands, the palatial 1,000-acre Palm Springs estate of the US Ambassador to Great Britain, Walter Annenberg, for a round of golf. (He had wanted to play polo, but it was St. Patrick's Day, and an anonymous caller had warned the Prince would be assassinated if he ventured near the polo grounds.) Charles was a miserable golfer ("I made the first hole in eleven shots!") but was amused when, seemingly out of nowhere, Bob Hope suddenly zoomed up in a golf cart just to say hello. After drinks with Frank Sinatra and dinner with then California Governor Ronald Reagan, Charles schmoozed at the Universal Pictures studios in Hollywood with Charlton Heston and Ava Gardner on the set of the disaster film *Earthquake*.

There was really only one star who fascinated Charles. "When they asked me who I most wanted to meet," the Prince told his longtime valet Stephen Barry, "I'm sure they thought I'd say Raquel Welch. But I said Barbra Streisand. I wanted to meet the woman behind the voice."

Charles had, in fact, been smitten with the singer since he was an undergraduate at Cambridge. At a time when most English college students were listening to the likes of Jimi Hendrix, Janis Joplin, Stevie Wonder, Dusty Springfield, and Aretha Franklin—or to pop groups as varied and exciting as the Doors, the Supremes, Led Zeppelin, the Who, the Rolling Stones, Cream, and the Mamas and the Papas—the Prince of Wales played Streisand's albums constantly. A personal favorite: the soundtrack from the 1968 film for which she won an Academy Award, *Funny Girl*. He saw it three times. A framed photograph of Streisand hung in his rooms at Cambridge and went up on the wall of his bedroom at Buckingham Palace after graduation. "Barbra Streisand," the Prince of Wales proclaimed proudly, "is my only pinup!"

At Charles's request, legendary Hollywood producer Hal Wallis arranged for the Prince to meet Streisand on the Columbia Pictures set of the *Funny Girl* sequel, *Funny Lady*. Columbia understandably saw the Prince's visit as nothing less than a publicity windfall. The press was kept at arm's length while the cavernous soundstage where Streisand was dubbing dialogue was cleared. As the movie star and her royal fan shook hands, four dozen disgruntled photographers standing behind a rope nevertheless snapped away furiously, blinding everyone with popping flashbulbs.

What Charles did not know was that Streisand had undertaken the filming of *Funny Lady* under duress. She had little enthusiasm for the project from the beginning but was contractually obligated to make the film. According to *Funny Lady* screenwriter Jay Presson Allen, Streisand was, at least figuratively speaking, "escorted to the set every day by a team of lawyers."

Charles sensed immediately that "something was wrong. . . . She appeared to be rather nervous and kept asking me questions in a rather tight-lipped fashion." Once the studio publicist declared the photo op over, Charles and Barbra retreated to a corner and kibitzed for fifteen minutes over coffee. When he asked her if she had plans to perform in England, she insisted she would never do another live show. "I only like performing," she said, "in front of people I know." She also wanted to spend more time with her son.

"Then why go on acting at all?" Charles shot back. Streisand, unable to come up with an answer, cocked her head and shrugged. The Prince of Wales later wrote in his navy journal that he "really wanted to get to stay and know her," but that she made it clear she had to get back to work. "I think I caught her on a bad day," he told his valet. "She had very little time and appeared very busy."

Their brief encounter did nothing to dampen Charles's enthusiasm. "People look at me in amazement," he wrote in his journal, "when I say she is devastatingly attractive and with a great deal of sex appeal. But I *still* contend she has great sex appeal after meeting her."

Streisand, overwhelmed by her own career concerns, wasn't made aware of the Prince's true feelings for her until years later. "Who knows?" she cracked. "If I'd been nicer to him, I might have been the first *real* Jewish Princess." She would discover years later that Charles still carried at least a small torch for her—and that they would eventually get a second shot at romance.

Charles was not the only Windsor who was an unabashed Barbra fan. The Queen had asked to meet Streisand after the London premiere of

Funny Lady. As Elizabeth II moved down the receiving line, Barbra broke a cardinal rule of royal etiquette by speaking to the Queen first. "Your Majesty," she blurted, "why do women have to wear gloves and the men don't?"

The Queen appeared startled, but then thought about if for a moment. "Well, I'll have to think about that one," she said. "It's tradition, I suppose."

Before the monarch could move out of earshot, Streisand said, "Well, I guess I *still* don't know. I think it's the men's sweaty hands that ought to be covered, not ours."

Charles's Southern California sojourn yielded other, unexpected surprises—such as Laura Jo Watkins, the willowy blonde admiral's daughter who just happened to be on the welcoming committee when the *Jupiter* docked in San Diego. Charles and the twenty-year-old California girl hit it off instantly, and she was invited to London to attend the going-away party for departing US Ambassador Annenberg.

The Prince managed to sneak Laura into his private quarters at Buckingham Palace, where, she later told her American friends, they made love. The secret romance appeared to be going smoothly until Charles invited Laura—who as an American and a Roman Catholic would at the time never seriously be considered marriage material—to watch him give his maiden speech in the House of Lords.

The speech, historic if only because it was the first time a member of the royal family had addressed the House of Lords in ninety years, was innocuous enough—all about making recreational facilities more widely available to underprivileged youth. Charles did manage to get a few laughs at the beginning when he quoted Oscar Wilde's maxim that "'if a thing is worth doing, it is worth doing badly.' The truth of that statement," the twenty-five-year-old prince went on, "I will leave to you to debate after I have sat down."

Unfortunately, the press paid little attention to what was said. Fleet Street was far more interested in reporting on the Prince's stunning American girlfriend—running photos of her on the front page, describing their "fairy-tale reunion" in London, and, in one instance, branding Laura "an unmarried Wallis Simpson."

With the press swarming about, Charles and his American lover were effectively cut off from each other—he at the palace and she at Winfield House, the Annenbergs' London residence. After they managed to rendez-vous at Kensington Palace, the headline in the *Birmingham Post* screamed, "Laura Jo and the Prince Had a Secret Midnight Meeting." Before long, Laura, disguised in a sailor's uniform, was smuggled to an RAF base and onto a military flight home.

When asked if he would ever marry a commoner, Charles said there was "no essential reason" why he could not marry someone who wasn't a member of a royal family or at least of the aristocracy. "If I'm deciding on whom I want to live with for fifty years," he explained, "well, that's the last decision in which I would want my head to be ruled entirely by my heart. It's nothing to do with class; it's to do with compatibility."

———————

The Prince of Wales was slightly taken aback when, after giving birth to a son in December 1974, Camilla—the one woman with whom he felt he was most compatible—asked him to be the godfather. "I don't know what to say," he confided to Lord Mountbatten. "We *are* still friends." Andrew Parker Bowles, perhaps not wanting to further offend their future sover-eign or jeopardize his military career, agreed to name the child Thomas Henry Charles—an obvious nod to the Prince of Wales. The gossip mill wasted no time speculating that Charles was Tom Parker Bowles's biologi-cal father—highly improbable given the fact that the Prince of Wales was at sea patrolling the coasts of New Zealand and Australia when the baby was conceived.

On a visit to Canada just a few weeks after the baptism, Charles en-countered someone who would help him forget Camilla—now and at var-ious key points over the next two decades. Unlike the other women in his life, she truly knew how to keep their relationship a secret. Valet Stephen Barry recalled that "there was one girl who managed to remain very nearly anonymous. The Prince saw more of her than anyone realized."

Janet Jenkins, who at thirty was four years older than Charles, worked as a receptionist at the British consulate in Montreal. They actually first became intimate in London when, after reconnecting at a party, he asked her out. "Toward the end of the date," said the very-married Jenkins, "Charles took me in his arms and gave me a deep, passionate kiss. I became weak in the knees, and I could barely stand up."

A year later, she met him again at her Montreal apartment while his Royal Protection Service detail waited in the hall. "After all the laughter, the talk, and the wine, it was also the first night we made love," recalled Jenkins, who delivered a verdict on Charles's romantic skills similar to the one Laura Jo Watkins had shared with a friend: "I found Charles to be a wonderful lover."

Charles poured out his heart to Jenkins in dozens of love letters. "I wish I could come roaring across the Atlantic to make you feel less lonely," he wrote her in July 1976. Soon he concocted a plan: he would fly to Montreal to watch his sister Anne compete as an equestrienne in the Summer Olympic Games. "If we went anywhere out, the press would be onto it in a flash, and that would be misery," he said. "If you could bear to see me, I would have thought your apartment is the quietest place. It will be something marvelous to look forward to as far as I'm concerned, and I can't wait to see you again." Later, as the Olympics drew near: "I do hope you will be there because it would be glorious to have a chance of being alone with you for a moment."

Even on the one or two occasions when their plans fell apart, Charles was attentive. During one of his visits to Montreal, he was unable to break away and rendezvous with Jenkins at the Ritz-Carlton Hotel—even though at one point he was just two blocks away. The best they could do was share a brief phone call. "It was marvelous to hear your voice again the other day from the Ritz," he wrote. "I am desperate being unable to see you."

Another time, the Prince lamented that he hadn't been able to put his royal duties aside and go to "places like Montreal where exciting ladies lurk behind bushes in order to pounce on unsuspecting naval officers! When are you coming back to the UK again? It really was such fun to see you in December—I only wish I hadn't had to rush off to catch a train & thereby ruin a gloriously cozy evening!" All of Charles's letters to Jenkins were signed "Much Love, Charles."

Jenkins, who wasn't a virgin or a member of the aristocracy, had no illusions about where their affair was headed. "I cared deeply for Charles," she insisted, "though I knew we would never marry." Perhaps because it was mutually understood that their relationship could only be extramarital, they were surprisingly candid with each other about their doubts and expectations. When Jenkins divorced her first husband, Charles wrote her words of reassurance: "Thank goodness you discovered the mistake early enough and didn't start a family." Then he added prophetically, "Making a mistake like that is, frankly, something which concerns me enormously."

Apparently another potentially disastrous mistake never occurred to Charles. There would be ample speculation over the years concerning children who may or may not have been sired by the Prince of Wales. When Jenkins gave birth to her son Jason in 1984—just nine months after one of her trysts with Prince Charles, who by then had been married to Princess Diana for three years and was the father of two sons—she identified her husband as the father on the birth certificate. Tongues wagged nevertheless.

In the meantime, the Prince of Wales had more on his mind than matrimony. As he prepared to make the adjustment from military to civilian life, Charles asked himself the most important question of all: What would he do now? There were the customary walkabouts, plaque unveilings, and tree plantings that comprised his day-to-day ceremonial duties. "My great problem," he confessed after six years in the Royal Navy, "is that I do not know what my role in life is. At the moment, I do not have one. But somehow I must find one."

More precisely, Charles would have to invent a role for himself—"make up the job," he said, "as I go along." After rejecting his mother's offer to make him governor-general of Australia—Charles did not want to deal with the fallout if he were called upon to dismiss the Australian prime minister, as a previous governor-general had done—Charles turned to Camilla for advice. Even more than the Queen Mother or Lord Mountbatten,

Mrs. Parker Bowles was now "the one who, more than any other, I can totally confide in . . . my best friend . . . my touchstone and sounding board."

Camilla pushed Charles to devote himself to the charities and interests that were closest to his heart. At the time, he wanted to establish a trust to help disadvantaged youth—urban minorities, in particular—by investing in small grassroots programs. After overcoming initial opposition from the Queen, who worried that any plan based on doling out cash to juvenile delinquents was doomed from the outset, Charles set up the Prince's Trust in June 1976.

As predicted, it was not exactly smooth sailing for the Prince of Wales's flagship charity—but not for the reasons outlined by the Queen. What Charles called "suspicion from Buckingham Palace" and "bureaucratic infighting" were the chief culprits in preventing the Prince's Trust from obtaining the funds it needed to get off the ground. That, and the fact that Charles himself was too distracted by other matters to give his new project his full attention. Once he finally did, the Prince's Trust would become a philanthropic dynamo throughout the Commonwealth, raising more than $2 billion for a wide range of charities—from environmental programs and art school to homeless shelters and health clinics.

Now that he was twenty-eight, the pressure to marry and produce an heir was increasing exponentially. Looking around at friends and contemporaries who were "becoming engaged left, right, and center," he wrote, "I am now becoming convinced that I shall soon be left floundering helpless on a shelf somewhere, having missed everyone!"

As passionate and considerate as he was with the women in his life, Charles did possess more than his share of idiosyncrasies. Among other things, he required all of his girlfriends to call him "Sir," even during their most private moments. There were also times, according to two of his former girlfriends, when, in the throes of passion, the Prince asked to be called Arthur—the king of Arthurian legend and a hero of Charles's since early childhood.

The Prince had once made the mistake of saying thirty was the perfect age for someone in his position to marry. Now, as he approached that milestone, the press was more frenetic than ever in trying to nail down the identity of the future princess bride. "It would have been a huge scoop," said veteran royals correspondent James Whitaker, "if he had any intention of settling down. The pressure was definitely on him to do so."

With Uncle Dickie's granddaughter Amanda Knatchbull still maturing in the wings, Charles cut a wide swath through the field of highborn ladies—all the while maintaining a close and fungible "friendship" with Camilla. Now his list of conquests expanded to include Louise Astor, daughter of Lord Astor of Hever; Bettina Lindsay, daughter of Lord Balneil; Lady Caroline Percy *and* Lady Victoria Percy, daughters of the Duke of Northumberland; Lady Camilla Fane, daughter of the Earl of Westmorland; Lady Jane Grosvenor and her sister Leonora, both sisters of the extremely wealthy Duke of Westminster; Lady Libby Manners and her cousin Lady Charlotte Manners, daughter of the Duke of Rutland; Caroline Longman, granddaughter of the Earl of Cavan; Lady Angela Nevill, daughter of Lord Rupert Nevill; Lady Cecil Kerr, daughter of the Marquis of Lothian; and Lady Henrietta FitzRoy, daughter of the Duke of Grafton.

There were three standouts in this blueblood crowd. Fleet Street reporters quickly unearthed a tantalizing tidbit about Lady Fiona Watson, daughter of the wealthy Yorkshire landowner Lord Manton: Using the alias Frances Cannon, she'd been paid $2,000 to pose for an eleven-page "Pet of the Month" spread in *Penthouse* magazine. "I can't believe this," gasped Lady Manton when the truth broke. "I just don't know what to say."

Lady Jane Wellesley, daughter of the Duke of Wellington, was for two years generally considered to be far out front in the race to become Princess of Wales. Speculation of an imminent engagement announcement ran so high that, when Lady Jane visited Charles at Sandringham, ten thousand people showed up outside the gates. Cornered by the press, Lady Jane snapped back: "Do you honestly believe I want to be Queen?"

Well, yes. At one point, it appeared as if Lady Jane may have torpedoed her own chances when she invited Charles and her friend Davina Sheffield, the pretty blonde granddaughter of Lord McGowan and sister-in-law of the Duchess of Beaufort, to a dinner party. In the coming months, Davina clearly had the inside track—until an old boyfriend came forward with details of their sexual relationship, and blew out of the water all hopes of Davina becoming the heir's virgin bride. By way of collateral damage, the competition for Charles's hand effectively ended their friendship. "They haven't," a friend said, "spoken since."

Although most of these dalliances were decidedly short lived, Charles, by all accounts, remained a gentleman at all times, never publicly uttering an unkind word about the women who drifted in and out of his life. Such was not the case, however, with the high-profile member of another European royal family. At a charity event in Monaco, the Prince of Wales was seated next to Princess Grace of Monaco's elder daughter, Princess Caroline. They did not even attempt to conceal their inexplicable—but genuine and intense—dislike for each other. He thought she was "irritating"; she dismissed him as "just plain boring." Charles told a reporter that "with our first meeting, the world had us married—and now the marriage is already in trouble!"

Barbra Streisand was still the Prince of Wales's number one pinup, despite the fact that their initial meeting proved, in the Prince's words, "less than satisfactory." But there was another actress he secretly dated during this period: Susan George, star of such steamy flicks as *Straw Dogs*, *Mandingo*, and *Dirty Mary Crazy Larry*. Their clandestine fling proved to be just that and no more, lasting three months before fizzling out.

Not every woman Charles took to bed was glamourous—or needed to be. According to Charles's friend, polo player Luis Basualdo, early on "it struck him that he could have virtually any young woman he desired." He more or less did, of course, and on his own terms. At the time, Basualdo was married to Viscount Cowdray's daughter, Lucy Pearson, and lived in the viscount's imposing West Sussex manor, Lodsworth House. "By 1977, Charles had joined my polo team, and we were together constantly," Basualdo said. "As we got to know each other, he dropped hints, he would mumble nervously about how hard it was for him to meet normal girls. After all, he couldn't just go to a pub and pick someone up. He didn't need to say more."

From then on, Basualdo served as Charles's go-between, rounding up the young daughters of tenant farmers and (unknown to Charles) threatening to have their families evicted if they didn't sleep with the Prince. "They were all young, some seventeen or younger," Basualdo told an interviewer, "but I told them to tell Charles they were nineteen." Charles, understandably, was particularly apprehensive—"absolutely petrified"—by the prospect of being caught with an underage girl. Eventually, Charles complained to Basualdo that the girls brought to Lodsworth House were "a bit young," and that he preferred "society girls of twenty-one or twenty-two."

Since these were "simple farm girls who were nervous about meeting" the Prince of Wales, Basualdo made sure they arrived at Lodsworth House early so they could have "a few drinks to loosen up." Charles himself never had more than two drinks—usually Pimm's—and "he didn't want the girls to get drunk, either."

Over several years, according to Basualdo, "Charles and I shared dozens of girls. Of course, I asked some of them what he was like in bed. They would laugh and tell me he was good. I never heard any complaints." One of the Prince's conquests was more specific. "He knows what he likes," she said, "and he knows what he's doing."

These accounts were still too vague for Basualdo, who often listened at the door to Charles's room. "I wanted to make sure there was more going on than chitchat. And I was nosy," he admitted. "I wanted to know what he was like in bed. I listened to his rhythm, the different sounds. Not counting foreplay, the final act usually lasted between seven and fifteen minutes. That's not bad." After his wife and nanny complained about the incessant headboard slamming that went on whenever the Prince of Wales visited, Charles was banished to an attic bedroom where, Basualdo said, "he could make as much noise as he wanted."

The press, amazingly, was totally unaware of Charles's sexual exploits. Instead, all eyes were on Lady Sarah Spencer, who, as the daughter of the 8th Earl Spencer, was near the top of the aristocratic pecking order. Sarah and her Spencer siblings, Jane, Diana, and Charles, had grown up in a cocoon of wealth and privilege—the result of a fortune built on sheep trading during the fifteenth century. For five hundred years, the Spencers had occupied a place at court. Sarah's paternal grandmother, Countess Spencer, had served as a lady-in-waiting to the Queen Mother. So had her maternal grandmother, Lady Fermoy, who was one of the Queen Mother's closest and most trusted confidantes. Sarah's father, John Spencer, had been an equerry to both George VI and Elizabeth II.

One of Lady Sarah's strengths was quiet forbearance. At the exclusive Cowdray Ball, Charles spotted a twenty-one-year-old Colombian beauty across the room. "Who is that girl in blue?" the Prince asked his friend Basualdo, and then "arrogantly just walked away from Sarah Spencer and started talking to her." Charles borrowed Basualdo's Daimler and disappeared to Lodsworth House for ninety minutes. "Sarah knew exactly what had happened," Basualdo recalled, "and never forgave me."

Despite her lofty pedigree, Lady Sarah was far from a perfect candidate for princely matrimony. At the height of her affair with Charles, newspapers reported that she'd had problems with alcohol, had once been expelled from boarding school, was now battling both anorexia and bulimia—and claimed to have had "thousands of boyfriends."

Charles seemed capable of overlooking all that. What really irked him, or so he told his polo-playing crony, was that Lady Sarah "wasn't as keen as him on sex." As a result, even though she was presumably his "steady girlfriend," Charles cheated on her "all the time."

If she couldn't be his bride, Lady Sarah would play an instrumental— if inadvertent—role in helping Charles find one. While paying a call on his then girlfriend at Althorp, Charles was introduced by Sarah to her younger sister Diana, sixteen and home from a year away at a Swiss finishing school. The scene was anything but romantic; both were standing in a muddy field at the time. "I introduced them," Sarah would say later with more than a trace of irony. "I'm cupid."

In truth, until this point, Lady Sarah and all the others were merely placeholders. Charles had waited seven years for one woman to come of age so he could pop the question, and now the time had come—the moment that would, Charles's beloved Grandpapa devoutly prayed, cement the names of Mountbatten and Windsor for all time.

Now nearly twenty-one, Lord Mountbatten's granddaughter Amanda had spent the last few years getting to know her cousin Charles. But these encounters occurred largely among other family members at Buckingham Palace, Windsor, Sandringham, Balmoral, Broadlands, and the tiny Caribbean island of Eleuthera where Mountbatten's daughter Patricia owned a house. Charles and Amanda grew very fond of each other—as cousins and as friends. They shared the same interests, the same offbeat *Goon Show* sense of the absurd, and the same devotion to Lord Mountbatten. But as the Prince himself acknowledged later, "There was never a spark."

Still, Charles felt obligated to propose to his cousin Amanda, and he did, aboard the royal yacht *Britannia* as it sailed toward Eleuthera. She turned him down, and for reasons he understood perfectly. Marriage to the heir would mean "the loss of independence . . . the surrender of self to a system . . . an intrusion more pervasive than attends any other public figure," he mused later. Without the intense, passionate love "that would have made such sacrifices worthwhile, the prospect was too daunting."

Mountbatten was deeply disappointed but wrote the Prince that "if the price were to spoil the future happiness of you both, then that would be a price I would not even contemplate." It was the kind of measured and understanding response that Charles had come to expect from his grandpapa, and not from his distant, demanding parents. Mountbatten was, the Prince of Wales declared, "my linchpin, trusted above all others."

Having dispatched his obligation to his great-uncle, Charles moved on to Venezuelan socialite Cristabel Barria-Borsage, and then to Anna Wallace, daughter of wealthy Scottish landowner Hamish Wallace. Known as "Whiplash Wallace" to her friends, the stunningly beautiful, fiery-tempered Anna was on the verge of accepting Charles's *second* marriage proposal when, at a Windsor Castle ball for the Queen Mother, the Prince ignored her and spent all his time dancing with Camilla Parker Bowles. "Nobody treats me like that!" she reportedly shouted at him as she stormed out of the party. "Not even you! I've never been treated so badly in my life!"

Through all the speculation revolving around his status as the World's

Princess Elizabeth and two-year-old Charles watch the royal procession from the roof of Clarence House during Queen Juliana of The Netherlands's state visit to London, November 1950.

2

The following summer, Charles and sister Anne pose with their parents, Princess Elizabeth and Prince Philip, on the Clarence House lawn.

3

4

On Charles's third birthday, he and Anne visit their grandparents King George VI and Queen Elizabeth at Buckingham Palace.

Flanked by the Queen Mother and his aunt Princess Margaret, four-year-old Charles
observes his mother's coronation on June 2, 1953, in Westminster Abbey. After the
ceremony, Charles joins his family in waving to a cheering crowd of more than one
million Britons from the Buckingham Palace balcony.

6

The Queen, Prince Charles, Princess Anne, and Prime Minister Winston Churchill on the platform of London's Waterloo Station, awaiting the return of the Queen Mother from her 1954 goodwill tour of the United States.

7

Nine-year-old Charles smiles gamely for photographers as he walks to class at Cheam the day his mother officially named him Prince of Wales.

8

A glum-looking Charles returns to Gordonstoun with skates in hand for a new school term in January 1963.

The twenty-year-old heir to the throne strolls down a street in Cambridge, where he was a student at Trinity College. Inset, the future monarch crowns a Cambridge University beauty queen in 1969. Below, Charles cracks up during a rehearsal of Trinity's theatrical revue in a fellow student's dormitory room.

11

10

12

A Royal Family tableau circa 1969: Prince Philip, Prince Edward, the Queen, Princess Anne, Prince Charles, and Prince Andrew.

13

Charles's investiture as Prince of Wales at Caernarfon Castle on July 1, 1969. A year later, he and Anne were part of an altogether different spectacle during their royal visit to the United States—waving to well wishers from the Truman Balcony of the White House with Richard and Pat Nixon.

14

15

16

Charles with his beloved Uncle Dickie, Lord Mountbatten, in 1970. Inset, Charles's first girlfriend: Lucia Santa Cruz, the stunning, Oxford-educated daughter of Chile's ambassador to the United Kingdom. She brought Charles and Camilla Shand together at a party in late summer of 1971. By the time Charles and Camilla were secretly photographed at a polo match four years later, their affair was in full swing—despite the fact that she was already married to Andrew Parker Bowles.

17

19

A bearded Charles aboard the aircraft carrier HMS *Hermes*, during his time serving as an officer in the Royal Navy.

20

In his ceremonial role as Prince of Wales, he donned many uniforms and costumes—like the full dress of a Kainai Chief, when he was given the tribal name Red Crow during a visit to the town of Stand Off, Alberta, Canada, in 1977.

Most Eligible Bachelor, Charles also maintained his "action man" image to the outside world. If he wasn't skiing in Switzerland, flying his own plane, surfing off the Australian coast, playing polo, or foxhunting—Charles overcame his fear of jumping his horse over fences and hedges just to please Camilla—then he was driving his Aston Martin through London streets with another dazzling young woman by his side.

Not every quest Charles undertook was for a bride—or in search of thrills. He would later admit that, in the mid-1970s, he "fell under the spell" of the South African writer, explorer, and spiritualist Laurens van der Post. In his bestselling book and subsequent popular BBC television series *The Lost World of the Kalahari*, Van der Post resurrected in vivid detail the ancient legends and forgotten myths of the South African bushmen. Van der Post and his second wife Ingaret, a Jungian psychoanalyst, became Charles's mystic mentors, encouraging him to reject convention and plumb the depths of his inner self—embracing, literally, the rocks and trees and other natural "spirits" that inhabited the world around him.

When Van der Post convinced Charles to talk to his plants, he didn't have to try very hard; at his various royal residences, particularly Balmoral, Charles confessed that he felt most comfortable when he was alone, communing with the local flora and fauna. He claimed to experience a "deep, religious connection" to the natural world that would "probably not sit well" with the Archbishop of Canterbury. It was around this time that Charles secretly underwent psychotherapy with Ingaret, and then with the Van der Posts' friend Dr. Alan McGlashan. (Years later Diana, Princess of Wales, would also be treated by Dr. McGlashan at Charles's urging.)

After his death in 1996 at age ninety, Laurens van der Post—whom Charles made a godfather to Prince William—would be exposed as a fraud, a con artist, a womanizer who fathered a child with a fourteen-year-old girl, and a "compulsive fantasist" who, according to British journalist J. D. F. Jones, plotted with his friend Margaret Thatcher to thwart Nelson Mandela's chances of becoming president of South Africa—among other things. When a doctor friend of Van der Post's was asked what caused the man's death, the doctor replied that Charles's guru was simply "weary of sustaining so many lies."

But not all of Charles's heroes would turn out to have feet of clay. In the wake of Amanda Knatchbull's refusal of marriage, Lord Mountbatten continued offering wise and loving counsel to his great-nephew. It was, Jonathan Dimbleby wrote in his authorized biography of Prince Charles, "Mountbatten's faith in his potential which had preserved his fragile sense of identity."

In mid-1979 Charles wrote a heartfelt letter to Mountbatten in which, for the first time, he spoke of how lost "we would be without you should you finally decide to depart." That August aboard the *Britannia*, the Prince was beguiled by Amanda's description of Mountbatten's summer retreat at Classiebawn Castle on Ireland's west coast. "I do wish I could come and see it," he wrote his great-uncle. "I know I would be captivated by it."

Just four days later, Charles was in Iceland as a guest of Lord and Lady "Kanga" Tryon, who owned a fishing lodge there. The Prince did more than fish during these trips to the Tryon fishing lodge; much of his time was spent in bed with his friend's bouncy Australian wife. "Sequestered so far away," said veteran journalist Christopher Wilson, "Charles fell swiftly in love."

Charles was fishing from a riverbank not far from the Tryon lodge when one of his aides rushed up and told him to brace himself for some terrible news. Had the Queen died? The Queen Mother? "My heart literally sank, and I felt quite sick," he recalled. "All sorts of hideous possibilities raced through my mind."

Nothing could have prepared him for what he was then told: the Irish Republican Army had blown up Lord Mountbatten's fishing boat, *Shadow V*, instantly killing Mountbatten, his fourteen-year-old grandson Nicholas, and a fifteen-year-old Irish boat hand. Nicholas's twin brother, Timothy, Mountbatten's daughter Patricia, and his son-in-law John all suffered serious injuries. Patricia's mother-in-law, Lady Brabourne, died the next morning, bringing the death toll to four.

"Agony, disbelief, a kind of wretched numbness swept over me," Charles recalled at hearing the news. This was followed by "fierce and violent determination to see that something was done about the IRA." (The bomber was tried, convicted, and served eighteen years in prison before being released in 1998 as part of the Good Friday Agreement ending hostilities in Northern Ireland. Still, paramilitary groups would continue carrying out bombings and other terrorist attacks as late as 2019.)

Within an hour of Dickie's assassination, Charles was on the phone to Camilla, sobbing his heart out. "Life has to go on, I suppose," Charles wrote in his journal, "but this afternoon I must confess I wanted it to stop. I felt supremely useless and powerless. . . . Life will never be the same now that he has gone."

Charles joined the rest of the Windsors to grieve at Balmoral, then journeyed by train to London for the nationally televised ceremonial funeral Lord Mountbatten had planned himself. As bands from all branches of the military played hymns and dirges, thousands of mourners turned out to watch Dickie's coffin make its way from Wellington Barracks to Westminster Abbey on a gun carriage pulled by 118 sailors from the Royal Navy.

Inside the abbey, the entire royal family was joined by hundreds of dignitaries from around the world in paying tribute to one of the towering figures of the twentieth century. Everyone was still clearly in shock just one week after Mountbatten's brutal murder, and none more so than Philip and Charles—the two men for whom Dickie had been nothing less than a father figure. Both princes wore their full-dress naval uniforms, but it was the heir to the British throne who had been chosen by Mountbatten to read his favorite passage from the Bible, Psalm 107. Sorrow etched on his face, a clearly distraught Charles delivered the famous lines in a quavering voice: "They that go down to the sea in ships, that do business in great waters; these see the works of the Lord, and his wonders in the deep."

Charles could not have known the impact his grief-stricken face was having on a young woman watching the funeral on television that day. Nor could he have remotely imagined how that young woman would change his life—and, in the process, the course of history.

Reporter: *Are you in love?*
Diana: *Of course!*
Charles: *Whatever "in love" is . . .*

Whatever happens, I will always love you.
—Charles to Camilla, in a phone call overheard by Diana

*We were told to treat Camilla as if she was mistress
of the house. It was as if Diana had never existed.*
— Ken Stronach, Prince Charles's valet, on the way Camilla and
Diana were treated during the marriage of Charles and Diana

*Forget her husband, her children,
her own mother. . . . He came first, always.*
—a member of the Parker Bowles household staff,
on Camilla's attitude toward Charles

FIVE

"YOU WILL NEVER BE KING!"

Charles would remember it as a seventeen-year-long blur of scandalous headlines, broken hearts, wounded children, and an unspeakable tragedy that simultaneously stunned the world and brought the monarchy to its knees. It all began in July 1980 with two people sitting on a hay bale at a Sussex barbecue. The first anniversary of Mountbatten's assassination was coming up, and Charles mentioned it to the young lady who sat with him, balancing a plate on her lap.

"I remember how desperately sad you looked," said Lady Diana Spencer, referring to television coverage of Mountbatten's funeral at Westminster Abbey. "I sensed your loneliness. And your need for someone to care for you . . ." Watching from a few yards away, Charles's former girlfriend Sabrina Guinness thought Diana's intentions were transparent. "She was giggling," Guinness said, "furiously trying to make an impression."

It was a bold move for Lady Sarah Spencer's blonde, blue-eyed little sister Diana—the rosy-cheeked, full-figured, denim-clad nineteen-year-old kindergarten teacher who Charles described as "jolly" and "bouncy" after their first brief meeting three years earlier. To be so open and direct with the Prince of Wales about so personal a matter required considerable chutzpah and the ability to appear convincingly sincere—qualities not often found in Britain's uptight, irony-laden upper classes. As it happened, Charles was very impressed with Lady Diana's warmth and what appeared to be her spot-on insight into how he suffered emotionally.

It also helped that Lady Diana, whose taste and interests were distinctly urban, appeared on the surface to be every inch the country girl. Her father was the Queen's equerry and another older sister, Lady Jane, was married to the Queen's assistant private secretary, Robert Fellowes, so Diana was occasionally invited along to Balmoral. During those outings, she always wore jeans, plaid shirts, and boots—and made it clear that she regarded herself as "a tomboy." Fellowes joined the Queen Mother, whose close friend and lady-in-waiting was Diana's grandmother Lady Ruth Fermoy, in backing Diana as a potential bride. Eventually the tables would turn, and Diana would come—with good reason—to consider Fellowes, the Queen Mother, and even her own grandmother as sworn enemies.

Soon Charles, blithely unaware that Diana's country girl persona was little more than a ruse, began singing the young woman's praises to members of his tight inner circle. The Prince even hinted to Camilla that Lady Diana might be the one. Of course, Charles probably wouldn't have taken a second look at Diana if he weren't under tremendous pressure to marry—pressure that the Duke of Edinburgh was applying in his usual sledgehammer style. "What in God's name are you waiting for?" he asked Charles during one Sandringham shooting party. "Can it be that difficult? Just pick one, and let's get on with it! You are *thirty-two* years old!"

In late August 1980 Charles, who preferred to court his newest love interest away from the prying eyes of journalists, invited Lady Diana to Balmoral for the weekend. There she once again played the part of a wholesome country lass to perfection, traipsing gamely along riverbanks and through muddy fields, laughing when she toppled into a bog and emerged covered in thick, greenish muck. The couple picnicked in the Scottish countryside, and Charles taught her to fish. Diana threw herself into every activity—including stalking deer that would be shot by male members of the royal hunting party—with unbridled enthusiasm. "She was a sort of wonderful English schoolgirl who was game for anything," said Charles's old friend Patti Palmer-Tomkinson, who was staying at

Balmoral with her husband at the time. "Diana was naturally young but sweet, and clearly very much wanted him."

Charles's interest grew exponentially when his brothers pleaded to be seated next to the beguiling Lady Diana at dinner. "She was so lovely, charming, so bright and full of fun and mischief," Palmer-Tomkinson recalled. "Every man gravitated toward her." Charles said later that he was "flattered" by all the attention other men were paying to the new lady in his life, and impressed that, even at such a young age, she moved with such grace and ease in royal circles.

Intrigued, Charles decided to continue courting Diana largely behind Palace walls, just beyond the reach of Britain's relentless tabloid press. At Sandringham, Diana hunted pheasant alongside her Prince, proved herself to be a confident equestrienne as she rode on horseback alongside Charles and the Queen, and once again captivated her royal hosts at dinner. By their fifth date, Charles admitted to a close friend that, while he could not yet say he loved Diana, she was so exceptionally fun and "warmhearted" that he was certain he could learn to.

Charles had, in fact, already assigned the task of helping him find a wife to the two women who he knew would have *his* best interests at heart: Camilla and Lady Tryon. There was no question in either woman's mind which mistress had the inside track. In 1980 Charles doled out $1.75 million (equivalent to $5.3 million in 2019) for a Georgian estate in Gloucestershire located two hours west of London—and only twenty-seven minutes from Bolehyde Manor in Chippenham, the Parker Bowles homestead. Charles had to instruct the Duchy of Cornwall to sell much of the village of Daglingworth to finance the purchase of Highgrove House from the family of former Prime Minister Harold Macmillan.

The three-story manor house with its neoclassical façade of gray stone featured nine bedrooms, four reception rooms, eight bathrooms, a nursery wing, stables, staff quarters, and 350 acres of farmland—modest by royal standards but appealing to Charles nonetheless because of its "faded but friendly elegance." Highgrove, which dates back to the late eighteenth century, also came with an interesting, if somewhat macabre, history. In 1850 the owner's granddaughter died after her gown caught fire during a soiree held for her brother in the ballroom. Years later, another fire nearly gutted the manor entirely. In 1956 Harold Macmillan bought the property; Charles, like everyone else in Britain's establishment, was aware that the Prime Minister's wife Dorothy carried on an affair with Lord Robert Boothby for thirty years, ending only with her death in 1966. Macmillan, though tortured by his wife's flagrant infidelity, never granted her a divorce—and never fell out of love with her.

In the coming years, Charles would beat a well-worn path from Highgrove to Bolehyde Manor and Camilla. They would also meet at various events, such as the Cirencester Park Polo Club Ball not far from Highgrove. According to Fleet Street veteran Christopher Wilson, the Prince and Mrs. Parker Bowles were seen "kissing each other, French kissing, dance after dance." At another gathering, Charles apparently found it impossible to resist Camilla's raw sexuality. He took one look at her slinky dress, said a guest, then "plunged his hands down the front and grabbed her breasts. In mixed company, that is not the done thing."

"To most of the population," Wilson said, "theirs was a passion which simply did not exist. But a privileged few were witness to an astonishing display of the almost animal attraction that the two now had for each other."

Camilla was not the only object of Charles's desire. There were also the Prince's frequent "comfort stops"—Kanga's words—made at the Old Manor House at Great Durnford, Lord Tryon's family seat. Kanga recalled later that the Prince of Wales would "ring out of the blue and say he would be passing by and would I mind if he stopped in." When he opened the door—always without knocking—she would be standing there with a glass of whiskey. Despite his deep and enduring devotion to Camilla, Charles went on record describing Kanga as "the only woman who ever understood me."

Not long after Charles and Diana had their fateful chat on a hay bale, the Prince's two most serious mistresses sat down together at the Parker Bowleses' home and compared notes on suitable royal brides. Each had a list of three candidates, but only one name appeared on both lists: Lady Diana Spencer. Even as late as 1980, virginity was a must when considering the mother of future monarchs—and a Palace physician would have to confirm this before any engagement was made. Charles's two mistresses were convinced that Diana was a virgin—one of the few available on their combined lists—and they were right. Diana, whose sisters called her "Duch" for Duchess, reflecting her long-expressed desire to marry the Prince, would say later that she knew she had to keep herself "tidy for whatever was coming my way."

Equally important, Diana's pedigree was impeccable. Unlike "the Germans," as she would call the Mountbatten-Windsors, the House of Spencer was one of Britain's most respected aristocratic families with roots dating back to the fifteenth century. Among historically important titles belonging to Spencer family members were the dukedom of Marlborough, the earldoms of Spencer and Sunderland, and the Churchill barony. Diana and Winston Churchill were actually fourth cousins twice removed.

Charles listened to Camilla and Kanga but still dragged his feet. He pointed to Andrew Parker Bowles's many affairs as grounds for her to get a divorce, insisting that he still wanted to make Camilla his wife. Of course, that was impossible. "Charles would have to basically step aside and let Andrew take his place in the line of succession," said Harold Brooks-Baker, longtime publishing director of *Burke's Peerage*, the nearly two-hundred-year-old genealogy and heraldry guide. "That wasn't about to happen. But Camilla let him stamp his feet for a while before bringing him back to reality. There was no way at that time that she was going to divorce, or that Charles was going to seriously consider marrying a divorced woman."

———

As time progressed and Charles continued to stall, Diana began to panic. She broke down several times, asking her sisters point-blank, "Why won't he ask me? Why won't he ask me?" It didn't help that the paparazzi were in hot pursuit, chasing her down at the kindergarten where she worked, at the Chelsea flat she shared with three friends, or simply walking down the street. "They simply won't let up," she complained to one of her roommates. "They hunt you down like an animal."

Through it all, Diana was careful to never let on to Charles or his minions that she was "frantic" that someone else had the inner track. "Never once did she ask about the other girls in his life," said Charles's valet Stephen Barry. "Not that I would have told her anything if she had."

Since she had been a guest of Charles's at Balmoral, there was added concern that Charles's failure to take action might compromise Lady Diana's reputation. "She was from one of the most important families in Britain, and, as far as anyone knew at the time, a very sweet, naïve girl," Barry said. "The Queen was becoming impatient, but Prince Philip even more so." Finally, Charles's father stepped in with stern words: "Either ask the poor girl to marry you or end it."

Charles, confronted with this ultimatum, then acted in what he described as a "confused and anxious state of mind." As soon as he returned from a skiing trip to Klosters, Switzerland, Charles drove to Bolehyde Manor and met Diana there. They strolled through the gardens, and, with Camilla peeking down from the second floor, Charles popped the question.

"Will you marry me?" he asked.

Diana brought her hand to her mouth, giggled, and answered, "Yes, please!" Then she threw her arms around him. Charles, taken by surprise, flinched. No matter. The giggling, which Charles later said he found "juvenile and unnerving," resumed.

Rather than choose a custom-designed ring, Diana quickly picked one out from an Asprey & Garrard jewelers catalogue: fourteen solitaire diamonds surrounding a magnificent 12-carat oval blue Ceylon sapphire set in 18-carat white gold. The cost: $45,000 (equivalent to about $145,000 in 2022). During their joint BBC television interview announcing the engagement, Charles predicted that his fiancée's being twelve years younger (the same age gap that existed between John F. Kennedy and Jackie Kennedy) would "keep me young," while Diana chirped, "With Prince Charles beside me, I cannot go wrong."

Not long after, Charles urged Camilla to meet Diana for lunch. The two women chatted, and Diana happily showed off her ring. They steered away from any discussion of Camilla's affair with Charles, but, throughout the lunch, the thought never left Diana's mind. Afterward, Charles pumped Camilla for information. "What did she say about us?" he asked anxiously.

"Nothing, nothing at all," Camilla replied, sticking to her original conviction that Diana was "very naïve" and knew nothing of their relationship. If Diana did know, both Camilla and Kanga Tryon had insisted all along, she was far too weak to do anything about it. "They thought Diana was the kind of meek person who would just go along the way everyone else did," Diana's friend Lady Elsa Bowker said. "They thought she would look the other way and just be happy to be the wife of the future king. They did not know her."

It did not take long for one thoughtless, offhand remark to push Diana over the edge. Just a few days after announcing their engagement, Charles put his arm around her waist, pinched it, and said, "Oh, a bit chubby here, aren't we?" Later, Diana would state publicly that this single comment so shocked and upset her at the impressionable age of nineteen that she soon became bulimic. At the height of her problem, she forced herself to vomit at least five times a day.

Had anyone bothered to scratch the porcelain-perfect surface, they would have realized that Diana was anything but unbreakable. Her mother abandoned the family to marry another, much younger man when Diana was only six, leaving the little girl and her three-year-old brother Charles to be raised by a succession of Dickensian nannies and governesses. In addition to the one who regularly clocked them with a wooden spoon for no reason at all, another banged Diana's and Charles's heads together when she felt they had disobeyed her. A bitter legal battle between Diana's parents eventually wound up with Earl Spencer getting full custody. Unfortunately, Earl Spencer remained so bitter about his wife's betrayal that for years he barely spoke to his own children—or, for that matter, anyone in the family. "Her own childhood was hell," Diana's friend Peter Janson said. "Her parents hated, despised each other."

As it turned out, Charles had much more in common with Diana than he did with Camilla. They were both open about their unhappy, abuse-filled childhoods, their estrangement from one or both parents, their feelings of abandonment. Yet this hardly spelled compatibility. "They were both just so broken and alienated," said Bonnie Angelo, who got to know both Charles and Diana as the London Bureau Chief of *Time* magazine. "He felt pressured to marry her, and she wanted to prove her own worth by snagging the future King of England, someone she had a crush on since she was a little girl. It was a recipe for disaster from the very beginning."

During the run-up to the wedding preparations, Diana was moved into rooms at Buckingham Palace and began learning the royal ropes from Charles's private secretary Edward Adeane and a handful of other aides. The strain, coupled with the bulimic episodes that were shrinking her waist from twenty-nine to twenty-two inches, quickly took its toll. "She went to Buckingham Palace, and then the tears started," her former roommate and friend Carolyn Bartholomew said of the five-foot-eleven Diana. "The little thing got so thin. I was worried about her. She wasn't happy, she was suddenly plunged into all this pressure, and it was a nightmare for her."

While Charles said later that he hadn't the slightest inkling that the "jolly" and "giggling" girl he had asked to marry him was prone to dark moods, he neglected to mention that initially the moods were his. Clearly irritated that he had acquiesced to pressure from Prince Philip and others, the Prince took it out on his young and vulnerable fiancée. At a charity gala at Goldsmiths' Hall in London, he sniped at her for wearing a stylish black dress. "Only mourners wear black," he complained. Princess Grace of Monaco overheard Charles's crack and pulled her into the ladies' room. They locked the door, and Diana proceeded to share with Princess Grace all the ways in which her future husband and the Palace were making life unbearable. "Don't worry," the former Grace Kelly told her, "it will get a lot worse!"

Most upsetting for Diana was the continuing presence of Camilla

Parker Bowles in her fiancé's life. Just as Charles was about to embark on a lengthy solo tour of Australia and New Zealand that would make her feel even more alone and isolated, Diana visited him in his office. She playfully jumped on his lap, but as soon as a call came in from Camilla, she bolted for the door. "She was saying good-bye to him before he left on his trip, and I didn't want to intrude on their privacy," Diana recalled. "Isn't that sad?"

At one point, Diana cornered Charles and confessed to being riven with doubt about their approaching nuptials. "I know all about you and Camilla, Charles," she said. "Do you still love her?"

"Camilla has been one of my most intimate friends, yes," he confessed to her. "But now that we are getting married, there is—there can never be—another woman in my life."

Diana was quick to pick up on the Prince's carefully chosen words. "But you didn't answer my question," she continued. "Do you still love Camilla?" Diana told her handlers on several occasions that she had asked Charles if he still loved Camilla Parker Bowles, "and he didn't give me a clear answer. What am I to do?"

Charles was still very much in love with Camilla—of that there could be no doubt. To make it clear to his mistress that they would always be a couple, he designed a gold chain bracelet for her with a blue enamel disc. Entwined on the disc in gold are the letters *G* and *F*—for Gladys and Fred, their pet names for each other. (Charles would later claim that *GF* stood for "Girl Friday"—an obvious attempt to make his relationship with Camilla seem more businesslike and platonic.)

Charles was not in his Buckingham Palace office when the package containing the bracelet arrived on his desk just two weeks before the wedding—but Diana was. "I opened it . . . and I was devastated," she recalled. "So rage, rage, rage!"

"Why can't you be honest with me?" Diana asked Charles, but rather than react, she said, "he cut me absolutely dead. It's as if he had made his decision, and if it wasn't going to work, it wasn't going to work. He'd found the virgin, the sacrificial lamb . . ."

That night, as planned, Charles met Camilla secretly and gave her the bracelet. They slept together that night and allegedly several times more before the wedding—including, according to reporter James Whitaker and Prince Charles's valet Stephen Barry, on the eve of the ceremony itself.

Consumed by anger and frustration, both bride and groom separately cried themselves to sleep the night before the wedding. Charles's capacity for seeing himself as victim was bottomless, and once again he chafed at the idea of being bullied into a marriage he did not want. The young woman whom Camilla once described as a "beautiful broodmare" intended to bear the Prince of Wales's children was already proving to be a handful. Diana, meanwhile, sobbed to her sisters just hours before the wedding, "I can't marry him. I can't do this." They famously replied, "Well, bad luck, Duch. . . . [It's] too late to chicken out."

To the outside world, the wedding of the Prince of Wales and Lady Diana Spencer at St. Paul's Cathedral on July 29, 1981, wildly surpassed all expectations. "This is the stuff," intoned Archbishop of Canterbury Robert Runcie, "of which fairy tales are made: the Prince and Princess on their wedding day."

For the couple at the center of all the pageantry and hoopla, it was more of a nightmare. Charles, waiting at the altar as his young bride glided up the aisle, had a clear view of several old flames and mistresses. Kanga Tryon was there, and Janet Jenkins, who could not take her eyes off Camilla and her "cool Cheshire cat grin." Neither could Diana, who said later the image of Camilla seated in the cathedral—"pale-gray, veiled pillbox hat, her son Tom standing on a chair"—was burned in her memory.

The spark in their marriage, if there ever was one, was extinguished early on. "The honeymoon was a perfect opportunity," Diana wrote to her lady-in-waiting, "to catch up on sleep." After cruising the Greek isles aboard the royal yacht *Britannia*—during which Diana mingled with the crew and kitchen staff and Charles holed up alone reading books by his guru, Laurens van der Post—the newlyweds spent a month at Balmoral. If Charles had hoped that somehow the magic of his "favorite place in all the world" would rub off on his bride, those thoughts were quickly dashed.

Charles was, in fact, still keeping in close touch with Camilla—and Diana knew it. According to one of his friends, the Princess of Wales had "reached the point of obsession" and more than once during the honeymoon "exploded into a tirade of anger" followed by long periods of "bewilderment and despondency."

Nevertheless, the façade of marital bliss did not crack. Before the marriage, much of the public viewed the overfamiliar Charles as a stuffy, bland throwback to an earlier era. The lively, outgoing, unpretentious Diana changed that perception overnight. "In the very beginning," said veteran *Times* correspondent Alan Hamilton, Diana "sprinkled fairy dust over the entire royal family. That was especially true of Charles, who all of sudden seemed so smart for having picked such a wonderful young woman to be his princess, the future Queen. People absolutely loved her, and that rubbed off on him."

With the birth of Prince William ("the Heir") in 1982 and Prince Harry ("the Spare") two years later, Charles's young family appeared picture perfect. Yet Harry's birth had marked a turning point in the marriage. Unlike his own father, who played squash and swam during his son's delivery, Charles was on hand and even choked back tears when Diana gave birth to William. "Fantastic, beautiful," the Prince told his wife after the arrival of the seven-pound, one-and-a-half-ounce William. "You are a darling." Diana's close friend Lucia Flecha de Lima, wife of the Brazilian Ambassador to the United Kingdom, remembered that Charles was "very enchanted" with William. He was there for Harry's arrival, too, but his reaction was startlingly different.

"Oh, God, it's a boy," Charles said, shaking his head. "And he even has red hair."

"At that moment," Diana said later, "something inside me closed off." At the christening, Charles doubled down on his comment, objecting to his newborn son's "rusty" hair. Diana's mother, Frances Shand Kydd, was incensed. "You should just be thankful that you had a child who is normal," she scolded, adding that many on Diana's side of the family had red hair.

Shand Kydd was unaware of the real reason for Charles's inexplicable criticism of Harry's looks. He suspected that Diana was having an affair with dashing and "rusty"-haired Captain James Hewitt of the Life Guards in the Household Cavalry, Diana's riding instructor. Eventually Diana would confess that she had fallen in love with Hewitt but that their relationship did not begin until 1986. However, evidence would ultimately surface that Hewitt first spotted Lady Diana Spencer at a polo match in Tidworth, Wiltshire, in June 1981—six weeks before she and Charles were married. Hewitt was playing for the army; Charles, for the navy.

Under hypnosis in 2005, Hewitt confessed that he and Diana made love for the first time in September 1982, just a few months after William's birth. The Princess was convinced she'd make "a very good army wife," and told Hewitt that she wanted to get a divorce and "settle down" with him—something, the riding instructor said, "we knew wasn't possible. . . . It was a dream."

In March 1984 Diana told Hewitt she was pregnant and they "stopped having a full sexual relationship," Hewitt said, "as it seemed more respectful." After Harry's birth in September, though, Diana and Hewitt picked up where they left off. After receiving an anonymous phone call suggesting that it would be "healthier" for him to call a halt to their affair, Hewitt asked British publicist Max Clifford how he and Diana might best proceed without blowing their cover. It was Clifford who recommended that Hewitt drop Diana as a pupil and start giving riding lessons to William and Harry. In the meantime, James insisted that he did not meet Diana until 1986—two years after Harry's birth.

The ploy worked. For eight years following Harry's birth, Diana and Hewitt continued to meet in secret—until, for reasons that would remain a mystery to Diana's lover, the Princess swiftly and unexpectedly called a halt to their affair. Harry's undeniable physical resemblance to Hewitt—a similarity that grew markedly stronger as he entered adulthood—coupled with similar facial mannerisms and characteristics that diverge from anything seen in the royal family, fueled speculation that James Hewitt was, in fact, Harry's biological father.

Yet in the early years of Charles and Diana's marriage, the public was blissfully unaware of any tensions between them—thanks in large part to the couple's adorable children. The little princes became Fleet Street darlings. From first steps, school uniforms, and playdates, to playmates, meltdowns, and growth spurts—their every mood and move was dutifully chronicled in newspapers and magazines around the world. "William and Harry pushed everything over the top," James Whitaker said. "The press and public were totally besotted with them. When they were very young, we were all very much in the dark about what was really going on. It must have been hell for those boys, but it was carefully hidden."

Charles, who persisted in maintaining his relationship with Camilla, turned a blind eye to his wife's pain. As early as January 1982, when she was three months pregnant with William and suffering from severe morning sickness, Diana and Charles began screaming invective at each other. As was usually the case, the subject was Camilla. The Prince was in his full riding gear and made no secret of the fact that he was walking out the front door at Sandringham to join Camilla for a ride through the Norfolk countryside. The argument moved to the top of the main staircase—right above the spot where the Queen and Princess Margaret were standing.

"I will throw myself down these stairs!" Diana threatened as her husband turned to leave. "I am so desperate, Charles. Please listen to me!"

But Charles didn't listen ("You're crying wolf," he said with a smirk), and the very pregnant Diana did what she threatened to do. Within seconds, the Princess of Wales lay sprawled on the foyer floor. Princess Margaret rushed to her side while the Queen, trembling, called for help. Bruised but otherwise uninjured—doctors assured her that her baby had not been harmed—Diana spent the rest of the day resting in her room. Charles, miffed at what he viewed as "more melodrama," went ahead with his plans to spend the afternoon with Camilla.

There would be many more such close calls. Over time the Princess would throw herself against a glass display case, shattering it; slash her wrists with a razor blade; and stab herself in the chest with a pocket knife. In taped interviews released nearly twenty years after her death, Diana recalled being prescribed large doses of the tranquilizer Valium by a string of psychiatrists—medication that did little to curb the self-destructive streak that grew more and more alarming. "I was in such a bad way," she admitted later. "Couldn't sleep, didn't eat, the whole world was collapsing around me." Each increasingly bloody incident was, said Diana, "a desperate cry for help."

It was a cry Charles refused to hear. He viewed Diana as "moody" and "spoiled," and chafed at the notion of being manipulated by the wife who derisively called him "the Boy Wonder" and "the Great White Hope" behind his back. It bothered him even more that the Princess had bestowed her own nickname on Camilla—"the Rottweiler"—although Camilla and her friends indulged in a little name-calling of their own. Whenever the subject of her rival came up in conversation, Camilla referred to her as "Barbie."

Adding to the turmoil, Charles was growing increasingly jealous of Diana's soaring popularity. His willowy, blonde, vibrant wife was proving to be an avatar of fashion on a scale not seen since Jackie Kennedy Onassis. During lunch with the Princess years later at the Four Seasons restaurant in Manhattan, writer Tina Brown described the impact Diana had just walking across the room: "She wears a mint-green Chanel suit with no blouse and a stunning tan. Making her way quickly across the crowded restaurant, she has the startling phosphorescence of a cartoon creation—too blonde, too tall, too painfully recognizable. Perhaps it's her height that's unsettling. It renders her more than just an acute natural beauty. She's like a strange overbred plant, a far-fetched experimental rose."

Even more important, Diana was something that Charles strived to but could never comfortably be: a thoroughly modern, reach-out-and-touch crowd pleaser. Over the years, Diana's visits to homeless shelters, cancer wards, children's hospitals, and AIDS clinics—sometimes accompanied by William and Harry—would place her among the world's most admired humanitarians. Her trademark warmth and willingness to engage with people in need struck a chord. For example, by shaking the hand of an AIDS patient in 1987—still relatively early in the deadly epidemic—without wearing gloves, she exploded the then prevalent myth that the disease could be spread simply by touch.

Charles, like his mother the Queen and all the Windsors, visited more than his share of hospitals, slums, and disaster sites. But he inevitably appeared awkward and standoffish compared with his down-to-earth wife. The fact that the Prince's Trust had already raised millions for charity by the time he married Diana could not offset the fact that he seemed aloof and uncomfortable around those who would someday be his subjects.

"No one foresaw the personality cult of Diana," said Lord MacLean, who was then Lord Chamberlain. "Diana was turning into a potential danger because all the attention was beginning to orbit around her, and in that marriage there can only be one sun: the Prince of Wales." Diana, for her part, felt underappreciated. "No matter what I do, no matter how many millions I raise for their charities," she complained, "it's not enough. It's *never* enough." Sometimes, it was too much. At one point, the Queen summoned Diana to Buckingham Palace and asked her to drop her support of AIDS research. "Why don't you," Her Majesty asked, "get involved in something a little more pleasant?"

It was not long before Charles and Diana were essentially leading separate lives—she at Kensington Palace, and the Prince at Highgrove. Fuming over his wife's refusal to, in his words, "behave rationally for a change," Charles kept in his breast pocket the letter that Prince Philip had written demanding that he propose marriage to Diana or risk damaging her reputation. When the subject of his rapidly unraveling marriage came up among friends, Charles would whip the letter out of his pocket with a flourish. "Look what they did to me," he would say, unfolding it. "I was forced into it!"

Now that she was for all intents and purposes chatelaine of Highgrove, Camilla made little effort to conceal her position in the Prince's life—at least from locals and their close circle of friends. When they weren't out riding together, Charles and Camilla took watercolor lessons from portrait painter Neil Forster, who lived nearby. "When Charles throws dinner parties for close friends," former royal security officer Andrew Jackson said at the time, "Camilla steps right into Di's shoes. She always comes alone, never with her husband. Camilla organizes the menu and sits alongside Charles. And she's the only person allowed into his walled garden."

In 1989, a year after Charles moved out of Kensington Palace, Diana barged into a fortieth birthday party for Camilla's sister Annabel. With Charles upstairs, she cornered his mistress in the ground-floor nursery. Diana told Camilla she knew what was going on and announced that she wasn't "born yesterday."

A stunned Camilla fought back. "You've got everything you ever wanted," she told Diana. "You've got all the men in the world to fall in love with you, and you've got two beautiful children. What more do you want?"

"I want my husband!" shouted Diana, who then apologized sarcastically for being "in the way. *Don't*," she went on, "treat me like an idiot!"

Camilla "ran out of the house as if she'd been shot out of a cannon," said one guest, "and Prince Charles sprinted after her." He returned and, red faced with rage, blasted Diana as she climbed into her car to leave. "I refuse," Charles told his wife, "to be the only Prince of Wales who never had a mistress!" Later that night at Highgrove, he phoned Camilla from the supposed privacy of his bath to apologize for Diana's outburst. At one point, Diana would share this tidbit with his mother the Queen. In fact, said Her Majesty's daughter-in-law, she often listened at Charles's bathroom door to the phone conversations he had with his mistress while lounging in the tub.

Charles knew that his wife was spying on him, and that she had turned to his mother for help. He also knew that the Queen had none to give. During one particularly emotional visit, Elizabeth II later told her private secretary, Diana "cried nonstop" as she begged for help in ending her husband's affair with Camilla. "What do I do?" Diana sobbed. "What do I do?"

"I don't know what you should do," replied the Queen, who had tried but failed to persuade her son to give up Mrs. Parker Bowles. "Charles is hopeless."

Yet the royal family's efforts aimed at getting rid of Camilla were half-hearted at best. Out of her blind affection for Charles, the Queen Mother had allowed the couple to tryst at Birkhall, her manor house on the grounds of Balmoral. Eventually the Queen would also order a separate, secret, and secure phone at Balmoral for the exclusive use of her son and his mistress.

Indeed, the Prince regarded his relationship with Camilla as nonnegotiable. He told his mother the same thing: that he had been railroaded into marrying a woman he didn't love and was not about to abandon the one he did. Highgrove became a primary trysting place for Charles and Camilla, as did Middlewick House, the Parker Bowleses' new five-hundred-acre estate conveniently located just thirteen minutes away.

Charles reportedly used his influence to make sure that Andrew Parker Bowles's various duties—he had been promoted to brigadier general and given the vaunted title Silver Stick in Waiting to the Queen—kept him far from Middlewick House for weeks or even months at a stretch. The Prince didn't have to try very hard. Andrew, who by now had resigned himself to being Charles's willing cuckold, often stayed in London during the workweek so he could indulge in extramarital shenanigans of his own.

Meanwhile at Highgrove and at Middlewick House, the Charles-Camilla affair took on all the properties of a bed-hopping, door-slamming music hall farce. No sooner would Andrew depart Middlewick House for London on Sunday night than all the exterior lights would be shut off so that Charles could drive up under cover of darkness—a weekly drill that members of Camilla's household staff called "the Blackout." Charles stayed the night, then departed before sunup—all of which prompted the servants to dub him the Prince of Darkness.

Charles's valet Ken Stronach was under strict orders from his boss to make it look to his wife—should Diana make a surprise appearance at Highgrove—as if Charles had spent the night home alone. Stronach left a half-eaten sandwich and an empty glass of sherry on the Prince's nightstand, alongside a newspaper with television listings circled in ink.

Stronach found the whole ritual absurd. "It didn't fool anybody," he said, "least of all Princess Diana."

A similar charade took place whenever the reverse happened, and Camilla snuck out to spend the night at Highgrove. No sooner would Diana leave Highgrove than Camilla would drive up and be escorted to a guest bedroom. Later in the evening, Charles would then order Highgrove's sophisticated security system turned off so that Camilla could move about the house freely—allowing her to sneak into the Prince's room. Stronach called this maneuver "a big risk," not to mention "a stupid thing to do. But he's blind to everything where the lady is concerned." Even more sophomoric was Charles's insistence that Stronach disturb the covers and sheets in the guest bedroom—but only on one side so that it appeared that only Camilla had slept there alone. "Even though everyone had orders not to tell the Princess or anyone that Camilla had been there, he actually believed he could make *us* think nothing was going on between him and his mistress. Really quite amazing."

For years, the Prince kept a framed photograph of Camilla next to his brass bed at Highgrove. Whenever Diana came to stay, Stronach scrambled to conceal the photo, along with any other telltale traces left behind by his employer's mistress: lipstick-stained glasses, half-full ashtrays—"anything that would have given them away."

What happened when Diana did, in fact, show up at Highgrove on weekends bordered on the slapstick. Camilla and Charles would meet at their special spot just inside the garden walls. Creeping back into his room, the Prince quickly changed into a new pair of pajamas. Stronach was left to scrub mud and grass stains—"obviously, they'd been doing it"—out of the old pair. "Prince Charles made love to Camilla Parker Bowles," Stronach said, "in the bushes of his Highgrove mansion while Princess Diana slept inside. Incredible."

Given all that was going on there, it was no surprise that Highgrove was a flashpoint in the Prince of Wales's marriage. Wendy Berry, the housekeeper at Highgrove, witnessed the slammed doors and pitched battles that were the hallmarks of day-to-day life when Charles and Diana were within the same four walls. During one skirmish, Charles's valet looked on while Diana, hurling epithets and mocking her husband's obsession with the dreary-looking Camilla, literally pursued the hapless Prince down hallways, up staircases, and from room to room. Since Harry's birth, Charles had for all intents and purposes unilaterally called a halt to their sexual relationship. "Why won't you sleep with *me*?" his wife asked point-blank.

"I don't know, dear," the Prince replied, his voice dripping with sarcasm. "I think I might be gay."

At one point, an exasperated Charles stood his ground and insisted on being given the respect that he felt his position warranted. "Do you know who I am?" he demanded imperiously.

Diana answered that he was "a fucking animal," and then delivered the coup de grâce: "You will never be King!" she shouted. "William will succeed your mother. I will see to that."

Charles never took such threats seriously. Diana was powerless to change the laws of succession, and he knew it. What he did not know was that the Princess, who surrounded herself with clairvoyants, tarot card readers, new age gurus, and "spiritual advisors" of all kinds, believed her astrologer's prediction that Charles would die before his mother and never sit on the throne.

Such grim prognostications aside, Charles had to deal with the plain fact that his wife was far more adept at manipulating public opinion to achieve her ends—and that she was not above using their children as pawns if required. "She is an absolute magician at turning things around and upside down," he fumed. "She bats her eyelashes, and everyone believes whatever she says, without question. How do I possibly compete with that?"

As it happened, Diana was not the only woman who was determined to take the Prince down a notch. In the pages of the *Manchester Evening News*, it was reported that Charles was so concerned about deepening racial divisions in Britain that he feared inheriting the "throne of a divided Britain." To prevent this, he allegedly contemplated stepping in himself to broker a peace. Traveling in New York, an angry Prime Minister Margaret Thatcher got on the phone to St. James's Palace and blasted him. "What the hell do you think you are doing?" she asked, pointing out that in the six years since taking office, her conservative policies had lifted the nation out of the economic doldrums. "I run this country," she reminded the Prince, "not you, Sir."

No one was more outraged than Charles, whose comments had been leaked by a member of his inner circle. The Prince wrote to his corpulent lifelong friend Nicholas "Fatty" Soames—who also happened to be Winston Churchill's grandson—that he was "incensed" and found "the whole thing extremely aggravating. I spend my whole time trying not to polarize things, and now someone has polarized me!"

Understandably, it was Diana who took center stage as far as William and Harry were concerned. But behind the scenes, Charles played an active role in raising his sons from the very beginning. Early on, Mummy and Papa differed on the boys' education. Charles wanted to hire a governess for the express purpose of educating William and Harry inside Kensington Palace. His wife, the former kindergarten teacher, argued that in order to be a well-adjusted adult—not to mention an effective monarch—William should "mix it up" with other children at a preschool. Charles remembered how, when he enrolled at Hill House school at the age of eight, he was "terribly shy. As a result, I never quite felt like I belonged. That's a feeling that never leaves you."

When they signed up William for Mrs. Mynors' Nursery School, located just a few short blocks from Kensington Palace, Charles wrote letters to several newspaper editors imploring them to leave the boy alone. Meanwhile, a panic button was installed behind the desk of William's Montessori-trained teacher, and classroom windows were replaced with bulletproof glass. On a chilly morning in September 1985, William, decked out in red shorts, red shoes, and a blue-, green-, and red-striped sweater, arrived at Mrs. Mynors' with both his parents. They were met by more than a hundred jostling photographers, each angling for just the right front-page shot.

Any other four-year-old might have been frightened by such pandemonium, but not William. He and his brother had already been exposed to their parents' seemingly endless screaming matches, the smashed crockery, and slamming doors. Unfortunately, the Heir reacted by lashing out. At one point during Harry's christening at Windsor Castle, William ran circles around the Archbishop of Canterbury, flapping his arms, barking like a dog, and occasionally bumping into the Queen and the Queen Mother.

Diana called William her "Mini-Tornado," and he proved she wasn't exaggerating when he touched down at the Queen Mother's Balmoral residence, Birkhall. William careened about the dining room, smashing glassware, tipping over chairs, and defacing a portrait of his great-great-great-great-great-grandmother Queen Victoria. Charles was mortified at his eldest son's behavior, and never more so than when William threw a full-blown tantrum before barking orders at the servants—many of whom the Prince of Wales had known all his life.

Teaching William some manners was one of the few matters on which Charles and Diana were in complete agreement. They had hoped that his teachers at Mrs. Mynors' Nursery School would be able to impose some structure on their son, but the royal toddler quickly put them in their place. According to staff members and several parents, William bossed around the other children ("My daddy is the Prince of Wales. If you don't do what I say, I'll have you arrested!"), shoved his way to the front of the line, grabbed crayons, chalk, and picture books out of the hands of his terrified classmates, and even started fights on the playground.

"Wills" was now a far cry from the adorable ten-month-old who'd accompanied his parents on their first major overseas trip to Australia in March 1983, when Diana had overruled the Queen's objections and insisted on bringing William along. This time she decided it would be best if he remained behind when the Waleses visited Washington in November 1985—the Princess of Wales's first trip ever to the United States. Much to

Charles's chagrin, his wife now took a firm hand in planning all their official trips abroad. Fearing that she and her husband would be surrounded by what she called "fossilized" politicians and diplomats, Diana insisted that the glamorous likes of Mikhail Baryshnikov, Neil Diamond, Clint Eastwood, Tom Selleck, and John Travolta be invited to the White House dinner held in the royal couple's honor.

This was the evening that an expressionless Charles watched as John Travolta twirled his wife around the dance floor. "I didn't know that I was supposed to dance with Princess Diana," the star of *Saturday Night Fever* said later, "but Nancy Reagan came up to me and said, 'This is her wish.'" So, following the First Lady's precise instructions, Travolta waited until the clock struck midnight, walked up to Princess Diana from behind, tapped her on the shoulder, and asked "Would you care to dance?" Diana, who wore a sleek midnight-blue velvet evening gown and pearl choker, dipped her head down at the floor and then up at him "in that Lady Diana way," said Travolta, "and we're off for fifteen minutes dancing. I'll never forget it. . . . I felt that I had taken her back to her childhood, when she had probably watched *Grease*, and, for that moment, I was her Prince Charming."

No one seemed to notice Charles, who was as surprised as everyone else that Travolta had "whisked" Diana "about the floor and everyone left them on their own—until I joined in eventually with a very good American ballerina, whose name I forget." It was a proud if completely overlooked moment for the Prince of Wales, who had taken lessons and fancied himself an accomplished dancer with some serious moves of his own. The "very good American ballerina" who stepped up to ask Charles to dance was Suzanne Farrell, principal dancer of the New York City Ballet and a favorite of its late founder, choreographer George Balanchine. As usual, Charles, who would later try to explain that he was "horribly jet-lagged," made little effort to appear as if he were enjoying himself. Instead, he complained there were "no lovely actresses or singers" at the glittering affair thrown by the White House, adding, "I had been rather hoping that Diana Ross would be there."

Still, for opera-loving Charles—who was seated between Nancy Reagan and the legendary soprano Beverly Sills and was transfixed by prima donna Leontyne Price's after-dinner performance of "Summertime" from *Porgy and Bess*—the US trip was pleasant enough. There was an opportunity to confer with President Reagan about his upcoming summit meeting with the new Soviet leader Mikhail Gorbachev, and, later, to tour the gardens at Oak Spring Farms, the four-thousand-acre Virginia estate of noted horticulturist, philanthropist, and art collector Bunny Mellon. She and her husband, Paul, heir to the Mellon banking fortune and one of the most successful breeders in the history of horse racing, were old friends of Charles's parents. While the Prince and the Mellons bonded over gardening and horses, Diana chatted happily with her luncheon companions: Jacqueline Kennedy Onassis and her children Caroline and John.

For Charles, there were also constant reminders that Diana—not her husband—was the one everyone had come to see. "Oh no, she's standing on the wrong side!" was the familiar refrain from spectators eager to see the Princess but positioned instead closer to the Prince. "It sapped my confidence," Charles told Jonathan Dimbleby later, "and made me long to escape." The Waleses attended a preview of the acclaimed "Treasure Houses of Great Britain: Five Hundred Years of Private Patronage and Art Collecting" exhibit at the National Gallery of Art, and Charles agreed to answer reporters' questions for a few minutes. He soon regretted that decision. With Diana sitting silently behind him, the Prince was pelted with questions not about the eye-popping exhibition and British art but about his wife. "I'm not a glove puppet," he shot back, "so I cannot answer that."

Before returning to England, there was one last stop: Palm Beach, Florida, where Prince Charles donned a bright-green shirt bearing the number 4 and scored a goal to help his polo team win a "friendly" match. At one point, a wayward shot hit him in the right shoulder; later, he almost fell off his horse but managed to recover. Diana, who had been watching the game beneath a yellow-and-white-striped canopy, awkwardly presented the two-foot-tall Princess of Wales Trophy to the winners: namely, her husband and his beaming teammates.

That night, the royal couple attended a gala at the Breakers Hotel to benefit one of Charles's charities, United World Colleges. UWC was founded in 1962 by Prince Philip's old mentor and Gordonstoun founder Kurt Hahn as a way to bridge the cultural and social gaps created by the Cold War by having young people from different nations study together on UWC campuses scattered around the world. Charles became president upon the death of Lord Mountbatten, and, like his great-uncle, he was criticized for using an anachronistic concept to create an international elite.

No matter. More than four hundred well-heeled contributors eagerly forked over $10,000 and up for tickets to the gala, which included such luminaries as Gregory Peck, Bob Hope, and Cary Grant. But it was the wheeler-dealer oil tycoon and Soviet sympathizer behind the event—and the self-appointed guest of honor—who had everyone buzzing.

Occidental Petroleum Chairman Armand Hammer, whose namesake great-grandson Armie Hammer would become a movie star a quarter century later, had contributed heavily to Charles's United World Colleges charity, and now he wanted the Prince to return the favor by attending the Palm Beach fund-raiser. Half the money from the gala—more than $4 million in the end—was funneled to the Hammer-funded UWC branch in Montezuma, New Mexico.

Hammer, however, had rankled many in the US business community because of his close ties with Moscow. When she learned of Hammer's involvement, Mary Sanford, the undisputed queen of Palm Beach society, resigned as a key organizer of the event and skipped town, taking several of her well-connected friends with her. Many of those regarded Hammer as a Communist fellow traveler—"a Soviet-sympathizing slicker of dubious character and integrity," wrote one columnist, who "has used guile, gold, and gall to rope in a lot of good, well-meaning people, including British Royalty, to help him organize a testimonial to himself." The Mayor of Palm Beach, along with the entire city council, went so far as to deny Hammer's application for a permit to allow the fund-raiser to take place. It took the intercession of Britain's Consul General—along with Hammer's pledge to donate an additional $75,000 to local charities—to get civic leaders to change their minds.

Rather than be concerned, Charles was amused by the uproar. Not only had Hammer pledged millions to several of the Prince's most important charities, but also he was footing the expenses for the entire affair and had arranged for the royal party to be flown from Washington to Palm Beach on his private jet. Hammer was not the only Palm Beach millionaire who had lavished gifts on the Prince and Princess of Wales: during their brief visit, Charles and Diana spent the night in a $2 million condominium that had been given to them as a wedding present by polo club president William Ylvisaker.

At the dinner that night, Charles lavished praise on Hammer before launching a surprise attack on critics of United World Colleges. He told his audience that he had "become completely fed up with hearing absolute nonsense" about the UWC being "a pet project of my great-uncle"—not to mention "snide comments about fund-raising." Charles's glittering, face-lifted audience cheered his remarks, giving him a badly needed boost at a time when the attention in any room always seemed to be sucked up by his glamourous wife.

Excited by the response and vowing to take a tougher stance from now on, the Prince headed to the dance floor with *Dynasty* vixen Joan Collins. "She was very amusing," he wrote in a letter on the flight back to London, "and with an unbelievable cleavage! All raised up and presented as if on a tray!"

It was only a matter of a few months before Charles was back in the United States hobnobbing with his superrich friends, sans Diana. This time he returned to Sunnylands, the Annenbergs' Palm Springs estate, for a weekend of basking in the sun and playing polo. There was also hard cash to be had. Charles was the guest of honor at a gala dinner—an event that raised a cool $1 million for Operation Raleigh, another educational charity of his that Walter Annenberg had bankrolled.

As was the case with so many American dynasties, the founder of the Annenberg fortune was steeped in scandal and outright criminal behavior.

Walter's colorful father, *Daily Racing Form* publisher Moses "Mo" Annenberg, built an empire through highly questionable business dealings and ultimately died in prison after being fined a then record $8 million for tax evasion in 1940. Walter and his siblings became billionaires, art collectors, and leading philanthropists of their generation—all, it was said, to put some distance between themselves and Mo Annenberg's notorious reputation.

The heir to the British throne couldn't have cared less. He reveled in the sheer excess of life at Sunnylands, which had a thirty-two-thousand-square-foot main house described by the *New York Times* as an "airy, Astrodome-size extravaganza of glass and Mexican lava stone, pink marble floors, and clustered paintings." Those "clustered paintings" included masterpieces by Van Gogh, Monet, Renoir, Cézanne, Degas, Manet, Picasso, Rodin, and Matisse—just to name a few. The *Times* went on to describe what most appealed to Charles about Sunnylands: the estate was, in the end, a "well-primped, mock-English country landscape in the desert, with trees, hills, ponds, waterfalls, its own golf course, and even an artificial swamp for bird-watching."

Then it was on to Dallas, where he was Nancy Reagan's date at yet another gala dinner—this time to celebrate the 150th anniversary of Texas. There, for the first time, he confided in the First Lady about the tensions within his marriage. She later told her confidante Betsy Bloomingdale that "all is not well" in the royal marriage. Charles "doesn't seem to know Diana at all," Mrs. Reagan observed. "She seems to be making him very unhappy."

It was telling that the Prince of Wales felt comfortable sharing his deepest doubts with the superrich and influential likes of Armand Hammer, the Annenbergs, and Nancy Reagan. For his entire adult life, Charles had undoubtedly studied hard, worked hard for his charities and causes, and played hard—particularly at polo, a sport at which he excelled but which would take a punishing toll on his body. Yet, like Princes of Wales before him, but very unlike his parents, Charles had developed an affinity for the outrageously rich and all they had to offer him in the way of perks:

villas in the South of France, private jets, yachts, and, of course, those endless galas that raised tens of millions of dollars for his pet projects and causes. Not surprisingly, this cast the elitist prince in sharp relief to his wife, who, despite her own glamour quotient, seemed more approachable—and more genuine. "Why is Prince Charles," asked the *Daily Mail* years later, "so fond of unsavory billionaires?"

"My Dear Mr. Hammer," he wrote to Armand Hammer after he and Princess Diana were flown home from America at the end of a royal tour aboard the billionaire's Boeing 727, "I have so many things to thank you for that I hardly know where to begin. Your kindness in letting us fly back in your 727 was enormously appreciated, and I am now thoroughly spoiled for any other form of flying." (After Hammer's death in 1990 at the age of ninety-two, it was discovered that Charles's benefactor had actually spied for the Soviet Union.)

By the spring of 1986, Charles made a point of openly taking vacations by himself. Staying at a Tuscan villa owned by another close friend, the Prince honed his talents as a plein air painter. "I paint all of my sketches out in the open," he explained, "regardless of the weather. This is why some of them have been exposed to the rain." While he was an avid student—on his frequent trips to Italy and France, Charles would spend up to five days straight doing nothing but painting outdoors—the Prince had no illusions about his talent. "My sketches," he confessed, "are the immediate expression of a true dilettante." Looking back at his earlier sketches, Charles added that he was "dismayed by their mediocrity."

In May, after spending weeks apart, Charles and Diana were in Vancouver on a swelteringly hot day to officially open the Expo 86 World's Fair. After visiting the pavilions of Saudi Arabia, the Soviet Union, the United States, and the United Kingdom ("voted unanimously by the critics as Expo's dullest," a BBC commentator proclaimed cheerfully), they arrived at the California pavilion. At this point, Diana was described as looking "hot, tired, and pale." While state officials were explaining a computerized bicycle exhibit, Diana touched Charles's arm, began to speak to him, and then collapsed. Diana's doctor, Surgeon Commander Ian Jenkins, rushed up to take the Princess's pulse as she lay on the floor. After a few minutes, she was helped to her feet and ushered into the women's room to recover. Charles, making no reference to his wife's collapse, resumed the tour.

Police scrambled, and an ambulance was called, but there was no need. Twenty minutes after she'd hit the floor, the Princess walked out the front door of the pavilion and climbed into a waiting limousine as thousands of spectators cheered. While one witness noted that the Prince may have at least "broken her fall," Charles made no effort to conceal his lack of concern for Diana's physical well-being at that very public moment. Later, he angrily characterized the fainting incident as just another attention-grabbing stunt. "You could have had the decency," Charles told Diana, "to do it behind closed doors and not in front of the cameras."

But the Princess of Wales was, in fact, quite ill both physically and emotionally. She suffered from bulimia, crippling anxiety, and suicidal depression. Yet Charles could only see her as a spoiled, self-indulgent narcissist. Nor did the Prince consider that, while he had Camilla to lean on and was surrounded by sycophants, Diana was working harder than anyone for the monarchy but getting no positive feedback whatsoever. "Her private life offered no consolation," recalled her private secretary, Patrick Jephson, "with a husband who saw her as a rival to be feared rather than a companion to be cherished. . . . Diana was a decency test for the Windsors, which some of them failed." One notable exception: Princess Margaret, who, as someone who had suffered deep wounds at the hands of the Men in Gray, saw Diana as something of a kindred spirit.

The Queen's sister was one person who could be counted on to lend a sympathetic ear. Another was Barry Mannakee, the royal protection officer who had been assigned to protect her in April 1985. Ruggedly handsome, thirteen years her senior, and the married father of two, Mannakee quickly fell for the Princess—and vice versa. He was very protective of Diana, and neither Mannakee nor Diana made any real effort inside Kensington to conceal their affection for each other. "They hugged and flirted quite a lot," said nanny Olga Powell. "I think it was obvious to everyone, including Prince Charles, what was going on." In a taped conversation with her voice coach Peter Settelen in 1992, Diana owned up to the affair in no uncertain terms. "I fell deeply in love with him," the Princess said. "He was the greatest fella I've ever had."

In late 1986 Mannakee was pulled off the Princess of Wales's detail on the grounds that the relationship between the bodyguard and the body he was guarding had turned "inappropriate." For his part, Charles, who devoutly wished someone would come along to brighten his wife's mood, preferred to look the other way. It was the approach he took toward all the men who drifted in and out of Diana's life. "I don't want to spy on her," he wrote in one letter, "or interfere in her life in any way."

Perhaps. But there were those within Palace walls who paid very close attention indeed—and who may have been willing to act on what they knew to protect the institution of the monarchy. On the evening of May 15, 1987, fellow police officer Stephen Peet offered to give Mannakee a ride home on the back of his Suzuki motorcycle. At around ten o'clock, a Ford Fiesta driven by seventeen-year-old Nicola Chopp turned from a side street, and Peat swerved to avoid a collision. In the process, the bodyguard was hurled into the rear side window of the Fiesta. Mannakee's spine snapped in two places, killing him instantly. Chopp was unharmed, but Peet sustained serious injuries. Mannakee was just thirty-nine years old.

The driver of the car claimed later that she had been pressured into admitting she'd caused the accident and testified about how that night she was blinded by "dazzling lights" from a "mystery car. I have always wondered if some more sinister forces were at work that night, although I could never prove it. I believe, with conviction, I was not the cause of Barry Mannakee's death." (In 2004 Lord Brocket, a polo-playing friend of the Prince of Wales, was serving time for fraud when a fellow inmate who had once been a police officer told him there was forensic evidence in a secret file concerning the case. The file reportedly shows that the Suzuki on which Mannakee was riding had been deliberately tampered with.) Ultimately, authorities would determine that Mannakee's death was simply the result of a straightforward auto accident and fined Chopp $135.

It fell to Charles to break the news of Mannakee's death to Diana as they flew aboard a royal jet to the Cannes Film Festival. The Princess was inconsolable. "She sobbed and wailed the entire time we were in the air," recalled the Prince, who by this time admitted to a sense of "utter detachment" when it came to his wife's emotional outbursts. Even if Charles had tried to comfort Diana, she acknowledged later that there was no way for her to "turn off the spigot." Yes, she said, "I was completely devastated. The affair was all found out, and he was chucked out. And then he was killed. And I think he was bumped off. But there we are. I don't . . . we'll never know."

For all the Sturm und Drang of their turbulent private lives, Charles and Diana were still able to come together for the sake of their boys. On January 15, 1987, the Princess accompanied William on his first day of school at Wetherby, a prekindergarten just five minutes from Kensington Palace at Notting Hill Gate. Charles hoped that the teachers there would "impose a little discipline on William, for all our sakes." Try as they might, things only got worse—particularly anytime that another child was the center of attention, even for an instant. During a small birthday party held for one of his classmates, William screamed that he hated the ice cream and cake and proceeded to toss his serving on the floor. When his teachers instructed the Prince to clean up his mess, his response echoed one of his father's favorite lines: "Do you know who I am? When I'm King, I'm going to send all my knights around to kill you!" Soon the teachers and students at Wetherby came up with their own nickname for the Waleses' eldest son: "the Basher."

Understandably, Charles and Diana worried, as did his paternal grandparents, about the impact all of this was having on their younger son. "William is setting a terrible example for Harry," the Queen told her husband. "Can you do something, Philip?" But even the usually intimidating

Duke of Edinburgh came up short when it came to disciplining William. During a family photo session aboard the royal yacht *Britannia*, Prince Philip could not get his grandson to cooperate. In the end, the portrait would show William standing in the foreground, his back turned defiantly toward the camera.

The senior royals were right to be concerned about Harry. One of Harry's nursery school teachers conceded that the Spare was never "quite the handful that William was." However, she added that "when William was horrid, Harry was horrid." At this point, the Mini-Tornado was more than just a bad influence on his younger brother. Left alone with Harry in the Kensington Palace nursery for just a few minutes, William lifted the toddler up and took him to an open window for some fresh air. A security guard arrived just in time to discover William dangling Harry by his ankles, three stories above the cement walkway below.

———

"Diana would have hit the roof," said Highgrove housekeeper Wendy Berry, "if anyone tried to spank the boys." That did not mean, however, that the Princess was entirely opposed to corporal punishment. When William walked up to a little girl at Windsor Castle and pushed her to the ground, Diana reacted instantly. Leaping to her feet, she ran over to William, grabbed him roughly, spun him around, and whacked him on his backside with her open palm. Then she made him apologize.

Papa and Mummy held their collective breath when William made his debut as a page boy at the wedding of Prince Andrew and Diana's earthy, rambunctious friend Sarah Ferguson. In contrast to the other pages and flower girls, who, if anything, seemed slightly intimidated by their surroundings, William dashed ahead and almost tripped over the bride's seventeen-foot train. Later, he fashioned a paper trumpet out of his wedding program and played it while Andrew and Sarah were pronounced man and wife.

Initially, Diana was pleased with the way William had performed at the wedding. But she had failed to see what the television cameras had captured—all the Basher's antics, from squirming in his pew and pushing the chin strap of his hat up his nose, to his habit of repeatedly sticking his tongue out at family, friends, and strangers alike.

No one was more disturbed by William's off-the-rails behavior than Charles. Having been victimized all his life by thugs and hooligans, the Prince of Wales knew one when saw one. "I know the difference between high spirits and cruelty," he told Camilla. "I cannot let William become what I detest most—a bully."

At Wetherby, William's teachers were authorized to do whatever was necessary—short of spanking—to turn the boy around. They punished him with time-outs, reprimands, and banishment from his favorite games. None of this seemed to work. Indeed, there were times when it seemed that, as one Kensington Palace staff member put it, "the only person who said no and really got results was Prince Charles." When Princess Diana was reluctant to discipline William, it was the Prince who had "no trouble at all ordering him back to the nursery if he misbehaved. I think they obeyed their father because they desperately wanted Papa back in their lives."

Earlier, when they were all technically together as a family at Kensington Palace, Charles had been a huge presence in his sons' daily lives. He routinely shared breakfast with William and Harry in the nursery, roughhoused with them on the floor, and threw himself into knock-down, drag-out pillow fights before tucking them into bed at night. Charles's bond with his sons seemed strongest when all three Windsor men engaged in horseplay—most memorably, a wrestling game they called the Big Bad Wolf, in which Papa, lying in wait to pounce on his "victims," played the title role.

Unfortunately, now that he had moved to Highgrove to be closer to Camilla, Charles saw his sons mostly when they came to spend the weekend—and to witness Mummy and Papa bicker and brawl relentlessly. According to Diana's friend Elsa Bowker, the Princess "liked to say 'boys will be boys.' But she was only fooling herself. What are two small boys to think when their mother and father don't get along? Children sometimes lash out when they are confused about things." Wendy Berry agreed. The boys "were old enough by now to be aware of the rows and tensions in their parents' marriage," she said. "No amount of playacting can ever fool a child."

With the help of the boys' new nanny, Ruth Wallace ("Nanny Roof"), Charles and Diana were able to convince William that he was not the center of the universe. Nanny Roof asked William how he felt when someone hurt his feelings, and then how he imagined other people felt when *their* feelings were hurt. "A lightbulb went off in his head," Diana recalled. "Oh, other people have feelings, too!"

By Christmas 1987 William was a little gentleman, extending his hand to introduce himself, opening doors for ladies, calling people "Sir," and always saying please and thank you. Nanny Roof credited Diana with setting "an excellent example. She went out of her way to be kind to average people." Soon the front-page headlines such as "The Basher Strikes Again!" and "William the Terrible Goes Berserk" were a thing of the past. Diana, said Elsa Bowker, had "always wanted the royal family to be human. But there was no kindness there, and she was a kind person."

The implication that Charles was not responsible for the turnaround in William's behavior—and, by imitation, Harry's sudden embrace of good manners—was unfair but understandable. The Prince of Wales's bred-in-the-bone sense of entitlement explained why he often treated servants and strangers with a chilly detachment. When Diana once asked him why he didn't simply fetch his own shirt from the closet just a few feet away, rather than ring for his valet, Charles replied indignantly, "That is his job. He is *paid* to do it." Yet he also had a deeply rooted sense of propriety, and what did and did not constitute acceptable behavior, for children as well as adults. Threatening to arrest a five-year-old girl if she refused to marry him—then laughing when she burst into tears—as William had done at Wetherby, was not acceptable behavior.

In early March 1988 Charles and Diana overlooked their differences long enough to embark together on a ski holiday at one of the Prince's fa-vorite resorts, Klosters. While Diana hunkered down in her chalet battling a cold and what she described as a "very bad case of the blubs," Charles struck out on the slopes with a small party that included his friends Charles and Patti Palmer-Tomkinson and Major Hugh Lindsay, a former equerry to the Queen.

Tackling the Haglamadd, a slope that was off the beaten path, they eventually arrived at the edge of a precipice and stopped. Suddenly they heard an ominous roar and looked up to see a chunk of ice break off the side of the mountain and come crashing down in their direction. "I've never forgotten the sound of it," Charles recalled later. "The whole moun-tain exploding outwards—vast clouds of snow. A whirling maelstrom. I thought to myself, 'My God, the horror.'" The group's guide, Bruno Spre-cher, pushed the Prince to safety as the resulting avalanche slammed into Patti Palmer-Tomkinson and Hugh Lindsay, carrying them over the four-hundred-foot-high cliff. Patti was dug out of the snow, and Charles at-tempted to keep her conscious by telling her that a rescue helicopter was on its way. She was in critical condition with numerous injuries but, after seven operations, would eventually make a full recovery.

Major Lindsay, however, had been killed instantly. Once his body was dug out of the snow, it was discovered that his skull had been crushed by the sheer force of the avalanche. Within hours Charles called Lindsay's widow, Sarah, who was six months pregnant, and described to her what had happened. Diana said later her "blood ran cold" at Charles's lack of emotion. She promised Sarah that she would never—"could never"—re-turn to Klosters, and she kept her promise. Charles, however, returned to the Swiss resort the very next year, "as if," Diana marveled, "nothing had happened."

The Prince was a dutiful godfather who kept his promise to pay for the child's education. But it was Diana who came to Sarah Lindsay's emo-tional rescue. "The Princess was fantastic," Lindsay said. "She used to ring me every Sunday evening. She was a dear friend—someone I could ring at midnight and say, 'Life is pretty grim.' Diana instinctively knew when I might be feeling down—the school holidays and so on," when her husband's absence was most keenly felt.

When Alice Lindsay turned one, Diana invited mother and daughter to Kensington Palace. There was a cake for Alice, and William and Harry joined in the birthday party. "The Princess of Wales," Sarah Lindsay said, "always knew how to cheer me up." The Princess and the widow would keep in touch for the remainder of Diana's life.

———

It was the Princess of Wales who needed the cheering up when, at the age of eight, William was sent to Ludgrove, an elite boarding school about thirty-five miles outside London in Berkshire. Both Charles and Diana had been profoundly scarred by their boarding school experiences, yet they reacted very differently to the notion of sending William away from home at such a young age. Inexplicably, Charles, who had been driven to the brink of suicide during his time at Cheam and Gordonstoun, picked up where his father Prince Philip left off, defending the idea on the grounds that it would "build character," "expose him to real other boys his own age," and, of course, "make a man out of him."

Diana had wanted William to live at home and attend school in London. She wept the day she took him to school and for weeks afterward. "She felt she was abandoning William the way she was abandoned as a child," Elsa Bowker said. "To a large extent, she blamed Charles."

Harry joined his brother at Ludgrove two years later. Whatever misgivings or doubts he may have always harbored about Harry's paternity, Charles lavished equal amounts of attention and affection on both his sons. Diana was most often shown hand-in-hand with her young children on the street, arriving at a playmate's birthday party or gamely joining a footrace as part of a school field day. But it was Charles who, away from the cameras, twirled his sons around on the lawns of Highgrove and Kensington Palace until they collapsed in tears of laughter.

Diana gladly deferred to Charles when it came to schooling William and Harry on the country pursuits that had been part and parcel of royal life for centuries. Foxhunting in the hills and valleys of Gloucestershire, fly-fishing at Balmoral, shooting parties at Sandringham, polo matches at Windsor and near Highgrove—these would be among the memories that cemented the bond between the Prince of Wales and his sons.

Charles had grown up surrounded by dogs—not only Her Majesty's ever-present corgis (who were detested by every other member of the royal family), but also the retrievers, setters, hounds, and terriers that populated the royal kennels at Windsor, Sandringham, and Balmoral. The boys were especially fond of Charles's Jack Russell terrier Tigga (inspired by the A. A. Milne character Tigger) and Tigga's puppy Roo—although they convinced Papa to change Roo's name to Pooh.

Tigga and Pooh were, of course, also highly trained hunting dogs who led the way whenever Charles and his sons struck out in pursuit of game. Sadly, one day Charles was walking in the woods with his dogs when Pooh suddenly ran off, triggering the largest dog hunt in UK history. A hefty reward was posted, and, over the course of several months, Charles employed the services of gillies (hunting and fishing guides), bailiffs, estate workers, gamekeepers, and even psychics to find Pooh—all to no avail. Oddly, Pooh's disappearance only made Charles resent Diana more. She had never attempted to conceal the fact that she loathed all of Charles's dogs, and early on even convinced him to get rid of his cherished Labrador, Harvey.

Leaving the great outdoors to her husband, the Princess confined herself to teaching William and Harry to swim in the Buckingham Palace pool, and otherwise focused on exposing them to the simple pleasures of a normal childhood. She took them to the movies (where she insisted they stand in line like everyone else), go-cart tracks, amusement parks, and fast-food outlets like McDonald's, Burger King, and her favorite, Kentucky Fried Chicken. Unlike Charles's time with the boys, spent usually on royal estates, Diana made sure her outings were leaked in advance to the press. "She could be very cunning in that way," said one Fleet Street editor. "There'd be an anonymous call, and the next day, we'd run a story of the loving Princess enjoying another day with her beautiful young sons—and without Prince Charles." The steady stream of such stories over the years "left people with the impression that the Prince of Wales really didn't care that much about his own kids."

From the standpoint of press exposure, Diana clearly had the upper hand. "KP," as the Princess called the twenty-eight-room Georgian brick building that had been home to William III, was located smack in the heart of London. Kensington Palace abutted 274 acres of lush public parkland, making it difficult for the boys to leave without attracting notice. A battalion of photographers camped outside the palace's ornate wrought iron gates, waiting to pounce the minute Diana's Jaguar emerged. Highgrove, tucked away in the Gloucestershire countryside, offered no such access. Once they arrived, the boys were free to ramble undisturbed across 350 acres of open land.

Not surprisingly, the press reported what it saw, leaving the public to conclude that loving mother Diana spent all her free time with William and Harry, while self-centered Charles seemed virtually absent from their lives. Jean Rook of the *Daily Express* complained that the Prince of Wales "is beginning to treat his sons like well-fed pets who know their place in the world of their utterly self-involved parent. Certainly it must hurt William and Harry to see their father more often on TV than in the flesh."

It also hurt Charles, who at times felt Diana "held all the cards" and felt powerless to do anything about his predicament. The boys' plain-spoken new nanny, Jessie Webb, brought in to replace the retiring Ruth Wallace in 1990, was more shocked by her employers' behavior than anything else. "Charles and Diana are both mental, you know," she said. "Those boys are going to need a lot of help if they're not going to end up as barking mad as their mum and dad."

Webb was not the only person concerned about the state of the royal couple's mental health—and the impact their take-no-prisoners warfare was having on William and Harry. When the family did gather at Highgrove, Diana and Charles were invariably locked in mortal combat. While Harry cowered in his room, William would often watch helplessly as his mother fled down corridors or locked herself in her room, sobbing. On one such occasion, Charles asked William to join him in the garden so he could try to explain what was happening. "I hate you, Papa!" the boy yelled. "I hate you so much. Why do you make Mummy cry all the time?" Then the boy bolted for his room.

Earlier, Diana and Charles had tried to make a point of at least occasionally sharing a meal with the boys when they were at Highgrove. William and Harry were eager to tell them about their schools and their games, and their parents, who basically ignored each other, deftly steered all conversation in their direction. Now Harry ate with the nanny, William and Diana ate on trays watching TV in her bedroom, and Charles dined alone in the large, opulent formal dining room. Diana's bed was "a refuge—a warm and happy place" for the young princes, said a former Highgrove staffer. Prince Charles was "specifically excluded, and it was very painful for him."

Diana did not hesitate to cast Charles as the villain—a role he was assigned every time a vacation or break ended and William begged his parents not to send him back to Ludgrove. Charles sympathized. After all, these were the same tearful pleas he'd made to the Queen and Prince Philip when he was a boy. "Of course boarding school could be bloody awful," he said, "but I told William, and later Harry, about some of the crazy teachers and lads I went to school with, and they'd start to laugh." He'd conclude each pep talk with the reminder that "everybody feels the same way you do. As soon as you're back with your chums, everything will be fine." There were crucial differences between Charles's boarding school experience and that of his sons: the atmosphere at Ludgrove was nothing like Cheam or Gordonstoun, and both William and Harry—two of the best-liked boys at the school—fit in right away.

After William was dropped off, Diana, who insisted on driving both William and Harry to school, would return to her car and break down crying. "You feel totally abandoned by the people who are supposed to love you the most," she said of her own boarding school days. "Why," she asked her bodyguard, "is Charles making us do this to our children? For

God's sake, he knows better than anyone what it's like to be a small boy shipped off like this."

Diana's fragile mental state was about to make headlines around the world, but Charles, too, had sunk into a deep depression. Rain or shine, the Prince of Wales spent entire days toiling inside the walls of his garden, then wound up collapsing alone in bed. Admitting that he felt he was on the verge of a nervous breakdown, Charles turned to one of his confidants, royal lawyer Arnold Goodman. "I have," he told Lord Goodman, "nothing to live for."

According to Goodman, the Prince was "showing the classic signs of depression"—and not just because his marriage was unraveling. Charles worried that he was either trapped in a loveless marriage or that a divorce—in the unlikely event that the Queen would allow it—would have grave repercussions for his children, the royal family, and the monarchy itself. In his considered opinion, the Prince of Wales was "suicidal."

This verdict was passed along to royal protection officers, who worried that the atmosphere at Highgrove was, in Inspector Ken Wharfe's words, "highly combustible." The clashes between Diana and Charles were now so raw that "violence seemed inevitable," said one bodyguard. Posing a special problem was the sheer firepower contained within Highgrove's walls. Guns were scattered about the premises—"shotguns, rifles, pistols, the whole lot"—and the detectives in charge of protecting members of the royal family were deeply concerned that "in the heat of anger," any one of these could be used to commit suicide, homicide, or both. There was also a legitimate concern that William and Harry might become collateral damage. Just to be safe, all guns were put under lock and key.

The perception of Charles as an absent, aloof father grew stronger—with help from publicity-savvy Diana and her network of friends and supporters. The Princess showed up alone for Harry's solo during the Wetherby Christmas recital and, during the boys' 1991 Easter break, took them skiing in Austria—again, without Charles. On the slopes, Diana's bodyguard, Ken Wharfe, stood in for Charles as a kind of surrogate father. At one point, William, under the weather with a nasty virus and struggling to keep up with his little brother, fell down in the snow and began crying. It was Wharfe who offered consoling words and stepped in to help William get back up on his skis and finish his run.

After making an official visit to Brazil in April, Charles returned to England and headed straight to the polo fields. At the end of May 1991, he was once again not in the picture when Diana took the little princes to visit a Royal Air Force base and a safari park. Later, the Prince of Wales was at a horse meet with Camilla when newspaper photographers snapped heartwarming shots of Diana and her sons frolicking at an amusement park. To be fair, most of Charles's sins are those of omission. "There's a certain kind of Englishman who doesn't take a lot of interest in his sons until they're able to kick a rugby ball, or, in his case, swing a polo mallet," veteran royals observer Anthony Holden explained. "Charles does begin to look increasingly like that rather disappointing, repressed, uptight Englishman." A longtime Windsor family friend tried to dispel the growing suspicion that Charles simply wasn't comfortable around his own children. "When the Prince of Wales does see his boys, he's all over them," the friend said. "But then he might not choose to see them again for a month or so."

Amazingly, no one seemed to notice the rift in the royal marriage until May 1991, when an enterprising reporter observed that Prince Charles and Mrs. Parker Bowles were vacationing at the same Italian resort—sans spouses. A few weeks later, as the newspapers were still waking up to their affair, Charles and Camilla were at Highgrove when royal protection officers called to say that one of William's classmates had been wielding a golf club and accidentally struck the Heir in the forehead just above the left eye. William had been knocked cold, blood was gushing from a wound in his head, and he was being rushed in a police car to the Royal Berkshire Hospital, not far from Ludgrove. "Operation Prince," the code name for a life-threatening emergency involving William, was now in full effect.

Prince Charles was "white with shock," recalled housekeeper Wendy Berry. "I knew it was something terrible the minute they called," Charles said. "My heart went cold." Wasting no time, he climbed into his blue

Aston Martin sports car and sped to the hospital. Meanwhile, Diana, who had been lunching with a friend in London when she heard the news, was on her way there behind the wheel of her green Jaguar.

When they arrived at the hospital, they were relieved to find William "sitting up," Charles said, "and chatting away." It was a rare moment of public togetherness, as he and his wife walked behind William's gurney, reassuring him as he was wheeled in for a CAT scan. The imaging procedure showed that the blow had fractured his skull, and that there was enough potential damage that he should be urgently transferred to a hospital that specialized in brain injuries. With Charles following close behind in his car, Diana rode alongside William in the ambulance to Great Ormond Street Hospital in London. Once there, doctors told William's worried parents that immediate surgery was necessary to assess the damage and make certain there were no bone splinters.

Charles, satisfied that matters were in hand, went ahead with his plans to attend a performance of *Tosca* at Covent Garden with Environment Secretary Michael Heseltine and Agricultural Minister John Gummer. Diana, in the meantime, whispered words of encouragement in William's ear as he was wheeled into surgery, and breathed a sigh of relief seventy-five minutes later when neurosurgeon Richard Hayward emerged to tell her the complicated operation had been a success. "Thank God," the Princess said, wiping away a tear. "She was literally shaking," said one of the nurses who had assisted in the procedure. "Just to see her standing there alone, with no one but her bodyguard. . . . I think we were all shocked that Prince William's father wasn't there, frankly."

After the curtain came down on *Tosca*, Charles called to check on William's condition. Told that the surgery had been a success and that Diana was still at the hospital, he boarded the royal train and traveled overnight with a group of Belgian officials for an environmental conference in Yorkshire. The next day, Charles visited William briefly at the hospital, then left again to see Camilla at Highgrove.

Diana boiled. According to her car-dealer friend (and, later, lover) James Gilbey, she reacted to William's accident with "horror and disbelief.

She can't understand her husband's behavior. . . . She thinks he is a bad father, a selfish father," Gilbey continued. "He will never delay, cancel, or change anything for their benefit." Fleet Street agreed. "What Kind of Dad Are You?" scolded the next day's headline in the *Sun*, echoing the growing sentiment that Charles was an uncaring, unfeeling father. "Charles," the Queen's cousin told one newspaper, "is treating William pretty much the same way Philip treated Charles."

The uproar surrounding William's brush with disaster was an unqualified public relations victory for Diana—and a crushing defeat for Charles. Moreover, he told the Queen that he was "tormented by the lies" about his feelings for his children. There was a simple solution, of course. In a detailed memo, the Prince's private secretary at the time, Richard Aylard, picked out some dates when Charles might spend time with William and Harry. The Prince of Wales scrawled "I'll try" across the memo and sent it back to Aylard, but in truth, said another aide, Charles "didn't try very hard." Even when the boys visited Highgrove, said former security guard Andrew Jacques, Charles seldom left his walled garden—"No Children Allowed!" read one posted sign—to play with them.

In the Prince's defense, Diana spent most of her time at Highgrove alone in the master bedroom (at this point Charles slept separately in his elaborate "dressing room"), where, again according to Jacques, there was a "well-thumbed marital guide" on the nightstand. "Diana believed that Camilla was like Wallis Simpson—that she must have had some sexual tricks up her sleeve," Lady Bowker said. "She tried to figure out if she was doing something wrong, or if there was something he wanted her to do, until she just gave up." In the end, added Lucia Flecha de Lima, "Diana had to accept that Charles had always been in love with Camilla, never with her. But at the time, Charles was still the love of Diana's life. I have no doubt about this."

———

Throughout the rest of 1991, there would be murmurings of unrest in the Waleses' marriage—and, much to the Queen's chagrin, an announcement in January 1992 that Prince Andrew and Fergie had agreed to separate.

The next month, Charles and Diana made a joint trip to India, where she struck a beguilingly lonesome pose in front of the Taj Mahal while her husband was off making a speech to a trade group. The image, clearly intended to send the message that the Princess of Wales had been all but abandoned by her heartless husband, worked.

All of these incidents generated sensational front-page headlines across the globe. But none compared with the media frenzy sparked by the publication of Andrew Morton's book *Diana: Her True Story* in the spring of 1992. Basically dictated in secret by Diana through a trusted intermediary—her friend Dr. James Colthurst—the book blew the lid off the Waleses' sham marriage, uncorking a series of sordid royal scandals in the process.

Even Diana was upset when one of her confidants, Stephen Twigg, went public in the *Sunday Express* defending her as the victim of the royal family's insensitivity. Seeking solace wherever he could find it, Charles invited his old paramour Janet Jenkins to Highgrove. She shared pictures of her now eight-year-old son Jason with the Prince, and then sat holding his hand for four hours straight as he explained to her why he now felt a separation was inevitable—and why he believed Diana might press for a divorce.

The fate of the Crown hung in the balance, but according to Jenkins, Charles was "consumed with worry" about the "psychological health" of William and Harry, "how all the fighting and bitterness would affect them in later life." That night, the Prince of Wales and his Canadian lover slept together one last time.

Diana had always believed that Philip was one of her main enemies at the Palace—his brusque and casually dismissive demeanor gave her no cause to think otherwise. But in a letter to her written in the summer of 1992, the Duke of Edinburgh made it clear that he blamed Charles for their disintegrating marriage. "We do not approve of either of you having lovers," Philip wrote. "Charles was silly to risk everything with Camilla for a man in his position. We never dreamed he might feel like leaving you for her. I cannot imagine anyone in their right mind leaving you for Camilla."

There were, in fact, high-level operatives in British intelligence loyal to Charles, and that August they struck a blow for the Prince's side. According to Wharfe, Diana's intimate cell phone conversations with James Gilbey were recorded and then broadcast at different times so that eventually they would be picked up by the press. She called him Sguidgy, and he listened patiently as she complained about Charles and her in-laws ("My life is torture. . . . Bloody hell! After all I've done for this fucking family"), shared details about her bouts with depression, and even spoke of her love for another man, James Hewitt. "Sguidgygate" caused an international sensation and, from Charles's standpoint, leveled the playing field somewhat by casting the Princess of Wales in a less-than-flattering light.

It would not be long before Diana partisans within Britain's intelligence services retaliated, broadcasting recordings of a three-year-old phone conversation between Charles and Camilla so that it could be picked up by the press. Five months after Squidgygate, the *Daily Mirror* published only brief extracts on the grounds that nearly all the tape was "so explicit that it is virtually unprintable." The entire transcript, which would not be released until the following January, provided a window into the tawdry, titillating, and unintentionally comical relationship between the future King of England and the woman who would, through a bizarre twist of events, eventually become his queen.

In addition to their assignations at Highgrove and Middlewick House, Charles and Camilla had arranged sleepovers at the homes of friends scattered throughout the kingdom. When Diana discovered later that many people she regarded as friends were among those her husband and his mistress relied on for trysting places, the Princess told Elsa Bowker that she felt "an unimaginable sense of betrayal—such deep, deep betrayal."

It was while sorting out the details of their next rendezvous that Charles and Camilla drifted into raunchy innuendo. Once the audio was made available to the public, Britons got their first taste of Camilla's whiskey-and-cigarettes contralto. Throughout the conversation, she lavishes Charles with praise, encouragement, and sympathy—all the things he believed his own mother and father had denied him. She praises his intelligence ("There's an awfully good brain working there") and his accomplishments ("I'm *so* proud of you"); in turn, he thanks her for suffering "all these indignities and tortures" from the less-than-understanding press.

The "sex tapes," as they quickly came to be known, would also confirm Diana's long-held suspicion that Camilla's hold on Charles was rooted in their physical relationship—a fact that became abundantly clear when, in the middle of their conversation about where to hop into bed next, Mrs. Parker Bowles suddenly began to sound if she were working on a phone sex hotline:

CAMILLA: Mmmmmm, you're awfully good at feeling your way
    along.
CHARLES: Oh stop! I want to feel my way along you, all over and
    up and down you and in and out.
CAMILLA: Oh!
CHARLES: Particularly in and out. . . . I fill your tank!
CAMILLA: Yes you do. . . . Oh, darling, I just want you now—
    desperately, desperately, desperately.

Although Charles's tasteless and bizarre wish that he be magically transformed into one of Camilla's tampons made headlines, there were moments that offered deeper insights into the relationship. "Your great achievement is to love me," Charles tells her rather imperiously. Camilla replies without hesitation, "Oh, darling, easier than falling off a chair." In fact, Charles listens as Camilla tells him she loves him eleven times—to his twice.

Charles couldn't resist ending the conversation on a distinctly adolescent note. He was going to hang up, he told his mistress, by "pressing the tit." (*Tit* is a Britishism for button.) Camilla's voice dropped an octave. "I wish," she purred, "you were pressing mine."

In that long-suppressed 1989 phone conversation that was only now coming to light, it was also clear that Camilla's role in the relationship also involved showing genuine interest in the issues that Charles was passionate about. She asks in the tapes if he will let her see one of his speeches, and lauds his intellect repeatedly.

Not that Charles needed much encouragement to share his opinion with others. A champion of holistic healing and other forms of alternative medicine, the Prince of Wales clashed frequently with members of the medical establishment, one of whom dismissed his ideas as "sheer quackery." He was also an outspoken environmentalist and an early advocate of organic and sustainable farming. His love of gardening, in combination with the Prince's lifelong quest for "spiritual enlightenment" spurred on by Laurens van der Post, led Charles to make one of his most startling claims in a 1986 BBC interview.

"I just come and talk to the plants, really," the Prince said as he strolled through his gardens at Highgrove. "Very important to talk to them. They respond." (Decades later, he confessed that he still talked to his plants—only now he didn't just talk to them but also "instructed" them.)

The issue that riled Charles most—and, in the process, ignited the most heated controversy—was modern architecture. In a May 1984 speech ostensibly given to celebrate the 150th anniversary of the Royal Institute of British Architects, the Prince of Wales stunned his hosts by accusing them of having "consistently ignored the feelings and wishes of the mass of ordinary people." He went on to decry the "glass stumps and concrete towers" of modern architecture, and called the proposed new wing at London's National Gallery a "monstrous carbuncle on the face of a much-loved and elegant friend" even as those responsible for the "carbuncle" squirmed just a few yards away.

At a time when his wife was dominating the news, Charles was delighted with the front-page coverage accorded his speech—and equally delighted when the National Gallery project was abandoned, though taking hundreds of jobs with it. "No person so close to the throne in the past," Harold Brooks-Baker observed, "has ever taken a stand with such unbelievably strong economic repercussions."

In 1988 Charles fired more shots across the bow of the architectural establishment with his BBC documentary and accompanying book *A Vi-*

sion of Britain: A Personal View of Architecture. As the author and narrator of the TV special, Charles roamed the country pointing out what he liked about Britain's changing architectural landscape—but mostly what he didn't. In the documentary, he describes a new parking structure as "a colossal fossil," the new National Theater as "a nuclear power station," and Birmingham's Central Library as "a place where books are incinerated, not kept." London's changing skyline of towering skyscrapers, he complained, resembled "a jostling scrum." A modernistic municipal building on the River Thames was simply "the monstrosity."

Prince Charles gleefully ambushed architects and designers but blanched at the idea that they had the right to defend themselves when he did. After noted architect Gordon Graham rebutted some of Charles's claims, he was confident there would be "no repercussions." His friends weren't so sure. "Nonsense," said Ian Coulter, a former advisor to journalist and politician Randolph Churchill, Winston's only son. "Gordon Graham gave up his knighthood with that speech. If the Sun King turns his back on you, you're in his shadow. Royalty has patronage and support, and if it's withdrawn, you're a dead man."

In this sense, Charles was every inch his father's son. Philip was notorious for insulting underlings and more than once had been caught shouting "You fool!" or "Moron!" at footmen who were too slow to open a car door or brought him the wrong thing for breakfast. "No infraction was too small for Prince Philip to rain down a torrent of abuse," said a former Buckingham Palace staffer, "if that was the mood he was in."

The notoriously thin-skinned Prince of Wales, who had grown to adulthood with a nineteenth-century sense of entitlement, was taken aback when architects fired back, calling him "archaic," "a luddite," and "lost in translation from the Middle Ages." Lord Rogers, one of Britain's leading architects, dismissed Charles as "architecturally ignorant" and accused the Prince of Wales of abusing his power by essentially scuttling projects while they were still on the drawing board.

Cambridge's Colin St. John Wilson assailed Charles for employing "ridicule and abuse" as his chief weapons in the architecture wars. "The

Nazis tried that," he said, pointing to Hitler's persecution of modernists and his embrace of neoclassicism, "and look what happened." Wilson went on to say that Charles's "firepower is colossal, but he has a total absence of scholarship." The Prince was taking England "full speed into the past."

Pointing to Charles's contention that he spoke for the average Briton when he condemned any architectural style not to his liking, Wilson said the Prince "invokes the man on the street but then hides behind the protocol of royalty." Battered by the critics, Charles cried on Camilla's shoulder. "Whenever he feels wronged," his former valet said, "he turns to Camilla, and she tells him what he needs to hear: that the rest of them are all fools, and that he knows what's best."

That was certainly the case when, in the wake of *A Vision of Britain*'s unexpected success, the Prince of Wales vowed to build his own version of Utopia in the Duchy of Cornwall. Inspired by the planned community of Seaside, Florida, where everything from house colors to the height of hedges was strictly controlled, the English town of Charles's dreams would incorporate principles of urban planning that most appealed to the Prince. With the help of self-styled "new urbanist" Leon Krier, Charles created Poundbury, a low-rise, pedestrian-friendly hamlet consisting of narrow streets and nondescript neoclassical and Tudor-style buildings.

Once it was completed, "the town that Prince Charles built" was blasted by the critics. Poundbury, wrote Hugh Aldersey-Williams in the *New Statesman*, was "an embarrassing anachronism." The *Guardian*'s Stephen Bayley found Charles's utopian vision "fake, heartless, authoritarian, and grimly cute," while critic Andy Spain skewered Poundbury as "a mishmash of styles from different centuries, all added together. It's a toy town, a museum of a mythical past. There is no soul, no heart." After Charles was told that the Queen and Prince Philip dropped in "for a quick look" at Poundbury while traveling through Dorset, he flew into a rage. "The project of my lifetime," he exploded, "and my parents give it twenty minutes of their time!"

Charles was not satisfied with building a town to match his own exacting standards of what a town should be. Convinced that Britain's colleges and universities were doing everything they could to quash neoclassicism in favor of modernism, he set up the Prince of Wales's Institute of Architecture in two classical stucco buildings in London's Regent's Park and gave it an annual budget of $3 million—some paid for by the Prince's Trust but funded mostly by Charles's wealthy friends. "This will not merely be a school of classical architecture," the Prince said, but it would also "introduce students to the delicate thread of wisdom that connects us with the works of our forebears." Building, he continued grandly, "should be a reflection of the order inherent in the universe."

In one of his characteristically preachy memos—this one to the institute's director, Dr. Brian Hanson—Charles claimed he wanted to teach students "reverence—reverence for the landscape and the soil, for the human spirit which is a reflection in some small measure of the Divine." To achieve these ends, the Prince of Wales came up with his own ten principles of architecture, which included respecting the land, harmony, density, flexibility, and "reclaiming our streets from the car"—catering first and foremost, in other words, to pedestrians. The architectural establishment's reaction to the Prince of Wales's Institute ranged from scathing to simply dismissive—"just more silly nonsense," said one Oxford architecture critic, "from *that man*."

On those days—and there were many—when he felt under attack, Charles retreated behind the walls of his gardens at Highgrove. Here the Prince of Wales had created an environment that was both laboratory and sanctuary. At Highgrove, he could experiment with animal husbandry and dabble in sustainable gardening, and he took special pride in his organically grown Brussels sprouts and his herd of black sheep.

Charles conceded that he had "absolutely no experience of gardening or farming" when he arrived at Highgrove. "The only trees I had planted had been official ones in very official holes." Before long, his gardens cov-

ered twenty-five acres divided into what Charles called "rooms": the Wild
Flower Meadow, Thyme Walk, the Stumpery, the Autumn Walk, the Tulip
Walk, the Southern Hemisphere Garden, the Walled Garden, the Carpet
Garden, and the Sundial Garden.

Later, the Stumpery would feature an arched pathway that led to two
small Greek temples. Every day, Prince Charles would walk to the arbore-
tum and there, inside a small private chapel called the Sanctuary, meditate
in front of a large stone with a cross carved into it.

Charles would need to meditate—and pray—as tensions continued to
mount until November 18, 1992, when at the last minute Diana canceled
plans for the boys to attend Charles's annual three-day shooting weekend
at Sandringham. At that point, Charles recalled, "something snapped." He
decided at that moment to ask for a separation. "There was no future in it
the way things were going. I had no choice."

The Prince of Wales knew that he was setting into motion a chain of
events that would inevitably rock the monarchy—an institution that was
already on shakier ground that it had been for years. One tabloid poll
showed that 63 percent of Britons felt the monarchy should be abolished.
Another survey indicated that up to 90 percent of the population believed
the royal family should pay taxes. Soon a Gallup poll would show that
80 percent of the Queen's subjects thought "too many members of the
royal family lead an idle, jet-set kind of existence."

Charles was entertaining his shooting party guests at Sandringham
when Buckingham Palace called with more shocking news. On the morning of Friday, November 20, smoke was seen billowing from the windows
of Windsor Castle near the Queen's private chapel. In one hour, the fire,
started when a workman's light ignited a curtain, was raging out of control, threatening to destroy the castle that had been a symbol of the British
monarchy since the days of William the Conqueror.

Prince Andrew, who had been staying at Windsor, quickly organized a
fire brigade. Sadly, the Windsor fire had broken out on Elizabeth and
Philip's forty-fifth wedding anniversary. The Queen was marking the milestone alone at Buckingham Palace while her husband was in Argentina on

behalf of the World Wildlife Fund—and, as it happened, seeing his old flame Susie Barrantes, ex-wife of Prince Charles's polo manager Ronald Ferguson and mother of Sarah Ferguson, Duchess of York. Fergie's mother was known in royal circles as "the Bolter" after she left Major Ferguson in 1974 to marry Argentine polo player Hector Barrantes, who died of cancer in 1990. "I always suspected," Ronald Ferguson said two years after their rendezvous in Buenos Aires, "that Prince Philip had an eye for Susie." (In a tragic coincidence, Susie Barrantes would be killed in an auto accident just one year after the Paris car crash that ended the life of Fergie's longtime friend Diana. Susie Barrantes was sixty-one.)

On this rainy November morning in 1992, the Queen rushed to Windsor as soon as she got the call from Andrew. Charles, not wanting to abandon his guests, saw no reason to rush—not even when television coverage showed the Queen, a tiny, hunched figure in a head scarf and rain slicker, gazing in helpless bewilderment as the fire burned for fifteen hours, consuming nine of the principal staterooms and severely damaging one hundred others. "She was," Andrew said of Her Majesty that day, "absolutely devastated."

Given his own sensibilities, Charles seemed less concerned about the historic castle than the art inside—one of the world's greatest collections, featuring six Gobelin tapestries and masterpieces by, among others, Rembrandt, Holbein, Van Dyck, Rubens, George Romney, and Sir Joshua Reynolds. Satisfied that the art and artifacts had been saved, Charles did not depart for Windsor until late in the day. Once there, he comforted his shaken mother before returning to Camilla and his friends at Sandringham. "The Queen was so upset," the Prince told an equerry. "She tried to hide it, but she was crying. It is the first time I have ever seen her cry . . ."

Elizabeth, shattered, turned to the only other person who truly understood the depth of her anguish. At Royal Lodge, her manor house in Windsor Great Park, the Queen Mother stayed up all night with her daughter, reminiscing about life when George VI was king and his two little princesses called the magical, turreted, fairy-tale castle their home.

Even before the conflagration at Windsor, the Queen was overwhelmed by several intertwining issues—all of which in one way or another involved her eldest son. Fueled by the run of royal scandals and a steadily worsening economy, there was growing consensus that the monarchy had become too great a burden on the English taxpayer. A movement was afoot in Parliament to force the monarch and Prince Charles to pay mandatory taxes on their sizeable private incomes and to fork over some of the annual revenue from their estates. Charles, who years earlier had voluntarily begun paying 25 percent of his income to the government, was all for the change. Under the new mandatory plan, he figured that the amount he turned over to the Treasury would be cut in half.

Urged on by Charles, the Queen agreed to voluntarily pay taxes on her private income from the Duchy of Lancaster—conservatively estimated in 1992 at $16 million (the equivalent of $28 million today). She also reluctantly yielded to pressure from courtiers to open the doors of Buckingham Palace to paying tourists—a major concession but a necessary one, given that it would wind up costing $59.2 million to restore Windsor Castle. The idea of charging people to wander through the staterooms of "Buck House," as the royals called home, was one that Charles had personally championed for years. "The White House gives tours to the public," he argued. "I see no earthly reason why we shouldn't—as long as people are willing to pay."

On November 24 the Queen, suffering from the effects of smoke inhalation and a heavy cold, addressed a luncheon in London's Guildhall scheduled to mark her fortieth year on the throne. Looking wan and defeated, Her Majesty confided to her audience that "1992 is not a year in which I shall look back with undiluted pleasure. In the words of one of my more sympathetic correspondents, it has turned out to be an annus horribilis."

She had no way of knowing just how much more *horribilis* things would turn out to be. The day after the Queen's Guildhall "Annus Horribilis" speech, Charles drove to Kensington Palace and told his wife he wanted a separation. Diana claimed that she was not surprised, although she was "very sad" nevertheless. Hours later, Charles and Diana each informed Her Majesty that a separation was their only recourse.

By asking the Queen to lay the groundwork for a separation, Charles telegraphed the message that divorce was inevitable. Even more problematic was the Prince's indiscreet affair with Mrs. Parker Bowles. He claimed at this point that he had no intention of marrying Camilla—after all, she was still married to someone else—but the Queen knew that her son was totally devoted to his mistress. She feared that if Charles moved ahead with his unspoken plans, it would provoke a replay of 1936, when her Uncle David gave up the throne to marry Wallis Simpson. "History is repeating itself," she told George Carey, the Archbishop of Canterbury, adding that Charles risked "throwing everything out the window" by divorcing Diana and marrying Camilla.

Charles, perhaps the most headstrong and least tractable of the Windsors, seemed unfazed by the possibility that a separation could threaten his future. "I am the heir to the throne," he told the Queen's assistant private secretary when the issue was raised. "Period."

Buckingham Palace's current head of household was not so certain. Could Charles, she wondered, be divorced and still, as monarch, head the Church of England? Could he ever remarry anyone—much less someone with a reputation as tarnished as Camilla's—and still hope to be king? At Her Majesty's insistence, Prime Minister John Major, who succeeded Margaret Thatcher in 1990, met secretly with the Archbishop, the Lord Chancellor, and the Foreign Secretary to come up with answers to these questions. Their halfhearted verdict: in an age when divorce was commonplace, it was "unlikely" that a divorce precluded Charles from becoming king.

That didn't mean they were entirely convinced. Prime Minister Major, whose own four-year-long extramarital affair with fellow Conservative member of Parliament Edwina Currie would cause a sensation, still worried that Charles's love life could be his undoing—and precipitate a constitutional crisis in the bargain. Everyone agreed that, for the sake of the monarchy, it must not appear as if Charles was in any way abandoning his own children.

On December 3 Diana drove to Ludgrove and broke the news of the separation to William and Harry. Charles, having agreed that she was better equipped to explain the breakup to their children, chose to remain at Highgrove with Camilla. As painful a task as it was for Diana, it left her feeling strangely liberated. "From Day One, I always knew I'd never be the next Queen," she said. "No one ever said that to me, I just knew it. . . . I just had to get out."

On December 9, 1992, Prime Minister Major stood in the House of Commons to announce that the Prince and Princess of Wales were separating. He stressed that the couple had "no plans to divorce, and their constitutional positions are unaffected." Carrying on almost matter-of-factly, he declared that "the succession to the throne is unaffected by it. There is no reason why the Princess of Wales should not be crowned Queen in due course."

No one took that last statement seriously. The notion that somehow Charles and Diana would find a way to reign alongside each other was absurd on its face, and, said one member of Major's cabinet, "everyone inside and outside the House of Commons knew it." Everyone, it seemed, but the Queen. As the chaotic year drew to a close, Her Majesty clung to the fantasy that her feckless son and his vexatious wife might somehow mend their differences. But as she looked back on the year that saw a cavalcade of royal scandals and the end of two of her sons' marriages—not to mention her beloved Windsor Castle nearly burn to the ground—the Queen wondered if she had failed as a mother. "Oh," she told her elderly former private secretary Martin Charteris over tea, "and I thought I'd brought them up so well!"

In an inexplicable departure from her usual modus operandi, Camilla stood on the front steps of Middlewick House and lied to the press. "If something has gone wrong, I'm very sorry for them," she said. "But I know nothing more than the average person in the street. I only know what I see on television."

The extent of Camilla's duplicity became crystal clear just a few weeks later, when on January 17, 1993, the average Briton was given the opportunity to actually listen in while the Prince of Wales and his mistress engaged in phone sex:

CHARLES: Oh, God, I'd just live inside your trousers . . .

CAMILLA: What are you going to turn into? A pair of knickers?

CHARLES: Or, God forbid, a Tampax. Just my luck! . . . To be chucked down the lavatory and go on and on forever, swirling round the top, never going down!

"At the time, the tape seemed to constitute a blow from which the royal family—and Charles in particular—would never recover," wrote Catherine Bennett in the *Guardian*. "How, after this, would the Prince ever dare to lecture his subjects on aesthetics, on spirituality?"

Prior to Diana, Prince Charles was voted the most popular royal by more than two-thirds of his countrymen. Now the Gallup poll showed that a staggering 96 percent of respondents had an unfavorable view of their next king—and 38 percent wanted Charles to step aside and let William wear the crown. Employing a concept that decades later would be echoed by an unlikely candidate for the US presidency, Charles fought back with the slogan "Let's put the 'Great' back into Great Britain." The slogan, along with many of the Prince's schemes and plans, fell flat.

Charles's reaction to all this bad news was simply to wallow in self-pity. "He lacked Diana's fighting spirit," a senior courtier said. "Prince Charles has always been a first-class whinger. He sulks, and it's all very 'Oh, woe is me. No one understands how I suffer.'" Behind his back, Palace aides and even a few friends called the Prince Eeyore, after the annoyingly down-in-the dumps donkey in A. A. Milne's *Winnie the Pooh*.

Soon a young woman who was also nicknamed after a children's book character would enter the lives of Charles and his sons, with near-catastrophic results. This time the children's classic was Beatrix Potter's *The Tale of Mrs. Tiggy-Winkle*, and the character was the anthropomorphic hedgehog that gave the book its title: Mrs. Tiggy-Winkle—"Tiggy" for short.

It looked like any other moving day: a jumbled landscape of packing crates, plastic bubble wrap, sheets of foam, and endless rolls of tape. Movers worked up a sweat maneuvering pieces of furniture through narrow doorways and down staircases, hauling cardboard boxes filled with clothes, books, and keepsakes down long hallways, then transporting everything two miles across town in a truck to start the whole process all over again—only this time in reverse.

Prince Charles was formally exiting Kensington Palace—where, despite his earlier relocation to Highgrove, he still kept many of his possessions—for York House, an addition to St. James's Palace that had once been home to Charles's great-uncle Edward VIII when he was Prince of Wales. Charles wanted to make his new, three-story, five-bedroom home the sort of place that William and Harry would want to stay. Toward that end, he hired interior decorator Robert Kime to redesign York House, which had been built in 1736 for yet another Prince of Wales: Frederick, the estranged son of King George II and the father of George III. Charles made sure the boys had their own computers, a screening room, a video game room, and a billiard table.

There was also a room set aside for the new nanny hired to take care of the boys when they were with their father. Pretty, tomboyish Alexandra "Tiggy" Legge-Bourke was four years Diana's junior and moved in the same social circles. Legge-Bourke was the daughter of a merchant banker and a Welsh aristocrat—her mother was a lady-in-waiting to Princess Anne—and had grown up on the family's six-thousand-acre estate in the Welsh mountains, Glanusk Park.

Charles remembered meeting Tiggy, who went to an exclusive girls' school run by Kanga Tryon's mother-in-law, when she was six and he was twenty-three. Tiggy was later enrolled at the same Swiss boarding school Diana had attended, Alpin Videmanette. Rounding out the similarities, Tiggy, like Diana, taught nursery school. In fact, she started her own school in Battersea, South London in 1985 and named it "Miss Tiggy-Winkle." The school folded after three years, but Legge-Bourke continued to be known as Tiggy.

Diana had just returned from taking William and Harry on a surprise trip to Disney World in Orlando, Florida—yet another public relations coup that left Charles looking like a sad excuse for a dad—when she was told her husband had engaged the services of a "surrogate mother" to help him take care of the boys. Diana was livid. "I don't need a substitute father for the boys when they're with me," she protested. "So why does Charles need a substitute mother when they are with him?" (Although the Princess was certainly more of a presence in the boys' lives than their father had ever been, she got plenty of help on the home front from their warm and caring Kensington Palace nanny, Olga Powell.)

Tiggy hit it off with the boys, quickly carving out a position for herself as less of a nanny and more of a playful big sister. They spent hours each day together, playing soccer, climbing trees, and splashing in the pool at Buckingham Palace. Always assigned a room adjacent to her charges, Tiggy even threw herself into the boys' nightly pillow fights.

Most important, Legge-Bourke provided Will and Harry with an avenue of escape from the mounting tensions in their parents' imploding marriage. On the threshold of adolescence, twelve-year-old William took his parents' separation especially hard. His grades at Ludgrove slipped dramatically, and servants could hear muffled sobs coming from his room at night.

That all changed with Tiggy's arrival. "She made them laugh," a Highgrove staffer said of the high-spirited Miss Legge-Bourke. "They needed that, perhaps, more than anything." The results were immediate. No longer dwelling round-the-clock on his parents' bitter split, William was able to focus on his schoolwork, and his grades improved significantly. Although good-natured, free-spirited Harry had shown few outward signs of anxiety, he had clearly been suffering in silence. Now that Tiggy had brought some stability to their lives, the eleven-year-old finally stopped sucking his thumb.

Diana, understandably, felt threatened. Now the papers were filled with photos of the nanny chasing the boys across muddy polo fields, taking them shopping, playfully tousling William's hair as they left church. A tabloid report that Tiggy was now calling the Princes "my babies" was the last straw.

Before long, Diana convinced herself that Charles and Tiggy were lovers. The Princess, said her private secretary Patrick Jephson, had "developed an increasingly lurid fantasy picture of Tiggy's private life." Eventually Diana came to believe that her estranged husband intended to have both her and Camilla "put aside" so that he could marry the comely young nanny—a theory she later shared with her solicitor, Lord Mishcon. For the time being, the Princess showered Charles with letters demanding that Tiggy's role in their children's lives be carefully circumscribed and that, among other things, she not "read to them at night, nor supervise their bath time." Diana also complained about Tiggy's pack-a-day smoking habit. "It amazes me," said the Princess, referring to the fact that Camilla was also an unapologetic smoker, "that Charles the health fanatic surrounds himself with these walking chimneys."

Charles complied to some extent, asking Tiggy to keep a lower profile and to avoid public displays of affection that could wind up in the press. For a short time, Legge-Bourke did her best not to be seen hugging the boys or having too much fun in their presence. But there was no denying that, with Charles immersed in his official duties and spending all his free time with Camilla, Tiggy was becoming a larger and larger presence in the boys' lives. "They're trying to brainwash my boys," Diana complained, "so they will forget me!"

Charles, meanwhile, was embarking on another personal crusade, this time in defense of Islam. Long an admirer of Eastern culture and religions—while strolling his gardens at Highgrove, the Prince often wore Moroccan garb—he agreed to be a patron of Oxford's Center of Islamic Studies in June 1993. Four months later, he donned black academic robes to address an audience of more than a thousand scholars in the university's Sheldonian Theater.

At a time when Al Qaida and other radical Muslim fundamentalist terror groups were on the rise, Charles condemned Western materialism, technology, and mass culture while praising Islam for having at its heart "a metaphysical and unified view of ourselves and the world around us. . . . Islam can teach us today a way of understanding and living in the world which Christianity itself is the poorer for having lost."

Charles reminded his audience of Christianity's long history of intolerance and violence, pointing out that Muslims view the Crusades as a period of "great cruelty, terrible plunder, and horrific atrocities." As for Muslim society being rigidly anti-female, Charles argued unconvincingly that "women are not automatically second-class citizens because they live in Islamic countries." As an example, he characterized the veiling of women—harshly enforced in some parts of the Islamic world—as "a personal statement of their Muslim identity." While bashing the craven materialism of the West as "offensive—and not just to Muslims"—the Prince conveniently ignored the blatant human rights violations and growing extremism that existed throughout the Middle East.

The picture Charles enthusiastically painted—one that ignored the openness of Western democracies and the terrifying specter of radical Islamic terrorism—made him an instant hero to much of the Muslim world. Ten days later, King Fahd of Saudi Arabia took the unprecedented step of meeting Charles as he arrived at Riyadh shortly before dawn, rather than waiting to receive the visiting Prince at his palace.

But at home, Charles's remarks were not received so warmly. "Does the Prince not know," asked one columnist, in a glancing reference to Camilla, "that the penalty for adultery under sharia law is death? It would seem particularly pertinent, considering."

*For a few seconds, I thought I was witnessing
the assassination of Prince Charles.*
—Robert Milliken, a reporter for the *Independent*

Fuck it. I'm entitled to a private life.
—Camilla, after finally divorcing Andrew Parker Bowles

SIX

JEALOUSIES AND INTRIGUES AND BACKSTABBING AND PLOTS

January 26, 1994, Australia Day
Sydney

The Asian man wearing a white shirt and blue jeans jumped up and knocked over a little girl as he rushed toward his target. Prince Charles, meanwhile, had been "feeling rather stupid" as he waited at the podium to hand out prizes to schoolchildren who appeared to be nowhere in evidence—"and still I stood there," he recalled, "cursing the organizers under my breath." Literally hurling himself on the stage, David Kang managed to get off two rounds before tripping and landing at the Prince's feet. Charles, adjusting his shirtsleeve, glanced in his assailant's direction with a slightly bemused look. Later, he cracked that "it must be one of the prize-winners who was particularly keen to receive his trophy!"

But it was no laughing matter. People in the audience screamed as chaos broke out onstage. Charles was surrounded by his bodyguards and Kang, a South Korean student who was protesting the treatment of Australia's "boat people"—Cambodian refugees stuck in Australian detention camps—was overpowered before being hustled away. It turned out that Kang, who merely wanted to draw attention to his cause, was shooting harmless blanks from a starter pistol. After a brief psychiatric evaluation, he was convicted of "threatening unlawful violence" and sentenced to five hundred hours of community service. Kang eventually graduated from the University of Sydney Law School and became a barrister.

"I'm all right," Charles told his security team immediately after the incident. "It was a bit silly to start shooting." The Prince's slow reflexes and supercilious attitude were interpreted as bravery, earning him high marks from his Australian hosts. "The Prince was fantastic—cool as a cucumber," said round-the-world yachtsman Ian Kiernan, who moments before had been named Australian of the Year. "He is a rugged individual." Before returning to the podium to continue handing out awards, Charles told Kiernan that he had once been charged by a bull elephant while in Kenya. "Now, *that*," the Prince said, "was scary."

The possibility of assassination lurked in the back of every royal's mind—and the Queen was no exception. "We were going riding one morning at Sandringham, and as we got on our horses, I remarked to the Queen that it was very misty," recalled her cousin Margaret Rhodes. "All she said was: 'I have just heard that the IRA have got a new rifle, and it can see through mist,' and off we rode. It wasn't a joke. It was something she had just learned. She's always known that someone might try to do something nasty to her. She's bound to think about that sort of thing." Still, Her Majesty, like the Prince of Wales, remained blasé about the possibility of being gunned down or blown up without warning. During one state visit to America, US Secret Service agents asked her to use an armor-plated limousine with blacked-out windows. "What's the point," she asked her communications secretary Charles Anson, "if I can't be seen?"

Nothing was scarier for Charles than the public reaction to his June 29, 1994, ITV television special, *Charles: The Private Man, the Public Role*. In the course of his two-and-a-half-hour prime-time chat with journalist Jonathan Dimbleby, taped to promote Dimbleby's forthcoming authorized biography of the Prince of Wales, Charles finally confessed that he had cheated on his wife.

DIMBLEBY: Did you try to be faithful and honorable to your wife
    when you took on the vow of marriage?

PRINCE CHARLES: Yes, absolutely.

DIMBLEBY: And you were?

PRINCE CHARLES: Yes . . . until it became irretrievably broken down,
    us both having tried.

In the same documentary, he dismissed press coverage of his marriage as "rubbish," and insisted he was not seeking a divorce from Diana. But, he added, he did not view divorce as a barrier to becoming king. For the first time, he also spoke about Camilla, calling her "a great friend" whose support he valued.

The TV special aired just one week after the Palace announced that the Queen was giving up the royal yacht *Britannia*—part of an ongoing campaign to placate critics of the monarchy by trimming its budget. Now all anyone could talk about was Charles's sordid confession. "Charles: I Cheated on Diana," blared the front-page headline in the *Express*, while the *Sun* trumpeted, "Di Told You So." The Queen was stunned, and so was Camilla—Mrs. Parker Bowles having been among several close friends and advisors who'd urged Charles not to discuss their affair.

The public had been well aware of the Prince's affair with Camilla for years, but his actually coming clean about it before a national audience of more than twenty-five million people was a different thing entirely. "It made everyone cringe," said a reporter for the *Times*. Journalist Brian Hoey agreed, claiming that "in one stroke" Charles had wiped out whatever popularity he had managed to build up. The headline in the *Daily Mirror*—"Not Fit to Reign"—seemed to echo the sentiments of millions.

By odd coincidence, Charles literally ran off the runway even as his claim to the throne seemed to be doing the same. On the day his taped interview with Dimbleby ran, the Prince was at the controls of one of the Queen's jets when it overshot the landing strip on the Scottish island of Islay.

While Charles's reputation unraveled, his now estranged wife took the opportunity to make a bold statement of her own. Rather than hole up in Kensington Palace, Diana swept into a gala at the Serpentine Gallery in London's Hyde Park looking glamourous and radiant in a low-cut black cocktail dress by Greek designer Christina Stambolian. The next day's papers ran photos of her throwing back her head and laughing, looking as if she didn't have a care in the world. Palace watchers promptly dubbed the one-of-a-kind black silk sheath "the Revenge Dress."

––––––––––

In typical fashion, Charles would not own up to the fact that the decision to publicly fess up to adultery on television had been his and his alone. Instead, he angrily blamed his private secretary at the time, Richard Aylard, for "talking me into it." The Prince of Wales, said a former assistant private secretary, "has no difficulty finding scapegoats among loyal members of his staff. When you work for him, you get used to being chastised for things you had absolutely nothing to do with. Prince Charles can't admit to himself that he is ever at fault."

As it happened, Diana's "revenge" would be short lived. Two months after Charles's televised confession of adultery, newspapers reported that the Princess had made hundreds of harassing phone calls to one of her married boyfriends, art dealer Oliver Hoare. It would eventually be proved that the calls were nothing more than a teenager's prank, but too late to undo the public's growing perception that she was unhinged.

In early October, Diana's reputation suffered another blow when Captain James Hewitt recounted their six-year affair in the pages of Anna Pasternak's lurid tell-all *Princess in Love*. The book, written with Hewitt's cooperation, detailed the dates, times, locations, and circumstances of their assignations—including one particularly steamy passage that described the couple's lovemaking on the bathroom floor. According to Hewitt, he and the Princess also trysted at Althorp, in Kensington Palace, and at Highgrove with William and Harry in the next room. "I don't see how this can go on," one privy councilor said. "It is making the Royal Family a worldwide laughingstock."

Less than a year earlier, Diana had rightly sensed her world spinning out of control and did something about it, announcing to the world that she was "taking the veil"—cutting back drastically on the number of charities she supported so she could reclaim some semblance of a private life. Now she found herself, as she put it to Elsa Bowker, "stripped bare for public consumption once again." The Princess was "deeply saddened" by this betrayal at the hands of someone she had trusted but even more concerned about how her boys would react. She said later that she "ran to them as fast as I could"—driving straight to Ludgrove to apologize.

Charles, who had long suspected that his wife was sleeping with her riding instructor, was also worried about the impact this new batch of sleazy headlines would inevitably have on his sons. On the other hand, he was happy for the public to learn once and for all that his wife had also strayed in their marriage. Camilla, meanwhile, was "over the moon," said Harold Brooks-Baker. "It was one thing to take lovers in aristocratic circles, but the *riding instructor?*"

But Charles and his allies were given little time to gloat. Two weeks later, the Prince detonated his own explosive device: Dimbleby's *The Prince of Wales*, in which, among other things, Charles whined that he had been bullied by his father, ignored by his cold and aloof mother, and victimized by his emotionally unstable wife. The first excerpts appeared on the eve of the Queen and Prince Philip's highly anticipated state visit to Moscow—the first ever by a reigning British monarch—and both were angry that their historic trip would now be overshadowed by more scandalous revelations.

Charles's mother and father were also wounded by Charles's cutting remarks. "No, no. That's not *true!*" the Queen protested to *her* mother when she read excerpts from the book depicting Elizabeth II and Philip as unfeeling, largely absent parents. "But Charles *knows* that, Mummy. Why does he say such things?" Eventually the Prince of Wales would feel guilty about his brutal attack on the Queen and the Duke of Edinburgh, but, for the time being, he actually seemed to enjoy causing them pain. "Prince Charles wanted to set the record straight," said his former deputy private secretary. "In his mind, it was a long time coming."

In stark contrast to the way they treated Charles, the Queen and Prince Philip both lavished attention and affection on all their grandchildren, especially William and Harry. From the age of five, William was invited to have tea alone with the Queen at least once a week. During these sessions, usually at Buckingham Palace or Windsor, Her Majesty quizzed her grandson the Heir about what he was studying in school, what subjects he most enjoyed, what sports he liked to play, who his friends were. She also dropped in a history lesson wherever she could—telling him the story behind a suit of armor or even giving him a peek inside the dreaded red boxes of state.

Now that he was an adolescent, William was even more the apple of Her Majesty's eye. "The Queen loved having Prince William around," her cousin Margaret Rhodes said. "She perked up whenever she talked about him." Philip, too, was impressed with his grandson—in part because at Balmoral and Sandringham, William was already proving himself to be the best shot in the family.

The easy rapport between Charles's parents and William—the kind of relationship denied him both as a child and as an adult—mystified and, to a certain extent, saddened the Prince of Wales. "Charles is jealous of all the attention William gets from the Queen," Diana told her hairdresser, Natalie Symonds. "I even feel a little sorry for him." It didn't help that polls seemed to show that the British people simply loved William more than they did Charles; a growing number were in favor of Charles stepping aside so that William could become the next monarch.

For all the brouhaha surrounding Charles's portrayal of himself as a child neglected by a heartless mother and father, other revelations in the book hit even closer to home. For the first time, Charles claimed that he had been forced by Prince Philip to marry Diana—and that he had never loved her. The next day, Diana headed to Ludgrove once again, this time to assure William and Harry that none of it was true. She could also "see in their eyes," she said later, that they did not believe her. "It pierced my heart like a dagger. I just wanted to cry."

Weeks later, twelve-year-old William angrily confronted his father during a weekend visit to Highgrove. "Why, Papa? Why did you do it?" he demanded. For once, Charles, who expounded on virtually any topic at the proverbial drop of a hat, merely watched in silence as William turned and walked away. "I supposed it would be painful for any child to hear that his parents don't love each other," Charles later said with a shrug. "But it was hardly a secret."

Given the opportunity to deny or at least temper his remarks, Charles instead doubled down on his statements in the book. When asked if the Prince of Wales had any doubts about cooperating with Dimbleby's authorized biography, Charles's spokesman stated flatly: "The Prince has *no* regrets." The day after the last installment of *The Prince of Wales* in the *Sunday Times*, Charles arrived in LA for a whirlwind five-day visit that included a benefit at the baronial estate of television producer Aaron Spelling; tours of the Los Angeles County Museum of Art, a high school, and a supermarket; and tea for three with former president Reagan and his wife Nancy at their Bel Air home. (Unbeknownst to the Prince, Ronald Reagan was in the process of writing his moving letter to the nation announcing that he had been diagnosed with Alzheimer's disease.)

The high point of the trip occurred in private. Six months earlier, Charles was in the audience at Wembley Arena in London when his old crush Barbra Streisand serenaded him with "Someday My Prince Will Come." Now she was among the dozens of name-over-the-title stars who turned out for a gala honoring the heir to the British throne. A few days later, Barbra met secretly with Charles in his suite at the Bel Air Hotel. At this point, Barbra had been through a failed marriage to actor Elliott Gould and high-profile relationships with, among others: comedian Tom Smothers; actors Omar Sharif, Ryan O'Neal, Warren Beatty, and Don Johnson; producer Jon Peters; film composer-producer (and ice cream heir) Richard Baskin; tennis great Andre Agassi; Dodi Fayed; TV newsman Peter Jennings; and, most recently, Angelina Jolie's Oscar-winning dad Jon Voight. (It would be another two years before she met her "soulmate" and future husband, actor James Brolin.) Not long before her encounter with Charles at the Bel Air Hotel, Barbra told CNN's Larry King that she hated being without a man in her life. "I want a partner," she declared. "I've had love and passion, and I want it again."

Once word got out that Charles had secretly rendezvoused with his Cambridge University crush Barbra Streisand, the Prince's spokesmen hurriedly issued an official explanation. The movie star and the Prince had simply had a "private tea." Given their extensive dating histories—and the fact that they were in a hotel room for the first time together with neither Camilla nor Diana around—it seemed "inevitable" to Harold Brooks-Baker that "sparks flew."

Their cover blown, Charles and Barbra went back to leading their very separate lives. But ten months later, Streisand flew aboard a Concorde supersonic jet to London to attend a fund-raising banquet for one of the Prince's favorite preservationist groups, the Foundation for Architecture. This time it was Elton John who, arriving at Highgrove for a small dinner party, was "surprised" to see Streisand there. What struck him as equally surprising was the absence of both Diana and Camilla. A member of the Highgrove staff remembered that, away from the handful of other guests, Charles and Barbra "were very affectionate toward each other"—so much so that, when the staffer came upon the couple in the Prince's study, "they were quite flustered."

Lady Elsa Bowker was among those who had "no idea" why Charles apparently "tried to conceal" his relationship with Streisand from Camilla. "She was never threatened by Charles's women—and there were many."

Andrew and Camilla Parker Bowles formally called it quits in January 1995. Camilla's spouse had been ridiculed for years as the world's most famous cuckold ("Andrew Parker Bowles is so patriotic," went the saying, "he laid down his wife for his country") and suffered through the painful revelation that Camilla spit out the word *It* when referring to her husband in the infamous Camillagate/tampon tapes: "I can't come to Highgrove, darling. 'It' is here." The Parker Bowleses' amicable and surprisingly quiet divorce, barely noticed by the press, ended a marriage that had lasted twenty-two years—one year shy of the twenty-*three*-year affair that Charles and Camilla had been carrying on under Andrew's nose.

The Parker Bowleses sold the family manse, Middlewick House, to Pink Floyd drummer Nick Mason for $2.5 million. With her share of the proceeds and a little help from some of Charles's wealthy friends, Camilla purchased Ray Mill House, a converted mill on twenty-seven acres conveniently located just sixteen miles from Highgrove, for $1.3 million. The Prince of Wales eased Camilla's transition by installing a sophisticated security system at the house, renovating the kitchen and bathrooms, replacing the windows, and designing the extensive gardens himself using trees and plantings from his own Highgrove nurseries. While the work was being done, Camilla boarded her horses and her Jack Russell terrier, Freddy, at Charles's estate. In the drawing room, a nineteenth-century portrait of Camilla's notorious great-grandmother Alice Keppel loomed large, just as it had at Middlewick House. "Camilla is clearly making a statement," said one guest. "She wants everyone to know she's proud to carry on the family tradition."

Charles and Diana tried to maintain a veneer of civility, at least around their sons. The Princess still worried that, in her absence, her sons were growing up Windsor. Notwithstanding her ongoing attempts to "keep the boys grounded" with visits to AIDS clinics, amusement parks, fast-food outlets, and homeless shelters, Diana was surprised at William's reaction when Charles "gave" him his own valet as a thirteenth birthday present. "William was totally delighted," said his nonplussed mother, "to have a manservant all his own."

Charles saw no reason for William *not* to have his own manservant at thirteen. The Prince of Wales had been given his first valet at twenty-one, when he was a student at Cambridge. "That was far too late," he told his private secretary. "I really needed one at Gordonstoun, but my father was still trying to toughen me up." Stephen Barry was the first to hold the job. "I was successful in knowing Prince Charles well," Barry said. "But I could never forget that he was the master and I the servant." Accordingly, Charles instructed William on what was and wasn't expected of a gentleman's valet. The most important rule, he emphasized, was that a valet "is not your friend. He's a servant—and you are his job."

Charles and Diana were all smiles when they stood behind William as he enrolled at Eton College on September 6, 1995. The Queen, Diana, and the Queen Mother all made it clear that they wanted William to attend Eton, and since Charles often spoke of Gordonstoun as "hell on earth," he had no desire to lobby for his boarding school alma mater. In fact, since the Prince of Wales had been virtually friendless at Gordonstoun, he was thrilled to hear from Old Etonians that the friends they made at the school were friends for life. "Charles was so lonely as a boy," Diana told a journalist friend. "He's never gotten over it."

There was one young teacher at Gordonstoun whom Charles did admire, Eric Anderson, and the fact that he was now headmaster at Eton was a plus. William's support system also included his housemaster, Dr. Andrew Gailey, who along with his wife Shauna could be counted on to keep a watchful and sympathetic eye on William. A few months earlier, the Prince and Princess put aside their differences long enough to invite the Gaileys to St. James's Palace for cocktails. Diana stressed to the couple that her son was "very strong" but also "very sensitive. He'll really need all the love and support you can possibly give him."

It would have been hard to find a school less like Gordonstoun than Eton, where the 1,300 students strolled emerald lawns in pin-striped trousers, waistcoats, and tails. Situated just a few minutes' walk from Windsor Castle, Eton was established in 1440 by Henry VI to groom young scholars for another educational institution that he also founded: King's College, Cambridge.

Among the sons of Arab sheikhs, European aristocrats, political leaders, investment bankers, and run-of-the-mill billionaires, William was still a standout. For one thing, he arrived at Eton with his own tracking device and a nineteen-man security detail. Yet Charles needn't have worried that William would be mercilessly taunted and bullied like he was. Unlike his father, who knew no one at Gordonstoun when he arrived, William came with a ready-made circle of friends that included Lord Mountbatten's grandson Nicholas Knatchbull and his cousin Lord Freddie Windsor.

Charles knew all too well why the Queen had campaigned for William to enroll there. At Eton, her grandson was just a seven-minute walk away; she could even watch him from her bedroom window as he played rugby on those famous Etonian fields. Nearly every Sunday for the next five years, a car would pick up William at exactly 3:50 in the afternoon and head across the Thames toward Windsor Castle. One minute later, the Prince would arrive at Granny's house for tea at 4:00 in the Oak Drawing Room—and the start of his unofficial weekly lesson in kingship. On occasion, they might be joined by the great-grandmother they called Gan-Gan—referred to by staff as the "Old Queen" to distinguish her from her septuagenarian daughter the "Young Queen." They "may have been the Queen and the Queen Mother," a footman said, "but when it came to William and Harry, they acted like grannies everywhere."

The family scene at William's Eton enrollment was so harmonious— and the press coverage so universally positive—that, for a moment, Charles forgot he was at war with his wife. Yet in early October Diana was once again on the defensive, this time publicly branded a "homewrecker" by British television personality Julia Carling because of her "friendship" with Julia's husband Will Carling, captain of England's national rugby team.

Carling and Oliver Hoare were only two of the several men Diana set her sights on during this period, including Canadian rocker Bryan Adams, legendary tenors Luciano Pavarotti and Placido Domingo, and US billionaire financier Theodore "Teddy" Forstmann. The Princess's romance with the silver-maned Forstmann, who was twenty-one years her senior, began in 1994 when he sat next to her during a black-tie dinner thrown by Lord Rothschild during tennis's Wimbledon Championships. From then on, Forstmann sent Diana flowers every week for the rest of her life. Diana fantasized about Forstmann running for president, with herself installed in the White House as First Lady. With her pick of bedrooms on the second floor of the Residence, the Princess toyed with the idea of moving into the Queen's Bedroom. "If I can't be queen here," she joked, "then I'll be Queen of America."

At one point in their relationship, Diana asked Forstmann to find an estate for her in fashionable Southampton, New York. "The idea of hob-nobbing with the Steven Spielberg set in the Hamptons appealed to her," said society columnist Aileen Mehle, better known as Suzy. "She was com-pletely starstruck, oddly enough. And she loved America and Americans." Forstmann found a sprawling property for Diana on the beach, but the Palace's Men in Gray nixed the idea because of security concerns.

Forstmann and the others took a backseat to one unlikely candidate for romance: paunchy, chain-smoking Pakistani heart surgeon Hasnat Khan. According to her hairdresser Natalie Symonds, the Princess was "wildly in love, totally obsessed" with thirty-nine-year-old "Natty" Khan—so obsessed that she donned a surgical mask and scrubs to watch him perform coronary bypass operations at London's Royal Brompton Hospital. Whenever she made these secret excursions to the hospital, Diana used the alias "Dr. Allegra."

Beginning in September 1995, Khan was regularly smuggled into Kensington Palace, usually hidden beneath a tartan blanket in the backseat of butler Paul Burrell's car. Occasionally, though, Diana would don a dark wig, glasses, jeans, and a leather jacket and do the smuggling herself. One time, the Princess greeted her physician lover at the front door wearing earrings and nothing else.

At one point, Diana was spending two hours a day studying the Koran, although she was concerned that, by converting to Islam, she might somehow jeopardize William's claim to the throne. According to Diana's friend Jemima Khan, who was then married to cricket player (and future Pakistan prime minister) Imran Khan, the Princess even flew to Pakistan—without bothering to tell Hasnat—to ask his parents if they would accept a non-Muslim as their daughter-in-law.

By the fall of 1995, Diana believed she had cause for optimism. Over the course of that entire year, she had made a calculated effort to work her way back into the Queen's good graces by taking on more public duties. Although Charles still bristled whenever Diana upstaged him with positive press, the Queen understood that Diana was "still an asset," said one official, "and that it was far better to support her doing more public engagements than to have her as a loose cannon."

Diana embraced the strategy—not only to rebuild her public image as a bulwark against Charles's ambitions but also to stave off the loneliness that had haunted her since the 1992 separation. After a triumphant official visit to France in late 1994, she set off on a high-profile, four-day tour of Japan in February 1995. There she was mobbed by frenzied fans chanting, "Diana-san! Diana-san!" The Princess of Wales followed up with more headline-grabbing trips to Venice and Moscow, followed by a return to Paris in September. On the drawing board was a visit to Argentina in November, and the following month Diana was to head for New York to accept the Cerebral Palsy Foundation's Humanitarian Award at a celebrity-studded black-tie gala.

With media attention focused once again on Diana's roller-coaster love life, Charles took a major step toward normalizing his relationship with Camilla. On October 18, 1995, a noticeably slimmer and decidedly more blonde Camilla waltzed into London's Ritz Hotel for the fiftieth birthday party of her chum Lady Sarah Keswick. She wore a black gown with a daring neckline and an ear-to-ear grin. Ninety minutes later, the Prince of Wales, who had scrupulously avoided being seen in public with his mistress, strolled in while the stunned paparazzi clicked away.

Once inside, the couple spent two hours together—dancing, dining, and schmoozing with the 150 other guests. Careful not to push his luck, the Prince left alone at midnight. An hour later, a beaming Camilla left on the arm of her still-loyal ex-husband, Andrew. Did she enjoy the party? reporters asked as she squeezed past them to get to her waiting car. "Yes, thank you," she replied brightly.

The next day, tabloids had a field day with the story, this time casting

Camilla as the homewrecker. Diana made a point of lunching at one of London's trendiest restaurants, Bibendum, that day—just so Fleet Street could run photos of her looking utterly unfazed by Camilla's "highly significant" debut. But the opposite was true. Now that she was determined to wed Natty Khan, Diana knew that she would have to do something to derail Charles's chances of ever becoming king. "Marrying a Muslim was going to put her in the line of fire," observed a courtier, who added that she was convinced Charles's spies knew about her romance with the physician and were about to go public with it. "She had to do something to deflect attention from that, something to make the public hate Charles and Camilla, and ensure that William would succeed the Queen." Camilla's first public appearance with Charles "sped up her timeline considerably. She knew what the Prince was up to: destroying his wife's reputation and gently moving Camilla to the center of the stage."

Nevertheless, Diana was also hatching alternative conspiracy theories. Around the time of Camilla's coming-out party, the Princess told her lawyer Lord Mishcon that both she and Camilla would be "set aside" by assassins working for British intelligence so that Charles would be free to marry Tiggy Legge-Bourke. "Camilla is in danger," she told Lord Mishcon. "They are going to have to get rid of us both."

"I could not believe what I was hearing," Mishcon said later. "It was very clear," recalled another of Diana's lawyers, Maggie Rae, "that Princess Diana thought she was going to be killed"—either in a staged plane, helicopter, or car crash. They did not share this information with anyone at the time, especially Prince Charles. "It seemed incredible, fantastic, that she could even be thinking such a thing," Lord Mishcon said. "We didn't want Prince Charles or the Queen to think the Princess was delusional."

Diana, it would be proven later, had every reason to suspect foul play was afoot. Both the MI5 and MI6—Britain's domestic and foreign intelligence agencies—as well as the American CIA eventually admitted that they had spied on Princess Diana for years, monitoring her calls, tailing her, intercepting her mail, monitoring and filming her every move. Convinced that her royal bodyguards were spying on her, Diana made the rash decision as 1994 drew to a close to dismiss them.

Several months later, in early 1995, something happened that further fueled Diana's suspicions. She was alone at the wheel of her green Audi convertible driving through central London when she approached a traffic light and stepped on the brake. Nothing happened. She kept slamming her foot on the brake pedal as her car rolled to a stop in the middle of the intersection. Luckily, no one struck Diana's car. Shaking, the Princess of Wales hailed a cab and went straight back to Kensington Palace. "The brakes of my car have been tampered with," she wrote to her friends Lady Elsa Bowker, Lucia Flecha de Lima, the spiritual healer Simone Simmons, and socialite Lady Annabel Goldsmith. "If something does happen to me, it will be MI5 or MI6."

Charles had been told from the release of the Camillagate tapes that someone with the technical ability inside the government had recorded the couple's steamy exchange and broadcast it so that it would be found by the press. But the Prince initially resisted the idea of a larger conspiracy, preferring to blame the press and the press alone. Still, as time went on, it became increasingly obvious even to the preternaturally naïve Prince of Wales that the court had been divided into warring camps—and that each had allies in MI5 and MI6. For the time being, Diana had shared her concerns only with her most trusted friends, and with her lawyers.

On Charles's forty-seventh birthday, the BBC announced that a wide-ranging interview with the Princess of Wales would be airing on the network's top-rated prime-time program, *Panorama*. Just the day before, Diana had phoned the Queen asking if she could spend Christmas with the rest of the royal family at Sandringham, but said nothing of the broadcast. The Prince, along with Buckingham Palace, St. James's Palace, Diana's lawyer Lord Mishcon, her private secretary Patrick Jephson, and others spent the next twenty-four hours scrambling to convince the Princess to pull the plug on the interview. When that failed, the Queen asked to at least see a transcript so that she would know what to expect. None was forthcoming. Not even the chairman of the BBC, Marmaduke Hussey, knew the details—a condition laid down by Diana, who feared he would share them with his wife Lady Susan Hussey, a lady-in-waiting to the Queen.

The *Panorama* interview, conducted in total secrecy with BBC correspondent Martin Bashir inside Kensington Palace, aired on November 20, 1995—the Queen and Prince Philip's forty-eighth wedding anniversary— and instantly caused an international sensation. Gazing up through heavily mascaraed lashes, Diana claimed that Charles's friends "were indicating that I was again unstable, sick, and should be put in a home of some sort. . . . I was almost an embarrassment."

In a wide-ranging interview that aired for fifty-five minutes (cut down from a full three hours), the Princess of Wales proceeded to talk with alarming candor about Camilla ("Well, there were three of us in this marriage, so it was a bit crowded"), her affair with Hewitt ("Yes, I adored him, I was in love with him"), whether her husband was suited to be king ("He'd find it a bit more suffocating"), her bulimia and depression ("I was at the end of my tether. I was desperate. I think I was so fed up with being seen as someone who was a basket case"), the Palace's ingratitude ("Nobody ever said, 'Well done,' but if I tripped up . . . a ton of bricks came down on me"), and her own desire to be "the queen of people's hearts. Someone's got to go out there and love people and show it."

At one point, she let it be known that she wanted William, not Charles, as the next monarch.

> BASHIR: Would it be your wish that when Prince William comes of age that he were to succeed the Queen rather than the current Prince of Wales?
>
> DIANA: My wish is that my husband finds peace of mind, and from that follows other things, yes.

Still, she made it clear that she was not seeking a divorce, and, at the end, struck an optimistic note:

"There is a future ahead. A future for my husband, a future for myself, and a future for the monarchy."

Watching with Camilla at Highgrove, Charles sighed, shook his head, and talked back to the television several times over the course of the broadcast. "My *God*!" he blurted at one point. "She has really done it this time."

Charles also expressed concern for how his sons would take this latest bombshell in their parents' turbulent marriage, but made no special effort to contact them, on the grounds that the teachers at Ludgrove and Eton would "know how to handle it." He also rightly assumed that his wife had already driven up to the school alone the day before to warn their boys about the coming storm. At the time, William was angry at his mother for doing the interview. However, in 2017 he would say that he understood her decision to speak directly to the media "because she was incredibly desperate, and the things that were being said about her were incredibly unfair"—things, William neglected to mention, that were being planted in the press by Charles's and Camilla's allies.

The Prince's friend Nicholas "Fatty" Soames proclaimed that Diana "seemed on the edge of paranoia." In terms of the initial public reaction to the Princess's blockbuster *Panorama* interview, Soames was distinctly in the minority. A Gallup poll conducted immediately after the program aired showed that 75 percent approved of the interview, 84 percent found her to be honest, and 85 percent felt she should be appointed as a "roving ambassador" for Great Britain. Conversely, nearly half of all Britons—46 percent—now felt that Charles was "unfit" to wear the crown.

Echoing the opinion of most viewers on both sides of the Atlantic, veteran American newswoman Barbara Walters deemed Diana's *Panorama* interview "superb." But this particular media triumph would come with a terrible price. Watching the interview with Prince Philip in her Buckingham Palace drawing room, the Queen was, according to her deputy private secretary, "seething with anger." Diana not only had the sheer audacity to appear on television without her permission, she had chosen to air the royal family's dirty laundry in public—and challenge Charles's right to wear the crown in the bargain. Her Majesty "was clearly just fed up—this was clearly the very last straw."

Thrilled at the outpouring of public affection in the wake of her BBC confessional, the Princess flew aboard the Concorde to New York, where her old pal Henry Kissinger presented her with the United Cerebral Palsy Foundation's Humanitarian of the Year Award before an audience of one thousand. She received a standing ovation—vindication, she told Kissinger, of her decision to take to the airwaves. Once back on home turf, Diana joined Charles at the annual Christmas lunch party they put on for one hundred staff members at London's Lanesborough Hotel. The Princess mingled cheerfully with her guests until she noticed Tiggy Legge-Bourke. Still convinced that Charles and the nanny were having an affair, Diana crept up behind her nemesis and whispered in her ear, "So sorry to hear about the baby."

A hush fell over the party as Tiggy, on the verge of collapse, was led to an adjacent room and wept. Diana's thinly veiled and unfounded insinuation—that the nanny had aborted Charles's child—was so malicious that the next day Legge-Bourke instructed her lawyers to demand an apology from the Princess. The letter arrived at Kensington Palace on December 18—the same day a liveried messenger delivered an envelope from Buckingham Palace bearing the Queen's royal seal.

After consulting with Prime Minister John Major and Archbishop of Canterbury George Carey, the Queen had sent handwritten letters to her son and daughter-in-law expressing anger over Diana's *Panorama* interview and Her Majesty's desire for an "early divorce . . . in the best interests of the country."

Diana was crushed. She had feared that perhaps she had overplayed her hand, but never imagined it might lead to this. "When she had to face the bitter truth from the Queen," said her friend Simone Simmons, "Diana fell apart. She couldn't sleep at night and started taking very strong sleeping pills. She was constantly in tears, reflecting over and over again on what might have been." The Princess told Lady Elsa Bowker that she "did not want a divorce" but that the Queen had "had enough of scandal, enough of the constant fighting between Diana and Charles."

Given the circumstances, Diana canceled her plans to join the Windsors at Sandringham. Instead, while William and Harry trimmed the tree and opened presents with Charles and the rest of the royals, Diana spent Christmas Day alone at Kensington Palace. Once the holidays were over, Charles returned William directly to Eton and took Harry on a ski trip to Klosters.

For the next four months, Diana and the Crown were locked in intense and often rancorous negotiations over the size and details of a final settlement. The Princess was no pushover. She made it clear that she wanted to continue to live at Kensington Palace, access to perks such as use of the royal fleet of jets and limousines, shared custody of the sons, of course—and $70 million in cash.

Exasperated, the Queen stepped in to break the impasse. Meeting one-on-one with her daughter-in-law at Buckingham Palace, Elizabeth— whom she referred to affectionately as "Ma"— listened patiently as Diana expressed wide-ranging concerns about her sons ("I don't want Charles and William flying on the same plane. If something happened, then Harry would become king, and it would just crush him"), her royal "HRH" status ("I think everyone agrees I've earned it—and I *am* William's mother"), and, without mentioning Camilla by name, her fear that Charles intended to remarry. Her Majesty unhesitatingly assured Diana that the Prince of Wales "will never remarry. He can't. He'll be head of the Church of England, and as long as you're alive, he can't marry anyone."

Unable to assuage Diana's doubts, the Queen insisted that she meet face-to-face with Charles to hammer out the details of the divorce. At four o'clock on the afternoon of February 28, 1996, Charles met with Diana at his offices in St. James's Palace. It was an emotional day for Diana—"The saddest day of my life," she called it later—because it was the day she and Charles were turning William and Harry into "children of divorce. I am a child of divorce. It is the very last thing I ever wanted for them." Yet she also told Charles that she loved him and that she would always love him because, she said, "You are the father of my children."

The meeting lasted forty-five minutes, and after it was over Kensington Palace issued a statement: "The Princess of Wales has agreed to Prince Charles's request for a divorce. The Princess will continue to be involved in all decisions relating to the children and will remain at Kensington Palace, with offices in St. James's Palace. The Princess of Wales will retain the title and be known as Diana, Princess of Wales."

———

Not so fast, Charles and his mother countered. Furious that Diana had jumped the gun by issuing her own statement, the Queen responded by saying that nothing had, in fact, been resolved and that all the major issues "remain to be discussed and settled." The War of the Waleses dragged on for another six months until the divorce was finalized on August 28, 1996. Charles was hosting members of a historic preservationist group at Highgrove when the divorce papers were delivered for his signature. After a brief stroll around his gardens, he went into his study, signed the papers, handed them to an equerry to be returned to St. James's Palace, and returned to his guests with a dry gin martini in hand.

Under the terms of the settlement, Diana would receive a lump sum payment of 17.5 million pounds—then about $28 million—plus $600,000 annually to run her offices. She would retain all of her titles, have complete access to royal aircraft, and be allowed to keep her royal jewelry—on condition that upon her death it would pass to her sons. As announced, the royal divorce agreement also stipulated that the shared custody arrangement that had been in effect since their separation would continue and that Diana would still be "regarded as a member of the royal family." She would also "from time to time receive invitations to state and national public occasions," and whenever she was in the presence of other royals, she would still be given "precedence" in accordance with her station as Princess of Wales.

Yet Charles, eyeing his own marital future with someone else, suggested to the Queen that Diana needed to be punished in some way for all the "trouble" she had caused. The Princess had desperately tried to hang on to the "Her Royal Highness" designation that was reserved for those in the line of succession, their spouses, and offspring. Those without the vaunted HRH before their name were required to curtsy or bow before every member of the extended royal family, and that meant she would technically be required to curtsy before her nieces Beatrice and Eugenie as well as William and Harry, not to mention their future wives. In the end, William told his mother not to worry. Once he became king, he promised, she would get her HRH back.

Both Charles and Diana repeatedly expressed concern for their boys' emotional well-being. However, neither they nor the Queen stepped in to offer them the professional counseling they clearly needed. "The boys put on a brave enough face," said the Princess's confidante Oonagh Toffolo. "They were away at school, but that didn't shield them from all the turmoil in their parents' lives. Diana worried about them, but she didn't think they needed professional counseling—which is strange, since she had seen therapists for years to treat her bulimia and depression. . . . And, of course, Charles pooh-poohed it every time the idea came up."

Charles appeared to be more concerned with what the divorce was costing him. Buckingham Palace leaked information indicating that the $28 million settlement would be paid out of the Queen's private trust, the Duchy of Lancaster, but in reality, she insisted it come straight out of Charles's pocket. According to Geoffrey Bignell, who handled the Prince of Wales's financial affairs for more than a decade, Charles was forced to unload his entire investment portfolio to meet the demands of the settlement. "Princess Diana took every penny he had," Bignell said. "I was told to liquidate everything—all his investments—so that he could give her the cash. He was very unhappy about that. That's when I stopped being his personal financial advisor because he had no personal wealth left. She took him to the cleaners."

Not that it had any noticeable effect on Charles's lifestyle. He could still count on an annual income at the time of $18 million from the Duchy of Cornwall—more than enough to fund even his lavish tastes. By 1996, the Prince was spending more than $100,000 each year on his bespoke wardrobe—only about $50,000 less than Diana, then unquestionably the world's most famous clotheshorse. Despite his avowed environmental concerns, he traveled everywhere aboard royal jets at an estimated cost of $1.3 million a year to British taxpayers. It was a level of comfort that Charles had come to expect. When a chartered British Airways 747 took a party of dignitaries to China for the handover of Hong Kong to mainland control, the Prince was horrified to find himself "on the top deck in what is normally Club Class. It took me some time," he wrote in his journal later, "to realize that this was not first class (!), although it puzzled me as to why the seat seemed *so* uncomfortable. I then discovered that others like [former prime minister] Edward Heath, [former home secretary] Douglas Hurd, the new foreign secretary, Robin Cook, several former governors of Hong Kong such as Lord Maclehose and Lord Wilson, and the leader of the Liberal Democrats, Paddy Ashdown, were comfortably ensconced in first class immediately below us. 'Such is the end of the Empire,' I sighed to myself."

The Prince of Wales insisted that his whims and idiosyncrasies be catered to throughout the day, and no one knew that better than Michael Fawcett. Charles's valet began his career in royal service as a footman to the Queen in 1981, and by 1995—after a period of cozying up to Charles as his assistant valet—was laying out the Prince's custom-made shirts on his bed at Kensington Palace each morning. Diana, among others, detested Fawcett and gossiped with friends about the nature of his relationship with her husband. Still, the valet became so indispensable to Charles that at one point the Prince admitted, "I can manage without just about anyone, except for Michael."

In addition to carefully selecting and laying out his boss's clothes, each morning Fawcett squeezed the toothpaste from a silver dispenser onto the Prince's monogrammed toothbrush, shaved his face with Penhaligon's Blenheim Bouquet shaving cream, helped him into his pants, buttoned up his shirt, laced up his shoes, and helped him slip on his jacket. In the evenings, one of Charles's two butlers prepared the Prince's cocktail—either a martini or a Laphroaig fifteen-year-old Royal Warrant whiskey on ice—but it was Fawcett who drew the Prince's bath, laid out his pajamas, and turned down his bed. When His Royal Highness was required to give a urine sample during his annual checkup, Fawcett willingly held the specimen bottle steady.

Fawcett was also in charge of Teddy, Charles's stuffed bear since childhood, which the Prince of Wales still literally clung to for comfort and slept with every night. The stuffed animal, now well into middle age and threadbare, required the constant and loving attention of Charles's nanny and surrogate mother Mabel Anderson, who was periodically brought out of retirement to make necessary repairs. Anderson, said a former assistant valet, "was the only human being allowed to take needle and thread to Prince Charles's teddy bear. He was well into his forties, and every time that teddy needed to be repaired, you would think it was his own child having major surgery."

Whenever the Prince of Wales traveled, it fell to his valet to make certain that he did so with his beloved teddy bear, his Prince of Wales hand towels, Kleenex Premium Comfort brand luxury toilet paper, and his custom-made white leather cushioned toilet seat. (When asked on a radio show in 2018, Charles publicly denied traveling with this seat despite confirmation from several royal protection officers and staff.)

The Prince of Wales's highly specific demands did not stop there. A former servant revealed that Charles's breakfast tray had to "contain a cup and saucer to the right with a silver spoon pointing outward at an angle of five o'clock. Butter must come in three balls and be chilled. The royal toast is always in a silver rack, never on a plate. Assorted jams, jellies, marmalades, and honey are served on a separate silver tray. Always a silver tray." Breakfast also included cereal, tea, some cut fruit—all small portions. "Prince Charles hated large portions. He would go absolutely crazy whenever he was served in America."

Charles never ate lunch ("I want to go to sleep immediately afterwards, so I skip it"), but at teatime he indulged in fruitcake from Wales. Dinner usually consisted of game shot by the Prince at one of the royal estates, or food grown or raised at Highgrove. Regardless of the main course, dinner nearly always included a green salad with a soft-boiled egg. This last dish, surprisingly enough, presented a special challenge. Chefs in the royal kitchen normally prepared several three-minute eggs before being satisfied that one had been cooked to meet the Prince's standards of softness. The rejects were discarded. (Again, in 2018 St. James's Palace issued a statement specifically denying that the Prince rejected six eggs for every one he consumed. The chef did the selecting, and the number varied from three to six. "I can't recall ever feeling I got it right on the first try," said a former chef at Balmoral.)

Often dinner guests at Highgrove or St. James's Palace would notice that their host ate a meal different from theirs, prepared specially for him. Charles made no effort to hide the distinction, insisting that he and he alone dine off Prince of Wales plates using Prince of Wales utensils. Prince Charles frequently brought along his own chef to dinner parties at the homes of others, for the express purpose of preparing him a separate dish. "We used to joke that he was afraid of being poisoned," a longtime Gloucestershire friend said, "but he really is just accustomed to getting precisely what he wants when he wants it, regardless of how that makes other people feel." Toward that end, his royal protection officers were often called upon to produce the ingredients necessary for their boss's dry martinis, and a small silver bowl of salt (he refuses to use a shaker) decorated with the Prince of Wales's three-plumed crest. "My people take such good care of me," he beamed when the bowl was brought around at a Windsor dinner. "They always bring my salt."

Woe be it to the staff member who fell short. At Highgrove, the head gardener awoke each day to a list of instructions and complaints written by his boss in red ink. The Prince of Wales then stood on his porch and, if he did not approve of the job his landscapers were doing, shouted orders at them through a green megaphone. Charles's attitude toward employees verged on "outright contempt," said one Highgrove staffer. "For someone who said he was bullied as a child, Prince Charles clearly enjoyed bullying us. He could be pleasant and courteous, but just as much of the time, he was moody and mean. He didn't think twice about shouting insults at you if you put a foot wrong."

Charles's former valet Ken Stronach, who for years was in charge of hand washing the Prince's underpants and tucking him into bed with Teddy, agreed. Not only was Charles prone to exploding at subordinates, but he also was capable of "flying into violent tantrums" if something displeased him. Stronach was in the room when Charles, in the middle of an argument with Diana, grabbed a heavy wooden bootjack and threw it at her, missing the Princess's head by inches. Another time, while vacationing at the villa of an aristocratic friend in the South of France, Charles was standing at his bathroom sink when he fumbled with one of his cuff links, and it fell down the drain. Flying into a blind rage, he pulled the sink off the wall, then smashed it, looking for the cuff link. Unable to find the missing jewelry, a wild-eyed Prince of Wales spun around and grabbed his valet by the throat. Stronach broke free, darted out a side door—and into a linen closet. Terrified, he huddled there for thirty minutes before he could hear Charles leave the bathroom. "Finally, the coast was clear," the valet recalled, "but I was still shaking."

It was not the only time the Prince of Wales ripped a sink from the wall in a fit of pique; the porcelain went flying yet again after a particularly furious row with Diana at Highgrove. Stronach, once again laying bare his boss's petulant streak, recalled that Charles became so frustrated at not being able to part his hair properly that he kept "hopping up and down and shaking his fists."

Once, when Charles was spending time with Camilla at Ray Mill House, Diana called Highgrove to check up on him. Her butler, Paul Burrell, happened to be at Highgrove at the time and answered the phone. The next day, Charles learned that Burrell had refused to cover for him and summoned the butler to his room. When Burrell asked if the Prince was ordering him to lie to Diana, Charles exploded. "Yes! *Yes*, I am!" he replied, picking up a book and hurling it at Burrell's head. The butler ducked, although he would hear the pages flutter as the book flew by. Charles was "still ranting and stamping his foot," Burrell recalled. "I am the Prince of Wales," Charles shouted, "and will be King!"

Imperious to a fault, the Prince also counted on those within his tight social circle to indulge his every impulse. Once, while a guest at a friend's country home, Charles wanted some fresh air. Unable to open the window, he picked up a chair and smashed it open. Not satisfied with the results, he smashed another. "You have to understand," Stronach said. "The Prince is accustomed to getting what he wants. And he wanted some fresh air."

As far as Stronach was concerned, not even Camilla had the power to calm Charles during the implosion of his marriage. "Only William and Harry could do that," said the valet, who recalled how the Prince of Wales dissolved in laughter when a maid stumbled upon the newly adolescent William's stash of "saucy magazines."

─────────

Charles was feeling particularly put upon in 1996, now that the public seemed to be squarely in Diana's corner. Without the full backing of Buckingham Palace or her husband, and despite her vow to cut back on her public duties, Diana still dazzled at a dizzying array of galas, openings, and celebrity fund-raisers. She raised millions for charity in the process. "Diana used her power," said Debbie Tate, who runs homes for abused children in Washington, DC, "just like a magic wand."

Diana's magic wand could not help the one mistress of her husband's that she genuinely liked. While the Princess's resentment of Camilla grew exponentially, she became extraordinarily fond of Charles's *other* woman, Lady Tryon. Kanga had been edged out of the picture by her onetime ally Camilla, and even though he was godfather to the son she had named after him, the Prince obliged by turning his back on her as well. Embracing the adage that "the enemy of my enemy is my friend," Diana made a point of being photographed as she visited Lady Tryon's high-end boutique in Knightsbridge.

Kanga Tryon's life had been far from fairy-tale perfect. Diagnosed as a child with a form of hip dysplasia called Perthes disease, she was put in leg braces at the age of nine and spent the rest of her life checking in and out of hospitals. In 1993 she won her battle with uterine cancer but fell victim to clinical depression—a condition made all the worse by what she understandably viewed as Camilla's betrayal. "It was a horrid, horrid time," said Victoria Tryon, one of Kanga's four children. "There were stories on the front page calling Mummy mad and all sorts of scandalous things." Kanga had "committed the cardinal sin of talking about the Prince."

While the Waleses' divorce gobbled up all the headlines in 1996, Kanga journeyed to a retreat in the Himalayas and then checked herself into a rehab facility in Surrey. After allegedly washing down painkillers with champagne and vodka, she plunged twenty-five feet from her second-floor window, fracturing her skull and paralyzing her from the waist down. Did she jump or was she pushed? The initial assumption was that Lady Tryon, disoriented and distraught over being frozen out of Prince Charles's life by Camilla, leapt from the window. But she told friends in no uncertain terms that she had been shoved out the window. Even her husband, who had argued bitterly and often with her about her relationship with Prince Charles, didn't believe she jumped. "She is a battler and has been through so much," Lord Tryon said. "She was a bit depressed, but she is just not the sort of person to have jumped."

Kanga underwent years of rehabilitation on her spine but never regained the use of her legs. For the rest of her life, she was confined to a wheelchair. In June 1997 Lady Tryon suffered a complete breakdown after she was told by her husband that he was divorcing her. That same day, after claiming repeatedly that "someone" was attempting to kill her, Kanga was detained at the Salisbury District Hospital—ironically, not far from Camilla's Ray Mill estate in Wiltshire—for one month under Britain's Mental Health Act. "She has flipped before," Lord Tryon said. "She has said in the past I am going to murder her."

Charles read the news about his ex-lover's plunge from a hospital window and her subsequent rapid decline with alarm, according to a royal butler. "Incredible," he told Camilla, staring at the front-page tabloid stories. "Poor, poor Kanga." He looked over at Mrs. PB, as the St. James's staff now called her, and shook his head as she sighed in agreement.

After her discharge from the hospital, Kanga moved into London's Ritz Hotel, not far from Charles's residence at St. James's Palace. Soon, while the Prince was in the middle of a polo match in July 1997, he spotted a woman seated in the crowd waving to him. When the match was over, Kanga reportedly "pursued" him in her wheelchair. The sad spectacle made its way into the papers. "She never stopped being obsessed with the Prince," Victoria Tryon said. That autumn, after returning from a trip to Australia and India, she underwent a minor skin graft procedure at a London clinic. Suffering complications from severe bedsores, she died from septicemia one day after Charles's forty-eighth birthday. Lady Tryon was forty-nine.

With Diana distracted temporarily by her hot pursuit of Hasnat Khan in mid-1996, Charles focused on one thing in the wake of his divorce: clearing a path for his eventual marriage to Camilla. That would require a serious image overhaul for the Prince, whose reputation had been savaged in the final years of his marriage. "The people dislike me almost as much as they adore Diana," he complained. "But, of course, they don't really *know* her—or me—do they?"

Since Diana began going rogue, the Firm was willing to look the other way when it came to Charles's mistress—on the grounds that she provided him with an emotional "safety net" when it came to dealing with his highly neurotic wife. Now that he was no longer saddled with Diana as his spouse, the Queen, Prince Philip, and the Men in Gray were pressuring him to dump Camilla.

They failed to take into account, however, that it was Mrs. PB who would take charge of efforts to salvage Charles's damaged public image. Camilla quietly asked her divorce lawyer, Hilary Browne Wilkinson, to help her find a public relations guru to "work some magic" on Charles's behalf. Wilkinson, who sat on Britain's voluntary watchdog Press Complaints Commission, did not hesitate to recommend Mark Bolland, the

PCC's tall, brash thirty-year-old director. Bolland had spent four years walking a proverbial tightrope: seriously addressing complaints lodged against Fleet Street without ever appearing to trod upon Britain's long tradition of a free and boisterous tabloid press. Somehow he had managed to maintain warm relations with most of the country's most powerful newspaper editors.

When he met secretly with Camilla at Ray Mill that August, Bolland was struck by how visibly anxious she was. In the course of their hourlong conversation, Camilla powered through a pack of unfiltered cigarettes, at times oblivious to the fact that her ash often hit the floor or the upholstered chair on which she was sitting.

Satisfied that Bolland was the right man for the job, Camilla arranged for him to meet the Prince at his St. James's office. Charles began by telling Bolland that the press had been "terribly cruel" to Camilla. "I want you to make people see Mrs. Parker Bowles through my eyes; let them see the marvelous woman I see. Once they do, I know they will love her the way I love her." It was obvious to Bolland from the outset that his new position was going to be as much about her image as it was about his.

Not everyone, however, was convinced that this was the right man for the job. The Men in Gray were not thrilled with Bolland's humble origins: his father was a former bricklayer turned small businessman, and Mark had attended a public high school. But what they objected to most was the fact that, in a pin-striped world of closeted homosexuals, Bolland would be the first *openly* gay senior courtier. According to Bolland, one minor royal sent several faxes to Charles's office saying, "Do you know Mark Bolland is gay?" Another one of the Men in Gray at Buckingham Palace hired a private detective to look into Bolland's sexuality.

None of which mattered to Charles, who was well aware that for years a substantial number of gay men had worked for the Windsors, several in the highest positions. There had always been a flourishing gay community at all the palaces, where gossip is the lifeblood of those privileged to attend to the needs of the royal family. One time, the Queen Mother heard two senior staff members whispering in the hallway. She opened her bedroom door and famously declared, "When you two old queens have stopped nattering, this old Queen is dying for a gin." What did Charles do when an old friend of the royal family confronted him directly about Bolland's sexuality? "I smiled politely," the Prince said, "and did nothing."

From his first day on the job, Bolland found the level of intrigue surrounding the Prince of Wales to be "staggering. It's a very medieval environment full of jealousies and intrigues and backstabbing and plots." Eventually Bolland himself would be considered a master of the game. Convinced that the Prince needed to be free of controversy, Mark succeeded in replacing Richard Aylard, Charles's comparatively outspoken and available private secretary, with the more circumspect Stephen Lamport. Doling out tidbits to a handful of favored journalists, Bolland could create a new public face for his boss and, just as important, for Camilla. He tightened his grip further when his romantic partner and future husband, Guy Black, replaced him as head of the Press Complaints Commission. As networking power couples went, the team of "Guy and Mark" was hard to beat. "One man is spinmeister to Prince Charles," noted the *Observer*'s Ben Summerskill, "the other keeps editors in hand."

Bolland realized quickly that Charles presented special challenges. "One of the Prince of Wales's problems—and it's a problem that's unique to him in the royal family—is the extent to which he is remote from public opinion," he said. "He doesn't read the newspapers, he doesn't watch television news, and he doesn't even really see letters that people write to him." Bolland wondered if Charles was simply too isolated from the people who would one day be his subjects. "I think it's a strange position when you have an heir to the throne who you feel is more out of touch than his mother, who's twenty-odd years older."

To accomplish his formidable task, Bolland hatched a top-secret plan called Operation PB (Operation Parker Bowles) and promptly set to work. That this was a distinctly uphill battle became painfully clear the first week in January 1997, when, during a highly rated national debate on the fate of the monarchy, the audience erupted in a resounding chorus of boos at the mere mention of Camilla's name. During the program, a record

2.6 million viewers called in to express their opinion. One-third wanted to abolish the monarchy altogether, with a full 56 percent of Scots wanting to fire the royal family.

Knowing full well that she had been cast in the public's mind as the scheming and deceitful Other Woman, Camilla made the calculated decision to start working from the outside in. But where to start? English shabby like the furniture she favored, Camilla was often seen in Wiltshire wearing boxy sweaters, frayed head scarves that reeked of cigarette smoke, muddy Wellingtons, and ripped riding pants. Her dyed blond hair was usually an uncombed tangle of split ends, her nails were bitten and dirty, and her teeth were stained yellow from decades of smoking.

Mrs. PB was just as . . . *relaxed* when it came to her home. Ray Mill House was always fully staffed—Charles paid for Camilla's housekeeper, cook, two maids, a driver, and a gardener—but it was a challenge to stay ahead of the mistress of the house. Mud-caked boots were piled in the hallway, wet towels lay in heaps on the bathroom floors, wads of used Kleenex were left on kitchen counters, and, in virtually every room, there had been left behind a plate with food on it or a glass with a lipstick-smeared rim. Given the chaos, it scarcely seemed to matter that the draperies and carpets at Ray Mill were faded and worn, or that the chintz-covered furniture was pocked with cigarette burn marks.

For years, Camilla had used self-deprecating humor to deflect criticism. Whenever she picked up the phone at Ray Mill, she often answered brightly, "Rottweiler here!" Yet now Camilla, even more than Charles, was committed to reinventing herself. If she could not match Diana's youth and beauty, she could at least be the best possible version of herself. Toward that end, Camilla consulted with dermatologists, dentists, cosmetologists, dieticians, fitness experts, and plastic surgeons. Gradually she would undergo a series of neck and face peels, laser treatments to smooth out her crow's-feet and the lines around her mouth, and Botox injections to remove the furrows in her forehead. Camilla's hair was newly cut, blonded, and coiffed by her personal hairdresser, Jo Hansford, and she paid $10,000 to have new caps put on her teeth. Mrs. PB would also manage to shed more than twenty-five pounds with a rigorous new diet and exercise regimen, transforming her from a size 14 to a size 10. Chucking the dowdy tweeds, the new and improved Camilla opted for clingy gowns and tailored suits by British designers such as Paddy Campbell, Antony Price, and the firm of Robinson Valentine.

On May 1, 1997, Charles and the rest of his countrymen were astonished when upstart Tony Blair and his Labour Party were swept into office, bringing a dramatic end to eighteen years of Tory Party rule. Despite the monarch's claim of impartiality, it has always been assumed that the Windsors—and the Queen in particular—were more in synch with the Conservatives. At their first meeting, the Queen seemed to confirm this by pointing out to Blair that he had not even been born when she welcomed her first prime minister as monarch—the giant of modern history she referred to simply as Winston.

Charles, however, hoped to form a bond with the new prime minister. Blair campaigned on cherry-picking the best ideas from both major parties: the social liberalism of Labour with the Conservatives' free market economic principles and "peace through strength" foreign policy agenda. While he was a fan of just the sort of modern architecture that Charles had railed against for decades, their stances on multiculturalism and the environment dovetailed nicely. Moreover, the new prime minister—the Queen's tenth—was, at forty-four, just four years younger than the Prince of Wales. Impressed with Blair's youthful enthusiasm, Charles could easily see the two contemporaries working together to shape a new, forward-looking Britain.

Unfortunately for Charles, Diana got there first. No one personified human-touch politics like the Princess of Wales, and when it was suggested by a senior courtier that Diana and the exciting young leader of the Opposition get together in early 1997, both jumped at the chance. The Queen was informed about these secret dinner meetings held far from Westminster and the palace, but there was always the danger that Diana would be accused of meddling in party politics once news of her friendship with Blair got out. "Princess Diana was thrilled by the cloak-

and-dagger of it all," said Labour Party spin doctor Alastair Campbell, who helped arrange the meetings. "He thought she could do a brilliant job as a kind of ambassador abroad for his vision of a modernized Britain. She was very excited about it." Spotted together chatting and laughing, the politician and the Princess forged a special alliance based in part on the fact that Diana found Blair "quite sexy"—and vice versa.

Even as Charles and Camilla plotted with Mark Bolland to win the hearts and minds of the British people, Diana was scoring one public relations triumph after another. Determined to focus public attention on the human suffering wrought by land mines, in January 1997 the Princess flew Sabena Airline to Angola, where there was an unexploded land mine for every one of its twelve million inhabitants. "This nation," she pointed out as soon as she arrived, "has the highest rate of amputees anywhere in the world."

Wearing a face shield and a flak jacket, Diana strolled bravely through a minefield marked with skull-and-crossbones pennants. Despite criticism from elements of her own government—at the time, Britain officially opposed a land mine ban—she would later visit war-ravaged Bosnia and hug children whose limbs had been blown off by mines. The startling images from these visits mobilized support for an anti–land mine treaty signed in Ottawa, Canada, by more than 120 nations. Almost as important to Diana was Charles's reaction. He phoned to tell her that he did not want the mother of his children taking any unnecessary risks. But he also praised her for her "incredible courage" and told his ex-wife that he was "so enormously proud" of her.

In July Diana would be invited to bring William and Harry along on a visit to Chequers, the Prime Minister's official country residence. While the Princes played outside with Blair's young sons Euan and Nicholas, the Prime Minister told Diana that he had just been discussing with President Bill Clinton of the United States what role she might play on the international stage. "I think at last I will have someone who will know how to use me," she told Lady Bowker. "He's told me he wants me to go on some missions. I'd really like to go to China. I'm very good at sorting people's heads out."

Oddly enough, it was Diana's continuing obsession with the reluctant Pakistani heart surgeon that made her feel more warmly toward the Prince. By early 1997, her obsession with Hasnat Khan had been thrown into overdrive. "Spread it around," she told her hairstylists Tess Rock and Natalie Symonds. "We're going to get married!" There was even a softening in Diana's attitude toward Camilla as a result of her own devotion to Khan. "She said at last she began to understand the undying love Prince Charles shared with Camilla Parker Bowles. She was wildly in love, totally obsessed by Dr. Khan."

Not every rival was looked upon so favorably by Diana. The Princess still resented Tiggy Legge-Bourke's "surrogate mother" status and, according to Tess Rock, "went potty" whenever she saw a photograph of the nanny with the boys. To placate Diana, Charles asked Tiggy not to seem "overly familiar" with William and Harry in public. Nevertheless, when William was confirmed in St. George's Chapel at Windsor in March 1997, the Princess was miffed that Tiggy had drawn up a guest list that was top-heavy with Windsors and short on Spencers. Diana and Charles had been getting along so well, as evidenced by the warmth they displayed toward each other at the confirmation, that the Prince finally decided it was best to remove Tiggy from his payroll. Legge-Bourke would still see the boys frequently, only for the moment strictly as a friend of the family.

The détente that now existed between Charles and Diana both delighted and bewildered their sons; the young princes had, in fact, never seen their parents behave so affectionately toward each other. Ironically, in the spring of 1997 Charles and Diana bonded over the fact that they had *both* been excluded by William from parents' day at Eton. "There will be press about," he told them, "but if you come, it will truly be unbearable." To compound the slight, William invited Tiggy instead. Charles warned his son that excluding his parents could be interpreted as a sign that Diana and Charles could not stand to be in each other's company, even to support their sons. Yet when Tiggy called Charles for advice, the Prince of Wales encouraged her to "pack a picnic lunch and some wine and have a good time."

William and Harry also noticed that, in stark contrast with the Diana of the past, the Princess now appeared determined not to offend their father or the Queen. That didn't mean she ran everything by Charles for approval. When William turned fifteen, Diana threw a small party at Kensington Palace that did not include any of her in-laws. Charles later learned the reason: for their pinup-obsessed son, the Princess had asked her chef to whip up a birthday cake decorated with six topless models. The Prince of Wales wasted no time telling the Queen, who thought "it was quite funny," he recalled. "She kept saying 'No. Oh, *no*. My heavens.'"

Charles did get a call from Diana the next day, however, after she kicked up yet another storm of controversy by taking William and Harry to see *The Devil's Own* starring Harrison Ford and Brad Pitt. First, Harry was underage, and Diana had to persuade the theater manager to let him in. Second, the movie was criticized for glamourizing the Irish Republican Army. Keenly sensitive to the fact that Charles's beloved great-uncle Dickie Mountbatten had been assassinated by the IRA—not to mention the political implications inherent in merely seeing the film—Diana called her ex-husband at St. James's Palace that same day. "I am so, so sorry, Charles," she pleaded. "I didn't know what it was about. We just wanted to see a movie, and we picked it out of the paper because William likes Harrison Ford."

"Don't worry," Charles replied. The Queen, he reassured her, "is a big fan of Harrison Ford, too."

Their rapprochement aside, the Prince and Princess of Wales still had Camilla to contend with. As she was about to embark on a long-planned trip to the United States in late June, Diana learned that Charles—in strict defiance of the Queen—was planning to throw an elaborate fiftieth birthday party for Camilla at Highgrove. The news did not sit well with the Princess, who called Mark Bolland directly to protest. Bolland was one of the few members of Charles's inner circle who, for the time being at least, Diana felt would give her an honest answer. "Mark, I'm very cross," said the Princess, who was willing to accept the fact that Charles loved Camilla but strongly objected to her rival flaunting her status as the Prince of

Wales's mistress. "What on earth's going on? People keep telling me that Camilla plans to make a big splash. . . . I don't know what to think. I'm *really* cross."

The next day, Camilla would indeed wind up in the newspapers—albeit for reasons that were not exactly to her liking. In a bizarre twist of fate, fifty-three-year-old designer Carolyn Melville-Smith was driving her Volvo in Wiltshire when a Ford Mondeo with Camilla at the wheel "appeared like a missile" and struck her car not far from Highgrove. "The next thing I knew," Melville-Smith recalled, "the other car was flying through the air, and I was in a ditch." The Volvo was on its side, and Melville-Smith's skirt was caught in the driver's-side door, trapping her inside.

Camilla, meanwhile, used her cell phone to call Charles. Melville-Smith claimed that, despite hearing her cries for help, Camilla chose not to respond to them in any way. Following Charles's instructions to stay put, she ran back to her car, lit a cigarette, and then sat on the curb rocking back and forth and crying until royal protection officers arrived. While Camilla said and did nothing, just yards away random passersby rushed to help Melville-Smith, calling for police and an ambulance, and reassuring the trapped woman that help was on the way.

Once police got to the accident scene, Camilla was administered a breathalyzer test—which she passed—and then taken to Highgrove to be treated by Charles's physician for a badly sprained wrist and a minor concussion. Melville-Smith, who at that point knew nothing about the other driver's identity, was taken by ambulance to a nearby hospital, where she was treated for minor scrapes and bruises. However, when the next day's newspapers reported that Camilla had come across an accident and heroically rescued the victim, Melville-Smith cried foul. She also laughed at the notion that Camilla was told not to do anything because the crash could have been a staged terrorist attack against a "special friend" of Prince Charles's.

"I am not a 'terrorist threat,'" objected Melville-Smith. "I was trapped in my car, yelling for help, and she did not come. I could have been badly hurt, and she just left me there." Later, Melville-Smith softened and decided not to press charges. "It would be really bitchy if I did pursue it," she said, "because Camilla has a hard enough time anyway, and she would only get more bad press." (Prosecutors were still mulling over whether or not to file criminal reckless driving charges against Camilla when Diana was killed in a car crash in Paris. Curiously, authorities decided not to pursue a case against Camilla because they did not want to compound the tragedy for Prince Charles in the days following his ex-wife's death.)

A few days after Camilla's accident, Charles was spending the weekend with the rest of the royal family at Sandringham. Everyone, including Prince Philip, asked how Camilla was doing—everyone, that is, but the Queen. Charles's mother was more convinced than ever that "that wicked woman," as Her Majesty called Camilla, was responsible for much of the misfortune that had befallen the House of Windsor. It was an opinion shared by the Queen's private secretary Sir Robert Fellowes and other key Palace officials who, in the words of one, wanted Charles to "send Mrs. Parker Bowles packing."

In the weeks ahead, Diana had no problem eclipsing Charles and his problematic lover. The Princess's whirlwind American tour included a reunion with her friend Mother Teresa at an AIDS hospice in the Bronx, breakfast with First Lady Hillary Clinton at the White House, and a celebrity-packed eightieth birthday party for *Washington Post* publisher Katharine Graham. At the Graham bash, the Princess was seated between her onetime love interest Teddy Forstmann and Hollywood megamogul Barry Diller. "She had been at the White House that day, and she said that Bill Clinton was the sexiest man alive," recalled Wall Street oracle Warren Buffett, who sat across from the Princess. "I can still see Barry's and Teddy's faces as she said it. I didn't ask her who the least sexy guy in the world alive was," Buffett continued. "I was afraid she might say, 'You!'"

Diana returned to London a few days later to make an appearance at a preview party for a charity auction of her gowns at Christie's in New York. The Princess was still fixated on Camilla's planned fiftieth birthday party ("Wouldn't it be funny if I jumped out of the cake in a bathing suit?"), and couldn't resist wearing a bracelet with interlocking *C*'s to the Christie's preview party ("You see, this one's for Charles, and this one's for Camilla!").

The sale itself had been William's idea as a way to raise money for the AIDS Crisis Trust and the Cancer Research Fund of London's Royal Marsden Hospital, although both Charles and the Queen had privately objected to members of the royal family hawking items as personal as clothing—regardless of where the money went. In the end, Diana's special brand of magic carried the day. Frenzied bidders shelled out $3.26 million for seventy-nine of the Princess's gowns—including the midnight-blue velvet dress Diana wore when she danced at the White House with John Travolta.

The Princess of Wales had been back in London only a few days when, on July 1, 1997, she celebrated her thirty-sixth birthday at a gala marking the Tate Gallery's centennial. Charles did not call to wish his ex-wife happy birthday—nor did the Queen or any other member of the royal family. But after the Tate gala, William and Harry sang "Happy Birthday" to their mother—for the very last time—as she blew out the candles on a cake prepared by the Kensington Palace chef.

For weeks, Charles had been preoccupied with planning the extravagant birthday bash he was throwing in honor of Camilla. He'd invited eighty friends—including her ex-husband, Andrew Parker Bowles—but no members of the royal family. The Prince of Wales's mistress had already taken a tentative first step into the spotlight a few months earlier when she became a patron of the National Osteoporosis Society, a charity she had been quietly working for since her mother's death from the bone disease three years earlier. But the exotic "Arabian Nights"–themed birthday party, held amid palm trees inside a massive tent where guests were served by staff in white robes and red fezzes, was considered a game changer for Camilla—a "trial balloon," said Harold Brooks-Baker, that would determine whether Prince Charles was "on shaky ground or not."

Camilla was among the first to arrive at the party with her sister, Annabel, driving through the Highgrove gates in a royal car with one of Charles's chauffeurs at the wheel. The guest of honor was wearing a slinky black dress and a diamond necklace that had been given to her by the Prince. Charles arrived not long after, making his presence clear by ordering his driver to go slow enough for waiting paparazzi to snap their pictures. Inside, Prince Charles and Mrs. PB made no effort to conceal their intimate relationship; they openly embraced, danced, laughed, whispered in each other's ears, and generally engaged in what a reporter for the *Telegraph* called the "easy familiarity of a longstanding couple."

Press coverage of the event was overwhelmingly positive, reflecting the public's changed attitude toward Camilla. Recent polls indicated that 20 percent of the British people had changed their minds about Camilla, and more than two out of three felt that the Prince of Wales should be free to wed his mistress. But on the question of whether or not Camilla should ever be queen, the answer was a resounding "No."

Camilla's allies rallied to her side, claiming that she'd been treated cruelly. "There was a public finger being pointed at her by the one person who is able to manipulate the media," said her longtime friend Charles Benson. "Because she is very beautiful, the Princess of Wales can be very persuasive when she's in the right mood. Diana had a nation crying for her, and, therefore, if they had her as a good fairy, they had to have a wicked witch, and that was poor old Camilla." A friend of Prince Charles's, Jane Ward, was encouraged by recent polls showing a softening in public opinion on the simple question of marriage. "We had the fairy tale that didn't work, and to me that is terribly sad," she said. "But maybe now it's time to move forward and for everyone to find some happiness."

Camilla, for one, was determined to seize the moment. In late July she asked Bolland to arrange a top-secret lunch at Highgrove with Tony Blair's image guru, Peter Mandelson. Although Camilla and Charles told Mandelson they had no intention of marrying, that was precisely their plan. "They kept saying they just wanted to have a normal life," an associate of Mandelson's said, "and that of course it was absurd to think they intended to become husband and wife. But Peter isn't an idiot."

Mandelson's advice was not to rush things—for the couple to continue operating in the shadows as they had done for years, with Camilla making strategically timed public appearances so as to "let the public get used to the idea of you as an actual person." At one point during the lunch, Charles turned to Mandelson and told him that he was concerned about his own image. "How do you think people see me?" the Prince asked.

"You command more affection, or sympathy, and respect than you realize," Mandelson said, softening Prince Charles up for what he was about to say next. "But many people have gained the impression you feel sorry for yourself, that you're rather glum and dispirited. This has a dampening effect on how you're regarded." He also pointed out in no uncertain terms to Charles that if he had any hope of winning back the loyalty of his future subjects, he had to make a concerted effort to appear less of a whinger.

No matter what Charles did or said—or how carelessly Camilla drove her car along country roads—there was no denying that the summer of '97 belonged to Diana. A week before Charles threw his highly publicized birthday bash for Camilla, Natty Khan walked out on Diana. Within days, he was back with a dozen red roses, begging for forgiveness. But it was too late. That same day, Diana and her boys boarded a Nice-bound Executive Gulfstream IV jet owned by Harrods, the iconic London department store. They were the honored guests of Harrods's controversial owner, the Egyptian-born, self-made billionaire Mohamed Al Fayed.

Spurned by Britain's establishment despite his vast holdings throughout the United Kingdom, Al Fayed had waged a years-long campaign to win over the world's most famous woman, donating generously to her charities and cozying up to her at various galas and banquets. Finally, when the two were seated together at a dinner following a benefit performance of *Swan Lake*, he invited Diana and her princeling sons to Castel Ste. Hélène, his sprawling $17 million estate in Saint-Tropez on the French Riviera. The Princess knew that by accepting, she would infuriate not only her in-laws, who regarded Al Fayed as a crass and preening social climber, but also Hasnat Khan. So naturally, Diana accepted.

As soon as they arrived in Nice, Diana, William, and Harry were driven to the harbor at Saint-Laurent-du-Var and piped aboard Al Fayed's newly acquired 195-foot yacht the *Jonikal*, with its fully equipped gym, saunas, helipad, mahogany-paneled staterooms, and crew of sixteen for the five-hour trip to Saint-Tropez. Two days later Al Fayed introduced Diana to his playboy son Dodi, and for the rest of the Princess's life the world press was filled with stories and photographs chronicling their steamy summer romance.

Dodi Fayed (he'd dropped the "Al" while living in the United States) had a history of problems with women and cocaine, but he and the Princess bonded over their shared experience as children of divorce. Unlike other men she had known, Dodi, who dabbled for a short period in the movie business (he produced the Oscar-winning *Chariots of Fire*, as well as *The Scarlet Letter* and *Hook*), had the time, money, and patience to devote himself completely to her.

Even when it came to matters of the heart, Diana valued her eldest son's opinion ("I call him my 'little old wise man,'" she told her hairdresser Tess Rock) and sought it out when it was time to return to London. William pointed out that, while Hasnat Khan made her cry, Dodi made her laugh. The Princess took her son's advice and, over the next month and a half, spent time with Dodi at his elegant Mayfair flat and aboard the *Jonikal* as it plied the waters off the South of France. All the while, Diana played to the cameras—simultaneously making Hasnat Khan jealous and completely overshadowing Camilla's milestone birthday celebration.

Diana seemed, in the words of her friend Lucia Flecha de Lima, "deliriously, rhapsodically happy." But reality struck when word came that her friend Gianni Versace had been gunned down outside his Miami Beach estate. Charles knew how close Diana had been to the noted Italian designer and called her immediately to say how sorry he was. "It means a great deal to me," she told Flecha de Lima, "to know that all the bitterness that was between us is gone now." Months earlier, Elton John had broken off his friendship with Diana when she bowed out of a book party arranged by Versace. Now they made up while comforting each other at Versace's celebrity-packed memorial service. Charles was especially moved by a widely published photograph of Diana putting her arm around a weeping

Elton—but not Camilla. "She smirked when she saw it," a Wiltshire friend recalled. "Camilla thought it was just one more brilliant publicity stunt on Diana's part."

———

As the Diana-Dodi affair heated up, there were the inevitable rumors of marriage. Although Diana accepted a $12,000 Jaeger-LeCoultre gold watch and a $3,000 Bulgari ring from Dodi that she wore on the fourth finger of her right hand, she made it clear to her close friends Annabel Goldsmith and Rosa Monckton that she had no intention of marrying her Egyptian playboy. While she described being with Dodi as "bliss," the Princess told Goldsmith that "the last thing" she needed was a new marriage. "I need it," she said, "like a bad rash on my face."

On this particular subject, Charles was torn. On the one hand, Dodi was a welcome distraction. As long as Diana was happy, she was less likely to perseverate on his relationship with Camilla. At the same time—and despite his oft-repeated praise of multiculturalism—the Prince shared his mother's less than charitable view of Al Fayed and his hedonist son. Rumors that this oddest of couples might marry were particularly upsetting to the Queen, if for no other reason than such a union would make a Muslim stepfather to the future head of the Church of England. "The whole idea," Brooks-Baker said, "sent the Palace into a *panic.*"

By way of easing his mother's fears, Charles told the Queen that Diana's friends were confident she had no plans to marry Dodi. "Yes, Charles," she replied. "But she has surprised us before, hasn't she?" For now, the Prince of Wales had a stock response for anyone who asked about his ex-wife's new love: "Whatever makes her happy makes me happy."

———

With the world captivated by his ex-wife's romantic escapade, Charles forged ahead with plans for Camilla to make another giant leap toward acceptance by hosting her first public event. Camilla and her sister, Annabel, announced "An Evening of Enchantment" that was to be held on September 13 to benefit the National Osteoporosis Society. Among those on the star-studded guest list: Mick Jagger, Elton John, Paul McCartney, Joan Collins, Eric Clapton, Emma Thompson—and Charles and Camilla's unlikely American pal, comedienne Joan Rivers.

Just to make certain that Diana did not overreact to news of Camilla's latest foray into the public arena, Charles obtained the Palace's permission to make a joint appearance with the Princess of Wales—their first since smiling for the cameras at William's confirmation six months earlier. As part of ongoing efforts to economize, the Crown had agreed to decommission the *Britannia*. Charles, who was scheduled to board the royal yacht at Cardiff for one segment of its farewell tour, asked Diana and the boys to join him. "Thrilled and touched" by Charles's invitation, the Princess accepted immediately—if for no other reason than William and Harry would "feel like part of a family again—even if it's only for a few hours. Every child of divorce knows how important that is." That phone call placed from Balmoral marked the last time Charles spoke to Diana.

Now, as their summer idyll neared its end, Dodi and Diana stopped over in Paris before flying home. No sooner had they checked in to the opulently appointed second-floor Imperial Suite of the Al Fayed–owned Ritz Hotel on the Place Vendôme than Diana dispatched a hotel staffer to find the Sony PlayStation Harry wanted for his thirteenth birthday—just two and a half weeks away. She had wanted to pick it out herself, but the paparazzi and crowds gathered outside the hotel made that impossible.

Charles, meanwhile, was winding down another flawless season at Balmoral spent fishing, hunting, horseback riding, and hiking with his sons. The royal summer in the Scottish Highlands had almost ended before it began. When William and Harry kissed their mother good-bye for the last time and journeyed to Balmoral the first week in August, they arrived to find the rest of the royals there with one major exception. Their father was AWOL spending a few days alone on Majorca just off the coast of Spain.

In the middle of his Spanish holiday, the Mercedes in which Charles was a passenger suddenly veered wildly out of control as it hurtled down on a winding mountain road. The Prince, who unlike Diana seldom wore a seat belt, was flung about the backseat as the driver struggled to negotiate a hairpin curve. Finally, Charles's bodyguard-chauffeur managed to slam on the brakes and bring the car to a screeching halt only seconds before it would have catapulted over a cliff to the rocks more than one hundred feet below. Charles and another royal protection officer, who was riding in the front passenger seat, were shaken but unhurt. A car that had been following close behind pulled up and two more plainclothes bodyguards armed with Glock 9-millimeter pistols—the rest of what is sometimes called the Prince's four-member close protection team—jumped out.

"Are you all right, Sir?" one asked as they rushed to the Prince's aid.

"My God," Charles said, catching his breath. "Did you see that? We were almost killed. Damn roads!"

As soon as they returned to their hotel, Charles downed a Laphroaig whiskey. Once his nerves were steadied, he phoned William and Harry at Balmoral with news that he'd be joining them in a few days. Charles laughed off his vehicular close call, but according to an Eton classmate, William was nonetheless concerned that Papa was taking too many risks. He wanted his father to tell his driver to be more cautious: "Be careful, Papa. Tell him to drive more slowly on those roads."

On August 30 the Prince of Wales sat down in his study at Balmoral and dashed off a letter to "My Dearest Diana" in which he asked if Harry, who was struggling with his studies at Ludgrove, should be held back an additional year before being sent to join William at Eton. Ending the note with "Lots of Love, Charles," the Prince sealed it and handed it to his secretary with strict instructions to have it messengered to Kensington Palace—so that the Princess could "have it on her desk when she returns from her holiday."

Several hours later, William called his mother. He started the conversation by expressing concern for his brother, who was being expressly excluded from a photo shoot marking William's return to Eton. "They only want me to pose, Mummy," the Heir explained, "and I don't want Harry to feel ignored." After Diana agreed to talk the matter over with Charles, mother and son chatted for twenty minutes about her Mediterranean holiday and his skill at bagging dozens of grouse, quail, partridge, and pheasant—all with a little guidance from the true marksman in the family, Grandpapa, the Duke of Edinburgh.

At this point, William and Harry had been apart from their mother for a month. Now, William told her, they were eager to spend time with her for at least a few days before heading back to school. "When is your flight arriving in London?" he asked her.

"Late Sunday morning—a little after eleven," she said.

"We can't wait to see you! Can we meet you at the airport?"

"Of course," Diana said without hesitating. *"Of course."*

From Day One, I always knew I'd never be the next queen.
—Diana

*Sometimes I think they just want to forget
about her. It's almost as if she never existed.*
—Diana's friend Wayne Sleep

You feel pain like no other pain.
—William in 2019, describing the impact of his mother's death

SEVEN

"OH, STOP COMPLAINING. WE ALL HAVE PROBLEM PARENTS"

Diana's sudden and brutal death on August 31, 1997, not only up-ended the House of Windsor and stunned the world but also seemed to have obliterated in a single stroke any chance for the Prince and his mistress to marry. The "Evening of Enchantment" charity ball to benefit the National Osteoporosis Society—their planned debut as a couple at a public event—was to occur two weeks later. Now it was scrapped, along with all the progress Operation PB had made in selling Camilla to the British people. The *Daily Mail* pointed out that, if the Prince still planned to remarry, "he knows, and Camilla knows, that this must now be put off to a date so far in the distance that some of their circle are actually using the word 'forever.'" Commentators agreed with veteran royals correspondent Judy Wade that if Camilla's car was seen anywhere in the vicinity of Highgrove, "it could be the end of them. The public simply won't tolerate it."

Within hours of hearing news of the crash, Charles began asking Mark Bolland and other advisors the same question over and over: "They're all going to blame me, aren't they?" Camilla knew better. Although Earl Spencer used his eulogy to blame the press for pursuing his sister into Paris's Alma tunnel that fateful night—causing the crash that killed her, the driver, and Dodi Fayed—most Britons believed Camilla had blood on her hands. Simply put, she had schemed to break up the Prince's marriage, driven Diana to the brink, and initiated the chain of events that ultimately placed the much-revered Princess of Wales in a car with Dodi to be chased to her death on a late-summer night. "They've got to blame someone—that much is true," she told one of her Ray Mill House neighbors. "But that someone is going to be me, I'm afraid."

Overnight, Camilla went back to being a pariah, easily the most loathed and reviled woman in the realm. Over the years, she had learned to live with the occasional boo, hiss, mumbled profanity, or disapproving glance. But this was different—and far scarier. A virtual prisoner at Ray Mill, she received dozens of death threats over the phone and in the mail. On the rare occasions when she did attempt to leave the house on an errand, strangers shouted obscenities at her, called her a whore, and, she later conceded, "made my life a living hell." Most of the unwelcome encounters went unreported, and St. James's Palace tried to shoot down the few that were—for example, the very accurate account of shoppers pelting Camilla with bread when she tried to shop at a local market.

It was "an appalling period" for Camilla, said Julia Cleverdon, who advised Prince Charles on his charities for more than thirty years. "He was in agony about it—he really, really was. And the fact that she was prepared to go through all this for him, I think illustrates what an incredibly strong relationship and partnership they've had."

Charles was rightly concerned for Camilla's safety. He doubled the contingent of armed royal protection officers guarding Ray Mill from four to eight. The Prince also worried that his own life was in danger—more specifically, that he could be assassinated while marching behind Diana's coffin during the Princess's funeral procession. Still shaken by what he now referred to obliquely as "what happened in Paris," an understandably morose Prince Charles penned four letters to be opened in the event of his death—one to William, predicting he would make a great king; one to Harry, urging him to support his brother; a love note to Camilla; and a letter to the British people basically saying how sorry he was that he would not have the opportunity to be their sovereign.

Yet Charles was not assassinated, nor was he booed. Quite the contrary. In the weeks and months following Diana's death, accounts in the press credited the Prince of Wales and Tony Blair with convincing the Queen to show Diana the respect in death that the royal family appeared to have denied her in life. Charles was also depicted correctly as a caring father, trying as best he could to help his sons recover from the devastating loss of the most important person in their young lives.

The day after Diana's funeral, the boys returned with him to Highgrove, where he swam, rode, and took long walks with them—all by way of distracting William and Harry with physical activity. Tiggy Legge-Bourke, who, with Charles's former nanny Mabel Anderson just happened to have been a guest at Balmoral when the terrible news came from Paris, also rushed in to help. Charles was grateful to both women for staying to comfort the boys and then traveling with the royal party to London so that they would both have a female shoulder to cry on. Most of the credit would go to Tiggy, whose tomboy streak came in handy during those first few days after the funeral when, as Charles said, "all William and Harry wanted to do was kick a soccer ball" around the Highgrove grounds.

Diana's feud with Tiggy aside, there was general agreement among the Princess's friends that she would have welcomed Legge-Bourke's presence at this soul-crushing time in her boys' lives—and would have understood that young Harry was especially vulnerable. Diana "smothered Harry in love," a friend noted, "and at least Tiggy was there to give him hugs and kisses." She also ran to Harry's room when he woke up crying in the middle of the night, tormented by nightmares about his mother's violent death. Tiggy would stay for hours, until Prince Harry went back to sleep.

On the surface, William appeared to be coping well—perhaps a little too well, friends and family suggested. Decades later, the Heir would speak of his confusion and inner turmoil at this time, and the feeling that "you had to put on a brave face and act as if nothing had happened. No one was telling us at the time that it was okay for us to grieve," he added. "You know, it was very much 'Let's get on with it.' So that's what I did." Earl Spencer was impressed with his nephew's "remarkable stoicism, almost leadership, in the quiet manner of his grief. His mother would be proud."

Windsors and Spencers alike showed up at Highgrove to celebrate

Harry's thirteenth birthday on September 15, and Diana's sister Sarah handed Harry the Sony PlayStation the Princess had gone to such lengths to buy in Paris on the eve of her death. Harry, who was learning from William and his famously dispassionate dad how to tamp down his emotions even in the presence of family, happily tore through the wrapping on all his gifts and blew out the candles on his cake without ever mentioning his mother.

Still, William told his father that he was "very worried about Harry" now that he was returning to Eton and Harry was off to Ludgrove. Charles insisted that Harry would be well looked after by the same two people who had helped William get through his parents' bitter divorce: Ludgrove headmaster Gerald Barber and his wife Janet. Moreover, Harry was free to call William at Eton anytime he wished. "The return to routine will be good for them," Prince Charles reasoned. "They need to see that life goes on."

Unlike Gordonstoun, where a virtually friendless Charles was emotionally and physically abused on a more or less continual basis, both Ludgrove and Eton provided safe havens of sorts for the young princes. Behind the brick walls and wrought iron gates of both schools, where students were instructed not to mention Diana or treat them differently, William and Harry were able to lose themselves in their sports and their studies. It helped that Harry, who, like his older brother, was a gifted athlete, made friends easily. Despite his popularity, though, Harry at times seemed "ineffably sad," said one of his teachers. Another recalled seeing Harry standing alone "with this terribly unhappy look on his face, bouncing a tennis ball against a wall for two hours. It seemed to me at the time that he had to be thinking about his mother. I didn't want to disturb him."

Four days after Harry's birthday, Prince Charles paused during a speech in Manchester to update his audience on how his sons were doing. He praised them both for being "quite remarkable" and for handling an "extraordinarily difficult time" with "quite enormous courage and the greatest possible dignity." He added, however, that "obviously, Diana's death has been an enormous loss as far as they are concerned, and I will always feel that loss."

William remained at Eton that fall, but since his brother's midterm break dovetailed with Charles's long-planned official tour of South Africa, he invited Harry along. The trip—coming just eight weeks after Diana's death—allowed for some important father-son bonding, not to mention the chance to show the world that he was a warm and caring dad. Tiggy tagged along to entertain Harry whenever official duties took his father away.

First, Harry and his Ludgrove chum Charlie Henderson went with Tiggy on safari in Botswana while Charles visited Swaziland and Lesotho. Later, the Princes met up in Durban, South Africa, where Papa was shaking hands with locals when he spotted Harry taking photos of him from the balcony of his suite at the Royal Hotel. The Spare was standing just below the hotel sign and waved to his father as the crowd below began chanting, "Harry! Harry!" Charles, clearly excited to see his son, pointed up and yelled to the crowd: "He's right there—under the letter *H*!" This was the sort of candidly affectionate, captured-on-film moment that St. James's Palace hoped would soften the future king's hard-boiled image.

The high point of the trip for Charles's thirteen-year-old son occurred in Johannesburg, where they attended a Spice Girls concert benefiting the Prince's Trust. Backstage, the Princes had their photos taken with Baby Spice (Emma Bunton), Posh Spice (Victoria Adams, later Mrs. David Beckham), Scary Spice (Melanie Brown, or Mel B.), Ginger Spice (Geri Halliwell), and Sporty Spice (Melanie Chisholm)—all of whom felt compelled to cover Diana's little boy with kisses. Photos of the encounter show Harry, wearing a navy-blue suit and a long purple tie, grinning from ear to ear. "The whole world had been crying for William and Harry, of course," Mel B. said at the time. "It's so wonderful to see him smile."

Father and son were blushing again when they were greeted by barebreasted women at the gates of the remote Zulu village of Duku. As the half-naked female villagers launched into a frenzied dance of welcome just feet from their seated royal guests, Charles turned to his wide-eyed son and said, "My, what amazing energy." Once again there were touching moments that conveyed the genuine, easy rapport between Charles and his younger son. At one point, Harry dissolved in tears of laughter when his father picked up a Zulu club and shield and jumped up and down like a warrior. Since Tiggy had not joined them on this particular leg of the trip, Harry asked his father for money to buy her a souvenir—a beaded bracelet—only to be reminded that royals never carry cash of any sort. Harry's bodyguard, Ian Hugget, coughed up the twenty-rand note (worth about $5) needed for the purchase.

———

Harry split off to return to school, leaving Prince Charles to deliver an address at a state dinner in Cape Town hosted by South Africa's President Nelson Mandela. Speaking of "the special importance to Africans of Diana's work to combat such things as AIDS, poverty, and the use of land mines," Charles went on to "convey my sons' and my own gratitude to all those South Africans who took the time and trouble to express their condolences."

Everyone stood up to applaud the Prince of Wales—including Earl Spencer, who was living in South Africa at the time. The two men, who had not spoken since Spencer delivered his provocative eulogy at Diana's funeral, shook hands and chatted amiably. Nevertheless, Charles, obviously still holding something of a grudge, had decided at the last minute to leave out a public tribute to the Spencer family that was included in the original draft of his speech.

No sooner did Charles and Harry return from their heartwarming father-son tour of South Africa than the young princes were hit with sobering news from the Inland Revenue service, Britain's answer to the IRS. Diana had left nearly all of her estate, ultimately valued at $35 million, to her sons. Now the government was taking a 40 percent tax bite out of the Princess's bequest, leaving William and Harry to split $21 million. Initially, Charles ordered his lawyers to take legal action against Inland Revenue but was talked out of it by his advisors. The Prince of Wales had wanted "to protect his sons' inheritance," said one, "but it would not have looked good if it appeared the royal family expected 'preferential treatment.'"

As Christmas 1997 approached—the boys' first without their mother—more disturbing details began to emerge about the crash in Paris. Most upsetting for William and Harry were accounts from eyewitnesses on the scene who reported that Diana was moaning and crying in pain as rescue workers pulled her from the twisted wreckage. Then there was Mohamed Al Fayed's insistence that Diana and Dodi were murdered by factions within the British government who could not tolerate a Muslim as stepfather to the future king. Al Fayed even went so far as to offer a reward of one million pounds ($1.62 million) to anyone who could produce the evidence that would prove his theory.

Charles knew there was no realistic way to shield William from the lurid stories popping up every day in the press. But Harry was another matter; just as they had done when William was a student at Ludgrove, Gerald and Janet Barber banned tabloids from the school and tightly controlled whatever information was coming to the students via TV and radio. Years later, Harry would praise these "sincere" efforts to protect him. He would also point out that they didn't work. "Of course I knew all the stories about the accident, everything," the Spare said. "It was absolutely everywhere you turned. No escaping it. But I never let on. It was easier to pretend that I didn't see and hear those ghastly, terrible things."

Over the next several weeks, Charles focused on getting his sons through the holiday season—and on trysting with Camilla, who was essentially under self-imposed house arrest, under the usual cloak-and-dagger conditions. On December 15 Camilla was spotted in public for the first time in four months, riding to the hounds with the Beaufort Hunt, one of the country's oldest foxhunting packs. It was also the very first time William and Harry, walking with Tiggy behind the pack, laid eyes on their father's mistress—at a considerable distance, on horseback with hundreds of other riders, and wearing traditional "rat-catcher" attire consisting of tweed hacking jacket, buff riding pants, black cap and black field boots. Charles was also among the rat-catcher-attired foxhunters, but nowhere in the vicinity of Camilla. Whenever the two set out on a hunt, they were careful never to be seen in close proximity to each other—"that," said the

Duke of Beaufort, who hosted the hunt on his fifty-thousand-acre estate, "would have given their enemies all the ammunition they needed."

Keeping with Windsor tradition, Charles and the boys spent Christmas with the rest of the family at Sandringham. By Christmas Eve, upward of a hundred staff members had spent weeks preparing a feast fit for, well, a queen. Their efforts aside, Charles always arrived with his own chef and a "hamper full of organic food," recalled royal chef Darren McGrady. "He liked his poached plums from Highgrove. His valet would come into the kitchen with three or four bottles of plums to be kept in the fridge."

After assembling in the White Drawing Room to put some finishing touches on the tree—always a Norfolk spruce cut down on the one-thousand-acre estate—the action moved to the Red Room, where large trestle tables were heaped with presents neatly stacked, labeled, and separated by lines of tape. As was always the case even in these most intimate of moments, the stacks of presents were arranged by rank, so that the Queen, Prince Philip, Charles, William, and Harry each had a table all her or his own.

Charles watched as his sons tore through their gifts—fishing reels, riding equipment—and then delicately unwrapped what they had given him: cuff links and a silver paperweight. The next morning, everyone attended Christmas-morning services at the Church of St. Mary Magdalene on the grounds of the royal estate—only this time, unlike what had occurred only months before at Balmoral, Diana's name would be specifically and loudly mentioned by Canon George Hall in his prayer for "all loved ones who have departed this life." The Queen—spurred on by her senior advisors—also mentioned Diana in her annual Christmas Day address, describing how "almost unbearably sad" the Princess's death had been and acknowledging how she shared the nation's sense of "shock and sorrow."

Watching his sons putting on a brave face during their first Christmas without Mummy, Charles was more determined than ever to do "whatever I can to help them forget." That meant spending as much time with them as possible—at Highgrove but also at St. James's Palace in the heart of London.

Immediately after Christmas at Sandringham, Charles took his sons on a ski holiday to Klosters. While the Prince of Wales was concentrating on his sons, the Queen launched a public relations offensive aimed at winning back those subjects she had alienated in the aftermath of Diana's death. For the first time, one of Britain's leading market research companies, Ipsos MORI, was brought in to assess the damage and help formulate a plan of attack. In a span of forty-eight months, the monarch would take several unprecedented steps—including a pledge to support Prime Minister Tony Blair's plan to end primogeniture, the thousand-year-old practice of making only the eldest male heir to the throne. She also released some of the Crown's most sensitive financial records—including information on the private holdings of the royal family—and formally proclaimed that all curtsying and bowing to members of the royal family be strictly voluntary. Since Diana had proven that even small public gestures could have enormous impact, the Queen also took her first ride in one of London's famous cabs, visited a McDonald's, and, incredibly, set foot for the very first time in a pub—the nine-hundred-year-old Bridge Inn at Topsham in Devon.

Keenly aware of William's and Harry's stratospheric standing in the polls, St. James's officials persuaded the Prince of Wales to take his sons along when he visited Canada in March 1998. William, who was making his first major public appearance since Diana's death, was clearly unprepared for the rock-star reception that awaited him when the Waleses arrived in Vancouver. At every stop, they were mobbed by thousands of girls squealing, "William! William!" and tossing cards, flowers, hankies, and teddy bears at the shell-shocked Prince. At every stop, William was greeted with cries of "I love you, Wills! Will you marry me?" At first, the Heir could only manage a nervous smile. But gradually, with a little chiding from the infinitely more easygoing Harry ("Go ahead, wave at that lot over there"), William learned to loosen up.

By the time they made their final scheduled appearance onstage at the Vancouver Heritage Center, William was clearly enjoying his newly discovered status as a global teenage heartthrob. When Charles and his sons were presented with the maple-leaf-emblazoned, red-and-white jackets and caps of the Canadian Olympic Team, which had competed in Nagano, Japan, the month before, William doffed his suit coat and slipped into the jacket before putting the cap on—backward. He then did a Michael Jackson–inspired shoulder roll and wrist snap before striking a pose. The result: pure pandemonium.

For Charles, it was a bittersweet moment. Just six months after their mother's death, they seemed to have put their grief behind them. They were, from their father's perspective, well adjusted and happy—deliriously so, now that young girls were throwing themselves at their feet. Yet once again, after years of struggling to emerge from his first wife's shadow, he was being shunted aside—this time by a public that had eyes only for Diana's boys. On the flight back to London with Harry (William and Tiggy flew home separately, in keeping with a Palace rule not to have two heirs fly together), Charles took one of his staff aside.

"God, here we go again, after all those years having people shove me aside so they could touch Diana," he said between sips of a chilled martini. "I'm so happy for the boys, of course, and it's terrible to feel jealous of your own children. But, you know, I just thought that was all behind me . . ."

However marginalized Charles may have felt, no one was, in fact, more isolated than his long-suffering and still much-despised mistress. Holed up at Ray Mill, Camilla followed the Canadian tour in the papers and on television—focusing in particular on Tiggy Legge-Bourke's near-constant presence in the background. Behind Tiggy's back, a resentful Mrs. PB referred to her as the "hired help" and, on occasion, "Big Ass." And she plotted to get rid of her.

Camilla was extremely territorial—a trait that led her to banish her onetime friend Lady Kanga Tryon from Charles's inner circle, not to mention wage her own war against Diana for the Prince's affections. Like the late Princess of Wales, she was jealous of the role Tiggy played in the young princes' lives, and suspicious of the curiously close bond that had always existed between the attractive young nanny and the Prince she had known since childhood. "Tiggy and the Prince were very playful with each other," one of Charles's former equerries observed. "They joked with each other, laughed a lot, there was an easy rapport—almost like a married couple. Make that a *happily* married couple."

Tiggy was gradually sidelined, thanks to some backstage maneuvering by Camilla. By the late spring of 1998, the nanny was no longer being asked to tag along on the Princes' trips to Sandringham, Highgrove, and Balmoral. In those rare cases when she was asked to step in, Tiggy could count on Mrs. Parker Bowles to offer stinging criticism of her job performance. On a trip to Wales that summer, the nanny looked on as her young charges rappelled down the face of a dam without safety harnesses or helmets. Camilla made certain Charles and even the Queen got a look at photos of the incident, accelerating Legge-Bourke's exit from the daily lives of the Princes.

———

In the meantime, Camilla made her first tentative step back into public view when she and her Prince cohosted what was billed as "A Weekend of Culture and Reflection" at Sandringham in March 1998. The black-tie, Edwardian-themed house party featured poetry readings, a string quartet from the Royal College of Music, and elegant candlelit dinners featuring $1,000 bottles of wine from Prince Charles's own cellars, as well as organic fruits and vegetables trucked the three and a half hours to Sandringham from the Highgrove Royal Gardens. One of the guests that evening was gossip columnist Aileen Mehle, who, along with Joan Rivers, Betsy Bloomingdale, and a handful of socialites and philanthropists, had been welcomed into the Prince's circle. "It was obvious that they were both extremely nervous about looking too comfy together," she recalled. "They were both very gracious, but also quite stiff, painfully self-conscious. It just seemed too soon after Diana's death. It was impossible not to ask yourself what she would have thought. I felt kind of sorry for Prince Charles and Camilla, if you want to know the truth."

Were Charles and Camilla still feeling, as Mehle suggested, "a shared sense of guilt"? Several weeks after their Sandringham affair, the Prince sought the answer to that and other nagging questions by embarking on one of his periodic journeys of spiritual self-discovery. This time he made a solo trip to the tenth-century, men-only Eastern Orthodox monastery of Vatopedi, perched seven thousand feet above the Aegean Sea on Mount Athos in northern Greece.

For the Prince of Wales, the Eastern Orthodox faith held a certain romantic appeal. His paternal grandmother, Princess Alice, had founded her own nursing order in Greece and wore the gray habit of an Orthodox nun. And although his father was exiled from Greece as an infant, Philip was baptized in the Greek Orthodox Church and had to convert to the Church of England to marry Princess Elizabeth in 1947. With its medieval cloisters, bearded, black-robed monks, relics (including the "Belt of the Virgin Mary" and the remains of Saint Herman of Alaska, the first Orthodox saint in America), Byzantine chants, elaborate mosaics, golden icons, and ancient rituals, Vatopedi spoke to Charles's need for mystery, mysticism, and meaning. Accordingly, the Prince of Wales stuck to the monastery's rigid schedule: up before dawn for prayer and meditation, all meals in the refectory, long stretches of silence and reflection, evening vespers by candlelight, and in bed by eight o'clock.

Of course, Charles was not exactly your average seminarian. The Prince had sailed to Greece aboard multibillionaire John Latsis's lavish, four-hundred-foot yacht *Alexander* (named after Alexander the Great) and arrived at the monastery's dock in a speedboat driven by his four-man security detail. During his brief stay at Vatopedi, Charles and his bodyguards occupied their own wing, and while the Prince did eat with his fellow pilgrims and their monk hosts in the rectory, all of his meals were prepared by a royal protection officer—a precaution taken to prevent the future king of England from being poisoned. That seemed highly unlikely: the Prince, who had raised millions of dollars for the Friends of Mount Athos charity, was always welcomed there with open arms.

Joking that his "spiritual batteries" were now "fully recharged," Charles repaid his hosts by throwing a party for Greek dignitaries at Highgrove. Camilla, taking another hesitant step into the limelight, was at his side—"doing all of the things," one of the guests recalled, "that any gracious wife would do. She welcomed us, made small talk, gave instructions to the staff. One got the impression that she was on top of things, handling all the small details—running the show, really." Being a royal hostess "seemed to come quite naturally to Mrs. Parker Bowles. She seemed very calm."

Camilla was anything but calm on June 12, 1998, when William left Eton for London to go to the movies with a small group of friends. He phoned Charles from the car just to let his father know that he'd be dropping in to York House to change his clothes. When Charles cautioned him that Mrs. Parker Bowles was there, William—who had always played the role of fixer and peacemaker in his parents' turbulent marriage—let his father know it was time he finally met Camilla.

The meeting, just nine months after Diana's death and nine days before William's sixteenth birthday, was a long time coming. The Princess had always leaned on him for advice, sharing even the most intimate details of her romantic life with the young Prince. So it was not at all surprising that, prior to Diana's death, neither William nor Harry had the slightest intention of ever meeting the woman responsible for shattering their parents' marriage. In April 1998, however, Charles cleverly arranged for Camilla's son and daughter—twenty-two-year-old Tom and Laura, nineteen—to join the royal party when he visited the Queen Mother at Birkhall. Although Camilla's fun-loving children would later run afoul of the royal family, at the time they instantly hit it off with William and Harry.

Now, just two months later, a trembling Camilla told Prince Charles that she was "terrified" and "couldn't go through" with meeting William. Instead, when he arrived at York House at four o'clock, she fled to the drawing room with her personal assistant Amanda McManus while he dashed upstairs to change. Understandably fed up with Camilla's foot-dragging, Charles took her arm and guided her toward William. Camilla, always cognizant of court protocol, curtsied and took the young Prince's extended hand. "You two have a lot of getting acquainted to do," Charles said awkwardly as he left his son and his mistress alone to talk over tea and soft drinks.

In typical fashion, it was William who tried to make Camilla feel at ease with talk about their shared love of foxhunting and polo, his life at Eton, and the fact that Harry had just passed his entrance exams and would be joining William at the exclusive boarding school. Thirty minutes later, William left to join his friends, and Camilla breathed a deep sigh of relief. Still, for the notorious Mrs. PB, it had been a nerve-wracking afternoon. "Darling," she told Charles, holding out her hand to show him it was still shaking, "I *really* need a vodka and tonic."

The fact that William was about to mark a milestone as important as his sixteenth birthday without his mother did not go unnoticed by Charles—nor by the Men in Gray. To satisfy the public's insatiable hunger for more information about the future sovereign, and to reward the press for keeping its promise to leave the Princes alone, the Palace released a profile of William. The piece was accompanied by photos and revealed, among other things, that William liked fast food and techno music, was increasingly leery about his new sex symbol status, yearned to go on an African safari, and actually liked wearing his Eton tailcoat. In exchange for cooperating, Charles agreed to stay at Highgrove while William celebrated his birthday with friends at Balmoral. William asked not to speak to any other members of the royal family—including the Queen, Prince Philip, and the Queen Mother—and only to his father and brother over the phone. "He just wanted to forget for one night," an Eton classmate explained, "that he was who he was."

In the coming weeks, William joined Camilla and his father for lunch, and met Camilla for a second tea. Charles, pleased with how well things were going between his elder son and Mrs. Parker Bowles, arranged for a similarly amiable encounter with Harry at Highgrove. "It was all about making Papa happy," a friend of the Princes said. "Princess Diana had told them their father loved Camilla, and even pointed to Charles and Camilla as an example of what real love looked like." It helped that Mrs. Parker Bowles was nothing like Diana—less a stepmother than, as one friend of Charles's put it, "a colorful aunt."

Stung by the widespread perception that paparazzi had chased Diana to her death, Fleet Street had kept a respectful distance from William and Harry. It was all part of an informal pledge to protect the boys' privacy, so when news of the secret meeting between Camilla and William was leaked a month after the fact, the Heir was livid. So, too, were the two Queens Elizabeth, but for very different reasons. The Queen Mother, who had perfected the art of "ostriching"—sticking her head in the sand—never spoke of Camilla to Charles. If she had, the Queen Mum reasoned, it could jeopardize her close relationship with the Prince of Wales.

The Queen felt no such compunction. She still urged Charles to jettison Mrs. Parker Bowles from his life in the interest of preserving public support for the monarchy. When the Queen's new private secretary, Robin Janvrin, refused to join William and Mrs. Parker Bowles for one of their teas at St. James's Palace because the Queen had withheld her permission, Charles was furious. "How many times do I have to say it?" he told his former private secretary Sir Richard Aylard. "Mrs. Parker Bowles is a nonnegotiable part of my life."

Perhaps, but the secret meeting between Mrs. PB and William was clearly designed to advance Camilla's prospects of becoming queen—and proved that Charles was not above using his children as pawns in the game. Many of Diana's friends felt this was an egregious affront to the Princess's memory. "Astonishingly insensitive" was how one friend described the meeting to journalist Richard Kay. Mrs. Parker Bowles had "caused Diana so much misery, it seems incredible that such a meeting should happen before the first anniversary of the Princess's death." Lady Elsa Bowker agreed, saying, "Diana would have been very upset that the woman who made her life hell was now being embraced by her sons."

Surprised by the uproar, Charles took off late that summer for an Aegean cruise aboard the *Alexander* with William and Harry—sans Camilla. In a brilliantly staged photo op, Prince Charles walked out onto the tarmac at Heathrow and kissed his six-foot-one teenage son good-bye before they took separate flights to Athens. "It was very touching," Mark Bolland said slyly. "Don't you agree?"

It had been seven years since the Prince and Princess of Wales had supposedly made a last-ditch effort to save their marriage by taking a "second honeymoon" aboard the *Alexander*—only to have it scuttled by Charles's constant canoodling with Camilla over the phone. This time around, the Prince of Wales did little to avail himself of all the *Alexander* had to offer: five decks, two pools, a movie theater, gold plumbing fixtures, a ballroom, and two helipads. Instead, the Prince spent hours standing alone on the deck, gazing at the horizon, lost in his thoughts. At one point, Charles turned to his host, Diana's friend the Greek shipping tycoon John Latsis, and said solemnly, "I just so wish she could be here with me."

"Diana?" asked Latsis, sensitive to the fact that the Princess had died only ten months earlier.

"Oh, heavens no," answered Charles, clearly miffed. "Camilla, of course."

———

Charles then had to deal with an emotionally wrenching milestone that loomed on the horizon. Everyone—but no one more than William and Harry—dreaded the approaching anniversary of Diana's death. Searching for distractions, the young princes decided to throw a surprise fiftieth birthday party for their father. To ensure that it would indeed be a surprise, they decided to host it at Highgrove on July 31, three and a half months before his actual birthday.

Not surprisingly, details were leaked to the *Sunday Mirror* just ten days before the party was to take place. An angry Charles went so far as to issue a statement saying that William and Harry were "upset" that the plans for the "secret party they were planning for their father" had been divulged. "They worked very hard to try to pull it off. . . . The Prince of Wales is sad that the newspaper involved did not handle the information it received with greater common sense and courtesy." William and Harry went ahead anyway, enlisting Prince Charles's longtime friends Emma Thompson, Stephen Fry, and "Mr. Bean" Rowan Atkinson to perform in a takeoff on another Atkinson vehicle, the hit British TV comedy *Blackadder*.

Not long after, Charles, William, Harry, and the rest of the royals fled to their usual summer sanctuary at Balmoral. While the outside world was inundated with articles and television specials commemorating Diana's death, the Prince of Wales took his sons fishing, riding, hunting, hiking, and picnicking with the Queen, Prince Philip, and the Queen Mother. This time, during services at Crathie Kirk Diana's name was actually mentioned. The congregation recited a "Prayer of Remembrance and Thanksgiving for Diana, Princess of Wales," in which she was praised as "a person who touched the hearts of so many people. She knew sorrow as well as happiness in her own life, and through this she grew in compassion for the suffering of others." Charles, who had been responsible for a considerable amount of Diana's suffering, dutifully recited the prayer with the rest of the congregants. Behind the scenes, he also stepped in to insist that on the first anniversary of Diana's death flags around the United Kingdom fly at half-mast. This time the Queen, clearly having learned her lesson the hard way, did not hesitate to issue the order.

Camilla was nowhere to be seen—and with good reason. As the first anniversary approached, the death threats mounted, and Charles pleaded with her to stay at Ray Mill House where the royal protection officers could protect her. "Is it going to be this way every year for the rest of my life?" she asked one of her bodyguards. "I'm not sure I can stand that."

In the fall, Charles was on hand when Harry joined his brother at Eton. William flourished there as both a scholar and an athlete. Ranking in the top 10 percent of his class academically, he was also captain of the swim team and excelled on the water polo, rowing, and rugby teams. He was also a member of the student leadership society called Pop, and was such an outstanding member of Eton's cadet force that he earned its coveted Sword of Honor.

Although Charles worried that Harry would wither in his brother's shadow, he needn't have. The Spare instantly charmed teachers and classmates alike, and would end up holding his own both academically and on the playing field. "Prince William is a gifted athlete, no question," said one of the boys' instructors at Eton. "He is focused, very determined, incredibly competitive. But Harry is a beast—just totally unafraid. He throws himself body and soul into every single sport. He will do anything to win, and, in that sense, he is much more the natural athlete than William." Agreed one of Harry's bodyguards, "William is very physical, but he is more hesitant, where Harry is absolutely fearless."

Harry was also smitten with all things military and would excel as a member of Eton's elite Combined Cadet Corps. The Princes' fascination with the trappings of the armed services—the uniforms and medals and marching bands—had as much to do with Diana as it did with Charles. The Spencers had a long and distinguished military history, and from the time her sons were toddlers, the Princess took them to British army bases to ride in tanks and watch parades. As for the Windsors, their link to military pageantry was obvious; William recalled that as small boys, he and Harry "completely lost our minds" whenever Charles dressed up in one of the many braided, bemedaled, beribboned ceremonial uniforms that he as Prince of Wales and the holder of more than fifty military ranks was fully entitled to wear.

Yet when it came to the young Princes' love of weapons, Charles and his family were the driving force. After killing their first buck at the age of fourteen, William and Harry were both "blooded" at Balmoral: dabbed on each cheek with the still-warm blood of their prey. Not long after, William took up foxhunting—all part and parcel of what Diana called the "glorious Windsor pastime of killing things."

That "glorious Windsor pastime" almost had fatal consequences later that year when William and Harry—with Charles's blessing—invited fourteen of their Eton pals to dine at Windsor Castle with Granny. Her Majesty met the Princes and their friends—the youngest of which were fourteen; the oldest, sixteen—over drinks in the Green Room. Wine was served at dinner: a white Burgundy with the sole, a Bordeaux with the pheasant, and, with the cheese plate, a tawny port. Once the Queen ex-

Diana and Charles deliver the requisite Buckingham Palace balcony kiss for the
cheering throng below following their wedding at St. Paul's Cathedral on July 29, 1981.

While Diana's
White House dance
with John Travolta
was the highlight
of the Wales' visit
to Washington in
1985, Nancy Reagan
was more charmed
by Charles's toast
during the state
dinner held in the
royal couple's honor.

23   Charles windsurfs off Majorca, August 1986. Later, the Waleses joined their hosts King Juan Carlos and Queen Sofia of Spain along with their children on the steps of Palma de Majorca's Marivent Palace.

24

Diana gleefully smashes a prop bottle over his head on the set of the 1987 James Bond film *The Living Daylights*.

Diana literally gives Charles the cold shoulder at a dinner hosted by Prime Minister Margaret Thatcher at 10 Downing Street.

His old flame Lady Tryon
curtsies for Prince Charles at
the Pink Diamond Charity
Ball in December 1990.
Charles flirted with his
longtime Hollywood crush
("My only pinup") Barbra
Streisand when he visited the
United States four years later.

Four princes and an earl—Philip, William, Diana's brother Earl Spencer, Harry, and Charles—walk behind Diana's coffin as it makes its way through the streets of London to Westminster Abbey on September 6, 1997.

A skilled polo player, Charles competed at Smith Square Windsor for the Queen Mother Cup in June of l998.

30

At another match the following year, he competed for the Dorchester Trophy at Cirencester Park—playing alongside both William and Harry for the first time.

31

Diana and Camilla were both jealous of the relationship between Charles and the boys' nanny Tiggy Legge-Bourke, who jokingly comforted the Prince of Wales after he lost the match.

32

Camilla's first public appearance with Charles was at her sister Annabel's fiftieth birthday party at London's Ritz Hotel on January 28, 1999.

Charles and his sons poke fun at each other for the cameras during a 2002 ski vacation at the Swiss ski resort of Klosters. But the mood turned somber when news came the next day that the Queen Mother—shown leaving church services at Westminster Abbey with Charles—suddenly took ill and died. The Prince of Wales participated in the "Vigil of Princes"—guarding his grandmother's coffin as she lay in state.

William and Charles check out the herd of Ayrshire cows at Highgrove in May 2004.

The newlyweds leave St. George's Chapel with the rest of the royal family on April 9, 2005. The Queen looked on as Camilla, now Duchess of Cornwall and Princess of Wales in all but name, struggled to keep her hat from being blown away in the wind.

cused herself at nine o'clock and retired to her private quarters, the Princes' teenage guests had the run of the castle's well-stocked liquor cabinets.

By eleven thirty at night, Harry announced that he wanted to go sledding. He escorted his guests to the pantry, from which they each grabbed a large silver serving tray and went outside to the steep, grassy hill beneath the castle's nine-hundred-year-old Round Tower. For the next thirty minutes, they hollered and yelled as they slid down the embankment. Their bodyguards, meanwhile, looked on patiently.

Just before dawn the next morning, each hungover young guest was issued his own 12-gauge shotgun and invited to hunt rabbit in the surrounding Windsor Great Park. Flanked by the usual contingent of gamekeepers, bodyguards, and barking dogs that were also an integral part of the royal hunting scene at Balmoral and Sandringham, the Eton gang paused for a civilized picnic lunch (wine included) and then more breaks throughout the afternoon that inevitably included sandwiches washed down with beer.

Several of the young men in the hunting party had never fired a gun before. No one had bothered to ask if they had. Charles, the Queen, or at least some of the more seasoned Palace officials might have paused long enough to realize that plying children with alcohol and then setting them loose on castle grounds with loaded shotguns might not be such a good idea. Charles, his judgment clearly clouded by centuries of royal tradition and a lifetime of privilege, was oblivious when it came to his sons' safety—not to mention the obvious threat posed to their guests. It was not the kind of thing that would have slipped past Diana, the quintessential hands-on mom.

It seemed inevitable, then, that an Etonian standing a few yards behind William would accidentally fire his shotgun, sending a buckshot whizzing past the future monarch's ear. Royal bodyguards, who up until now kept whatever reservations they may have had to themselves, sprinted toward William and his horrified, gape-mouthed friend, pistols drawn. William explained that the other boy was inexperienced, and there was no harm done. No more than ten minutes passed before the hunt resumed as if nothing had happened.

In reality, the Heir had come heart-stoppingly close to losing his life in one senseless instant. If the worst had happened—and just one year after his mother's accidental death—it would have been hard to imagine the monarchy surviving such a blow. Amazingly, when he was informed of the incident that could have been prevented with a little commonsense parental vigilance, Charles merely shrugged it off. "No one was hurt?" he asked. "William is surrounded by people whose only job is to protect him. If there really was any danger, I'm sure they would have stepped in."

As far as the Prince of Wales was concerned, there were more important matters to attend to: for example, the six lavish parties that had been planned during the monthlong runup to his fiftieth birthday on November 14, 1998. The milestone weighed heavily on the Prince's mind—so much so that he began to openly complain at dinner parties and other private functions that his seventy-two-year-old mother was standing in his way. "We were all completely shocked," said the wife of one of Charles's teammates at the Beaufort Polo Club, "when the Prince of Wales slammed down his knife and fork on the table and said rather loudly, 'How long does she expect me to wait? Why doesn't she abdicate?'"

At another event, this one a reception attended by Lord Mishcon, Charles became "agitated in the extreme" discussing the Queen and her Buckingham Palace handlers—particularly her private secretary, Sir Robert Fellowes. "There is a time when you simply have to exit the stage," complained Charles, who felt his plans for the future were being thwarted by "Mummy's" intransigence. "That dreadful Fellowes and the rest of them keep telling the Queen she can stay there forever. I don't know why she doesn't just step aside and relax. She's worked hard enough. She's earned it. *I've* earned it."

Tensions between the two primary royal camps—all the Queen's men at Buckingham Palace and Charles's loyal staff at St. James's Palace—were clearly ramping up, with the Prince's team advocating a rebranding of the monarchy with its man in charge. "We believe," one aide told the *New*

York Times, "the Prince is the voice of what the monarchy is going to be in the twenty-first century."

TV producer Gavin Hewitt poured gasoline on the flames when he approached Charles about a BBC documentary for *Panorama* timed to coincide with this milestone fiftieth birthday. While the Prince of Wales did not appear in *Prince Charles at 50: A Life in Waiting*, he did agree to an in-depth off-camera interview and gave Hewitt unfettered access to friends and members of his staff. Although many of his comments would remain secret for years, the Prince complained to Hewitt that he felt "tortured" over his private life, claiming it was being "turned into an industry for others' profit."

When Hewitt asked about Camilla, Charles shot back, "I thought the British people were supposed to be compassionate. I don't see much of it." Besides, he added, "What makes people think they have the right to ask these questions? All my life, people have been telling me what to do. I'm tired of it. My private life has become an industry. People are making money out of it."

Charles continued to vent, ostensibly off the record, about other issues. Still irked by having to give up the royal yacht *Britannia* (which was costing nearly $20 million annually just to keep afloat), the Prince railed against the "false economies" wrought by "small-minded" Treasury officials who were "incapable of seeing past a balance sheet."

The most provocative comments leaking from St. James's Palace were aired in a separate documentary for London Weekend Television's *Charles at 50*. While the Prince himself was no longer reticent about what his life would be like "when I will be doing my mother's job," his aides boldly spoke of their boss "moving up to number one." One of Charles's men remarked tetchily, "The Queen quite likes being queen, and she doesn't give up much."

In fairness, the Queen had been increasingly willing to have Charles stand in for her at important events. For example, she dispatched him to represent the Crown at the handover of Hong Kong to China in June 1997 (when he complained bitterly about having to fly commercial) and to Northern Ireland in August 1998 after an IRA car bomb detonated in the sleepy town of Omagh, killing twenty-nine. But it was also clear that the heir to the throne and his St. James's Palace courtiers were becoming increasingly impatient.

Over the past year leading up to the half-century mark, the Prince of Wales had seen a stunning reversal of fortune. The most convulsive event of his life—the death of Diana—had freed him from having to compete with the most beloved being on the planet for the public's affection. No longer the most loathed member of the royal family, he was now seen not as a pompous philanderer and clueless twit but as a loving father and a world-class philanthropist whose Prince's Trust charities had made a huge impact on British society. After plummeting in the polls from 82 percent in 1991 to 41 percent in 1996, he had made a staggering comeback. As 1998 drew to a close, fully 63 percent of Britons felt Charles would make "a good king."

A key factor was undoubtedly the rise to power of Tony Blair and the Labour Party. For years, Charles was the only member of the royal family aside from Diana who advocated enlisting the private sector to open up opportunities for minorities, young people, and the unemployed, and who spoke out on issues such as health care, organic farming, and climate change. "Suddenly," Mark Bolland said, "his views became part of the political language of this country." As for Blair's policies, Prince's Trust chief Tom Shebbeare claimed that "a lot of what the government's doing, to our delight, they really filched from us."

Even more important was the charm offensive masterminded by Bolland. For the first time, Charles had in his corner someone who knew how to massage the press. "I think he was maligned and treated unfairly," Bolland explained, "and I hope in this job I can help him understand the modern media. I believe in the monarchy, and he's going to be it. He's only going to survive if he can take the proper path."

At Bolland's urging, Charles brought on board Brown Lloyd James, the London PR firm headed up by former Beatles personal assistant Peter Brown, ex–*Daily Express* editor Sir Nicholas Lloyd, and Howell James, who at one point ran the political office at 10 Downing Street. BLJ's other clients included Christie's, the BBC, designer Ralph Lauren, and composer Andrew Lloyd Webber. Not long after being hired, the Prince's new handlers persuaded him to actually chat with the reporters who covered him on a daily basis—and to whom he had not spoken a single unscripted, personal sentence in more than a decade. The ice was finally broken on a flight from South Africa to Swaziland, when the Prince stunned the press corps by strolling into the coach section of the plane and joking with reporters about, among other things, having to remain blasé while being greeted by those "energetic" bare-breasted natives at nearly every stop. "Chattering Charles Plays Royal Tour Joker," blared the front-page headline in that day's *London Evening Standard*.

The Prince had loosened up privately as well. One weekend, Bolland's home phone rang, and Charles, who seldom had the satisfaction of dialing a call himself, casually asked his PR man if he was doing "anything exciting."

"Actually, I was emptying the dishwasher," Bolland answered.

"Oh, yes," said the Prince. "And now I am supposed to say, 'What's that?'"

Not that he didn't still often revert to the old, morose, self-doubting, tantrum-tossing Prince of yore. At a Highgrove dinner party in the late fall of 1998, Charles asked Peter Mandelson what Tony Blair's cabinet thought of him, and once again Mandelson made the mistake of answering honestly. "They think you go about feeling sorry for yourself," he said, clearly wounding the Prince to the core. Moving to the front hall, a dejected Charles began asking his guests one by one if the cabinet members were right. "I don't think any of us can cope with you asking that question over and over again for the next month," Camilla said bluntly, fulfilling her get-a-grip role in the relationship. "Well, then," he replied forlornly, "how about for just the next twenty minutes?"

There were always those who were quick to defend Charles's cloying sense of self-doubt. "He's scarred by intense, brutal, unfair criticism," said Chris Patten, the last British governor of Hong Kong, "and he's had to endure more than almost any other human being." Yet even Charles's lifelong friend and mentor Dr. Eric Anderson acknowledged that the Prince's sensitivity was a "major weakness of his. It would no doubt be easier if you had the hide of an elephant to stand the slings and arrows that are hurled from the media, but he is actually quite thin-skinned and sensitive to what is said about him." Another woman in charge of a Prince's Trust charity got so fed up that she blurted out, "Oh, stop complaining. We all have problem parents." The Prince, she went on to say, "does moan about so."

This was not a problem shared by the most important person in his life. When Camilla's friend Linda Edwards asked her how she coped with all the "horrible stories about her," Camilla replied, "Well, I don't see a lot of it. But I was always brought up to get on with life and not sit in the corner and weep and wail."

When Charles was weeping and wailing these days, it was often about his mother's unwillingness to step aside—particularly in light of the fact that, during the crisis triggered by the Princess of Wales's death, the Queen had shown how out of touch she was with modern Britain. With the help of Tony Blair, Charles had virtually rescued the monarchy, and now he was more than ready to "move up." With the Prince's explicit approval, Bolland told the producers of *Charles at 50* that Charles would be "privately delighted if the Queen abdicated." So potentially incendiary was the comment that the show's producers checked and double-checked it for accuracy with St. James's Palace. Each time, Charles's most senior advisors stood by the quote.

It was not difficult to imagine what Charles III would be like. "When he moves up to number one," one staffer mused, "he obviously takes on responsibilities and sheds others. As King, he can't run around and lecture everybody. But then, knowing him, he probably will." *Charles at 50* gave viewers a peek at what changes the Prince already had in mind for the monarchy. For starters, he would move out of Buckingham Palace—which would be used as the monarchy's London headquarters but also opened up to tourists and used for ceremonial events. He would reside instead at Windsor Castle. St. James's Palace, Highgrove, and the immensely lucrative Duchy of Lancaster properties now owned by the Queen would go to the new Prince of Wales, William.

Strongly implying that only he had the vitality and the vision necessary to streamline the monarchy, Charles wanted to toss out the Civil List—the allowance voted on by Parliament to fund the Queen and her family—for a self-sustaining Sovereign Grant that would end the unseemly ritual of having to go crown-in-hand to the House of Commons every year. Unfortunately, that would require returning to the monarchy the Crown Estate, which George III had signed over to the government in 1760. (In 1998 the Crown Estate, which included all of London's Regent Street and half of St. James's in West London, among other things, was generating an annual income of about $200 million. By 2022, its holdings would be valued at around $20 billion.) Charles's plan involved taking a flat 15 percent of the total net revenues to fund the monarchy, removing the necessity to debate the sum in Parliament each year. In addition, the Prince wanted to pare down the royal family itself by kicking his brothers Andrew and Edward off the payroll, while promoting his sister Anne to a place of prominence as his "royal partner."

"Mention the top job, and the Prince's staff talk in the future, not the conditional tense, about when, not if," said the *New York Times*'s Warren Hoge. "They are confident to the point of arrogance that their once-belittled man can bring stature to the post." One told Hoge that it "will be nice" to have a monarch "who's thoughtful. We haven't had one for a while."

Prince Charles was on a tour of the Balkans when *Charles at 50* aired, sparking a media frenzy. Within minutes, he phoned his mother to deny that he had ever said or thought such a thing and how "distressed" he was by the mere mention of the word *abdicate*. The whole idea was "ludicrous," he said in a statement that also praised the "duty and loyalty" of the Queen as "an example to us all."

Charles's apology fell on deaf ears. Her Majesty was furious. "She had heard the rumors about what Prince Charles was saying behind her back, and that was hurtful enough," a former private secretary said. "But when he allowed Bolland to go public, that was firing a shot across her bow." It also "made Her Majesty just dig in that much more." The Queen Mother never forgave the Duke and Duchess of Windsor for pitching her frail husband onto the throne, and at age ninety-eight, she was more adamant than ever that Camilla was as toxic an influence on Charles as Wallis Simpson had been on Edward VIII.

The Queen shared her mother's view. Further complicating matters was the Queen's own firmly held belief—at least for the time being—that she had made a solemn pact with God to reign as long as she was physically and mentally capable. As the head of the Church of England, she viewed the vows she made during her coronation service as so sacred that for years she battled efforts to release film of the moment when she was anointed queen. "Throughout her reign," Gavin Hewitt said, the Queen "has been determined to . . . protect her legacy by passing on the monarchy in good health. Her son's undefined private life is seen as threatening what she has worked so hard to preserve. The Queen is not only against their ever marrying but believes the public would never accept a Queen Camilla or Charles as king with Camilla by his side."

Having seriously overplayed his hand by publicly challenging the Queen at what he wrongly perceived to be her weakest moment, Charles retreated. Continuing the Prince's ongoing campaign to rebrand himself as what Bolland called "a good bloke," the ITV network broadcast a celebrity-packed, two-hour birthday gala. At one point during the program, "Ginger Spice" Geri Halliwell did her best Marilyn Monroe impression while singing a sexy version of "Happy Birthday" to the future king ("Happy *birthday*, Your Royal *Highness*").

On November 12 there was another party, this time at Hampton Court Palace, with Camilla making a furtive appearance but still cautiously staying out of camera range. Charles's handlers prodded him to show up the next day in Sheffield, where he joined with one of the stars of *The Full Monty*—the hit British film about six unemployed steelworkers who become male strippers—to bump and grind to Donna Summer's "Hot Stuff" in an unemployment line. The Prince was clearly uncomfortable, but once the brief gag was over with, the understanding crowd clapped sympathetically.

On Charles's actual fiftieth birthday, Saturday, November 14, the Queen hosted a party for 850 at Buckingham Palace. Not surprisingly, Camilla was not invited. The guest of honor and his staff had been informed that Her Majesty was still fuming over all the abdication chatter emanating from St. James's Palace. If she was still angry, the sovereign was shrewd enough not to let on. In a rare but still tepid display of public affection, the Queen began her brief remarks by calling her son Charles, and he returned the favor by addressing her as Mummy.

Charles's Highgrove bash, planned with military precision by Camilla, was another benchmark in their relationship. By way of acknowledging his passion for organic growing, Camilla used wildflowers, branches, leaves, vines, and tree stumps from the newly finished Orchard Room to re-create his walled garden indoors. This time Camilla made it clear she was no longer willing to "skulk about." She instructed her driver to slow down for photographers as her limousine pulled up to the estate, then emerged wearing a décolletage-bearing emerald-green velvet gown and a spectacular diamond, turquoise, and sapphire necklace.

Most of the 340 guests had already arrived when William, fresh from cadet field exercises at Eton, burst in wearing combat gear. He bounded upstairs and was back within minutes wearing a tuxedo. At the dinner, William raised a glass of pink champagne to toast the birthday boy. Later, he and Harry—the evening's self-appointed DJs—huddled with Camilla over a daunting stack of CDs before she picked out a disco tune that she remembered was a hit around the time when she and Charles rekindled their affair: the Village People's "YMCA."

With Camilla's children, Tom and Laura, standing next to them, the young princes looked on in mock horror as Charles and Camilla took to the dance floor and rocked out to music by the Bee Gees, ABBA, Queen, Chic, and Gloria Gaynor. Once the clock struck three, William and Harry, also fans of *The Full Monty*, put on Hot Chocolate's "You Sexy Thing," whipped off their shirts, and began unbuttoning their pants while the remaining guests roared with laughter. The routine would become the boys' signature "party piece" whenever they got together with friends.

Notably absent were the Queen, Prince Philip, Charles's siblings, and the Queen Mother—all continuing to show solidarity with the monarch over her refusal to meet or even be seen with Camilla. Princess Margaret, still more willing than not to disobey her sister, was on hand. So were Stephen Fry and Rowan Atkinson, to perform in the requisite cringe-inducing skits, and Geri Halliwell read a poem she had written specially for the occasion. "Charming Prince, you're in your prime," she said before delivering the most jarring note of the night: "That chair is yours, it's almost time." Charles winced noticeably but recovered quickly.

Perhaps most important for Charles's infamous mistress, many of the crowned heads of Europe—both incumbent and exiled—showed up, including royals from Spain, Denmark, Greece, the Netherlands, Belgium, Luxembourg, Bulgaria, and even several Arab countries. For the first time, Camilla was receiving them as hostess—a major step up in terms of protocol, and clear evidence that she was capable of assuming royal duties in the future.

Ten weeks later, Charles and Camilla marked another milestone, and Mark Bolland made certain there would be hundreds of journalists there to cover it by tipping them off three days in advance. On January 28, 1999, the Prince and his mistress stood together for twenty seconds on the steps of London's Ritz Hotel, where they'd come to join in celebrating the fiftieth birthday of Camilla's sister Annabel Eliot. The timing and the location for this event—their first official public appearance as a couple—was no accident. Of all the parties, events, and galas Camilla could have chosen to make this particular statement, this marked exactly ten years since the Princess of Wales had cornered Camilla and scolded her at Annabel's fortieth birthday party.

This time, at Bolland's insistence, Camilla toned down her wardrobe for the masses. Instead of a ball gown with a plummeting neckline and jewels worthy of an empress, she wore a conservative black cocktail dress and a pearl choker. None of which mattered to those Diana loyalists who recognized the significance of the date. One noted that "people often say Camilla is such a sweet and uncomplicated woman. But all you have to do is look at how she plots, schemes—the deception."

In a matter of weeks, and with the help of precisely timed leaks from St. James's Palace, paparazzi shot Charles and Camilla hunting in East York-shire, and at the Royal Shakespeare Theatre in Stratford-upon-Avon. With Bolland continuing to pull the strings, Operation PB scored another tri-umph in May, when Camilla returned to the London Ritz—this time to host a banquet for the National Osteoporosis Society. Confident in her new role as Charles's official companion, she wore a diamond brooch bearing the distinctive ostrich-plumed emblem of the Prince of Wales. Later, she was Charles's guest at a glittering Buckingham Palace dinner for wealthy Americans who contributed millions to his Prince of Wales's Charitable Foundation. It was another first for Camilla, made all the more intriguing by her dramatic entrance into the White Drawing Room alongside Charles through a secret door hidden behind a massive cabinet and a thirty-foot-high gilt-framed mirror. The door, through which the Queen usually en-tered, connected the staterooms to the royal family's private living quarters.

Operation PB was dealt another setback that same month, however. At a time when Camilla could not afford to be portrayed in anything but the most favorable light, her son Tom admitted to snorting cocaine at the Cannes Film Festival. Coming four years after his 1995 arrest for possess-ing marijuana and the drug Ecstasy, the cocaine headlines uncorked a flood of unseemly revelations about Camilla's only son—most memorably the time he attended a "Fetish Party" done up like a dominatrix in fishnet stockings and stiletto heels.

Never particularly involved in raising her children—that was left to their nannies, governesses, and boarding school teachers—Camilla held back. Instead, in his role as godfather, Charles was enlisted to give the young man a stern lecture. "Your mother is very upset," the Prince told him. "For God's sake, think of what all this is doing to her." He also warned Tom to keep his distance from his newfound buddies William and Harry until he got his cocaine problem in check.

The Parker Bowles family name would wind up in the headlines again when Emma Parker Bowles, Camilla's niece and William's first serious crush, was also treated for alcohol and cocaine abuse. When a tabloid discovered that she had spent a month drying out in an Arizona clinic, Emma described the whole affair as "very upsetting." In fairness, around the same time a number of people in William's inner circle were battling substance abuse: His cousin Nicholas Knatchbull, Lord Mountbatten's great-grandson and the Heir's closest chum at Eton, would end up going into rehab twice in two years. Tara Palmer-Tomkinson, the daughter of Charles's longtime skiing pal Charlie Palmer-Tomkinson and his wife Patti, was also being treated for cocaine abuse that year. Even a particular favorite of the Queen, the boys' cousin Lord Frederick ("Freddie") Windsor, was sucked into drug dependence. "It's very difficult," he warned Charles's sons, "to avoid getting into this sort of thing when you move in these circles."

Of course, the difference between Tara Palmer-Tomkinson, Nicholas Knatchbull, and Freddie Windsor was that they were not Camilla's children. Months later, when Camilla's longtime friend Emilie van Cutsem confided to Charles over dinner that she had heard Tom had relapsed, Camilla retaliated by spreading false gossip about the Van Cutsem boys. "Even with people she's known for years," an American acquaintance said, "Camilla is ruthless if there is any hint of betrayal. She is highly suspicious of women, and if she feels threatened by you in any way, you're dead."

The Tom Parker Bowles drug and fetish party scandal was a major setback for Charles and Camilla, who had been making great strides toward public acceptance as a couple. Now the Queen, who showed no signs of softening her stance on Camilla, warned Charles that the young princes should not consort with his mistress's wayward son. "Once it looked as if Prince William and Prince Harry were being dragged down by the Parker Bowleses as well," a courtier remarked, the Queen "became very cross." In an unusual display of unity on the Parker Bowles issue, Buckingham Palace and Charles's advisors agreed that Tom should not be seen in public with either

William or Harry. Camilla, too, was asked to stay out of the public eye until the scandals had died down.

The Prince of Wales's protests fell on deaf ears when the Queen banned Camilla from attending the June 19, 1999, St. George's Chapel wedding of Charles's brother Prince Edward and Sophie Rhys-Jones, who bore more than a passing resemblance to the late Princess of Wales. Charles, who had already agreed to share best man duties with his brother Andrew, showed up as planned at the ceremony and the somewhat toned-down reception for six hundred, but he made no secret of his displeasure over Camilla's forced absence. Was this a sign that there had been a major setback in Charles's campaign to win the Crown's approval of Camilla? "The Queen," replied a Palace spokesman, "made it clear that any rapprochement is out of the question."

Charles, whose mantra now was "I am so sick and tired of people telling me what to do," was less than compliant with his mother's wishes. Camilla joined him and the boys aboard the *Alexander* when they embarked in July on a ten-day cruise of the Aegean. What's more, Charles disregarded the damaging news about Tom Parker Bowles's drug use and invited him along, as well as his sister Laura.

The Prince of Wales and his mistress were once again accused of showing a callous disregard for Diana's memory. It had been only eight years since, on the occasion of their tenth anniversary, the Prince and Princess of Wales made one final attempt at saving their marriage by taking a "second honeymoon" aboard the *Alexander.* "Each of these places represented something in the rivalry between Diana and Camilla," a friend of the Princess observed. "Camilla was simply going back to each spot to make it clear that she had won. It made a lot of people angry."

Despite it all, Charles was convinced that Camilla could be a valuable asset to the royal family as a goodwill ambassador abroad, and to prove it he sent her off on a solo trip to New York. It was a daring move. As popular as the late Princess of Wales remained in England, she was idolized in the United States—often referred to by the Prince and his wary spinmeisters as "Diana territory."

With Mark Bolland at her side, Camilla boarded a Concorde on September 19, 1999. After a brief stay at the East Hampton mansion of Scott Bessent, the up-and-coming, openly gay protégé of billionaire investment titan George Soros and a major contributor to Charles's charities, Camilla helicoptered into Manhattan in the middle of a storm—"Darling it was *terrifying*, I thought I was going to die," she later told Charles—and checked in to a $1,100 suite in Diana's favorite hotel, the Carlyle on Madison Avenue.

Never straying far from Bolland, Camilla made a quick visit to the New York Academy of Art and caught a performance of *Cabaret*. The highlight of the trip was a lunch cohosted by ninety-seven-year-old Park Avenue society grande dame Brooke Astor and television news legend Barbara Walters. Among the guests were Henry Kissinger, UN Secretary General Kofi Annan, media mogul Mort Zuckerman, billionaire (and future New York City mayor) Michael Bloomberg, designer Oscar de la Renta, *Vogue* magazine editor Anna Wintour, and actor Michael Douglas and his actress wife, Catherine Zeta-Jones.

As a young woman, Astor had actually met Alice Keppel, and Camilla was eager to learn what she could about her great-grandmother. Unfortunately by the time Astor encountered Keppel in the 1930s, Edward VII had been dead more than twenty years, and the King's ex-mistress was considered a social pariah—cast out by the upper classes who regarded her as wanton and predatory, and not just because of her affair with Edward. It seemed that while she was married to the long-suffering George Keppel, Camilla's great-grandmother bore two children out of wedlock by two different lovers: Sonia, who was widely assumed to be King Edward's child, and Violet, whose father was Lord Grimthorpe, the designer of Big Ben. If Sonia was indeed Edward VII's daughter, this made Camilla and Charles second cousins.

Brooke Astor also refrained from telling her guest that Mrs. Keppel was no great beauty, or from mentioning that Camilla's great-grandmother met "a very sad end" living out her final years in a room at the Ritz Hotel in an alcoholic haze and dying of cirrhosis in 1947. Mrs. Astor did, however, cause something of a scene by loudly congratulating Camilla on following in Alice Keppel's footsteps. Camilla's great-grandmother "would have been so proud of you," Astor told her wide-eyed guest. "You're keeping this mistress business in the family! Two generations providing mistresses!" Another guest, Carnegie Foundation president Vartan Gregorian, recalled that Camilla was "gracious" and "laughed at the 'mistress business' remark." But, he added, "It was an extraordinarily awkward moment."

Camilla took some solace in the fact that Mrs. Astor, who may have been suffering from dementia, was equally blunt with other guests. When Zeta-Jones passed by, Astor pointed at her and asked Gregorian, "Who is that woman?" When he responded that Zeta-Jones was a "great actress," Astor replied loudly, "Well, she's wearing the wrong dress for this occasion!" According to Gregorian, Zeta-Jones, who was standing directly in front of Astor, "pretended not to hear."

By the end of the luncheon, it was clear that New York's draconian antismoking rules, which made it almost impossible for Camilla to smoke anywhere, were taking their toll. Camilla "nearly had a nicotine fit," said one guest, who noticed that "the first thing she did when she got outside was light up and take a long drag on her cigarette."

More anxiety-provoking was another celebrity-sprinkled reception that came to an abrupt end when someone phoned in a credible bomb threat. The moment the bomb squad arrived, Camilla slipped out a side door, lit up again, and cracked, "Well, *that* was fun!"

Her smoking habit aside, Mrs. Parker Bowles had clearly charmed her American hosts. The media coverage was almost universally positive, and Charles was careful to make sure that the Queen's new private secretary, Robin Janvrin, delivered copies of the laudatory articles straight to her desk—"so that she can read them before she starts working on the boxes."

Back on home turf, Camilla was quickly trotted out by Bolland for another high-profile fund-raiser—this time a black-tie dinner for the Prince of Wales's Charitable Foundation at Edinburgh's sixteenth-century Holyrood Palace, the official residence of the monarch in Scotland and once the home of the ill-fated Mary, Queen of Scots.

Once again Mrs. PB charmed the rich Americans on the guest list with her approachability and earthy good humor. "She's just one of those people who gets the off-color jokes and loves to laugh," her pal Joan Rivers said. "Camilla doesn't take herself seriously, and she'll shoot Prince Charles down when maybe he's getting a little pompous. But don't be fooled, she's a very smart woman and very aware that she has to be careful. Camilla always knows what she's doing because if she does the wrong thing, it can hurt Charles—and she obviously loves him completely."

Now that Camilla had stayed overnight in all the royal residences—Buckingham Palace, Windsor Castle, Sandringham, Balmoral, and Holyrood—while the Queen was not present, Mrs. PB began to feel more like one of the family. That did not extend to interfering in the lives of the young princes—with one unfortunate exception. In mid-1999 Camilla urged William to go public with his passion for the controversial blood sport of foxhunting, something that up until that point he had wisely kept under wraps. "Camilla was passionate about the hunt," said a fellow member of the Beaufort Hunt Club, "and she actually thought William would improve the sport's image if people saw him doing it. Obviously, she was very wrong."

Obviously. William had been hunting on royal estates for years. But when newspapers ran photos of the tweed-jacketed heir on horseback with two hundred members of the Beaufort Hunt, animal rights activists were aghast. Although people such as Camilla and the Windsors saw it as a sacred British tradition, surveys indicated that most UK citizens viewed foxhunting as indefensibly cruel. The *Express* scolded William for his "upper-class arrogance" and accused him of showing a "blatant disregard" for public opinion. "Shame-Faced" proclaimed the front-page headline in the *Mirror*, which now described William as "haughty and provocative." William was even denounced on the floor of Parliament. MP Mike Foster blasted the young Prince as "arrogant and insensitive" for making the decision "to so publicly endorse hunting."

Charles was appalled—and defiant. "These people have never done it. I mean, they can't even afford to do it, and therefore have no idea what they are talking about," he complained to another member of the Beaufort Hunt Club. "Imagine trying to tell us what we can or cannot do? The impertinence!"

For his part, William brushed aside his critics just as he dismissed his father's request that he refrain from partying at the high-profile London clubs he now frequented—establishments such as Crazy Larry's, K-Bar, and Chinawhite. Unlike some of his aristocratic pals, William never strayed from the straight and narrow when it came to drugs. Underage drinking was something else again. The Rattlebone Inn, a four-hundred-year-old pub just four miles up the road from Highgrove, was a particular favorite of William's—and would later be the spot where Harry got into serious trouble. More than once, the young princes ducked into an alleyway behind the pub and hid while local police raided the place in search of illegal underage or after-hours drinkers. Had they been caught, it was unlikely the boys would have been arrested; their royal protection officers, who had been instructed to blend into the crowd but always be close at hand, would have intervened.

Charles watched with some amusement as William coped with his new sex symbol status. In addition to the usual bevy of highborn beauties who flitted on the periphery of the royal family—saucer-eyed blondes and leggy brunettes with names like Emilia d'Erlanger and Davina Duckworth-Chad—at least two Americans had caught the Heir's eye. That summer and into the fall of 1999, William exchanged torrid e-mails with model Lauren Bush, granddaughter of former US President George H. W. Bush and niece of future President George W. Bush.

Not long after, a bona fide American pop icon launched her own cyber assault on the Prince's heart. When singer Britney Spears learned that William had taped a poster of her on his wall at Eton, the two began a correspondence that one of his more discreet pals characterized as "naughty." William invited Spears to be his official date at the millennium party he was planning to usher in the twenty-first century—an extravaganza he liked to call the Willenium—but her concert schedule made that impossible. Instead, they agreed to rendezvous in London on the first

Valentine's Day of the new millennium. Charles could feel his son's frustration when those plans were also leaked to the press, and St. James's Palace was forced to issue a denial that spoke of the "nonsense put out by public relations firms" while still failing to deny the torrid notes he and Britney lobbed back and forth over the internet.

—————

As the year 2000 approached, Charles offered Highgrove as the location for William's much-ballyhooed bash. "William won't want to see the place destroyed," Papa reasoned. "He loves the place almost as much as I do. At least this way the mayhem will be contained." But William was fed up with leaks that caused him to change his plans or abort them altogether. He decided instead to forgo a major public event and get "very seriously, seriously drunk" with friends at a cramped, decaying village hall near Sandringham. Two days later on a flight to Wales, he told a British Airways flight attendant that he was still suffering from a hangover.

Charles took the dawn of the new millennium more seriously. "It was bittersweet for him, I think," mused *Times* royal correspondent Alan Hamilton. "Prince Charles grew up thinking that, of course, by now he'd be king—that he'd be the monarch who bridged the twentieth and twenty-first centuries. These milestones mean something to him. He is a man who is intensely aware of history and his place in it."

That was almost painfully evident in Charles's five-minute-long "Thought for the Day," recorded at Highgrove and broadcast by BBC Radio 4 on January 1, 2000. In a speech that resonated as a defense of religion, Charles managed to invoke Plato, Rilke, Einstein, Dante, and "Our Lord Jesus Christ" while attacking genetic engineering, a pernicious lack of spiritualism, and the effrontery of anticreationists. "After all," Charles noted, "the likelihood of life beginning by chance is about as great as a hurricane blowing through a scrapyard and assembling a Rolls-Royce."

Buried in the heavily Christian text were references that gave some small insight into the kind of monarch that Charles—the first English king of the third millennium—might turn out to be. "Of course, there is all the difference in the world between renewing what is old and replacing old with new," he mused, suggesting that he intended to do the latter. "The millennium provides us with an opportunity to abandon the poles of blind optimism on one hand and total despair on the other, and to rediscover a much older emotion: hope."

Where was Charles the moment the twentieth century became history? With Camilla at Highgrove, ushering in the new millennium with a few close friends. Eventually the Prince of Wales and his longtime love ended up alone in the garden, holding hands. "After all we had been through," she said, "we want to be alone together. There was no one else who could possibly have understood the feelings we had that night."

I promise you there is no intention, no plan, no plot, no conspiracy.
—Charles's aide, denying plans to make Camilla
acceptable to the public as the next Queen

*Tempting fate is not Camilla's style, but she did see it as a sign
that her days as a demon figure were coming to an end.*
—Mark Bolland, on polls showing a slight
improvement in her approval rating

The bag can now come off my head.
—Camilla

EIGHT

"OUR MANIFOLD SINS AND WICKEDNESS"

I t's all up to the Queen now, isn't it?" Charles asked Mark Bolland matter-of-factly. "How long can she keep up this abominable nonsense?" In May 2000 the Prince of Wales made a strategic decision to face religious objections to his union with the notorious Mrs. PB head-on. He essentially brought her as his date to the weeklong General Assembly of the Church of Scotland at Holyrood Palace. In addition to being the future head of the Church of England, Charles took his place at the General Assembly as Lord High Commissioner—substituting for the Crown—with Camilla literally at his side. He walked away fully confident that, at least in terms of the Scottish church, there would be no objection to the divorced Prince marrying his divorced mistress—at least not on religious grounds.

Two weeks later, Charles and Camilla got the major breakthrough they had been praying for and working toward. At a Highgrove barbecue ostensibly held to celebrate the sixtieth birthday of Charles's friend King Constantine II, who ruled from 1964 until Greece abolished its monarchy in 1973, Camilla entered the room and was startled when the Queen walked directly over to her. Mrs. Parker Bowles performed a deep, formal curtsy, and the Queen reacted with a smile. The two women chatted amiably for ten minutes before the Queen used her usual signal that she was done—switching her handbag from one hand to the other—and moved on to the next guest.

During the 1970s, the Queen and Camilla had encountered one another in passing, but this was their first known meeting in more than twenty years. Less than a month later, Camilla wore a pink Versace gown to attend the Prince of Wales's Charitable Foundation dinner at the foundation's headquarters in a renovated warehouse in London's trendy Shoreditch neighborhood. Expecting to pose for photographers as they had outside the Ritz Hotel, Charles and Camilla, startled by antimonarchist demonstrators across the street, quickly ducked inside. Among the guests at the gala: actress Lauren Bacall, Sir Richard Branson, Donatella Versace, model Elle Macpherson, and Joan Rivers. Looking over the warehouse setting and the industrial décor—barbed-wire place settings, black rubber tablecloths—Bacall sighed. "This looks more like Detroit than London," she cracked to another American at the dinner. "Looks like the monarchy has fallen on hard times."

For Charles and Camilla, there was another choreographed breakthrough moment the following week. Once again Mrs. Parker Bowles was hosting another fund-raising affair for the National Osteoporosis Society, this time at London's Somerset House to celebrate the organization's fifteenth anniversary. She and Lord Rothschild were standing in a receiving line when Charles emerged from his limousine with Queen Rania of Jordan. "Hello, you," the Prince said as he approached Camilla, bussing her briskly on each cheek. It was the couple's first kiss in public—fleeting, blink-and-you-missed-it, but their first public kiss nonetheless.

It did not go unnoticed that Camilla was wearing a magnificent $200,000 diamond necklace that had once belonged to the Princess of Wales. "It's simply heartbreaking to see someone else wearing Diana's things," said her friend Vivienne Parry. The gesture of wearing something as conspicuous as the necklace—particularly on what was only their third public appearance together—signaled Charles's intention to "move things along."

While Charles and Camilla flitted from one glittering event to the next, there was still a steep hill to climb if they were ever to reach full acceptance by the Queen. Her Royal Highness took advantage of William's eighteenth birthday on June 21, 2000, to throw a party for seven hundred guests at Windsor Castle—not only for her favorite grandson but also for the other milestone birthdays that year: Prince Andrew's fortieth, Princess Anne's fiftieth, Princess Margaret's seventieth, and—most significantly—the Queen Mother's centennial.

Ironically, the birthday boy himself opted out, claiming he was cramming for his final exams. Instead, William remained just minutes away, holed up in his rooms at Eton. But all the other royals celebrating birthdays were at the party, as were Charles, Harry, Prince Andrew's ex-wife, the Duchess of York (it was her first appearance with the royals since Diana's death), and even Andrew Parker Bowles.

Camilla, however, was intentionally left off the guest list. She was also excluded from the Queen Mother's official one hundredth birthday pageant in July, when Charles sat next to his beloved Granny as she rode in an open carriage on the Horse Guards Parade, the large parade ground off Whitehall in central London. The day's festivities included full-dress parades (the Queen Mother was used to reviewing troops, having done it since 1927), Royal Air Force flyovers, and the requisite appearance by the entire royal family on the Buckingham Palace balcony—the kind of historic day that Charles hoped Camilla would be permitted to join someday. But not today, and certainly not if the Queen Mother had anything to say about it. "Prince Charles was so torn between those two women he loved so much," Margaret Rhodes said. "But the Queen Mother was not going to budge."

While Charles was busy with his relatives, Camilla focused on other things: namely, ridding herself once and for all of any competitors for her Prince's affections. Camilla, like Diana, had long resented the bond that existed between Tiggy Legge-Bourke and Charles—not to mention the big-sister role she played in the lives of his sons. In October 1999 Legge-Bourke married Charles Pettifer, a divorced father of two and a former army officer. (Harry made quite an impression at the wedding when, on a dare, he grabbed a goldfish out of a bowl and swallowed it.) Charles, well aware of Camilla's grudge against Tiggy, declined to attend. From this point on, Tiggy was no longer around to talk William out of his dark moods or console a still-fragile Harry. But she hadn't exited their lives completely. Tiggy and the young princes talked on the phone "constantly," she said, "the way people who care deeply for each other do."

With their former nanny now concentrating on her own family—two years later, Harry would become godfather to her son Freddie—Camilla turned her attention to Charles's secretary, Sarah Goodall. Just twenty-four years old when she was hired in 1988 to handle the Prince's correspondence, Goodall was a fixture at St. James's Palace and Highgrove, and was often at Charles's elbow when he traveled abroad. Just eight months after Diana's death, Goodall was one of only five people invited to accompany Charles when he and Camilla vacationed at Birkhall. The Prince's mistress was "not happy to see Sarah there," a Balmoral staffer said. "Mrs. Parker Bowles had these stolen moments with Prince Charles, and she wasn't eager to share them with anyone."

Throughout their stay at Birkhall, Charles and his secretary engaged in the same sort of lighthearted banter that characterized their relationship in the office. Following her usual modus operandi, Camilla sidled up to Sarah at dinner and befriended her with talk of horses, charity work, and even their mothers' health problems. Then Camilla, complaining to Charles and to Goodall's boss Mark Bolland that his longtime secretary was "entirely too forward" with the Prince, launched a concerted campaign to neutralize her.

"Camilla made it clear she did not want me working there," said Goodall, who after more than ten years on the job felt herself being "ganged up on for no reason." The situation deteriorated until one day she turned up at her St. James's Palace office and was told she had been sacked. Given only a few minutes to clean out her desk and surrender her security pass, she was then escorted out by grim-faced Palace guards. "Charles is not strong enough to say 'no' to Camilla," Goodall said. "Or to have said, 'I like her, I'm keeping her.'" Bolland would later agree with Goodall's assessment. "Prince Charles is very, very weak," he stated. And Camilla? "She isn't."

As the Windsors faced the third anniversary of Diana's death, Charles took solace in the fact that his sons appeared, on the surface, at least, to be flourishing. This was due, Papa firmly believed, to the fact that the press had largely adhered to its self-imposed ban on covering Diana's sons. Now that William had turned eighteen, that gentlemen's agreement was about to expire. In an attempt to get Fleet Street to continue its hands-off policy—at least until they had made it through college—Buckingham Palace released a series of photographs and a video showing William strolling through Eton's cloisters, cooking paella, and competing at water polo and soccer. Having never actually sat down for an interview before, the young Prince grudgingly agreed to answer questions submitted in writing by Peter Archer, the British Press Association's esteemed royal correspondent. The bombshell revelations included the fact that his dog Widgeon had given birth to eight puppies, that he still liked pop and dance music, and that he, like most of his fellow Etonians, would take a traditional "gap year" of self-exploration before starting college.

Determined to test his stamina both physically and mentally, William secretly flew to the tiny Central American nation of Belize to train with a unit of the Welsh Guards. He was in the jungle and out of phone contact when his father e-mailed him his final exam grades using an army link: a C in biology, a B in art history, and an A in geography. This overall B average nevertheless placed William in the top 7 percent of all British students.

Charles watched with pride as his elder son promptly plunged headlong into another adventure: a three-week stint scuba diving on Rodrigues Island in the Indian Ocean. His companion on the trip was Mark "Marko" Dyer, a tall, redheaded former Welsh Guards officer handpicked by Charles to be his sons' main minder. Dyer, who fished, motorbiked, and swam with his young charges on the Rodrigues Island expedition, picked up where Tiggy left off.

"Charles is very busy, as I'm sure you've noticed, and he can't be there all the time," Camilla once explained to Joan Rivers. "They really need a male figure in their day-to-day lives aside from their bodyguards, and that's what Mark does." Both Camilla and Charles objected to press reports calling Dyer, who at thirty-four was twenty years younger than the Prince of Wales, a "second father" to William and Harry. "He's more of a big brother," Camilla said, "and he does it brilliantly."

By way of equal time, Dyer was also on hand when Harry celebrated his sixteenth birthday by visiting the historic Ifield Tavern in Chelsea, a pub frequented by such notables as Madonna and Brad Pitt. "It was lovely," Prince Harry told the pub's owner, Ed Baines. "I'll tell my grand-mother to pop in next time she's in the area!"

However charming and carefree both young men may have seemed to the outside world, their mother was never far from the Princes' minds. When one of Diana's most trusted aides published a damning tell-all about her, William did not hesitate to rise to her defense. Charles stood by his son—literally—when, on September 29, 2000, he stepped before televi-sion cameras to denounce *Shadows of a Princess* by Diana's former private secretary Patrick Jephson. Prince William told reporters that both he and Harry were "quite upset about it" and that his mother's "trust had been be-trayed. Even now she is being exploited."

William, whose beige Burberry crewneck sweater and jeans contrasted with Charles's bespoke double-breasted suit, thanked the press for its re-straint in covering him and his brother, and went on to describe plans for his gap year. The Heir would soon be off to the region of Patagonia in Chile, where he would join 110 volunteers to chop wood, repair homes and public buildings, paint houses, and tutor local children. During the press conference, the public got a glimpse of the easy rapport between fa-ther and son. When reporters asked if Prince Charles had "chipped in" to pay for the trip, William said with a smile, "He might have helped slightly." Once the laughter died down, Charles interjected, "I chip in all the bloody time!"

It hadn't really dawned on Charles—or any other members of the royal family, for that matter—that this was the first time anyone outside their circle had ever heard William's voice. The press embargo had worked so well that his clipped, upper-class speech pattern—reminiscent of Charles's but with a dash of actor Hugh Grant—came as a welcome surprise. Already the tallest member of the royal family at six foot two, William was more than merely physically impressive; he exhibited a degree of poise and confidence that his father had still yet to achieve.

The Queen, who had watched the entire press conference live on television, "was very pleased indeed with her grandson's performance," said a Palace spokesman. According to Charles's spokeswoman, Colleen Harris, holding the press conference was "absolutely Prince William's decision—and those were his words."

For Charles and Camilla, the stir created by *Shadows of a Princess* was strictly win-win. He was genuinely proud of how William comported himself with the dignified self-assurance befitting a future king. The Prince of Wales was also delighted to see any member of his late wife's senior staff savaged—particularly by his own son. But most important, Jephson's book depicted Diana as unbalanced, scheming, spiteful, spoiled, and at times downright malicious—someone who combined "a radiant smile with a knife between the shoulder blades."

For the first time, the public was getting a glimpse of the darker side of the complicated Princess—the neurotic, self-destructive, and occasionally manipulative side—and not from an enemy but from one of her closest confidants. "I wondered how long it was going to take," Charles told one of his senior aides, "for *someone* to tell the truth about her."

As far as the public was concerned, Charles was being increasingly perceived as a loving father to two of the world's most cherished young men—both of whom had distinctly different personalities. William, described by his friends as deliberate, thoughtful, stubborn, and at times moody and withdrawn, had "very definite ideas about things," Peter Archer noted. This was "something he got from both his mother and his father. No one is going to make William do something that he doesn't want to do." Charles's younger son seemed less introspective and deliberative—the sort of person "who does what is asked of him without reservation or complaint," Archer said. Harry was "less inquisitive than his brother and more eager to please." But appearances were deceiving. Years later, Harry would confide to a friend that, three years after his mother's death, he was "completely lost, crying myself to sleep, but hiding it all very well."

Camilla was not hiding much at all when, on vacation with Charles in the South of France, she peeled down the top of her bathing suit so he could slather her with sunscreen. Fleet Street, still currying favor with the Prince in an attempt to gain more access to William and Harry, declined to publish the topless shots. However, European tabloids showed no such restraint—much to the Queen's consternation.

Her Majesty still viewed the relationship between her eldest son and his resilient mistress as fundamentally immoral, and she was not alone. For years, whenever Charles made an official visit to Wales, he stayed at historic Powis Castle. That came to an abrupt halt when the castle's owner, the Earl of Powis, learned that the Prince and Camilla had used it as a secret trysting spot. From now on, the Earl informed St. James's Palace, Powis Castle was off-limits to the Prince of Wales and his mistress. "You don't sleep in the same bed if you are not married," he said. "That applies to everyone."

While Harry remained with his nose in his books at Eton, William was enlisted to pave the way for Camilla's ultimate acceptance by the public—and to nudge the Queen one step closer to at least meeting with his father's mistress. On February 7, 2001, William made his first official public appearance at a gala celebrating the tenth anniversary of Britain's Press Complaints Commission—all by way of thanking the press for keeping its distance. The gathering of more than 550 guests, most of them journalists who were instructed that the event was to be strictly off the record, would also be the unlikely setting for the first joint appearance of Camilla, Charles, and William.

Complicating matters was the fact that the Queen had made it clear that Camilla was not to be seen publicly with either of her grandsons. To accomplish this, Charles and William arrived at Somerset House in central

London but split up as soon as they were inside. Fifteen minutes later, Camilla entered at the opposite end of the reception room, working the crowd without ever coming near the Princes. After an hour and a half spent nibbling on canapés and sipping Chablis, Charles and William made their exit. Once she was told the Princes had left, Camilla waited another half hour before finally departing alone.

Although Camilla was never seen with Charles or William, it was widely reported the next day that all three were at the high-profile event. "It was definitely a victory for Camilla," journalist Richard Kay said. "It left one with the general impression that she was being accepted into the family." The Queen, outraged that William would be dragged into the Mrs. Parker Bowles matter, reacted with a sharp rebuke. "Inform St. James's Palace," she told her private secretary, "that Mrs. Parker Bowles is not to be seen with either Prince William or Prince Harry. It's bad enough people have to tolerate seeing her with my son."

Once William returned from Chile, he worked for a month as a hired hand on a farm owned by one of the Princess of Wales's friends near Highgrove. Now that he'd made his debut at the PCC gala, he was off in early March for a four-month stint tracking wildlife, digging ditches, and fixing fences on game preserves in southern Africa. William was still abroad when, on June 17, 2001, Prince Charles paid a call on his mother at Buckingham Palace. "Please, Mummy," he pleaded, "can't you be kinder toward Camilla?" When the Queen replied succinctly that neither she nor Charles's grandmother would deign to be seen in public with his mistress, Charles stormed out.

For the next sixty days, Charles and his mother dug in, refusing even to speak to each other. The situation was particularly tense at Balmoral, where, despite her steadfast opposition to Camilla, the Queen Mother allowed Charles and his mistress to stay at Birkhall in her absence. Although the two royal residences were just a few miles from each other, the Queen made a point of shunning the couple; Charles waited in vain for an invitation to the castle or for his mother to at least drop in privately. "It was very strange," recalled a Balmoral caretaker. "The Queen likes to drive herself around up here—and she drives very fast. She would speed up and go right past Birkhall without stopping."

While his mother stood her ground, Charles once again found himself in the peculiar position of having to defend Diana's memory—if only for his sons' sake. William was still in Africa when he learned that the Countess of Wessex—his uncle Edward's wife, Sophie—was caught in a tabloid sting operation making derisive comments about the late Princess of Wales. "A lot of things came out after Diana's death about the way she behaved," Charles's sister-in-law told the undercover reporter who posed as a potential client for her public relations firm. After lambasting Diana as "publicity mad" and "scheming," Sophie went on to attack "the fanatical Diana diehards who'll always blame the Prince of Wales for everything."

In fact, Sophie defended Charles as "great fun, he really is. For instance, with William and Harry, he's so laid back. I mean, what you don't see is when the Prince of Wales is messing around and being funny and silly . . . He plays around with the boys all the time; they mess around with each other. He'll always have a go at putting a wig on or doing something silly." She also praised the Prince of Wales for being "a man who has always been ahead of his time. He was damned as a complete quack. People laughed at him for his views on architecture and the environment, but now they're starting to take notice."

Unfortunately, she also described her mother-in-law the Queen rather flippantly as "an old dear," and conceded that Charles and Camilla ranked "number one on people's unpopular-people list. People don't want Camilla to be queen." When asked if the Queen would ever allow the Prince and Mrs. PB to marry, Sophie replied, "I think it's hard, especially while the Queen Mother is alive."

The Queen, understandably, was outraged—not only because of Sophie's indiscreet comments about the royal family as well as numerous political figures, but because the Countess of Wessex was seeking to capitalize on her position. As much as Charles may have welcomed the Countess's unkind words about Diana (not to mention her characterization of him as a man ahead of his time), Charles pressured Sophie to write letters of apology to everyone involved and to resign from her public relations firm.

During the summer of 2001, a series of scandals unfolded that would shake the monarchy to its foundations—and test the mettle of the man who would be king. Charles had no idea that Harry was first exposed to marijuana at the age of fourteen while visiting the Mountbattens at Broadlands. The young Prince was reportedly handed a "huge" joint by his cousin Nicholas Knatchbull, and after taking one puff "went really red," according to Knatchbull's girlfriend Jessica Hay. "I think he was embarrassed."

This time Harry, still two years under Britain's legal drinking age of eighteen, had been left to his own devices at Highgrove while his father and big brother were away. The Prince of Wales, at his mistress's urging, had done his best to make Highgrove an appealing sanctuary for William and Harry. Christened Club H, Highgrove's basement area boasted a dance floor, a jukebox, video games, a state-of-the-art sound system, and a fully stocked bar. Not yet seventeen, Harry already had a pickup line that seemed impossible to top: "Would you like to come back to my palace for a drink?"

Unfortunately, without Charles, William, or Tiggy to restrain him, Harry was spending more and more time down the road at the Rattlebone Inn, knocking back pint after pint of Stella Artois with vodka and gin chasers. At one point, after mock fighting with his friends over a game of pool, Harry was thrown out. Charles might have been able to look the other way, except that a maid at Highgrove noticed the scent of marijuana following one of Harry's Club H parties. Bodyguards assigned to protect the teenager had been reluctant to say anything that might get him in trouble, but they confirmed to Charles that Harry was indeed smoking pot—and frequently. Soon it was revealed that he had also been caught sharing joints with friends in a toolshed behind the Rattlebone Inn.

Having seen Camilla's son and so many others in the royal orbit fall victim to drugs, Charles sprang into action—or, at least, that is what the public would later be led to believe. In truth, months before Charles was informed of Harry's pot smoking, Mark Dyer had taken the young Prince to spend the day talking to recovering heroin and cocaine addicts at south London's Featherstone Lodge rehabilitation center. This encounter with hardcore drug offenders was sobering, but not sobering enough. In the coming months, Harry—now nicknamed the Sponge—was drinking himself blind on a near-nightly basis. "Harry would never come in and have one drink," said Nick Hooper, a bartender at the Vine Tree pub near Highgrove. "With him it was binge, binge, binge. . . . His speech was always slurred, and he would stumble about."

Charles did nothing to curb Harry's drinking—even though newspapers were now running photos of the Spare, red faced and bleary eyed, exiting clubs in London, more often than not out a side door. "Alcohol is something Prince Charles understands," Harold Brooks-Baker said. "Everyone in the British aristocracy drinks—and often to excess. The Queen Mother has four or five stiff drinks every day. Doesn't seem to have done her any harm."

Decades later, Harry would look back on his teenage drinking as an early indication of more serious mental health issues. "I can safely say after losing my mum at the age of twelve, I shut down all of my emotions for the next twenty years," Harry confessed. "My solution was to stick my head in the sand, refusing to ever think about my mum because why would that help? It's only going to make you sad. It's not going to bring her back. So from an emotional side, just don't have emotions about anything."

It would be six months before tabloids finally learned of Harry's marijuana use, the extent of his binge drinking, and his visit to Featherstone. The sordid details of Harry's drunken escapades—one bartender remembered the Prince bolting out into the street to throw up, then returning unaware that his jacket was "smeared with vomit"—shocked the nation. Upset that he had been the cause of more scandalous headlines, Harry admitted to one friend that he felt "like a complete idiot. Nobody understands how difficult things are for my father. I just feel that I've let him down."

Still, there was an upside to the "Harry Pothead" affair. Ignoring the fact that Mark Dyer, not Charles, had taken Harry to Featherstone to be scared straight, St. James's Palace rearranged the timeline to make it look as if it had all been Papa's idea. Bolland cast the Prince of Wales in the role of Everydad: an attentive hands-on father grappling with issues faced by parents everywhere.

Not that everyone agreed with that rosy assessment of Charles's parenting skills. "Harry always depended on his mother for guidance," Diana's brother Earl Spencer said, "and on William." With his older brother away on safari in Africa, Harry was essentially cast adrift. The Princess of Wales and her elder son, Spencer said, would "never have let things get out of hand the way Charles did."

At the same time that Charles was coping with Harry's drug and alcohol problems, he was confronted with another bombshell crisis when police raided the home of Diana's trusted butler Paul Burrell in August and charged him with pilfering 342 items worth an estimated $7.7 million from Diana's Kensington Palace apartments. The man the Princess used to call "my rock" had tried without success to convince authorities that the possessions in question had either been entrusted to him for safekeeping or were gifts to him and his family from Diana.

Burrell wrote to Charles and then to William, asking them to vouch for his credibility. But none of the Windsors, all of whom were well aware of Diana's close relationship with Burrell, spoke up. "Why was the royal family not defending me?" the former butler asked. "I thought I was being fed to the lions."

Seeing disaster ahead if Burrell were tried and forced to spill secrets about the royal marriage on the witness stand, Mark Bolland arranged for Charles to meet with Burrell after a polo match on August 3, 2001. Midway through the match, however, the Prince of Wales was pitched from his horse and knocked unconscious. Even as their father was taken to a nearby hospital for observation, William and Harry resumed playing. Charles's accident turned out to be the pretext for canceling the meeting with Burrell. In reality, Scotland Yard had presented Charles and William with damning evidence that the butler was selling Diana's things in the United States—so-called proof that turned out to be entirely fabricated.

As a result of Charles's diffidence and the royal family's desire to distance themselves from scandal, the case dragged on for two years, pushing Burrell to the brink of financial ruin and thoughts of suicide. It was not until the second week of his trial, in October 2002, that prosecutors were forced to reveal what they were really looking for when they raided the butler's house. An informant had told investigators that inside a mahogany box marked *D*, they would find some of the Princess's most scandalous secrets: scathing correspondence from Prince Philip, the signet ring James Hewitt had given her, and a taped conversation she'd conducted with former Kensington Palace valet and footman George Smith in 1996.

Smith, who was drinking heavily and suffered from clinical depression, claimed that his troubles began in 1989 when he was allegedly raped by one of Prince Charles's manservants. Tossing more gasoline on the bonfire, Smith also swore that he had witnessed the same man in a compromising position—which he spelled out in graphic detail—with a senior member of the royal family.

Diana had, in fact, called Charles when she heard Smith's story and demanded that the aide be fired. Charles angrily refused his wife's request ("Do not pay attention to staff tittle-tattle"), and even spent $200,000 to cover the manservant's legal expenses. According to Charles's lawyer, Fiona Shackleton, the Prince of Wales had only one thing to say about the valet's startling accusations of rape: "George must go." Charles authorized a lump sum payment of $59,000 to Smith, who left his position at Kensington Palace and eventually dropped the matter—a chain of events that would inevitably lead to charges of a cover-up.

In the meantime, however, Charles understood that for the sake of the Crown—and his future claim to it—the "rape tape" must never be played in open court. Yet the Queen's private secretary, Robin Janvrin, made it clear to Charles that her position remained the same: she was not about to interfere in any matter before the courts. The Prince's last chance to persuade the Queen to step in was in the backseat of Her Majesty's Rolls-Royce as the Queen, Prince Philip, and Charles rode to a memorial service at St. Paul's Cathedral for 202 victims of a terrorist attack in Bali.

"Paul Burrell will be testifying in just a few days," Charles told his parents. "You really must do something now, before it's too late."

The Queen was silent, but her husband spoke up. "It's a bit tricky for Mummy," Prince Philip told his son, "because she saw Paul, you know."

"What?" asked Charles, incredulous. "You mean he came to see you? When?"

Stunned, the Prince of Wales listened as his mother recounted their meeting at Buckingham Palace shortly after Diana's death—a meeting at which he informed Her Majesty that, with her permission, he intended to hold the Princess's things for safekeeping.

"But Mummy, why haven't you said anything?" Charles demanded.

"Well, I didn't think it was significant," she answered. What the Queen didn't tell her son was that she had also taken Burrell aside and cautioned him, "Beware, Paul. There are powers at work in this country about which we have no knowledge." Burrell later described the Queen as "deadly serious. She was clearly warning me to be vigilant."

Within hours, Charles spoke with his new private secretary, the Queen's former treasurer Sir Michael Peat, who in turn passed along the new information to Scotland Yard. The next day, before Burrell could take the stand, the case was abruptly dropped.

"It's the Queen!" said Burrell, fighting back tears. "It's all thanks to the Queen."

"My brother and I are very glad for Paul," William said. "We always knew he was completely innocent, of course." For Charles, however, it was too little, too late. Smith's sensational allegations had already been uncorked. "I Was Raped by Charles's Servant," screamed the full-page headline in the *Daily Mail*, which also accurately observed that "Panic Grips the Palace."

There was more to come as a direct result of the Burrell case. Once his sworn deposition to prosecutors was leaked to the press, Burrell quickly sold his story to the *Daily Mirror* for $468,000. Among other things, he revealed for the first time that Diana was so besotted with Hasnat Khan that she considered tricking him into marriage by becoming pregnant. While Charles and Camilla once again appreciated any unflattering revelations about the late Princess of Wales, the Prince worried about what impact it was all having on his sons. In a public statement, Burrell tried to reassure William and Harry that he would "never betray your mother or you for as long as I live. Some things will go to my grave with me."

A different strategy was put in place to contain Burrell. The royals refrained from criticizing the former butler and even went out of their way to publicly support him. For a time, this tack seemed to work. When a tabloid attacked Burrell as "Paul the Betrayer," St. James's Palace issued a statement denying that the royal family was angry with him. At the same time, a spokesman for the Queen insisted that the sovereign was not at all "furious or unhappy" with Burrell, as the press was reporting. A year later, however, Burrell would hang even more of the royal family's dirty linen out to dry in his memoir *A Royal Duty*—including one letter from Diana in which she predicted she was about to be the victim of a staged auto accident and another, written shortly before her death, in which she eviscerated her ex-husband. "I have been battered, bruised, and abused mentally by a system for 15 years now," the Princess wrote. "Thank you, Charles, for putting me through such hell and for giving me the opportunity to learn from the cruel things you have done to me."

So why didn't Charles simply insist prosecutors drop the case against Burrell when he first had the chance in the summer of 2001? "The Prince isn't strong . . . and he was at his weakest, really," observed Mark Bolland, who had urged the Prince to act decisively. "He's not strong about many things. He's not a strong person, and in this particular case, he was very, very weak, and I think that was frustrating for everybody." As a result, Bolland went on, the Burrell case "was a complete fuckup that should never have happened." Prince Charles "should have done more to stop it. But he's not a terribly strong person. He lacks a lot of confidence, and so if he's in a situation where there's a lot of pressure . . . he does find it very hard to stand up for himself." Bolland, who left shortly after the case against Burrell was dropped to start his own public relations firm, added that the Prince of Wales "doesn't have a lot of self-belief. He doesn't have a lot of inner strength." In the end, Charles's media guru concluded, the Burrell case and all the sensational headlines it spawned over two years was "one of the biggest mistakes Prince Charles has made."

In the Prince's defense, during this period, scandals and crises popped up like a carnival game of whack-a-mole, and Charles was usually the only royal willing to wield the mallet. One of the most unexpected occurred after William began his college career in the fall of 2001. While Cambridge alumnus Charles lobbied for his school and the Spencers pushed for Oxford, William instead chose to enroll in Scotland's University of St. Andrews, alma mater of his Eton housemaster and mentor Andrew Gailey. The Queen, who often stated that Balmoral was simply her "most favorite place," liked the idea of St. Andrews as well; with Scottish nationalism on the rise, it could only help matters for the future king to become the first British monarch to have attended a university in Scotland.

Famous as the spot where golf was invented in the 1440s, St. Andrews had a student body of just six thousand and offered a more intimate, small-college atmosphere than either Oxford or Cambridge. The campus was located seventy-five miles north of Edinburgh but could not have been more remote. Shrouded by fog and jutting out into the North Sea, St. Andrews might as well have been on the far side of the moon. It didn't seem that way, however, when Charles maneuvered his racing-green Vauxhall estate car onto the North Street approach to St. Andrews and past a crowd of four thousand screaming spectators held back by police barricades. The Prince of Wales was so startled by the size of the crowd that he misjudged the angle into the narrow archway beneath St. Andrews's medieval clock tower. Unable to conceal his embarrassment, Charles backed up and made a second try.

"I almost turned around and fled," confessed Charles, who managed a wan smile but worried that local police might not be able to keep "the mob" under control. Papa shouldn't have worried—at least not about the press. St. James's and Fleet Street struck a deal that reporters and camera crews would be given free access to Prince William the day of his arrival on campus—as long as they agreed to depart within twenty-four hours.

Charles's youngest brother, Prince Edward, apparently hadn't gotten the memo. Trying to establish himself as a television producer, Edward had signed on to produce a documentary series for the American cable TV channel E! Entertainment called *Royalty A to Z* and dispatched a two-man camera crew to film William as he settled into his residence hall, St. Salvator's ("Sallies" to students), and took a quick tour of the campus grounds. When local officials asked them to leave with the rest of the working press, the *Royalty A to Z* camera crew replied that they had special permission from William's Uncle Edward to stay and keep shooting. In fact, they said they had been instructed to tag along on William's entire first week as a university student.

Charles was "incandescent with rage," as Bolland described it, and at first refused to take his brother's pleading phone calls. When he finally did deign to speak with Edward, the Prince of Wales "flayed him alive." Charles "didn't expect his own brother to stab him in the back like that," another St. James's spokesman said. "He saw it as an act of betrayal, pure and simple."

Not surprisingly Edward, his reputation now almost as badly bruised as his wife's, hastily withdrew the crew, canceled his participation in the documentary series, and, within months, abandoned altogether his dream of having his own career as a television producer. But even without intrusion from the media, William, who majored in art history and geography, found it hard to adjust to campus life. Within weeks, he was complaining to Charles that St. Andrews was too isolated, that he missed his friends and family, and that he was "feeling trapped." Each weekend, he drove the seventy-five miles south to Edinburgh to connect with old Eton pals attending school there, or made the five-hour train ride to visit Granny, Grandpapa Philip, and Great Gran—the Queen Mother—at Balmoral.

"It's easy to feel cut off," observed William's Eton chum David Walston, "if you're not around the few people you can really count on."

That Christmas, feeling isolated and very much alone—despite having already made friends with a young coed named Kate Middleton—William implored his father to let him transfer to Edinburgh University. But Charles's advisors nixed the idea. It would risk branding Prince William a pampered whinger like his father—something the Crown was determined to avoid. At the same time, Kate Middleton, who was also having doubts, was being urged by her parents to stick it out at St. Andrews. When William and Kate returned to school, they agreed to make a go of it for one more year—and then leave together "if we feel then," Kate said, "like we do now." Looking back on his early "wobbles" concerning St. Andrews, William dismissed the idea that he was merely missing his family. "I don't think I was homesick," he said. "I was more daunted."

Charles and the royal family were dealt two emotional hammer blows in early 2002. On February 9 Her Majesty's once-beautiful, infamously high-living Princess Margaret, a lifelong smoker, died at age seventy-one after suffering a series of strokes and eventually succumbing to a heart attack. As children, Elizabeth and Margaret called each other Lilibet and Margo; to Charles, she was always Aunt Margo, a glamourous and fun figure who clenched a long silver cigarette holder in her teeth while playing piano duets with her nephew when he was a little boy. Toward the end of her life, Charles visited Princess Margaret, now bedridden and blind, and spent hours reading to her.

Just hours after the death of his "darling aunt," Charles recorded a touching tribute that was broadcast on British television. "This is a terribly sad day for all my family, but particularly for the Queen, of course, my mama, and for my grandmother the Queen Mother," he began, going on to praise Margaret's "wonderful, free spirit" and to talk about how much "she loved life and lived it to the full. My aunt was one of those remarkable people who, apart from being so vital and attractive—she was incredibly beautiful—was also talented." Princess Margaret played the piano "flawlessly" by ear, Charles reported, sang "like an angel," and "had this wonderfully sharp mind. . . . We shall all miss her dreadfully."

Rather than console the Queen at Windsor Castle, Charles rushed to the side of his grandmother at Sandringham. The Queen Mother, who along with her husband, King George VI, was a symbol of Britain's fighting spirit during World War II, accepted her youngest child's death with dignity. Margaret Rose's death, said the indomitable Windsor matriarch, was "a merciful release" from pain and suffering.

The Queen Mother was frail, but managed nonetheless to attend Margaret's funeral and interment at St. George's Chapel. Before heading off on another ski vacation in Switzerland with William and Harry, Charles dropped in on his grandmother at Windsor Great Park with an early Easter present: a potted jasmine from his greenhouse at Highgrove.

Less than forty-eight hours later, on the afternoon of March 30, 2002, the Queen Mother was at Windsor for the Easter weekend when she suddenly grew tired. Elizabeth had been out riding and was just returning to the Windsor stables when doctors summoned her to her mother's side. When the Queen arrived, she found the Queen Mother sitting upright in a chair by the fireplace in her bedroom, dressed in a lounging robe. Elizabeth, who had been told to hurry and was still wearing her riding clothes and muddy riding boots, knelt by her mother's side. They spoke for only a few moments before the Queen Mother slipped into unconsciousness. At three fifteen in the afternoon, with Elizabeth, Margaret's children Sarah Chatto and David Armstrong-Jones (known professionally as David Linley; he is now Earl of Snowdon), and the Queen's niece Margaret Rhodes all weeping at her bedside, the Queen Mother died peacefully.

Unquestionably the most beloved member of the royal family, the Queen Mother had connected with every generation. To William and Harry she was Great Gran, a kindred spirit who loved racy jokes, Balmoral, and gin and tonics. The Queen Mother, who loved to imitate Ali G, the would-be rap icon created by comedian Sacha Baron Cohen, was excited by her great-grandson's decision to attend St. Andrews, which was surrounded by twenty-two pubs—more per square mile than any other community in Scotland. "If there are any good parties," she told William, "invite me down!"

Margaret Rhodes called the twin losses of the Queen's only sibling and her mother a "terrible wallop of grief." Neither was unexpected, but that did little to lessen the impact. "It doesn't matter how old someone is," Tony Blair said, "or how long you've had to prepare. It was a terrible shock."

The Queen was still choking back tears when she called Charles at the Hotel Walserhof in Klosters less than a quarter hour after the Queen Mother passed away. "Papa was shattered, absolutely destroyed," William told his friend Guy Pelly. While Charles and his sons had remained phenomenally stoic even under the gaze of millions during Diana's funeral, all three men broke down. "It was just watching my father cry," Harry explained later. "Just couldn't take it."

The first phone call Charles made was not to his brothers or to his sister—or to any member of the royal family—but to Camilla. "Charles was terribly upset that he wasn't there when his grandmother died," she told one of her Wiltshire neighbors. "It really bothered him. He felt he let her down in some way."

Ignoring the rule that prohibits two heirs to the throne from flying together, the Queen dispatched an RAF jet to pick up all three princes and ferry them back to London. Already dressed in black as they boarded the plane—all royals travel with mourning attire for just such an eventuality—Charles turned to remind William and Harry that it was Easter morning. No sooner did they arrive at Royal Lodge, the Queen Mother's Great Windsor Park residence, than the Queen emerged and summoned Charles, William, and Harry upstairs to the Queen Mother's bedroom. There Charles walked slowly up to his grandmother, knelt by her bedside, and hung his head. According to Margaret Rhodes, the Queen Mother looked "thirty years younger" in death than she did in life.

As he had for Princess Margaret only weeks earlier, Charles took to the airwaves again, this time to praise his grandmother as "the original life enhancer—indomitable, timeless, somehow able to span the generations . . .

wise, loving, with an immensely strong character and a natural grace. . . . Above all, she understood the British character, and her heart belonged to this ancient old land."

Turning to his own relationship with his grandmother, Charles paused for a moment, his tongue planted in his cheek as he tried to subdue his emotions. On a side table next to him were two framed photographs of the Queen Mother, dressed all in pink in one shot and vibrant blue in the other. "For me," he said, "she meant . . . everything. I have dreaded, dreaded this moment. Somehow I never thought it would come. She seemed gloriously unstoppable. Ever since I was a child, I adored her. . . . She was such fun. We laughed until we cried. Oh, how I will miss those laughs." In the end, Charles stated simply that "she was the most magical grandmother you could possibly have, and I was utterly devoted to her. Her departure has left an irreplaceable chasm," he said, staring down at his hands as he was suddenly overcome with emotion, "but *thank God* we're all the richer for the sheer joy of her presence and everything she stood for."

The Queen must have thought at the time, one courtier observed, that it was not the sort of tribute she could ever expect from her son. The bond of affection between Charles and his grandmother did not exist between Charles and his mother—at least not to that extent—"and the Queen knows it. What they've always had," Margaret Rhodes mused, "is more in the nature of respect than love, or at least the love between a parent and child in the way most people think of it." In a separate, decidedly more formal address to the nation, the Queen thanked her people for the "outpouring of affection" that was "overwhelming. . . . I thank you also from my heart for the love you gave her during her life and the honor you now give her in death."

On the eve of his grandmother's funeral at Westminster Abbey, Charles joined the Queen Mother's other three grandsons—Andrew, Edward, and Margaret's son, David—in a fifteen-minute "Vigil of the Princes" as she lay in state at Westminster Hall. Charles and Andrew wore their medal-bedecked, gold-braided full-dress naval uniforms while Edward and David wore mourning suits—each standing at a corner of the coffin, heads bowed. Charles did this not once but twice as an estimated half million mourners filed past.

The funeral route from St. James's Palace to Westminster Abbey was lined with more than a million mourners. Inside the Abbey, three generations of present and future British monarchs—the Queen, Charles, and William—were among 2,200 crowned heads, titled aristocrats, world leaders, and other dignitaries who had come to pay their respects. Throughout the service, a wounded-looking Charles stared at the coffin, draped with the Queen Mother's personal blue, red, white, and gold standard. Resting atop the casket was her coronation crown, ablaze with 2,800 diamonds, including the eye-popping 105-carat Koh-i-Noor.

In the common room at St. Andrews, William's roommate and secret girlfriend, Kate Middleton, was content to watch the funeral service on television. Camilla was another matter. Despite the fact that the Queen Mother forbade Camilla's name from being spoken in her presence, Charles pleaded with his mother through intermediaries to allow his mistress to attend. Positioned a discreet distance from the royal family, Camilla was there in person—albeit on the sidelines—to lend Charles moral support. She was also there to finally bid farewell to the woman who had blocked their marriage.

That spring, polls would show an uptick in the couple's popularity as a majority of 57 percent said they approved of Charles and Camilla getting married. The Prince of Wales pointed to these new figures as evidence that the Queen should no longer ban the love of his life from high-profile affairs. "Just imagine how many times she has heard, 'No dear, I'm afraid you've got to stay home tonight,'" Harold Brooks-Baker said. "Totally humiliating."

Charles demanded that Camilla be allowed to join in the upcoming Golden Jubilee festivities celebrating Elizabeth II's fiftieth anniversary on the throne. He got his wish when Camilla was invited to sit in the royal box at the classical concert kicking off the celebrations on June 1, 2002. Camilla, seated directly behind Charles, was clearly nervous; when her image was projected on a giant screen, she was fiddling with her hair and licking her lips. The Queen and Camilla never spoke to each other—in fact, the monarch scrupulously avoided making eye contact—but no matter. This was the first time the two had ever been seen together, in a manner of speaking, by the general public.

Charles was glad to see Camilla unwind two days later, when she was again seated with the royal family—this time at the Jubilee's "Party at the Palace" pop concert in the Buckingham Palace gardens. In stark contrast to Charles, Camilla was more attuned to pop music and sang along when Phil Collins launched into his remake of the Supremes' hit "You Can't Hurry Love." Later, while milling backstage with performers such as Tom Jones, Tony Bennett, Paul McCartney, and Elton John, Camilla maintained her composure when Ozzy Osbourne's wife, Sharon, walked up to her and squeezed her breasts. "You've got gorgeous old tits!" Sharon said cheerfully. Camilla, apparently flattered, just smiled and nodded.

Diana's name was never mentioned during the Jubilee celebrations—a sin of omission that did not sit well with the Princess's fans. "You would not have seen a pop concert on the grounds of Buckingham Palace," the Queen's biographer Robert Lacey observed, "had it not been for Diana." Before long, Earl Spencer weighed in, criticizing the royal family for trying to keep William and Harry away from their Spencer relatives.

Indeed, Charles had banned his sons from attending Spencer's wedding at Althorp to his second wife, former nursery school teacher Caroline Freud. The Earl went on to complain that, with the exception of a chance meeting at a charity gala, he hadn't seen the Prince of Wales since Diana's funeral. Nor had Charles visited Diana's grave at Althorp. "Not a single time," Earl Spencer said, "in five years." (William and Harry both had, each year on their mother's birthday.)

In September 2002 Charles once again found himself in the peculiar position of having to join his sons in defending his late wife's memory while simultaneously savoring the fact that every portrayal of Diana as unbalanced served to bolster his—and Camilla's—standing in the polls. Since her death, the most tawdry revelations had come from those closest to her. James Hewitt, Patrick Jephson, and Paul Burrell were now joined by Diana's longtime bodyguard Ken Wharfe. In the pages of *Diana: Closely Guarded Secret*, Wharfe revealed, among other things, that Diana routinely paraded around in front of him in the nude and always kept a vibrator in her purse that she playfully brandished when she thought no one else was looking.

During his six years as the Princess of Wales's chief minder, Wharfe had become something of a surrogate father to William and Harry. When the boys attended Wetherby, it was Wharfe—not Charles—who showed up on father-son day to compete in the fathers footrace. Now Wharfe's book destroyed that bond. "It's just total treachery, that's all," William told Guy Pelly. "Harry is *really* upset." So was Granny. "The Queen is very perturbed," said her private secretary, Robin Janvrin. "She is extremely worried about the effect all this will have on her grandsons."

In a statement, Charles blasted Wharfe's steamy tell-all as "a disgusting betrayal" and called for Scotland Yard chief Sir John Stevens to take legal action against the retired bodyguard. "It really shakes the foundations of their entire belief system when something like this happens," one former Palace official said of the royal family's need to "count on the discretion of the people who work for them. They simply can't afford to have their butlers and bodyguards running around spilling family secrets."

Despite pressure from St. James's Palace, Sir John's hands were tied in the Wharfe matter; bodyguards employed by Scotland Yard were not covered by the same confidentiality agreement binding royal household staff since 2000. Attention would soon turn back to James Hewitt when it was discovered that he was trying to peddle sixty-four torrid love letters Diana had written him while he was serving in the 1991 Persian Gulf War. His asking price: $16.5 million.

"I felt your lips on my body last night as I slept," Diana wrote in one of the letters to her lover. "They were everywhere." In another, she complained that Hewitt had twice refused her plea to make love to her in a meadow adjacent to his mother's house. She called him "a beast one lusts after," and, in several of the love notes, referred to Hewitt's penis as "my friend." In others, she asks about pornography she has sent him in the field, and slyly refers to his affairs with other women.

Hewitt tried to spin the letters as "historic" and "unique. It's the first time a member of the royal family is writing to a serving soldier at war." But, once their contents were splayed across front pages everywhere, Hewitt once again found himself being denounced as "the Love Rat."

At the same time, Charles and the Queen were coming under siege for not doing enough to honor the Princess of Wales's memory. It was proposed that a statue of Diana be placed outside Kensington, or that Heathrow Airport be renamed either Princess Diana Airport or Princess of Wales Airport in her honor. Charles and the Queen nixed both ideas on the grounds that they were "inappropriate."

At the same time that surveys were showing increased support for Charles and Camilla, they also indicated that the overwhelming majority of Britons agreed with Earl Spencer that Charles and his supporters were trying to "marginalize" Diana by telling people "she never mattered." It didn't help that the one Diana monument Charles did greenlight—a $4.7 million memorial pool in Hyde Park by Seattle landscape architect Kathryn Gustafson—was initially dismissed as a "drainage ditch" and a "puddle."

William and Harry were willing to defer to their father, and remained silent on the matter. "We were each too busy trying to process our grief," said William, who claimed he and his brother never got the counseling they needed and were basically left to their own devices. "Only we didn't realize it at the time."

On the surface, William still appeared to be the more serious of the two, given to brooding and long silences. "Harry is quick to share his emotions with other people," Peter Archer said, "and while that may get him in trouble in the short run, it's healthy in the long run. William tends to block unpleasant things out, to push them to the back of his mind, rather than face them." More accurately, both young men were concealing their pain, confusion, frustration, and anger behind a mask of false bravado.

More than once during this period, William snapped. As he and his father returned from a foxhunting expedition on horseback, the nineteen-year-old spotted a man with a camera and charged at him. "Prince Charles went by first, and then William saw me and just went mad," photographer Clive Postlethwaite recalled. "He rode toward me with his eyes wide and his teeth showing."

"Fucking piss off!" shouted William as he plowed straight ahead, forcing Postlethwaite to drop his camera and jump out of the way.

Charles understood his son's frustration when it came to dealing with the press. At around the same time, the Prince of Wales once again found himself in hot water over his habit of writing hundreds of long, rambling letters to cabinet members and government officials expressing his opinions on everything from foxhunting, climate change, education, architecture, and meditation to political correctness, nursing care, alternative medicine, urban planning, and sustainable farming. These letters, eventually known as the "Black Spider Memos"—a reference to the Prince's distinctive, spidery script—ruffled feathers because traditionally the monarchy was expected to be politically impartial.

Charles, unlike the Queen, made a point of wearing his opinions on his gold-braided sleeve. To the Lord Chancellor, Lord Irvine, he complained bitterly about the proliferation of lawsuits. Pointing to a decision by the government to chop down chestnut trees out of a concern that passersby would be injured by falling chestnuts, the Prince bemoaned "the very real and growing prospect of an American-style personal injury 'culture.'" In a letter to Prime Minister Tony Blair that was leaked to the press, he defended "country pursuits" such as foxhunting and claimed that "if we, as a group, were black or gay, we would not be victimized or picked upon." According to Mark Bolland, "These letters were not merely routine and noncontroversial, but contained his views on political matters and political issues." In several, Bolland said, Charles frequently "denounced the elected leaders of other countries in extreme terms."

On occasion, His Royal Highness did more than just put pen to paper. At one point, Prince Charles, who described himself as a "close friend" of the Dalai Lama, protested China's occupation of Tibet by boycotting a Buckingham Palace banquet in honor of Chinese president Jiang Zemin. In case there was any doubt, Bolland later described Charles's action as a "deliberate snub."

"This is someone," fumed MP Ian Davidson of the Labour Party, "who was born with a mouthful of silver spoons—a megawealthy farmer who's looking for things to do—so he fires off letters. If he wants to be involved in politics, then he should stand for election."

Once again made the object of ridicule, Charles complained bitterly to his staff about the "constant drip" of leaks that were "obviously intended to make me look like an imbecile." St. James's Palace went on the defensive, claiming Prince Charles took "an active interest in all aspects of British life" and believed that "part of his role must be to highlight problems and represent views in danger of not being heard." Adding that the Prince could fulfill this role only "if complete confidentiality is maintained," a Palace spokeswoman allowed that Prince Charles was "fully aware that while he has every right to advise, it is ministers who decide."

More trouble bubbled up on the home front when William made the unwise decision to take out his frustrations on the road. Charles's longtime friend and Gloucestershire neighbor, seventy-six-year-old Earl Bathurst, was driving his white Land Rover along a narrow country lane near Highgrove when William came out of nowhere and roared past him on the left at twice the legal speed limit. "He drove on the grass to overtake me," the Earl said. "I thought he was just a yob [hooligan] driving a rather crummy VW Golf which anybody might have. I was very annoyed."

The encounter didn't end there. Succumbing to some road rage of his own, the Earl blew his horn and flashed his lights—but instead of slowing down, William stepped on the gas. "There were clouds of dust," Bathurst said. "I thought he was bound to stop, but not a bit of it." Enraged, the Earl took a shortcut through the trees, pulled in front of the VW, and managed to block its path. At that point, a Vauxhall Omega pulled up, and William's bodyguards jumped out to confront the Earl. It was only then that he realized the "yob" in the car was Prince William. "They thought I was trying to take him out," Bathurst said. "I could have been shot."

Without ever bothering to leave his car, William simply drove past Bathurst while the man was being questioned by the royal bodyguards. "He just drove on round us," Bathurst recalled. "It wasn't very civil, to be honest."

Ever since William first got behind the wheel, his father had worried about his son's penchant for speed. But confronting a fellow member of the aristocracy—and a Highgrove neighbor to boot—was unacceptable. As soon as he was informed of the incident, Charles picked up the phone and called Bathurst directly to apologize for his son's behavior. Bathurst was not impressed, particularly since an unrepentant William had clearly refused to do the apologizing himself. "Prince Charles must tell his son," Bathurst told authorities, "to obey the rules like everybody else."

In this instance, as in so many others, Camilla defended William's behavior as "normal for his age" and reminded Charles that he, Prince Philip, and the Queen were infamous for their lead-footed driving styles. According to staff members at Highgrove, Charles's chain-smoking mistress also "gave a wink and a nod" to William when he smoked—they both were partial to Marlboro Lights—until a major health scare prompted her to quit. Stricken in May 2003 with back pain so severe that she had to be hospitalized, Camilla was warned by doctors that the habit had already taken its toll on her heart and her lungs. Moreover, she was told that studies had shown a link between smoking and osteoporosis, the disease that killed her mother and her maternal grandmother. Terrified at the prospect, she quit cold turkey.

Camilla made no effort to talk William and Harry out of smoking ("It took me forty years to quit! Why on earth should they listen to me?") or to persuade them to cut back on their marathon partying. Unfortunately, by the fall of 2003, Charles was routinely being briefed on his sons' less-than-wholesome nocturnal activities. Although William and Kate Middleton were still very much a couple, he and his brother routinely drank themselves into oblivion at London nightspots such as Purple, the Sofa So Bar, Boujis, and Mahiki—the Mayfair club owned partly by Guy Pelly. Photographs of the bleary-eyed princes openly groping young women at clubs—and then literally being carried out by their bodyguards—would eventually be fodder for the tabloids, igniting another brushfire that Charles would eventually have to extinguish.

In the meantime, the Prince of Wales was distracted by another of his many projects: the renovation of his new home, Clarence House. The Queen Mother's home for nearly a half century, the four-story, 172-year-old palace with a staff of ninety was now to be the official residence of Charles and his sons—and the unofficial residence of Mrs. PB.

Camilla's own tastes ran to English shabby, but now that she was moving inside the walls of a royal palace, the Prince of Wales's mistress wasted no time pulling down the Queen Mother's frayed drapes and threadbare furniture. Robert Kime, the British designer she had hired to gussy up York House, Highgrove, and Ray Mill House, was now confronted with the delicate assignment of upgrading Clarence House without erasing the memory of Charles's adored Granny.

Kime, guided by Camilla and with Charles overseeing the whole project, chose wisely to merely burnish rather than redo the public spaces on the main floor: the book-lined Lancaster Room; the Morning Room, with its Chippendale gilt wood furniture, blue-gray silk damask drapes, and paintings by Claude Monet and Augustus John; the light-filled Garden Room, used for formal receptions; the Main Hall, lined with portraits of previous royal occupants (not to mention the crimson-draped Horse Corridor hung with portraits of all the Queen Mum's favorite thoroughbreds)—all would have been instantly familiar to her.

Unlike other royal residences, the off-limits private quarters upstairs were far more opulent than the rooms that were open to the public. There were seven bedrooms in all, including Charles's and Camilla's adjoining his-and-hers suites on the second floor, the young princes' rooms on the third, and a separate suite of rooms for Camilla's father, Major Bruce Shand. While Camilla opted for eighteenth-century Chinese wallpaper in her sitting room, the design-minded Prince of Wales took complete charge of what his bedroom would look like: soft pink fabric for the walls, a massive carved mahogany Georgian four-poster with curtains that could be drawn on all sides, and cobalt-blue draperies. For his study, the Prince handpicked a white-and-blue-striped fabric for the sofa in his study and silver leaf wallpaper.

At Charles's insistence, paintings, drawings, and photographs of his adored grandmother were everywhere—atop grand pianos, on fireplace mantelpieces, on coffee tables, and on nightstands. Even the basement screening room, which boasted seats upholstered in red velvet, was turned into a shrine to Elizabeth's departed mum.

Dominating an entire wall was an enormous Cecil Beaton photograph of the then slender, young queen, looking winsome and twirling a frilly parasol as she modeled a piece from the Norman Hartnell–designed "White Wardrobe" that caused a fashion sensation when she toured France in 1938. "You feel the Queen Mother's presence in every room," a visitor commented.

"Yes," Camilla replied, widening her eyes and clearing her throat for comic effect. "You most certainly do."

The bill for Camilla's remodeling of Clarence House: just over $10 million. The new lady of the house and her father, Major Shand, had scarcely moved in when there were howls of protest in the press. To quell the critics, Charles grudgingly agreed to foot the bill for the cost of refurbishing Camilla's suite of rooms and those of her father.

Charles was heartened when, in an interview marking his twenty-first birthday, William sprang to his father's defense. The Heir said his father had "been given quite a hard time recently," and that he hoped "people would give him a break. He does amazing things. I only wish people would see that more because he's had a very hard time, and yet he's stuck it out and he's still very positive."

———

William also made it clear that he intended to chart his own course as a future monarch—even if it meant standing up to his father and the faceless puppet masters at Buckingham Palace. "I like to be in control of my life," the Heir said. "If I don't have any say in it, then I lose complete control, and I don't like the idea of that. I could actually lose my identity." Conceding that "a lot of people" considered him "hugely stubborn," William maintained that he had to stand up for himself. "If you don't stick to your guns," he said, "then you lose control."

Although he shared his father's stubborn streak, he had no use for the trappings of aristocracy. Charles had spent his entire life surrounded by a small, sycophantic army of butlers, valets, aides, and equerries who catered to his every whim. He was also accustomed to being addressed either as "Your Highness" or "Sir." William insisted he had no need for an entourage or to be put on a pedestal. "Out of personal choice," he explained, "I like to be called William. I want to come across as me."

William also made it clear that, while he had enormous respect for all that his father had accomplished, he intended to focus on aiding the homeless—a particular interest of his mother's—rather than work to promote any of Charles's favorite charities. "I was influenced a lot by my visits to shelters with my mother when I was younger," he said. "My mother used her position to help other people, as does my father, and I hope to do the same."

Charles was also pleased to hear what William had to say in the interview about his brother. "My brother is a very nice guy," he said of the Spare, "and extremely caring." Harry had been a fairly dismal student at Eton—his D in geography was the lowest grade in his class—but he had excelled as a member of the Combined Cadet Corps and planned to enter Britain's elite Royal Military Academy Sandhurst. However, since Sandhurst was reluctant to accept cadets under the age of twenty, Harry would take two gap years off instead of one. His first gap-year assignment: spending three months Down Under playing polo and working as a jackeroo—one of Australia's famous ranch hands—on Tooloombilla Station, a forty-thousand-acre spread in Queensland. He was paid the standard $160 a week, but that scarcely mattered to antimonarchists who objected to Australian taxpayers footing Prince Harry's $1 million–plus security bill.

When Charles and the Queen offered William the use of Windsor Castle for his coming-of-age party, the Heir, still smitten with Africa after his gap-year experience in Kenya, opted for an *Out of Africa* theme. Granny approved—but with the proviso that all three hundred guests be cautioned to avoid any "racial overtones" in their costumes or overt references to Britain's colonial past. The Prince of Wales dug deep into his Highgrove closet for a dashiki in bold stripes, while the Queen showed up as the "Queen of Swaziland" in an elaborate white African headdress, white sheath dress, and white fur wrap. William and Kate Middleton came as Tarzan and Jane—he in a black-and-yellow-striped loincloth, she in a daring leopard print dress. Earl Spencer, Prince Philip, Prince Andrew, and Harry all came in safari outfits of one sort or another, while other guests dressed as characters from *The Lion King*, witch doctors, and Foreign Legionnaires. Careful not to draw too much attention to herself, Camilla, wearing a red-and-blue tribal costume and a striking red-feathered headdress, slipped in quietly through a side entrance.

The $800,000 affair, which included monkeys swinging from palm trees, elephant rides for the guests, and music by the Botswanan band Shakarimba, also signaled a thaw between Diana's Spencer relatives and the Windsors. With Papa's blessing, William insisted that all of his Spencer aunts and uncles not only be invited to the party but also that they spend the night at the castle. For the first time, Diana's siblings, William, Harry, Charles, Camilla, Prince Philip, and the Queen were all spending time together under the same roof. At the height of the festivities, Charles presented William with his present: a $165,000 Argentine polo pony.

Before the older celebrants called it a night, William took to the stage a few minutes before midnight to thank his guests for coming. In the middle of the Prince's remarks, a man done up like Osama bin Laden in drag—dark glasses, turban, beard, red high heels, pink satin evening gown—leapt onstage and grabbed the microphone out of William's hand. Self-styled "comedy terrorist" Aaron Barschak began singing his own version of "Diamonds Are a Girl's Best Friend," then kissed William on both cheeks before being hauled off by bodyguards. William, none the worse for wear, danced and drank in his loincloth until dawn.

The birthday boy's father was not so calm. How, he demanded to know, could a gate-crasher wend his way past scores of uniformed and armed undercover officers and wind up onstage with the future king of England? Camilla did her best to calm down her Prince, but to no avail. "My God!" Charles said. "What if he had been a suicide bomber? He could have wiped us all out!"

This was, in fact, the thirteenth major breach in royal security since the Queen was awakened one evening in 1982 to discover an intruder had broken into Buckingham Palace and was sitting on the edge of her bed. Then there was the nude paraglider who landed on the roof of Buckingham Palace in 1994, and the day Princess Anne answered her bedroom door only to encounter a tourist asking for directions to Victoria Station. Charles's private quarters at Buckingham Palace and St. James's Palace had been broken into several times, although in those instances the perpetrators were never identified.

Barschak himself was surprised how "unbelievably simple" it was to mingle with the royal family. "I was amazed I got in," he said. "The police immediately started giving me directions. I was astounded that nobody asked for my name or ID . . . or why I was carrying a bulging rucksack [backpack]. I could have had anything in it."

Prince Charles and the Queen pressed for answers from Scotland Yard chief Sir John Stevens, who, in turn, ordered that David Veness, the assistant commissioner in charge of Royal Protection, launch a thorough investigation. In the interim, all Stevens could do was issue an abject public apology to the royal family "for the appalling breach of security, which should not have happened, whatever the circumstances."

The press seemed less concerned with security breaches than it was with William's love life. Speculation centered on Jessica "Jecca" Craig, whose father owned the fifty-five-thousand-acre game preserve in Kenya where William spent part of his gap year. During his four months there, William squeezed in a brief romance with Jecca, and now she was his guest of honor. What no one realized at the time was that, before inviting Jecca, William explained everything to his true love Kate Middleton. When the Palace realized that Craig's sometime boyfriend, shipping heir Henry

Ropner, had been inadvertently left off the guest list, they scrambled at the eleventh hour to send him an invitation.

Her skimpy "You Jane, Me Tarzan" attire aside, Kate wisely chose to avoid the spotlight at the party, choosing instead to blend in with the couple's friends from St. Andrews. It had been only a few weeks since William made a secret trip to the Middleton family home in Berkshire to belatedly celebrate Kate's twenty-first birthday, then slipped out under cover of darkness and quietly returned to Clarence House—all without tipping off the tabloid press.

The clandestine visit to Kate's home marked the first time William had the opportunity to meet her parents, and they all hit it off instantly—despite the fact that the Middletons' roots were decidedly working class. Kate's mother, Carole Goldsmith Middleton, was a descendant of coal miners from County Durham and spent part of her childhood in public housing. Unable to afford college, she signed on with British Airways as a flight attendant straight out of high school. Michael Middleton, Kate's father, had a few interesting family connections: he was related to Beatrix Potter of *The Tale of Peter Rabbit* fame as well as to the legendary Shakespearean actress Ellen Terry and Academy Award–winning actor Sir John Gielgud. He even shared an ancestor with the royal family—seventeenth-century statesman Sir Thomas Fairfax—making Kate and William fifteenth cousins.

Michael had been a flight dispatcher for British Airways and was in charge of the airline's ground operations at Heathrow when the couple met, promptly fell in love, and, after living together for a year, tied the knot. Catherine—she would not be called Kate until she was well into her teens—was born on January 9, 1982, and was joined by a sister, Philippa ("Pippa"), twenty months later. Shortly after their brother James was born in 1987, Carole rented a storage space and launched Party Pieces, a mail-order business designed to, she explained in her prospectus, "inspire other mothers to create magical parties at home and to make party organizing a little easier."

Soon Party Pieces was filling thousands of orders for everything from party hats, noisemakers, paper plates, and balloons, to invitations, lanterns, costumes, and games. After Michael quit his job at Heathrow and joined the family firm, Carole made the shrewd decision to set up a Party Pieces website in 1992. Within two years, their mail order business was grossing more than $3 million annually—enough to purchase Oak Acre, a Tudor-style compound in the unremittingly quaint Berkshire village of Bucklebury.

Kate's educational experience was not unlike William's. She attended several exclusive private schools—St. Andrews School in the nearby town of Pangbourne, followed by two elite boarding schools: Downe House and Marlborough College in Wiltshire. At Downe House, Kate got a taste of the bullying Charles was exposed to as a child—not as extreme, of course, but enough for Kate's parents to transfer her to Marlborough. Kate was studious and athletic, with a quiet reserve that belied a mischievous streak. During her four years at Marlborough, she flashed her derriere so frequently from her residence hall window that Miss Middleton was given the nickname "Middlebum."

William didn't to get to know that aspect of Kate's personality until she famously paraded down the runway in sexy lingerie as part of St. Andrews's annual Don't Walk charity fashion show sponsored by Yves Saint Laurent. The Prince, who had paid $375 for a front-row seat, leapt to his feet and cheered. "We were all wowed," their friend Jules Knight said. "Here was this reserved girl we knew up onstage, looking like a smoldering temptress." It was "a side to her we didn't know existed," Knight added, "and it was a turning point in people's perception of her. Everyone took note, including Will."

By the time Kate showed up at William's birthday party in a revealing leopard print dress, she had already been to Sandringham—albeit as one of fourteen St. Andrews students William invited to a shooting party. While William and Kate stayed with their pals at Wood Farm, a five-bedroom "cottage" on the estate grounds, Papa was at the main house playing host to the Queen of Denmark. "I want you to meet my father," William reassured Kate, "but he's always got these things to do."

It was only after the *Out of Africa* party that it dawned on Charles just how serious his son was about Miss Middleton. When they returned to St. Andrews in the fall of 2003, William and Kate moved out of the house they had been sharing with roommates near the campus and took up residence at Balgove House, a roomy, fuchsia-covered cottage on the outskirts of town. The Heir had to get his father's permission to move in with his girlfriend for a number of reasons, not the least of which was the $2.5 million price tag for bulletproof windows, panic rooms, new security cameras, and a separate building to house a permanent contingent of four armed guards.

Charles's initial impression of Miss Middleton was generally favorable, although he was not convinced the relationship would last. There were too many reports of William "snogging" (kissing) and dancing wildly with other attractive young women at pulsating nightspots in London and Edinburgh. Camilla, however, recognized early on that this supremely poised descendant of coal miners was a serious contender for William's affections—and as such, a threat.

Although Mrs. Parker Bowles was technically a commoner because she had no title, she was also a genuine aristocrat—a direct descendant of William the Conqueror and the granddaughter of a baron. Having struggled to gain acceptance by the Queen for so long—and still finding it just out of reach—Camilla could scarcely be expected to look kindly on someone with essentially no social standing at all. Unimpressed by the Middletons' up-by-the-bootstraps saga, Camilla told Charles that she found William's girlfriend "pretty, but rather dim." Later, as Kate came closer to gaining acceptance by the Queen, Camilla would draw Charles's attention to the nickname that had been bestowed on Kate and her socially ambitious sister Pippa. "Apparently they're called the 'Wisteria Sisters' because they're beautiful," Camilla reported, "and they have 'a ferocious ability to climb.'" She also repeated her strongly held belief that neither William nor Harry should marry before the age of thirty-five.

What Camilla wanted was for William to marry one of the highborn, titled English roses he had dated before meeting Kate, or better yet, someone from one of the royal houses of Europe. It was understood that, once a match had been made, William was free to take a mistress or go back to playing the field. "Camilla is a kind of snob when it comes to the royal family," Brooks-Baker said. "She's down-to-earth herself, but she believes the royals should stay up there on that pedestal and keep the riffraff out."

Camilla was most disturbed about the negative things she was hearing about Carole Middleton from mutual friends in Berkshire. They were telling her that Kate's mother was strictly nouveau riche, and completely lacking in breeding and background. She was pushy, they said—a chain-smoker and a gum chewer who dressed like someone half her age. "Really, Charles," Camilla said in front of St. James's staff members, "I'm not impressed with these Middleton people."

Charles had other, more pressing matters to attend to in late October 2003. Mark Bolland was still lobbing grenades at his former employer in the wake of the two-year-long Burrell case, warning in the *News of the World* that the Crown would collapse if Charles and his fellow Windsors continued to be "blissfully unaware of real people's problems. The royal family will at last reap the bitter harvest from the seeds their courtiers are now sowing," he wrote, adding that the Windsors should stop being "frightened of the ghost of Diana" and "learn lessons" from the late Princess. "It is still not too late. Why not just embrace what good she represented and her dynamic force for change?" If the Queen and the Prince of Wales didn't "start to understand the way a modern, democratic society works in an age of global communication," Bolland concluded ominously, the monarchy would soon discover that "the line between invisibility and irrelevance is no line at all."

Invisibility is what Charles craved when he returned from an official trip to India and Oman to find that he was embroiled once again in the latest in a seemingly endless stream of lurid sex scandals. Eight months earlier, Charles's trusted valet Michael Fawcett resigned from his $180,000-a-year job after it was revealed that one of his duties had been to sell off more than $150,000 worth of royal gifts and turn the proceeds over to the Prince—a task for which he earned the Palace nickname Fawcett the

Fence. The valet's reported $800,000 severance package, supplemented by an additional $750,000 to buy a house and a $160,000-a-year retainer to arrange parties and other events for the Prince, sparked indignation when the details were leaked to the *Daily Mail* and the *Times*.

Now, a year after valet George Smith claimed he had been raped by one of Charles's senior servants and had witnessed "a member of the royal family" in an awkward position with another man, the *Mail on Sunday* was about to identify the Prince of Wales as the mystery royal. At the same time, Paul Burrell made public secret tapes Diana recorded in the early 1990s in which she complained that Charles was "too close" to Fawcett. "What can one do when your husband is in an unhealthy relationship with a servant?" She recalled that Charles and Fawcett seemed "uncomfortable and uneasy" when she surprised them one evening in one of the Prince's private rooms.

"I feel completely isolated," Diana said at the time. "Charles confides more in Fawcett than he does with me." Later in the tapes, the Princess accused Charles and the Queen of being "trapped in the Dark Ages," and in part blamed the royal family's dismissive attitude toward her on the valet. "They look down their noses at me," she said. "It's just awful. I am sure Fawcett is behind it. He has far too much influence."

Before the *Mail on Sunday* could detonate its bombshell, Fawcett's attorneys obtained an injunction blocking publication of the allegedly false and defamatory story. "Gagged!" shrieked the paper's front-page headline the following day. The court order, however, did not apply to the *News of the World*, which asked point-blank on its front page, "Is Charles Bisexual?" "Emphatically not," answered Mark Bolland, who nonetheless admitted that Charles's own private secretary, Sir Michael Peat, had once asked if he thought the Prince of Wales slept with men as well as women.

Camilla, who dismissed the idea of Charles being anything but heterosexual with one word—"laughable"—advised the Prince to "loftily sweep aside" the stories and "go about doing the wonderful things you do, darling." In this instance, however, Charles made the unwise decision to meet the accusations head-on. He instructed his private secretary to go on television and issue a flat-out denial on his behalf. Calling the charges "totally untrue and without a shred of substance," Peat went on to insist that "the speculation needs to come to an end. The incident which the former employee claims to have witnessed did not take place."

Unfortunately for Charles, Peat's "denial" included a flat-out admission that Charles was indeed the royal in question. Why was Peat dismissing the story as "nonsense"? Because, the private secretary declared, "the Prince of Wales has told me it is untrue, and I believe him implicitly."

"By the time he was finished," said journalist Richard Kay, "Sir Michael had talked around the unspecified rumor so much that no one of average intelligence could have been in any doubt that it was one of a sexual nature involving the Prince and a royal servant." Not surprisingly, Fleet Street's reaction was anything but restrained.

"Charles on the Rack—Crisis Grows over What the Servant Saw," screamed the headline in the *Daily Mail*. The *Mirror* went with "Me and Servant: It's All Lies! Charles's Astonishing Denial," and the *Independent* decried a "Right Royal Whitewash." "The Palace Is Under Siege over Sex Rumor Frenzy" bellowed the respectable *Guardian*. Even London's staunchly promonarchy *Sunday Times* asked: "Prince Charles: Nothing to Fear, Nothing to Hide?" Editors on the other side of the Atlantic weren't any kinder. "Hear the One About Prince Charles and the Valet?" asked *Salon*. "'Princess Charles' May Go on TV to Deny Bi-Sex Rumors," smirked the *New York Post*.

A senior courtier described the Prince's denial as "a moment of madness that could destroy Charles." Polls over the next few days seemed to confirm those fears. One showed that fewer than 39 percent of Britons now wanted him as their next monarch. An overwhelming majority wanted William to succeed the Queen. Under the headline "Why the Palace Is Under Siege over Sex Rumor Frenzy," the *Guardian*'s John Arlidge wrote that Prince Charles had "put himself in the thick of it" and "turned a private drama into a public crisis."

The Prince of Wales withdrew to Highgrove to talk to his plants, stroll his gardens, and tend to his prized herd of black sheep. On his fifty-fifth birthday, he ventured outside to visit a nearby senior living community, where staff members and residents surprised him with a cake. As they burst into a shaky rendition of "Happy Birthday," Charles stared blankly. "We wanted to cheer him up on his birthday," said one of the organizers of the visit, Lady Emily Blatch. "We thought," she added in a masterpiece of understatement, "he might need it."

Charles could at least take pride in his sons. By all accounts, William had settled down with Kate Middleton in their cozy farmhouse, and the two were doing well in all their classes. Still working on revamping Harry's image as a hard-drinking party animal—no sooner did he return from Australia than he began staying out until four in the morning at clubs in and around London—Charles's aides decided on sending the Spare to work with AIDS victims in Africa. But before he departed, Harry went on another bender at Boujis, the smart South Kensington club owned by the Princes' former aide and pal Marko Dyer. It was nearly three o'clock when his two bodyguards helped a soused Harry out of the club and into a waiting car.

A few days later, under the headline "Spoiled and Lazy Harry Is One of a Kind," *Express* columnist Carol Sarler slammed the young Prince as "a national disgrace" who "rarely lifted a finger unless it's to feel up a cheap tart in a nightclub." Not only was Harry guilty of "drinking, drugging, and yobbing" (hooliganism), she continued, but his planned two-month stint in the African nation of Lesotho, where 30 percent of the population suffered from AIDS, was nothing more than a public relations ploy to recast his image. Harry, Sarler said, "only reluctantly agreed to spend part of the trip staring at poor people."

Furious, Charles instructed his new communications secretary, Patrick "Paddy" Harverson, to fire back. Not only was Sarler's attack "beyond the pale . . . completely wrong, unfair, and unfounded," but the portrait she painted of Prince Harry was "grossly inaccurate and ill-informed." To prove their point, an ITV camera crew followed Harry as he hauled water, dug ditches, built bridges, and played with AIDS-infected orphans.

Diana would undoubtedly have been pleased to see her boys fully embrace her brand of hands-on giving. She would have been less thrilled to see them embrace Camilla as their stepmother. While they were both cordial to their father's mistress, neither William nor Harry made an effort to spend time with her. Conversely, Charles declined to force the issue, realizing that his sons were busy with their own lives. "They are kind of like Ron and Nancy Reagan," their American friend Joan Rivers said. "It's all about Charles and Camilla. She loves him, and he loves her—and he really doesn't *need* William and Harry to love her too. It would be nice if they *liked* her, and I think they do."

Camilla was still a constant presence in Charles's social life, accompanying him to private and semiofficial events within the United Kingdom. But she was still denied an official role, particularly if the assignment was overseas. When Charles flew to Washington for Ronald Reagan's funeral on June 11, 2004, and returned the same day, Camilla didn't go. "It was terribly sad. Nancy was crushed," Charles told Camilla at a small dinner party a few days later. "That's the way it's going to be with us," Camilla said before joking, "That's why I'm going first!"

The limbo Charles and Camilla found themselves in might have gone on indefinitely were it not for a game-changing incident that fall. Edward van Cutsem, Charles's twenty-nine-year-old godson, was to marry twenty-four-year-old Lady Tamara Grosvenor, daughter of the Duke and Duchess of Westminster, at Chester Cathedral. The Queen and Prince Philip were invited, and William and Harry were to serve as ushers. Charles and Camilla had been invited by the groom, but at the last minute Edward's mother asked the Prince of Wales and his mistress not only to sit in separate pews but also to arrive and leave in separate cars. In keeping with protocol, that meant Charles would sit up front with the rest of the royal family, and Camilla would be relegated to the back of the church.

Camilla felt it was one indignity too many, and Charles agreed. They decided to boycott the Van Cutsem wedding and to come up with a strategy that would let them plan one of their own. The Prince of Wales had always been reluctant to confront his mother, but now Camilla was insisting that he take a stand. Charles told the Queen in no uncertain terms that he was going to go ahead with plans to marry Mrs. Parker Bowles—whether she approved or not. "And whatever Mrs. Parker Bowles wants," Richard Kay remarked, "Mrs. Parker Bowles gets."

There were strategic reasons as well for tying the knot. Charles could see that William had fallen deeply in love with Kate Middleton, and there was already talk of an imminent engagement. Given the fact that most of his countrymen already wanted William to succeed the Queen, that preference was likely to become even stronger if he became a husband while Papa still shilly-shallied with his aging mistress. Charles knew that William, who often became emotional when discussing how unfairly his father had been treated in the press, would never steal the crown from him. But the Prince of Wales was also savvy enough to realize that the monarchy relied, more than ever, on public support. "If they don't love me the way they love the Queen because they'd rather have someone else," Charles told his deputy private secretary, "then I might as well just stay right where I am."

As 2004 drew to a close, the Queen informed her private secretary, Sir Robin Janvrin, that she felt "powerless to stop this." During the royal family's Christmas holiday at Sandringham, Elizabeth II reluctantly bestowed her long-withheld consent. Before she did, though, the Queen extracted from Charles the promise that he would not seek to make Camilla his queen after he assumed the throne. Charles insisted that Camilla had no ambition to become either Princess of Wales or wear the crown of a queen.

Charles asked for and got his sons' blessing. At Highgrove, just before New Year's Day 2005, he got down on bended knee ("Of course. What else?" Camilla said later) and asked for Camilla's hand in marriage. Ironically, the ring—an emerald-cut diamond with three diamond baguettes on either side, all weighing a total of 8 carats—had belonged to the Queen Mother.

The plan was to announce the wedding on Valentine's Day 2005. There would be many distractions along the way—not the least of which was

Harry's decision to attend a costume party wearing the short-sleeved khaki uniform of Nazi tank commander General Erwin Rommel's Afrika Korps, including the eagle badge of the dreaded Wehrmacht on the chest and a swastika armband. Apparently, Harry had no concept of Nazism or what the swastika in particular symbolized.

Alongside the headline "Harry the Nazi," the *Sun* ran a full-page photograph of the partying Prince in his costume, holding a cigarette in his left hand and a drink in his right. The large red, white, and black swastika band on his right arm leapt off the page. Reaction was swift. Members of Parliament, Holocaust survivors and their families, the Israeli Foreign Minister, and several World War II veterans groups immediately condemned the clueless Prince. Hitler biographer Sir Ian Kershaw pilloried Harry for "grotesquely bad taste," Rabbi Marvin Hier of the Simon Wiesenthal Center criticized him for committing a "shameful act," and former royals press spokesman Dickie Arbiter claimed that "once again Prince Charles has been let down by his wayward son. It can't go on."

Charles, who was in Scotland at the time, could be heard by one security officer "shouting at the top of his lungs" at Harry over the phone from Balmoral. ("Mein Fury: Charles Rages at Nazi Harry," read the *Sun*'s headline the following day.) "Prince Charles was apoplectic, and by the time he was finished, poor Prince Harry was shaking." Papa also questioned why William, who wore an inoffensive lion costume, didn't step in to prevent his younger brother from making such a colossal error in judgment. "I don't think either of them really fully appreciate who the Nazis were and what they did," Charles confided to a major American donor, "which, considering my family's history in standing up to them, is really quite remarkable."

Still, Harry was mortified that he had "let down the family" yet again. Charles grudgingly accepted the boy's tearful apologies and instructed Clarence House to issue a press release. "Prince Harry has apologized for any offense or embarrassment he has caused," the brief statement read. "He realizes it was a poor choice of costume."

For many, this tepid "apology" did not go nearly far enough. The leader of the Conservatives in Parliament, Michael Howard, demanded that Prince Harry go on television "and tell us himself just how contrite he is." Concerned that Harry's costume might prove a boon to neo-Nazi groups, Jewish leaders invited Prince Harry to participate in ceremonies commemorating the sixtieth anniversary of the liberation of Auschwitz. It had to be explained to the young Prince that Auschwitz was a Nazi concentration camp where one million Jews perished.

Charles, convinced that public outrage over Harry's behavior was overblown, made it clear that his son would not be apologizing on television. Nor would Harry be visiting Auschwitz. Instead, he would make a "private personal apology" to the Chief Rabbi of the United Hebrew Congregations of the Commonwealth, Dr. Jonathan Sacks. There would be no more comments on this matter, Paddy Harverson told the press, from Prince Charles or any member of the royal family. Prince Harry made a "heartfelt apology for making a very bad mistake."

Not everyone was satisfied. Backbenchers in the House of Commons were now calling for Harry to be barred from attending Sandhurst, on the grounds that he was "simply not suitable," said Labourite Doug Henderson. Harry "let the country down," chimed in Lord Levy, Britain's envoy to the Middle East. "The Prince's behavior has sent shock waves through the international community." *Daily Telegraph* columnist Tom Utley, calling Harry "a complete thicko," noted that the wayward Prince seemed "utterly clueless" about what a swastika symbolizes. "What the hell did they teach him during his five years at Eton? We are talking stupidity on an absolutely monumental scale."

Once again Diana's friends rushed to point out that nothing of this sort could have happened on her watch. To be sure, Charles had never been as close to the boys even when they were small. Although the Prince stepped up as a caring father in the wake of his ex-wife's death, he had not been a constant presence in his sons' lives once they were shipped off to boarding school. With the exception of their headmasters and security officers, some of whom had grown close to the Princes but still did not rise to the level of father surrogates, William and Harry were essentially left alone to cope with the pressures of daily life.

Charles, hoping to forestall another media disaster, finally hired a separate private secretary for William and Harry in the aftermath of the "Harry the Nazi" episode. Jamie Lowther-Pinkerton, a forty-four-year-old father of three, had served as a major in the Irish Guards and worked as the Queen Mother's equerry. A veteran of the first Gulf War, he had also served in Britain's elite Special Forces, chasing down narcotics dealers in Colombia in the 1990s. The Major and the boys hit it off instantly; for the next eight years, Lowther-Pinkerton would be available on a round-the-clock basis—there to provide William and Harry with the fatherly advice they needed to stay out of trouble. In the process, he would become their most trusted aide and a de facto member of the family.

Charles's plan to announce his engagement to Camilla on Valentine's Day fell through on February 10, 2005, when Prime Minister Tony Blair's office leaked it to the press. Just days before, the Queen had consulted 10 Downing Street before granting her official permission under the Royal Marriages Act. "The Duke of Edinburgh and I are very happy that the Prince of Wales and Mrs. Parker Bowles are to marry," read Her Majesty's less-than-effusive statement. "We have given them our warmest good wishes for their future together."

That night, the couple hosted a dinner for environmentalists at Windsor Castle, where the Queen lit up the round tower in their honor. Later Camilla, wearing a red dress and smiling from ear to ear, flashed her engagement ring for the cameras. The blushing fifty-seven-year-old bride-to-be burbled, "I'm just coming down to earth."

———

Charles, meanwhile, was having to cope with two major losses in his sporting life—activities that had been centerpieces of his life since he was a teenager. Despite his bombarding Tony Blair and other ministers with Black Spider memos inexplicably defending foxhunts as "romantic," the government's ban went into effect in February 2005. In a final show of defiance, the Prince of Wales was cheered by his fellow riders as he went out with the Meynell and South Staffordshire hunt in Derbyshire just three days before the ban went into effect. (Camilla had already given up fox-hunting because, she said, "it was wreaking havoc with my back.")

A few months later, Charles hung up his polo mallet for good. He had competed in the stratospherically expensive sport—the high-living Prince once disingenuously called polo "my one great extravagance"—for more than four decades. "Without polo," he said when he was in the middle of his tumultuous marriage to Diana, "I will go stark, staring mad. I will go on as long as I bounce when I fall off." But the sport had taken its toll on the royal personage: over the years, he had been thrown from his horse numerous times, breaking bones and severely injuring his back. In one instance, Charles's pony threw him off and then kicked him in the face, leaving a two-inch scar on his left cheek. Now, as he prepared to wed the love of his life, he "felt the time was right. I wish to bow out gracefully, but regretfully."

Besides, there were plenty of other challenges facing Charles and Camilla—not the least of which was whether the two divorcees would be allowed a church wedding, and if the Queen would be willing to attend the ceremony at all. While the details were worked out, William and Harry took the groom on a "stag week" ski trip to Klosters. At one point, the trio sat on a stone wall and posed gamely for a battery of photographers. With reporters only a few yards away and open microphones inches in front them, Charles griped about the press. "I can't bear that man," he said of the BBC's Nicholas Witchell as Witchell stood directly in front of them, looking at Prince Charles in total amazement. "He's so awful, he really is. . . . Bloody people. I *hate* doing this."

The infinitely more media savvy William tried to calm down his father. "Keep smiling," he murmured to Papa under his breath. "Keep smiling."

If it was all an act, William seemed terribly convincing. Asked what he thought of the upcoming wedding, he replied enthusiastically, "Very happy, very pleased. It will be a good day." He even joked about his responsibilities as a witness at the civil ceremony. "As long as I don't lose the rings," he cracked, "I'm all right!"

Saturday, April 9, 2005
Windsor Castle

Charles and Camilla knelt side by side in the nave of St. George's Chapel—burial place of ten kings including Henry VIII and spiritual home of the Order of the Garter—and hung their heads in an abject and obvious display of shame. Before them stood the imposing figure of Dr. Rowan Williams, the white-bearded, crimson-robed Archbishop of Canterbury. With large leather-bound copies of the 1662 *Book of Common Prayer* opened before each of them, the bride and groom read the Act of Penitence; written by King Henry VIII's Archbishop of Canterbury, Thomas Cranmer, this is considered to be the strongest confessional prayer in the Church of England.

Technically, what transpired inside the medieval stone walls of Windsor Castle was not a wedding at all; Charles and Camilla officially tied the knot earlier during a brief civil ceremony at Windsor Guildhall. This was a forty-five-minute service of prayer and dedication, and the Archbishop grudgingly agreed to perform it only if the bride and groom made some public apology for the egregiously adulterous behavior for which they were so famous. Still kneeling and gazing down at the prayer books before them, Charles nervously scratched behind his right ear as the moment arrived when he and Camilla were forced to beg for absolution. Although the Prince of Wales twiddled his thumbs throughout, both husband and wife were red faced as they read aloud along with their 750 assembled guests:

"We acknowledge and bewail our manifold sins and wickedness, which we, from time to time, most grievously have committed, by thought, word, and deed against thy Divine Majesty, provoking most justly thy wrath and indignation against us.

"We do earnestly repent and are utterly sorry for these our misdoings. The remembrance of them is grievous unto us. The burden of them intolerable."

Leaving no doubt as to what he expected of the newlyweds, the Archbishop instructed them—first Charles and then Camilla—to be faithful to each other in their marriage, to understand the covenant of marriage, and to take each other "for richer, for poorer, for better or worse . . . till parted by death." Perhaps not satisfied that he had driven the point home sufficiently, the cleric asked again if they had resolved in their hearts to be "faithful" and to "forsake all others." After all, up until this point, neither had shown any particular interest in abiding by any marriage vows.

"That is my resolve," Charles answered diffidently, "with the help of God." Camilla followed suit, and then they touched hands as the Archbishop proclaimed, "Let the rings be symbols of your faithfulness." Their wedding bands were made from gold sliced off the same large Welsh nugget that provided the gold for Charles and Diana's wedding rings as well as the wedding rings worn by the Queen and Prince Philip.

Publicly owning up to their "manifold sins and wickedness" was only one of several important concessions Charles and Camilla were compelled to make—chief among them the Prince of Wales's vow that when he became king, he would not insist that Camilla be his queen but rather England's very first "Princess consort." For the time being, rather than be known as Princess of Wales—a title still identified so strongly with Diana—she had agreed to assume one of her predecessor's lesser appellations: Duchess of Cornwall. It was certainly grander than what the Palace's Men in Gray originally had in mind: simply "Camilla Windsor," with no title at all.

By way of at least making his marriage to Camilla more palatable to the public—polls showed that only 7 percent could accept her as their queen—Charles was more than willing to go along with the "soft sell" strategy mapped out by Mark Bolland and Peter Mandelson. With good reason. None of it really mattered. Whatever they called her, Camilla was now—in tradition and law—Princess of Wales by simple virtue of her marriage to the Prince of Wales. This meant that among all women in the royal family, she was second only to the Queen in rank. Once Charles became king, she would automatically become queen for the very same reason—and not just Queen of England. The English monarch is also head of state in sixteen of the British Commonwealth's fifty-three member nations, making his wife queen of those nations as well. (Entering into a morganatic marriage that specifically barred her from becoming queen was nixed by Charles early in the process.)

Whether or not these few concessions really mattered, the planets had aligned in such a way as to make marriage to the love of his life possible—and Charles seized the moment. His motives were not entirely romantic. Pressure had been mounting ever since the previous Archbishop of Canterbury, George Carey, urged him to "make an honest woman" of his longtime mistress. In addition to the Church of England publicly calling for the Prince to put an end to his "sinful" affair with Camilla, the Queen resigned herself to the inevitable. As much as she blamed Camilla for destroying her son's marriage and damaging the monarchy, Elizabeth II wanted him to re-marry now rather than later—so that the people could grow accustomed to the idea of a King Charles and Queen Camilla.

That is, if Charles succeeded his mother. William and his longtime girlfriend Kate Middleton appeared headed for the altar as well. Polls continued to show that a vast majority of British citizens wanted William as their next sovereign—a feeling that would only grow stronger if William married his popular college sweetheart while Papa was still cavorting with his older mistress.

Then there was the money to consider. The House of Commons had appointed a special committee to look into Prince Charles's financial affairs and determined that he was spending half a million dollars on Camilla annually—some of that courtesy of the British taxpayer. "One might excuse spending that much on a royal spouse," one MP noted. "But lavishing public funds on the Prince of Wales's paramour will not sit well with Parliament—or the British people."

For Charles, there were other financial matters to contend with. Namely, should he become the first Prince of Wales—the first member of the royal family, in fact—to insist his bride sign a prenuptial agreement? Because he had no such agreement with Diana, he had been forced to reach into his own deep pockets to pay her $28 million settlement. In the end, and against the advice of his lawyers, Charles did not raise the issue of a prenup with Camilla at all. On the contrary, he went out of his way to ensure that his second wife would always be financially independent by setting up a $20 million trust fund that guaranteed her an annual income of at least $700,000. (The only catch was that, upon her death, the $20 million would be paid back into the royal coffers.)

However generous the terms of the trust fund were, it did not preclude Camilla from demanding a settlement in the event of a divorce. The Prince "simply didn't care," said a royal lawyer. "He was adamant that the marriage has to be based from the start on trust and good faith"—things that were certainly missing from his first attempt at matrimony.

With the financial and legal hurdles cleared—the Lord Chancellor, Lord Falconer, ruled that under the Human Rights Act of 1998 a divorced future king was free to marry in a civil ceremony "like anybody else"— there was still one last pothole on the road to wedded bliss. Pope John Paul II died on April 2, 2005, and his funeral was the same day as the originally scheduled wedding date: April 8. Elizabeth ordered her son to postpone his wedding by one day so that he could stand in for her in Rome—"anything she could do," said one of the Queen's ladies-in-waiting, "to stave off having to watch Charles marry Camilla, even if only for one day."

Or for two hours. Over a period of weeks, Charles implored his mother repeatedly to attend the actual 12:30 p.m. wedding service at Windsor Guildhall, but she said she did not want to get in the way of the "low-key" nature of the civil ceremony. Her absence—and that of Prince Philip—was widely perceived as a royal snub, as both the Queen and the Prince of Wales knew it would be.

Indeed, at the 2:30 p.m. service of prayer and dedication, Camilla's new mother-in-law made no effort to conceal her feelings. "Cross" and "sour" were the words used in the press to describe the look on the Queen's face throughout the service. "Sullen" was another. Through much of the ceremony, she stared straight ahead, occasionally squinting down at the program in her lap or pausing to emit an audible sigh of resignation. She confided later to her cousin that it was hard to forget that her mother was directly beneath their feet, buried alongside her husband, George VI, in the St. George's Chapel vault. The Queen Mother was so fed up with the way Diana treated her adored grandson that by 1991 she forbade anyone from uttering the Princess's name in her house. But it was Camilla whom she truly despised. Like the notorious American divorcée Wallis Simpson, Camilla rained scandal down upon the royal family and, in the process, pushed the monarchy itself to the brink of extinction.

"The Queen Mother could not figure out what it was Charles saw in Camilla," Margaret Rhodes said, "any more than she could understand what her brother-in-law, Edward VIII, saw in Mrs. Simpson." The Queen Mother described both women as "wicked" and "two peas in a pod." She also made her daughter promise that she would not allow Charles to marry Camilla—"no matter how happy he thinks she will make him."

It had been a promise Elizabeth II felt bound to keep. The Queen Mother "held a certain power over the Queen," Harold Brooks-Baker said. "She may have looked sweet and grandmotherly, but she had a wicked wit, and she could hold a grudge forever." Until her mother's death in March 2002 at age 101, the Queen kept her word. "There was," said Colin Henderson, the Queen's head coachman in the Royal Mews, "an unwritten instruction that 'that woman' does not cross the threshold" of Buckingham Palace—"or, for that matter, any royal residence."

Charles was undeniably devastated by news of his Granny's passing. After all, she had always provided him with the loving support ("the hugs—those wonderful, all-enveloping hugs") and tenderness that no one else in the family seemed capable of giving. But it was equally true that the Queen Mother's death removed the last major obstacle to securing the Queen's permission to marry, if not exactly her blessing.

For this particularly fraught occasion, Elizabeth II wore an off-white suit and a matching hat. Wearing even off-white, said one courtier, was "an interesting choice, given wedding protocol that makes it rather clear that white is a color that is really reserved for the bride, whether she chooses to wear it or not." But then again, he continued, "perhaps the Queen is sending the message that she regards the marriage a bit of a sham and the bride rather a joke." Members of the royal family often use jewelry to send signals, and it was hard to miss the Australian wattle brooch of blue and yellow diamonds sparkling on her left lapel—an important piece, but not as stunning or historically significant as the Queen Victoria diamond brooch the Queen wore to Princess Diana's funeral at Westminster Abbey.

"It was inevitable that they would marry, and the Queen just wanted them to get it over with," longtime royals correspondent James Whitaker said. "But it didn't mean she had to like it." Her Majesty was certainly not alone. A *Daily Telegraph* poll conducted just days earlier showed that a majority of Britons felt his marriage to Camilla would weaken the monarchy and that 69 percent of Britons did not want Charles to succeed the Queen. A *Sunday Times* poll also reflected the public's outrage, with 58 percent preferring William as their next monarch, and 73 percent flat-out rejecting the idea of Camilla as queen.

Camilla tried to dismiss the big event at Windsor as just "two old people getting hitched." But, in truth, the whole affair seemed to be taking its toll on the fifty-seven-year-old bride. On the eve of her wedding, Camilla mysteriously came down with a scorching 103-degree temperature that royal physicians could attribute only to "massive amounts of stress." The next morning, Camilla simply refused to get out of bed. She was, she would later admit, "panic stricken" that she and Charles would be confronted by hundreds of Diana fans at Windsor protesting the marriage. With Camilla literally hiding beneath the covers, her daughter Laura, her sister Annabel, her dresser Jacqui Meakin, and a housemaid cajoled and pleaded—until Annabel finally threatened to put on her sister's clothes and marry the Prince of Wales herself. Finally, Camilla reluctantly climbed out of bed and slowly got dressed.

On the ride to Windsor Guildhall, Charles reassuringly pointed out that most of the people lining the streets were smiling and friendly. But not everyone. Directly across from Guildhall hung a banner that read "Illegal, Immoral, Shameful," while another read "Long Live the Queen, Diana Forever: King Charles, Queen Camilla—Never!"

Not surprisingly, security was tight, with plainclothes officers milling among the spectators, uniformed police with bomb-sniffing dogs examining bags and packages, and snipers positioned on rooftops. Inside Windsor Guildhall, Camilla was shaking so badly that one of her friends feared she would collapse "before she could say 'I do.'" While Charles and his bride did not kiss at any time during the service—in fact, they would not be seen kissing at all on their wedding day—Camilla's son Tom Parker Bowles was relieved that "everything went as planned." Standing together on the Guildhall steps as the newlyweds waved at the mostly sympathetic crowd, William tried to ignore the scattered "boos" and catcalls. "Well, I'm happy with that," he said. His new stepbrother nodded in agreement. "Yup," Tom said. "Me too."

One person whose absence was noted: Kate Middleton, by this point a source of frenzied speculation. As undoubtedly fond of her as he had become, Charles would not countenance having his bride upstaged by someone as young, stunning, and appealing to the masses as Kate. It was generally understood, a friend said, that this was "at long, long last Camilla's moment."

The bride was still trembling when she made her entrance at St. George's Chapel, but she had never looked more glamourous. For the civil ceremony, Camilla had worn a cream silk chiffon dress, a matching oyster silk coat created by London designers Robinson Valentine, a large white hat decorated with French lace and feather trim, and a diamond-and-pearl Prince of Wales "feathers brooch" pinned to her right lapel. Charles was fittingly attired in a morning suit—gray pin-striped trousers, gray double-breasted vest, black coat, pale-blue shirt, blue-and-green-patterned tie, a flower in his left lapel.

Now as she walked down the aisle on the arm of her new husband, Camilla looked regal in a Valentine-designed floor-length hand-painted porcelain-blue silk shantung coat worn over a matching chiffon dress, and a striking Philip Treacy–designed feathered gold headdress tipped with

Swarovski crystals—a look that appealed to Charles, who rightly observed that Treacy intended for the crystal-tipped baby ostrich feathers to look like "glistening shafts of wheat." Camilla's bridal bouquet consisted of lily-of-the-valley and white, yellow, and purple primroses with a sprig of myrtle. The myrtle, sent by a well-wisher from Cornwall, had traditionally been featured in royal bouquets since Victorian times—and always by the women who were destined to become queen.

At the end of the service, everyone stood to sing "God Save the Queen," with the obvious exception of the Queen herself. (When asked why by an American friend, she replied with a sly grin, "Do you really think I should just stand there and sing, 'God save . . . me'?") The bride and groom then departed arm in arm through the chapel's West Door, followed at a distance by Prince Philip and the Queen. Once outside, they were welcomed by warm applause and cheers from the crowd.

The Prince of Wales took a deep breath, squinted into the sunshine, and smiled. "Well, here we are then," he said to Camilla.

"I was rather nervous," she admitted, holding on to her elaborate ostrich feather hat to prevent it from sailing off in the wind.

"Well, we're married now," he reassured her. "Right, to the plan now. . . . Look over at all the well-wishers. Lovely, isn't it?"

"Oh yes," Camilla nodded as she continued to struggle with her headpiece. "This hat is no good in the wind." Turning around, she scanned the crowd for her mother-in-law. "Where's the Queen?" she asked anxiously.

"They'll be along soon," Charles said. "She'll be having a good old chat."

The Queen was taking her time, perhaps contemplating whether she was ready for her first-ever appearance alongside the problematic Mrs. Parker Bowles.

Eventually Her Majesty did materialize on the steps behind them. "That all went rather well," she muttered to Charles.

"Yes," he answered blankly.

In an instant, she turned to go. "We're leaving now," the Queen told her son.

Surprised, Charles knew another important moment—the image of Camilla standing next to the Queen—was slipping through his fingers. "Oh," he pleaded with his mother, "I really want a picture of us all." The Queen had no intention of cooperating, and within seconds she and the Duke of Edinburgh were climbing into a royal Rolls that ferried them back up Castle Hill. Charles had managed to convince her, however, to host a tea-and-finger-food reception in Windsor's opulent state apartments for eight hundred of the couple's friends. Among them: Prime Minister Tony Blair and his wife, Cherie; King Constantine and Queen Anne-Marie of Greece; rocker Phil Collins; Italian fashion designer Valentino Garavani; British TV host and journalist Sir David Frost; actors Richard Grant, Edward Fox, and Joanna Lumley; longtime chum Joan Rivers; and even Andrew Parker Bowles with his new wife, Rosemary.

The Queen, famously fanatical when it came to the sport of kings, could not ignore the fact that the wedding fell on the same day as horse racing's Grand National Steeplechase. Her Majesty began her wedding reception speech by saying she had "two important announcements to make. The first is that Hedgehunter has won the Grand National! The other is that my son is home and dry with the woman he loves. They have been over difficult jumps—Becher's Brook and the Chair—and all kinds of other terrible obstacles. And now," she added, "they're in the winner's enclosure." At no time did she mention Camilla by name.

In his speech, Charles thanked "my dear Mama" for footing the bill and "my darling Camilla, who has stood with me through thick and thin and whose precious optimism and humor have seen me through." The Prince went on to thank his bride once more "for taking on the task of being married to me." As the newlyweds left the reception, William and Harry made a point of bussing their stepmother on both cheeks. At the reception, the Queen and Prince Philip finally bit the bullet and posed for wedding portraits—their first with Camilla next to the sovereign. William and Harry also posed with their beaming father and his bride—the first time they were photographed with Camilla, as well.

Behind the scenes, Charles—egged on by his handlers at St. James's—

had begged his mother to make some public sign of affection toward Camilla; if the once-notorious Mrs. Parker Bowles was ever to be fully accepted by the public as the wife of the future monarch, then such a demonstration of goodwill was needed. But as one of her earliest private secretaries, Martin Charteris, once commented, "This queen does not like being told what to do. And why should she? She is the Queen."

Nevertheless, Her Majesty, determined to restore some degree of tranquility within Palace walls, did pull off one precisely timed and well-executed gesture as her son and his new wife paused on the castle steps before departing for their honeymoon at Balmoral: Quickly, the Queen surprised Camilla by offering her cheek for a good-bye kiss, and then watched impassively as Charles and his trembling bride climbed into their waiting Bentley.

William and Harry, meanwhile, had spent more than an hour decorating the wedding car with Mylar balloons and graffiti that read "Prince+Duchess, C+C," and the obligatory "Just Married." Charles, who admitted later that at this point he was "more relieved than anything else that it was over," managed a broad smile as his sons waved good-bye, shouting, "Thanks for coming! Thanks for coming!"—the words the Prince of Wales and Camilla repeated robotically as they shook hands in the receiving line.

For the next two weeks, Charles and Camilla spent their honeymoon indulging in their favorite country pursuits at Balmoral on the banks of the River Muick. More precisely, they stayed not at Balmoral Castle but at the newly refurbished Birkhall, once the Scottish home of the one person who had so successfully blocked Prince Charles's marriage to his longtime love—the Queen Mother. Nevertheless, Charles still cherished the memory of his grandmother. She called Birkhall, built in 1715 and purchased by Queen Victoria in 1849, a "small big house, or a big small house." Camilla had proposed that Birkhall, the site of six royal honeymoons, be updated and the furnishings replaced, but Charles would have none of it. The frayed upholstery, faded draperies, and soiled carpets were repaired, not replaced. The tartan wall covers also remained, and the Queen

Mother's blue gardening coats were left hanging on wooden pegs near a rear doorway right where they were the day she died. Perhaps the most striking reminder of the Queen Mother—quite literally—was her collection of eleven grandfather clocks in the dining room that chimed loud and long every hour but not quite in unison, stopping all conversation in its tracks. "It's no use trying to talk," the Queen Mother would admonish her guests, "until they're all finished."

During her first few months as a bona fide member of the royal family, Camilla took it slow. She rode in a royal carriage at Ascot, and again at Trooping the Colour—the Queen's parade marking the monarch's "official" birthday in early June. Afterward, she made her debut appearance on the Buckingham Palace balcony with the Queen, Charles, and the rest of the royals. Few noticed that Camilla was wearing her wedding dress—the same ensemble she wore to her civil ceremony at Windsor. This was at Charles's insistence. "Prince Charles believes it is Camilla's right," explained an equerry, "to appear on that balcony in her wedding dress the way Princess Diana and other royal brides have." Charles "wanted her photographed with him on that balcony in her wedding dress, alongside him," added another senior courtier. "That's all there was to it. But it does show how his mind is working and where he hopes it will lead."

A month later, bombs planted by Islamist terrorists went off on the busses and subways of London, killing fifty-two people and wounding more than seven hundred others. Within hours, Charles and Camilla were visiting victims at St. Mary's Hospital in Paddington. Charles was proud of the way Camilla, looking into the faces of people who had been horribly injured, "managed to hold it all together. She's a very compassionate, strong human being," he added. "But she wept later."

In the wake of the terrorist attacks, Britons were eager for good news, and it came in the form of a royal graduation. After living together on campus for three years, Big Willy and Babykins—the nicknames William and Kate Middleton had for each other—graduated from the University of St. Andrews on June 23, 2005. He earned a master of arts degree in geography, while Kate walked away with a degree in art history—making her the only future queen with a university degree. Queen Elizabeth and Prince Philip were there, as were Harry, Camilla, and of course, Charles. For all their firepower, the senior royals took a backseat to the undeniable stars of this particular show: the tall, blond heir to the British throne and his stunning, chestnut-maned commoner girlfriend.

Vice-Chancellor Brian Lang seemed to have William and Kate in mind when he rose to give his commencement address. "I say this every year to all new graduates: you may have met your husband or wife." Lang paused for the expected laugh, then continued. "Our title as 'Top Matchmaking University in Britain' signifies so much that is good about St. Andrews, so we can rely on you to go forth and multiply."

First, however, William would have to fulfill the six-month postgraduate schedule mapped out for him by Buckingham Palace: a short stint with financial institutions in the city, working on a small farm in Papa's Duchy of Cornwall, volunteering at a children's hospital, riding with RAF search-and-rescue teams in Wales—before beginning his forty-four weeks of punishing military training at Sandhurst.

It was during this period that he drew even closer to the Middletons. Those weekends that William didn't spend with Kate at the Middletons' flat in Chelsea, he drove the thirty-three miles from Sandhurst to Oak Acre in Bucklebury. There, away from omnipresent servants and fawning courtiers, he felt he could unwind in a way he never could at Highgrove or Clarence House. Given the tumult of his own parents' doomed marriage, this up-close-and-personal glimpse of what appeared to be a truly happy family life struck William as "a revelation." He enjoyed being in their company, and they, in turn, treated him like one of their own. William and his girlfriend's parents had grown so close, in fact, that the Heir began calling Mike Middleton "Dad."

If Papa was jealous of Kate's father, or even aware that William had been embraced so warmly by the Middleton family, he gave no sign of it. "Prince Charles was confident in his role as 'Papa,'" a former equerry said. "The word *Dad* does not have the same meaning for him. Members of the royal family don't call their fathers Dad. Papa, or Pa, or Father—never

Dad." Besides, "the Prince of Wales was focused on making the British people fall in love with Camilla."

On November 2, 2005, the Prince of Wales and the Duchess of Cornwall embarked on their first official trip abroad: a much-anticipated six-day tour of the United States. On board their jet (chartered at a cost of $370,000) was a sixteen-member entourage that included a valet, a butler, a dresser, a physician, a makeup artist, a hairdresser, and several secretaries. More than fifty British journalists also made the trip. Camilla, who had already encountered criticism for wearing the same red coat and tartan wrap three times in one week, packed fifty dresses. Charles made do with a dozen suits and blazers.

The Prince of Wales's concerns were not merely sartorial. America was still, as he often said, "Diana Country." The Prince worried that die-hard fans of the late Princess of Wales might turn out to jeer him and Camilla, pelt them with eggs, or, worse yet, attack them in some way. Charles, anticipating the worst, ordered that security for the trip be doubled.

Their first stop was Ground Zero for the dedication of a memorial stone at what would eventually be named the Queen Elizabeth II September 11th Garden, created to honor the sixty-seven British victims of 9/11. That was followed by a glittering champagne reception at the Museum of Modern Art. On the front page of the next day's *New York Post* was a photo of Camilla wearing an ill-fitting blue velvet dress and the headline "Queen Camilla Is New York's Frump Tower." "If it was Diana they were looking for, forget it," columnist Cindy Adams sniped. "Glamorous, Camilla definitely ain't." Actress Elaine Stritch disagreed. "I don't care what other people say," Stritch told the new Princess of Wales, "you look terrific. No bullshit, you look great!"

At the White House, Charles and Camilla enjoyed an informal lunch with President George W. Bush and First Lady Laura Bush, and would return that same evening to be guests of honor at a black-tie dinner. The entire time, protestors stood outside the White House Gates, chanting and waving placards that read "You're No Diana." That was painfully clear that night when, in contrast to the dazzling evening gown Diana had worn to dance the night away with John Travolta twenty years earlier, Camilla opted for a more matronly black cashmere jacket and black pleated skirt.

In between their meals at the Executive Mansion, Charles and Camilla accompanied the First Lady on a tour of a charter school in Southeast Washington. Then the Duchess split off to give a speech about osteoporosis at the National Institutes of Health in Bethesda, Maryland, while Charles accepted the prestigious Victor Scully Prize for his contribution to the public understanding of urban planning. The Prince announced that he was donating his $25,000 prize, named for a renowned Yale University professor and architecture historian, to rebuilding Gulf Coast communities devastated by Hurricane Katrina three months earlier.

From Washington, Charles and Camilla made an unscheduled stop in New Orleans to survey the damage done by Katrina and were visibly shaken by what they saw. Camilla, who spent much of the day lugging around a shopping bag filled with Mardi Gras decorations given to her by a survivor, scrambled up the side of a rebuilt levee in a tight skirt and high heels to get a better look.

From New Orleans, they flew to San Francisco—where, during a visit to a homeless center, Prince Charles was repeatedly called "Your Honor"—and then drove north over the Golden Gate Bridge to visit organic farms in picturesque Marin County. There, while browsing an open-air market, Camilla sampled vegetables, fruits, cheese, and even organic wine as she strolled from one stall to another. In her only faux pas on the trip, she did not offer to pay for anything—something both Diana and Charles were always extraordinarily careful to do.

Over time the American press and public gradually warmed to the somewhat drab older couple, although anyone expecting them to generate the kind of excitement that Diana did was inevitably disappointed. "Princess Diana was everybody's favorite movie star," commented Letitia Baldrige, who had been Jackie Kennedy's White House social secretary. "Camilla is no movie star."

The press accounts back home, however, painted the tour as an unmitigated triumph—proof positive that Charles and Camilla were a royal force to be reckoned with, even in "Diana Country."

In light of Camilla's stellar performance in the United States, it came as a shock when the Queen decided to specifically exclude the Duchess of Cornwall from the state prayers for the royal family that, after a separate prayer for the sovereign, are recited at all Church of England Sunday services. "Almighty God, the fountain of all goodness," the prayer reads, "we humbly beseech thee to bless Philip, Duke of Edinburgh, Charles, Prince of Wales, and all the royal family." Prior to being stripped of her royal status after her divorce from Charles in 1996, Princess Diana had always been included by name in the prayer.

Charles was well known within Palace circles for his flashes of temper, and in this case he angrily demanded to know from the source why she was snubbing his wife. The Queen pointed to new surveys showing that three out of four Britons still opposed the idea of Camilla becoming queen. "Too many people are still unhappy with the marriage, Charles," Her Majesty explained, adding that she didn't "want to appear insensitive."

On the bright side, now that she was a full-fledged member of the royal family Camilla was entitled to attend the Windsors' lavish Christmas festivities at Sandringham. Far more important for the former Mrs. Parker Bowles, the loyal but embattled mistress who had been relegated to the shadows for so long, this was the first time in decades she could spend Christmas with the man she loved.

In March 2006 Charles and Camilla embarked on a two-week tour of Egypt, Saudi Arabia, and India. For Camilla, an emotional moment came at a Commonwealth cemetery at El Alamein, Egypt, when she visited the graves of two men who had fought alongside her father during World War II. As Charles looked on, she placed a bouquet of white roses on the graves with a personal note from Major Bruce Shand. "The gallantry and sacrifice of two fellow 12th Lancers on 6th November 1942 will never be forgotten by me," it read.

"I've a huge lump in my throat," Camilla said. "Very moving."

In Cairo, Camilla covered her face with a veil to enter the thousand-year-old Al-Azhar mosque, but inadvertently flouted Wahhabite Islamic law when she forgot to wear a head scarf for her formal introduction to Saudi King Abdullah Bin Abdulaziz Al Saud. In Riyadh, Charles became the first Westerner to give a speech at Imam Muhammad ibn Saud Islamic University, considered by more reform-minded Saudis as the heart of intractable Islamic conservatism. His decidedly uphill theme: religious tolerance.

As the trip progressed, temperatures soared. The 108-degree heat "almost did me in," admitted Camilla, who at several points was on the verge of collapse. The one time she actually did collapse had nothing to do with the heat, however. While signing a guest book at a Sikh shrine in the Indian state of Punjab, the Duchess went to sit down, only to discover too late that the chair was no longer there. A flustered and somewhat indignant Charles got his wife back on her feet, but she merely dusted herself and continued shaking hands. It amazed the *Telegraph*'s Caroline Davies that Camilla somehow "managed to keep smiling all the way down as she hit the floor."

———

On April 21, 2006, Charles joined the rest of his countrymen in celebrating the Queen's eightieth birthday. Countess Mountbatten observed that Elizabeth II was "as happy as I have ever seen her," despite Charles's characteristically stiff if heartfelt video tribute to "my mama." He even inadvertently lent credence to his earlier description of the Queen as a cold and aloof parent, describing how frustrated he was as a small boy trying to talk to his mother over the phone during long absences—"when all one heard was the faintest of voices over an incessant crackle and static."

Not unexpectedly, the fact that the Queen was now an octogenarian stirred up talk of abdication—even though the overwhelming consensus was this was something Her Majesty would never even consider doing. Still, at fifty-six, Charles was only three years younger than Edward VII when he succeeded Victoria. For both men, the wait had grown all but unbearable over the years. "Most people must find out what job is right for them, and then they spend their whole life doing it," a friend of Charles's observed. "Now, imagine being born to do only one job and then having to wait around a bloody lifetime to do it!"

There was one secret society inside the Palace that addressed such matters as the succession: the Way Ahead Group. At the end of 1992—her annus horribilis that saw Windsor Castle nearly burn to the ground and two of her sons' marriages founder—the Queen called what Palace officials referred to as a "crunch summit" to map out a future for the monarchy. Lord Airlie, a favorite of Her Majesty's and at the time Lord Chamberlain, set up the Way Ahead Group with the Queen as chairperson and a membership composed of senior royals and a handful of advisors whose identities remained confidential. The details of their twice-yearly conversations—so sensitive that MI5 swept the conference for listening devices before each meeting—were not disclosed to anyone; even the Prime Minister was kept in the dark.

The group's early meetings paved the way for many new policies—from the sovereign agreeing to pay income taxes to finally taking steps toward ending primogeniture, the centuries-old rule that places male children ahead of female children in the line of succession. In 2006 Charles urged his mother to admit twenty-four-year-old William into this sanctum sanctorum of royal decision-making. For the next six years, William and Charles actively participated in Way Ahead debates that shaped the monarchy in the post-Diana era—until the Queen called a halt to the meetings because she felt they had outlived their usefulness.

While William was undergoing rigorous training at Sandhurst—and later serving as Lieutenant Wales with the Blues and Royals Regiment of the Household Cavalry—his girlfriend was relentlessly pursued by paparazzi as Diana had been. Kate handled it surprisingly well—but not William, who feared she might meet the same fate as his mother. He turned to Papa for help. Charles usually distanced himself from such problems, but, in this case, he hired the royal law firm of Harbottle & Lewis to issue a string of stern warnings aimed at getting Britain's voracious tabloids to back down. Papa also hired a bodyguard to protect her around the clock when she was in London—protection that she was not legally entitled to because she had no formal standing. Still, by going the extra mile, Charles had signaled to the world at large that Kate Middleton was likely headed to the altar with his son.

In May 2006 Charles and Camilla would, in fact, be hosting a wedding reception at Ray Mill House as mother and stepfather of the bride. A year after Tom Parker Bowles's marriage to fashion journalist Sara Buys, Camilla's daughter Laura was marrying Harry Lopes, a onetime Calvin Klein underwear model and grandson of the late (and extraordinarily rich) Lord Astor of Hever. Once again William and Kate were the undisputed stars of the evening, eclipsing not only Charles and Camilla but also the bride and groom. "There was a terrific buzz as they came in," said the minister who performed the ceremony.

In a matter of weeks, Camilla's extended family gathered once again— this time to bury the Duchess's father, Bruce Shand, who had died at the age of eighty-nine. Charles described Camilla as "absolutely devastated" by the Major's death. Shand, who had the Wodehousian habit of ending every sentence with "what?," was a caricature of the perfect English gentleman. He was also unwaveringly loyal to his daughter, to the point where he once angrily confronted the Prince of Wales, wanting to know why it was "taking so damned bloody long" for the couple to marry.

By early 2007, Charles was about to ask his son the same thing. Now that William was launching what he intended to be a serious military career—as heir to the throne, he would undergo training in the Royal Navy and the Royal Air Force as well as the army—the twenty-four-year-old complained to his father that his relationship with Kate had begun to feel "claustrophobic." No matter that the preternaturally patient Kate, dubbed "Waity Katy" by Fleet Street, had given him plenty of leeway to visit clubs and even flirt with other women.

There were other pressures brought to bear on father and sons that year, not the least of which was the release at the end of 2006 of the portentously titled 832-page *Operation Paget Inquiry Report into the Allegation of Conspiracy to Murder Diana, Princess of Wales and Emad El-Din Mo-hamed Abdel Moneim Fayed.* John Stevens, now Lord Stevens, ran the investigation, and questioned both the Prince of Wales and Charles's father, the Duke of Edinburgh. At the end of a grueling three-hour interrogation at Clarence House, Charles was "stunned" by Lord Stevens's final question: "Did you, Your Highness, plot to murder the Princess or have anything to do with her death?"

"No," Charles answered, clenching his fists. "I did not." His father was even more insulted by Lord Stevens's line of questioning, but Diana's provocative statements in the final months of her life—repeatedly accusing Prince Philip of plotting "to get rid of me in a staged automobile accident"—made it imperative for Stevens to press the issue.

The *Operation Paget Report*, which had taken more than two years to complete, confirmed the findings of the original accident investigation. Notwithstanding the Princess's strangely accurate premonitions, the man driving the Mercedes sedan in which she and Dodi Fayed were riding that night was drunk, and none of those who perished in the car was wearing a seat belt.

Operation Paget did give a new sense of urgency to a more immediate problem: Now that he would be away on military maneuvers, who would protect Kate from being relentlessly pursued—perhaps even to her death—just as William's own mother had been?

Charles had grown fond of Kate over the years, impressed not only by her beauty, poise, charm, and wit, but also by what he called her "obvious strength of character." Camilla told her brother, Mark Shand, that what her husband most liked about Kate was that, unlike William's mother, she seemed "not at all neurotic." It was no small irony that, ultimately, it was Prince Charles's affection for Kate that led him to recommend to William that he break up with her. Do you, he asked his son point-blank, "intend to marry her in the end?"

William, who had often heard Camilla say that no man should marry before the age of thirty-five, made it abundantly clear that he was not ready to marry anyone. Charles, remembering how his own father had pressured him to marry—with disastrous results—advised his son to "end it now." By stringing the young woman along, he told William, he was being "completely unfair to Kate." Moreover, press interest in her was only bound to intensify as time went on, exposing her to even more risks.

Within hours, William broke up with his longtime love in a cell phone call, reducing her to tears. "The future king and his long-term girlfriend Kate Middleton," the *Times* intoned solemnly the next day, "have parted." The tabloids were somewhat less restrained. "Wills and Kate Split," screamed the front-page headline in the next morning's *Sun*, while the *Daily Mail*'s front page was taken up entirely with only two words: "It's Over!"

Where William took his father's advice, Kate consulted her mother Carole. Together they devised a strategy to win back William by having Kate hit London's social scene with Pippa, date other wealthy and titled young bachelors—including some of his friends—and generally appear as if she didn't have a care in the world. Their friend Jules Knight believed the young Prince "suddenly felt that he had made a huge mistake."

Six weeks to the day after William called it quits, he invited Kate to Clarence House and begged her to forgive him. It would be more than a month before the public learned they had reconciled—when she suddenly materialized at William's side on July 1, 2007, at the pop-star-studded Concert for Diana marking the tenth anniversary of the Princess's death and what would have been her forty-sixth birthday.

Things still moved at a snail's pace in the relationship, but Charles fully understood why. The Prince of Wales, who had always seen himself as a man of action, looked back on his years in the Royal Navy as one of the great experiences in his life. Now he could see the excitement in William's eyes whenever he spoke of his military training and how he wanted to join his fellow soldiers on the battlefield. However, the military brass was not about to put the heir to the throne in harm's way. Harry was another matter. Once the Spare was sent to the front lines in Afghanistan in December 2007 ("When Harry was in Afghanistan, I worried the whole damn time," Charles said), William pleaded for a chance to join him. "It was very difficult for William not to go," Charles later said. "But I did say to him 'You know, look, when I was in the navy . . . I had the same problem. They wouldn't send me anywhere!'"

Nonetheless, William asked Papa to put pressure on the Queen to intercede. In late April 2008 Granny granted William's wish to serve with British forces in Afghanistan—but only for thirty hours. His top-secret but highly perilous assignment: pilot a C-17 Globemaster troop transport to the front lines in Afghanistan and pick up the body of a fallen British soldier.

Just three weeks later, Kate stood in for William at the royal wedding of his cousin Peter Phillips, the oldest of Princess Anne's two children, and Autumn Kelly. It was the setting for Kate's first face-to-face meeting with the Queen. "It was in amongst a lot of other guests," Kate said of her first conversation with her future grandmother-in-law. "The Queen was very friendly and welcoming."

Charles was as surprised as everyone else when, rather than joining the Firm full-time at the end of 2008, William signed up instead for five years with the Royal Air Force as a search-and-rescue helicopter pilot. The next year, he and Kate moved into a rented five-bedroom farmhouse on the Welsh island of Anglesey, not far from the RAF Valley air base where he was stationed. While Charles had been widely criticized for spending money on his mistress, no one complained when it was revealed that an additional fifteen bodyguards were assigned to protect William and Kate at a cost of $2 million annually.

The world held its breath for another year as Charles watched the tabloid press unearth one unpleasant story after another about his future daughter-in-law's family. Most notable were photos of Kate's brother, James, nude and in drag, and a series of exposés about Kate's wild uncle Gary Goldsmith, the tattooed, profanity-spewing, cocaine-loving tech industry mogul who hosted his niece and Prince William at La Maison de Bang Bang, his crudely named estate on the Spanish island of Ibiza.

Before they became public, Camilla had gotten word of Uncle Gary's antics and presented them to Charles as further proof that the Middletons were "unsuitable" in-laws. But the Prince, who had already broken up the couple once, was not about to shatter his son's heart a second time. Even after the *News of the World* broke the story with the headline "Kate Middleton Drug and Vice Shock: Tycoon Who Boasts of Hosting Will's Villa Holiday Supplies Cocaine and Fixes Hookers," Charles and the Queen had only praise for Kate. The main reason had nothing to do with loyalty or kindness. Polls showed that, with Kate at his side, William's popularity was sky-high. A solid 64 percent of Her Majesty's subjects wanted him as their next king—and an all-time-record low of 19 percent wanted Charles.

———

For most of 2010, 22 Squadron C Flight's newly minted helicopter pilot was at the controls of his Sea King Mk 3, airlifting heart attack victims off oil rigs in the Irish Sea and rescuing hikers stranded in the rugged Snowdonia Mountains. Early that year, however, Granny dispatched William on a mission of a different sort. While Kate remained home in Wales, William journeyed to Australia and New Zealand on his first overseas tour.

Charles was initially all for sending William Down Under—until he read the headlines questioning why the Queen had passed *him* over for the job. By choosing her grandson to make the trip instead of her oldest son, Her Majesty inadvertently encouraged talk that William was now her "shadow king"—and that he was the person she was preparing for the top job.

Once again William was upset by any suggestion that he was trying to upstage his father. Prince Charles, he said, "is a marvelous, generous man who has really made an enormous impact on the world. My father is a great man in his own right, but, unfortunately, not everyone sees that." As for Kate: "She and my father adore each other."

———

For Charles, William's love affair with Kate was a double-edged sword. On the one hand, she was an obvious asset for the royalty, giving the people a vision of the monarchy extending well into the twenty-first century. On the other hand, this golden young couple full of promise undermined the Prince of Wales's standing and cast an even darker shadow over his own future as the next sovereign. "Camilla understands this better than anyone," said a veteran member of the St. James's Palace staff. "But Prince Charles doesn't really have the stomach for Machiavellian games like she does."

Charles's reaction was not unexpected when William told him that he was at last ready to pop the question. "Well, finally!" he said. "Thank God. It's about time, don't you think?" The Queen, who more than once had asked Charles to nudge his son toward an engagement, was also relieved. In October 2010 William took Kate to the slopes of snowcapped Mount Kenya, got down on one knee, and proposed with his mother's famous 18-carat diamond-and-sapphire engagement ring—"my way of making sure my mother didn't miss out on today."

A month later, on November 16, the happy news was announced over Twitter and the Queen's Facebook page. Charles professed to be "thrilled. They have been practicing long enough!" Camilla, who had been sniping at Kate and the Middletons for nine years, was at once effusive and perplexing. "It's the most brilliant news!" she said. "I'm just so happy for both of them. It's wicked."

Three days later, Charles and Camilla found themselves in hot water again. In an attempt to simultaneously explain his world philosophy and sound alarm bells about climate change à la former US Vice President Al Gore's eye-opening 2006 documentary *An Inconvenient Truth*, Charles filmed his own based on his book *Harmony: A New Way of Looking at Our World*. NBC agreed to air the documentary in prime time on November 19, along with an exclusive interview of the Prince conducted by the network's star news anchor at the time, Brian Williams.

Williams and Prince Charles sauntered across pasturelands and then sat down to chat in the dining room of the Castle of Mey, a former home of the late Queen Mother on the north coast of Scotland and now one of Charles and Camilla's five residences. The conversation covered a number of topics—the environment, William and Harry, the media—but one out-of-the-blue question clearly took the Prince by surprise: "Does the Duchess of Cornwall become Queen of England if and when you become the monarch?"

Charles paused for a moment. "That's, well . . . We'll see, won't we? That could be."

Reaction was swift. "Queen Camilla?" asked the headline in the *Guardian*. "Prince Charles Does Not Contradict U.S. Interviewer." The BBC reported that the Prince of Wales could have "stuck to the Clarence House script" and insisted he was abiding by his premarital pledge to make Camilla only Princess consort and not queen. But instead, the BBC went on, the Prince chose to give "a rather stumbling answer . . . which confirmed what people suspected, that he wants Camilla crowned alongside him as Queen Consort."

Less than three months later, Camilla herself weighed in, leaving little doubt that she and her husband had no intention of keeping the promise they made in 2005 to win public support for their marriage. The Duchess of Cornwall was visiting a children's center in Chippenham, Wiltshire, when an eight-year-old girl walked up and asked her, "Are you going to be Queen one day?"

Taken aback, Camilla thought for a moment, shrugged, and said, "You never know."

He's trying to save the world, damn it!
If you can't stand the heat, get out of the kitchen!
—Elizabeth Buchanan, Charles's former aide

To this day, Prince Charles is a deeply insecure person.
—Mark Bolland, Charles's former media advisor

Camilla soothes things.
She anticipates what can go wrong.
—Anne Glenconner, friend and
former lady-in-waiting to Princess Margaret

NINE

"OFF WITH THEIR HEADS!"

Westminster Abbey
April 29, 2011

The ten massive bells of the ancient abbey pealed, the throng cheered, and a shaft of golden sunlight sliced through the clouds to fall directly on the 1977 Rolls-Royce Phantom VI just as the bride emerged. Wearing a dress of ivory silk overlaid with lace, diamond chandelier earrings, and the dazzling Cartier Halo tiara—on loan from the Queen—Kate Middleton turned to wave, and the crowd exploded in cheers. While sister Pippa, no less striking in a simple white sheath, grabbed the bride's nine-foot-long train, Kate took her father's arm and proceeded through the abbey's massive West Door.

On a day brimming with symbolism, even the car in which they arrived had special significance. Five months before, Charles and Camilla were attacked in the very same Rolls-Royce by an angry mob demonstrating against a decision by Prime Minister David Cameron's new Conservative government to balance the budget by tripling university tuition fees. Separated momentarily from their security detail, the terrified couple hunkered down in the backseat as the crowd chanted, "Off with their heads!" and hurled rocks and bottles at the car. At one point, someone managed to reach inside through one of the shattered windows and jab the Duchess of Cornwall in the side with a stick before royal protection officers could finally come to the rescue.

Rather than ride to her wedding in another car, Kate insisted that the badly damaged Phantom be fully restored to its former glory—all by way of making it perfectly clear that the institution of the monarchy was as resilient as it had ever been. No one appreciated the gesture more than Charles, who just nine days earlier had marked another sobering milestone. On April 20, 2011, he surpassed Edward VII as the heir who had waited longest to ascend to the throne: fifty-nine years, two months, and thirteen days. Ironically, the Queen, looking even more vital than usual as she eagerly awaited her grandson's marriage, turned eighty-five the next day.

The Wedding of the Century was watched live on television and via the internet by an estimated three billion people in 180 countries—topping the record for a global audience set by Diana's funeral fourteen years earlier. They were not disappointed. As royal spectacles went—and Charles had played a major role in nearly all of them since his mother became queen—the marriage of Prince William to his college sweetheart Kate Middleton went off without a hitch. William, dressed in the crimson and braided ceremonial uniform of a colonel in the Irish Guards, his RAF wings pinned to a sky-blue garter sash, waited patiently at the altar with his best man, an equally dashing Prince Harry, at this side.

Sitting in the front pew with the rest of the groom's family, Charles wore the equally flamboyant Royal Navy Number One Dress, a ceremonial admiral's uniform with medals, badges, and ornamental gold braiding on the right shoulder that indicated he was aide-de-camp to his mother, Elizabeth II. At the Prince of Wales's side was his black-and-gold ceremonial sword. Philip, not to be outdone, wore his scarlet Grenadier Guards uniform with a sash signifying that he was a Knight of the Garter. The Duke of Edinburgh also carried a silver-sheathed sword—one that was less fancy but visibly larger than his son's.

That morning, the Queen, who had already proclaimed the couple's wedding day a national holiday, named her grandson and his bride the

Duke and Duchess of Cambridge, Earl and Countess of Strathearn, and Baron and Lady Carrickfergus. She also invited the Middletons to design their own coat of arms and then ordered that it be "impaled" (merged) with William's, symbolizing the union of the Windsors, the Spencers, and the Middletons. Now, as William slipped a wedding ring cleaved from a unique nugget of Welsh gold on Kate's finger (William chose not to wear one), the couple seemed not the least bit nervous. Like Diana before her— but unlike Camilla in her wedding to Charles—Kate intentionally omitted the word *obey* from her vows. When the Archbishop of Canterbury pronounced them man and wife, a roar went up outside the abbey.

Inside, the mood was happy, if understandably more restrained. For her part, the Queen had tried to make the process for the newlyweds as easy as possible. When William and Kate asked her what to do after they were given a wedding guest list with 777 names on it—nearly all people they didn't know—the Queen told them to "tear it up and start with your friends. It's *your* day."

In stark contrast to the glum, dyspeptic expression she maintained throughout Charles and Camilla's wedding service in 2005, the Queen "never stopped grinning for an instant" reported one church official who witnessed the ceremony. Camilla, meanwhile, was described as "nervous and distracted." As for Charles: "The Prince of Wales had that look he often has—eyebrows raised, benign smile. I assume he was overjoyed. Hard to tell."

Once outside, William and Kate climbed into the open horse-drawn 1902 State Landau used for the most important royal occasions and rode past more than one million cheering well-wishers who lined the route to Buckingham Palace. Pandemonium struck when they joined the rest of the royal family on the palace balcony, and the newlyweds were so eager to please that when it appeared they had disappointed the crowd with their first kiss, they did it again with a little more passion. Charles, in full military regalia, maintained the same distant, detached look he had inside the abbey. Camilla was busy trying to rein in her fidgety granddaughter Eliza Lopes, at three years old the youngest of the bridesmaids.

There were the requisite formal photos, followed by an intimate Queen's Breakfast for 650. Afterward, William and Kate surprised the crowd by driving through the Buckingham Palace gates in Charles's midnight-blue 1970 Aston Martin convertible with JUST WED license plates and taking a victory lap before zooming off to Clarence House to change. That night, the Prince of Wales hosted a glittering black-tie banquet for 300 at Buckingham Palace, where there were the usual speeches and toasts. Charles stood up and looked down on William's balding pate, felt his own, and said with a shrug, "It must be hereditary." Then he turned sentimental, recalling how he gave a pedal car to William when he was a small boy and told him the only thing he shouldn't do was drive it into the cedar tree in the yard. "Of course," Charles said, "he drove the car into the tree, which was more or less the end of the car and the tree." After praising Kate ("A wonderful girl; we are so lucky to have her in the family"), Charles cracked that he hoped his elder son would care for him in his old age. "Now I'm worried," the groom's father said, "that instead he'll push my wheelchair off a cliff."

Just one year after hosting William and Kate's Wedding of the Century, Britain was ready to party again. This time there would be a seemingly never-ending series of country fairs, garden parties, luncheons, teas, banquets, concerts, street fairs, and receptions over the four months leading up to the Queen's Diamond Jubilee—a four-day extravaganza in June celebrating Elizabeth II's sixtieth year on the throne. Only one other British monarch had reigned as long: her great-great-grandmother Victoria.

Unlike her Golden Jubilee ten years earlier, however, this time Her Majesty was willing to share the spotlight. Charles and his team at St. James's Palace saw the opportunity to showcase the Prince of Wales as well, and the Queen's canny private secretary, former British intelligence officer Sir Christopher Geidt, agreed. Geidt, Charles's private secretary Clive Alderton, and his communications secretary Paddy Harverson collaborated on a scheme to "make it clear this wasn't just a celebration of the

Charles makes a heartfelt effort to connect with young victims of Hurricane Katrina during his and Camilla's visit to New Orleans in November 2005.

Charles and Camilla accompany the Queen at the 2007 Commonwealth summit in Kampala, Uganda.

Although Charles nearly torpedoed Kate Middleton's chances of ever landing her prince by urging William to break up with her in 2007, he was thrilled when William and Kate finally tied the knot in 2011.

41

42

For the first time in seventeen years, Charles joined Her Majesty at the State Opening of Parliament in 2013—a clear sign that he was taking on more of the monarch's official duties as he prepared to step into what Palace insiders call "The Top Job."

Proving that they are game for anything, Charles and Camilla always throw themselves into native dances. From top: The Prince during a visit to Mexico City, and Camilla on their royal tour of Crete. During a visit to Australia, the heir to the throne manages to look dignified while receiving a traditional aboriginal blessing with a didgeridoo.

44

45

Three Kings. A twenty-two-month-old Prince George steals the show when he makes his debut on the Buckingham Palace balcony during Trooping the Colour ceremonies in 2015—just six weeks after the birth of his sister, Charlotte. At a charity polo match the following day, Charles keeps one eye on his rambunctious grandson while Kate greets a friend. On her third birthday, Princess Charlotte showers kisses on the newest Cambridge, little brother Prince Louis.

At an April 2018 Buckingham Palace dinner, Charles weeps with laughter at the wit of Canadian Prime Minister Justin Trudeau.

Scenes from a Royal Wedding. When Meghan Markle's father was unable to attend her wedding to Prince Harry on May 19, 2018, Charles stepped in to walk her down the aisle. Later, the newly minted Duke and Duchess of Sussex depart in an open carriage. Center: A wedding portrait, featuring the United Kingdom's first divorced, biracial, American princess.

50

51

52

Meghan shares a laugh with her grandmother-in-law, who welcomed the Sussexes' son, Archie Harrison Mountbatten-Windsor, into the royal fold on May 6, 2019.

53

54

In a rare candid moment on the Buckingham Palace balcony, Charles chats with Harry and Meghan while Camilla, the Queen, and Kate watch Charlotte make faces at the crowd below. George, meanwhile, looks skyward for signs that the RAF flyover is about to begin.

55

Charles tenderly kisses the Queen's hand at the 2017 funeral of the Countess Mountbatten, daughter of his mentor (and Her Majesty's second cousin) Lord Mountbatten.

past," Harverson said, "but an exciting look forward at the future of the monarchy." Specifically, Charles, William, Kate, and yes, Camilla, would be at her side whenever possible. They would also serve as her ambassadors, filling in for the monarch whenever she herself could not be there in the flesh.

Beginning in February, the Queen crisscrossed the country—usually with Prince Philip—visiting cities, towns, and small villages, while her children were dispatched to every corner of the Commonwealth: Charles and Camilla to Canada, Australia, and New Zealand; Anne to Africa; Andrew to India and the Caribbean; William and Kate to Singapore, Malaysia, and the South Pacific. Harry was sent to the Bahamas, Belize, and Jamaica as, in the words of one courtier, "the fun-loving stand-in for his grandmother."

Charles specifically wanted to underscore the importance of the Commonwealth and his future role as the head of it. Over her sixty-year reign Elizabeth II, who keenly appreciated the fact that one-third of the world's population still lived in Commonwealth nations, had somehow managed to single-handedly keep the global confederation from unraveling. Fifteen of the fifty-three former British colonies and dependencies that make up the Commonwealth had kept the British monarch as their sovereign even after gaining their independence—an arrangement that held fast almost entirely because of the personal affection the people in those countries felt for Elizabeth.

Without her on the throne, there was genuine concern that countries with strong antimonarchist movements and where Charles was not particularly popular—Canada and Australia, for instance—would opt for republicanism, signaling the beginning of the end for what remained of the British Empire. "I think the appropriate time for this nation to move to be a republic," former Australian prime minister Julia Gillard said, echoing the sentiments of several other Commonwealth nations, "is when we see the monarch change." (There were similar concerns about Scotland, where the population had voted down independence from the United Kingdom in part, said political analysts, because of the Queen's popularity there.)

While her children were on the road that March of 2012, Elizabeth II journeyed in the Gold State Coach—"the Pram," as Camilla wryly called it—to Westminster Hall for the purpose of unveiling a new stained window bearing her coat of arms. More important, she would also address both houses of Parliament for only the sixth time in her six-decade reign. The regal tableau included gold-helmeted officers of the Household Cavalry with their plumed gold helmets, sabers, and ceremonial three-hundred-year-old battle-axes, the elaborately adorned State Trumpeters of the Life Guards, and, lining the grand staircase, Beefeaters in their trademark crimson-and-gold dress uniforms dating back to sixteenth-century Tudor England. Seated next to the Queen was Prince Philip, looking impassive on his own marginally smaller but still opulent throne.

With members of the House of Lords and the House of Commons looking on, the Queen thanked her family ("Their support across the generations has been beyond measure") and particularly her deadpan husband. "Prince Philip is well known for declining compliments of any kind," she cracked as he stared straight ahead, expressionless. "But throughout he has been a constant strength and guide." Making it clear that part of the Jubilee celebrations would also be aimed at paving the way for future generations of monarchs, the Queen went on to say specifically how "proud and grateful" she was "to the Prince of Wales and other members of the royal family" for touring the world on her behalf.

The festivities picked up steam in mid-May with the four-day Diamond Jubilee Pageant and Royal Windsor Horse Show, an international equine spectacular branded by Palace media mavens as "the World Comes to Windsor." During the pageant and throughout the course of the Diamond Jubilee celebrations, Her Majesty would host the largest assembly of crowned heads since she assumed the throne: an emperor and empress, an emir, a sultan, a grand duke, and twenty-four kings and queens.

The jubilee's climax was stretched out over the first weekend in June, and, in the planning, Charles had made sure to sideline his brothers and sister. With the exception of giving the Queen and Prince Philip their due, the Prince of Wales insisted that otherwise the spotlight fall on him and his wife. Jubilee weekend started Friday night with Prince Charles's hour-long BBC-Television tribute to his mother. By turns tearful and exuberant, the Prince offered commentary on his parents' personal photos and shaky home movies as he sat in the library at Balmoral, looking much like any other baby boomer overcome by nostalgic glimpses into his own past.

In one scene, the Queen and Queen Mother laugh as they mock-struggle to push baby Charles uphill in a pram. In another, Winston Churchill shows up at a family picnic, and in yet another, eight-year-old Charles and his little sister Anne are at Holkham Beach near Sandringham, buried up to their necks in sand. Eighteen years earlier, Charles had accused his mother of being distant, cold, and aloof. Now he went out of his way to laud her for her "amazing poise and natural grace."

On Sunday, June 3, hundreds of street parties were held across the nation as part of the jubilee celebrations. One of the largest was in central London, where 2,500 people sat at a giant picnic table—actually five hundred end-to-end trestle tables—and waited to be served what was billed as "the Big Jubilee Lunch." Some in the crowd had been expecting the Queen herself, or perhaps William, but were not disappointed when Charles and Camilla showed up as the surprise guests of honor. The Duke and Duchess of Cornwall were greeted with wild cheers and then sang along to "God Save the Queen" before taking their seats. Camilla never took off her raincoat or her kid gloves, but she blended right in, happily chatting with locals about the food they had brought to the party in Tupperware containers. "Ah, sausage rolls," she said, sampling one woman's dish. "You can't beat a sausage roll, can you?"

Later, while Charles complained about that morning's rainy weather ("It's been ghastly, hasn't it?"), Camilla opened a box and produced a large Union Jack cake. "Here, you!" she said to the Prince. "I've been up all night making this." She smiled. "Okay, well, I haven't. It was my idea, though, and it is the thought that counts. I am not sure you would want to eat anything I made anyway!"

From there, Charles and Camilla headed for the Chelsea Harbour Pier, where they joined the Queen and the Duke of Edinburgh on a forty-one-foot tender from the decommissioned royal yacht *Britannia*. Charles and the Queen, who could both be brought to tears just talking about *Britannia*, savored this brief, nostalgic ride down the Thames to Cadogan Pier where a more suitable vessel awaited them. There they joined William, Kate, and Harry aboard the *Spirit of Chartwell*, a 210-foot luxury cruiser that had been transformed into a lavish, flower-bedecked royal barge. The *Spirit of Chartwell* could easily have accommodated the Queen's entire family, their spouses, and children, but that was not the idea. Once again, to make it clear that Charles was next in the line of succession, the Prince of Wales thought it best that Anne, Andrew, Edward, and their families ride in separate, far less grand boats. Mama agreed.

Along with more than 1.2 million Britons who lined the banks of the Thames twelve deep, the royal party watched in a driving rain as the flotilla of more than a thousand vessels passed in review: cutters, dragon boats, tall ships, trawlers, fireboats, Viking longships, a Maori war canoe, a pirate ship, and, most movingly, a motorboat steered by the last survivor of Dunkirk. The one thing they all had in common: these vessels had been drawn from every corner of Her Majesty's extended realm, the Commonwealth of Nations.

For her appearance aboard the *Chartwell*, the Queen decided to wear white, and asked that Camilla and Kate do the same. While the Duchess of Cornwall complied, the Duchess of Cambridge had apparently not gotten the memo: Kate came in a scarlet dress by Alexander McQueen, with a feathered chapeau to match.

"Oh, Kate, what were you thinking?" asked the *Daily Mail's* Amanda Platell, one of several journalists who took Prince William's wife to task for trying to upstage the Queen. "While the rest of the royal party sensibly opted for a muted palette, determined not to outshine the woman at the center of it all, the Duchess of Cambridge opted for a scarlet dress so bold and bright it just screamed: 'Look at me!'" One of Charles's former advisors was convinced that Kate's wardrobe choice was calculated and was probably the brainchild of one of Prince William's media gurus at Kensington Palace. In a family whose members "vie for attention every day," Charles's former advisor said, Camilla "couldn't have been happy. Every time the spotlight is on William or on Kate, for that matter, it undercuts the Prince of Wales just a little bit. He feels it, and she feels it."

While the press focused on the color palette of Kate's wardrobe, no one seemed to notice that the Duke of Edinburgh, who in six days would turn ninety-one, stood in the rain for four hours straight without ever bothering to visit the head. Once the maritime portion of the day's festivities was over, he was rushed to the hospital with a severe bladder infection and had to forgo the three-hour jubilee pop concert in front of Buckingham Palace.

At the end of the concert—which featured Sir Elton John, Sir Paul McCartney, Stevie Wonder, Annie Lennox, Ed Sheeran, Sir Tom Jones, and Dame Shirley Bassey of "Goldfinger" fame, among others—Charles noted that "the only sad thing" about the evening was that Prince Philip was too ill to attend. "But ladies and gentlemen," he added, "if we shout loud enough, he might just hear us in hospital." The crowd of more than a half million people started chanting "Philip! Philip! Philip!" Charles bent down and, as fireworks exploded over the palace, tenderly kissed the Queen's hand.

The following day, Charles and Camilla attended a National Service of Thanksgiving for Elizabeth II at St. Paul's Cathedral and then joined her at a "Queen's Luncheon" with London tradespeople at Westminster Hall. A million people lined the streets to catch a glimpse of Her Majesty as she rode in the horse-drawn 1902 State Landau coach back to Buckingham Palace. Since Philip had yet to be discharged from the hospital, Charles suggested that his mother forgo her usual practice of going solo under such circumstances. Instead, the Prince of Wales urged her to allow him and Camilla to ride with her, freeing up a second carriage to accommodate William, Kate, and Harry.

Not only did the Queen agree to Charles's plan, but also she allowed Camilla to sit next to her—"pride of place," as the *Times* called it—and no one was more surprised and delighted than Camilla herself. Veteran royal commentator Robert Jobson noted that the monarch "was sending a very strong message that the Duchess of Cornwall deserved to be there." (The next year, Philip was back beside the Queen in the royal carriage, this time sitting ramrod straight in the full uniform of the Grenadier Guards—tall bearskin hat included.)

Stepping out onto the Buckingham Palace balcony, the Queen was visibly startled by the thunderous ovation that went up from the throng. "Amazing," she said to Charles. "Oh, my goodness, how extraordinary." The cheers were not only for the sovereign, of course. In addition to her heir, *his* heir, Camilla, Kate, and Harry rounded out the royal balcony tableau. Add Prince Philip, and you had what Palace insiders now called "the Magnificent Seven"—a vital new face for the monarchy.

For the Prince of Wales, the Diamond Jubilee also marked a turning point. Bookended by the venerated sovereign and his storybook-handsome son, Charles was now seen as an indispensable bridge to the future. "When you see them all standing on the balcony," a senior courtier observed, "Charles is the one who really leaps out at you now. He has trained longer and harder than anyone to be the monarch—you can see the experience, even wisdom, in his face. He is starting to look like a king."

There was no question, however, who still commanded center stage. Less than two months later, Charles and Camilla were waiting for the Queen to arrive at the opening ceremonies of the 2012 London Olympics when suddenly an image of corgis racing up the Buckingham Palace stairs was broadcast on giant screens inside the stadium. Charles, who along with other members of the royal family had no idea what was about to happen, looked at Olympic organizing committee chairman Sebastian Coe and "laughed rather nervously," Coe recalled. "He wondered where on earth this was going." When the film cut to the back of the Queen, the Prince of Wales thought it was an impersonator—until she turned around. "It was then that everyone, including Prince Charles, realized, 'My God! It really is the Queen!'"

In the film clip, actor Daniel Craig of James Bond fame winds up boarding a helicopter with the Queen and parachuting with her into Olympic Stadium. While William and Harry shouted, "Go, Granny, go!" their father and Camilla roared with laughter. "When the Queen suddenly appeared in the royal box to officially open the games," Lord Coe said, "no one was more stunned than the Prince of Wales."

As the summer of 2012 drew to a close, Charles could breathe a sigh of relief that—fifteen years after their mother's death—both his sons appeared to be flourishing as senior members of the royal family. Now that a $7.6 million renovation to their quarters at Kensington Palace was complete, William and Kate were able to move into the palace's apartment 1A. Formerly the home of Princess Margaret, apartment 1A was actually a four-story, twenty-room Georgian brick manor with a walled garden and private tennis courts. The Queen would also spend $3 million on upgrades to Anmer Hall, a ten-bedroom, eighteenth-century stone-and-brick mansion on the grounds of Sandringham; within two years, Anmer Hall would become the Cambridges' principal residence, as William embarked on a new career as a pilot for the nearby East Anglian Air Ambulance service. The civilian job paid $60,000 a year, all of which William—who had inherited $18 million from his mother's estate when he turned thirty—donated to charity.

Charles also took solace in the knowledge that Harry's rabble-rousing days seemed to be behind him. The Spare filled in for the Queen at the closing ceremonies of the Olympic Games, and now, having completed his training as an Apache attack helicopter pilot, was about to be deployed to Afghanistan for a second time. "Only the best of the best become Apache pilots," said one of Harry's instructors at Naval Air Facility El Centro in California. "Harry is one of the very best of the very best."

After a relatively scandal-free eighteen months, Charles and the Queen—both of whom were on holiday at Balmoral—were blindsided by what happened next. On August 21, 2012, the Prince of Wales was informed that some "compromising" photos had turned up on the internet and were now winding up on the front pages of newspapers across the United States. The cell phone snapshots clearly showed Prince Harry cavorting in the buff with an equally nude young woman in his $8,000-a-night Las Vegas hotel suite. They were, Prince Charles was told, apparently playing strip billiards.

Charles's law firm of Harbottle & Lewis sprang into action, demanding that the Press Complaints Commission block publication of the photos in the United Kingdom. Their argument: that the moment captured on film was "entirely personal" and that Prince Harry had "a reasonable expectation of privacy" in his own hotel suite. The Prince of Wales wanted to go further, promising legal action if any newspaper in Britain dared publish the embarrassing snapshots.

Fleet Street wasn't having it. "Heir It Is! Harry Grabs the Crown Jewels!" hollered the *Sun*'s headline alongside a photo of a naked Prince, clutching his genitals in a halfhearted effort to conceal them. The *Daily Mirror* blared, "Harry Naked Romp!," while the *Daily Mail* reported, "Palace Fury at Harry Naked Photos."

Charles was furious—and not just at the press. He wanted to know why Harry's royal protection officers hadn't prevented the photos from being taken in the first place. There were, in fact, other photos showing one of Harry's bodyguards horsing around with him in the hotel hot tub. "I'm not exactly sure how you can protect Prince Harry when you are wearing your swim trunks in a Jacuzzi," said Dai Davies, former head of the royal protection squad at Scotland Yard. "For starters, where is his gun?"

This time Dickie Arbiter, the Queen's former press secretary, didn't mince words about the Spare. Harry, he told Charles, was a "loose cannon and shouldn't be left alone." Once again Harry's scandalous behavior was denounced on the floor of Parliament, this time by Labour MP Stephen Pound. This newest episode was, he said, "a new low, even for the royal family."

Despite his firm belief that Harry's privacy had been "egregiously violated," Charles gave the obligatory stern fatherly lecture on what it meant to be a Windsor. "My father's always trying to remind me about who I am and stuff like that," said Harry, who this time refused to make any public apologies but did make the trip to Balmoral to apologize to his father and his grandmother. "But it's very easy to forget about who I am when I am in the army. Everyone's wearing the same uniform and doing the same kind of thing. I get on well with the lads, and I enjoy my job. It really is as simple as that."

Harry's army buddies—both male and female—quickly rallied to his defense online by posing naked but concealing their private parts behind helmets, flags, and all manner of military hardware, including rifles and tanks. On Facebook, "Support Prince Harry with a Naked Salute" became almost as popular as the cell phone image that started it all.

Cheeky tableaus notwithstanding, Harry was mortified that he had let down his guard in Vegas. "It was a classic example of me being too much army and not enough Prince," he said later. "At the end of the day, I let myself down, I let my family down." Besides, he went on, "There's no such thing as privacy now. Everyone's got a camera on their cell phone. You can't move an inch without someone judging you. That's just the way it goes. I'm not going to sit here and whinge about it."

Still, as soon as Harry returned from his second tour of duty, the Prince was on the brink of a nervous breakdown—as he had been "many times" before. "I have probably been very close to a complete breakdown on numerous occasions, when all sorts of grief and sorts of lies and misconceptions and everything are coming to you from every angle," he conceded. Harry characterized the two-year period following his brother's wedding as one of "total chaos. I just couldn't put my finger on it. I just didn't know what was wrong with me."

While performing royal duties, Harry was often gripped by panic attacks that led to a fight-or-flight response. "During those years, I took up boxing, because everyone was saying boxing is good for you and it's a really good way of letting out aggression," he said. "And that really saved me because I was on the verge of punching someone, so being able to punch someone [in the ring] was certainly easier."

Whether it was because he simply failed to recognize the symptoms of clinical depression in his son or because he still clung to the royals' time-honored, stiff-upper-lip credo, Charles failed to take action. Fortunately, William stepped in to tell his brother he should seek professional help. "Look, you really need to deal with this," he told Harry. "It is not normal to think that nothing has affected you." It was also during this critical period of anxiety, depression, and bottled-up rage that Harry seriously considered renouncing his title and living out the rest of his life as a commoner. "I wanted out," he said later, "but then decided to stay in and work out a role for myself." The reason: "I don't want to let down the Queen—or my father."

Or his mother. Following in Diana's footsteps, Harry had journeyed to the South African kingdom of Lesotho in 2004 to help build a clinic for AIDS-infected orphans. While cradling an HIV-positive infant in his arms, Harry mused, "I've got a lot of my mother in me, basically, and I just think she'd want us to do this—me and my brother." Two years later, he returned to establish Sentebale (Forget Me Not), a new charity for children orphaned by AIDS.

Ironically, the things that both William and Harry believed their mother would "want us to do" brought them closer to Charles's ideal of public service. Two years after the Las Vegas scandal, Harry would seek to honor his military comrades by founding the annual Invictus Games, in which wounded, sick, or injured veterans compete in a variety of sports. *Invictus* is the Latin word for "undefeated." Beyond that, William and Harry—now joined by Kate—continued to champion many of the more than one hundred charities Diana had supported, raising millions of dollars for AIDS and cancer patients, battered women, children's hospitals, and the homeless.

No one, of course, had raised more money for charity than Papa. Nor had anyone worked harder on behalf of the monarchy. In 2012 alone, Charles racked up a staggering 592 official engagements. (The Queen came in second with 425 appearances that year.) Amazingly, the Prince of Wales still had time to churn out lengthy, highly detailed Black Spider memos at the astonishing rate of 1,800 or more each year. Education, ar-

chitecture, organic farming, wildlife preservation (from the Chatham alba-
tross to the Patagonian toothfish), badger hunting, herbal medicines,
overseas funding to restore huts in the Antarctic used in the early twentieth century by explorers Robert Scott and Ernest Shackleton—the Prince's
deepest thoughts on these and other pressing issues were dispatched on a
daily basis to government officials, from the Prime Minister on down.

Calling himself a "dissident" and—more or less self-deprecatingly—"the
Meddlesome Prince," Charles made it clear that as king he intended to become far more politically involved than his predecessor. Toward that end, he
did not shy away from making his views known on more controversial issues. In one of his memos to 10 Downing Street made public in 2015,
Charles criticized the government for not replacing military hardware that
had performed poorly in the desert—specifically the Lynx helicopter. "I fear
that this is just one more example of where our armed forces are being asked
to do an extremely challenging job (particularly in Iraq) without the necessary resources." Later, after half the Lynx helicopter fleet in Iraq was
grounded because of the searing heat, Prime Minister Tony Blair conceded
that Prince Charles had been right.

However, such admissions were few and far between for the infamously oversensitive Charles, who grew increasingly frustrated in his essentially thankless role as monarch-in-waiting. In the wake of Harry's
latest scandal, he seemed even touchier than usual, fuming over even the
smallest criticism in the press and lashing out indiscriminately at underlings. When he wasn't raging against perceived enemies or shouting at the
help, Charles was given to long stretches of brooding. Even Camilla, who
could always be counted on to bolster her Prince's spirits, found the task
increasingly difficult. "It is so frustrating," she complained to her friend
Joan Rivers, "when he does his Eeyore thing: You know, 'Oh, poor, pathetic me.' Sometimes I just want to scream."

So did many of the Prince's own staff members. Charles had a knack
for pitting even his most loyal and trusted aides against one another, resulting in turf wars at St. James's Palace that, wrote *Time*'s Catherine Mayer,
were "common and bloody." Mayer went on to say that "the court of the

heir to the throne crackles with tension," and even likened Clarence House to Wolf Hall—a not-so-subtle allusion to novelist Hilary Mantel's horrific account of scheming, treachery, and carnage in the court of Henry VIII.

Charles clearly intended to be an activist king, and as such he would wield an arcane form of power that in modern times had been dismissed as purely ceremonial—the power of Royal Assent. Once a bill was passed by both the House of Commons and the House of Lords, it required Royal Assent before it became law. This was accomplished by the monarch signing a letters patent—the written legal instrument that confers power from the Crown—in much the same way that a sitting US president signs a bill into law.

Ironically, abuses by the two previous kings named Charles forced Parliament to curtail the authority of the throne. Charles I had dissolved Parliament in 1629 after it sought to limit his capricious exercise of power. Eleven years of what would be known as the Personal Rule, or the Eleven Years' Tyranny, followed, during which Charles I ruled unchecked by Parliament. This led to the English Civil War, which brought Oliver Cromwell to power as Lord Protector, and Charles I's beheading in 1649.

Charles I's son was only slightly less inclined toward throwing his weight around after the restoration of the monarchy in 1660. Charles II not only withheld Royal Assent but also dissolved Parliament altogether in 1681 and ruled as an absolute monarch until his death four years later. As the power of Parliament grew, the Crown became less inclined to defy the will of the people's elected representatives. The last time it happened was in 1708, when, on the advice of her ministers, Queen Anne withheld Royal Assent from a bill that would have set up a militia in Scotland—an armed force that could, she feared, eventually turn against her.

Over the ensuing three centuries, the monarchy's political power eroded steadily, leaving it to survive as an enduring but politically toothless symbol of imperial grandeur and national unity. Now when the Queen dissolved Parliament, it was at the request of the Prime Minister, so that new elections could be held. When Parliament passed a bill, royal assent was always granted. As legal scholar John Kirkhope pointed out, the monarch's perceived duty to essentially rubber-stamp legislation has been seen in modern times as little more than the "quaint and sweet" vestige of a bygone age. The sovereign may be head of state, but her role today was strictly ceremonial.

Or was it? As the result of a lawsuit to release previously sealed documents, Britons were shocked to learn in 2013 that both Charles and the Queen had actually thwarted the will of Parliament on dozens of occasions. Employing their little-known prerogatives of Queen's Consent and Prince's Consent, Elizabeth II and the Prince of Wales had the right to veto any legislation curtailing their authority even before it was debated in Parliament. Most glaringly, the Queen vetoed the Military Action Against Iraq Bill in 1999, which would have transferred the power to launch air strikes against Iraq from the sovereign to Parliament. For his part, over the previous decade Charles had used his Prince's Consent power to essentially veto twelve government bills. The Queen and her son wield "real influence and real power," Kirkhope observed, "albeit unaccountable."

Bowing to pressure from St. James's Palace, the Queen made subtle efforts to transfer even more power to Charles. She still would not allow him to sit in on her weekly meetings with the Prime Minister—a request he had made following the death of Diana—but the monarch did not prevent the Prince from conferring with the Prime Minister and assorted government leaders on his own. Charles was also given copies of highly classified government documents from Her Majesty's red leather boxes of state (his boxes were green), and he increasingly performed ceremonial duties normally undertaken by the sovereign. By 2013, he was routinely standing in for the Queen when foreign ambassadors arrived at Buckingham Palace to present their credentials, and conducted a record number of investitures in his mother's absence.

Bestowing knighthoods and other honors was something neither Charles nor the Queen took lightly. When it was suggested that William should step in to perform several investitures as part of his kingly training, Papa took him firmly in hand. The night before his first investiture, Charles rehearsed with his son, using a ceremonial sword to show him the proper way to bestow a knighthood: a tap of the sword on the left shoulder, a sweep high above the recipient's head, and then a second tap on the right. "Careful on the upswing," Charles cautioned his pupil with a straight face. "Mustn't lop off an ear or something."

The badges and medals that invariably had to be pinned onto the dresses and jackets of recipients were also problematic: although Palace aides had already attached hooks to the honorees' clothing so that these awards could be simply hooked on, they often refused to stay fastened. William's very first "victim" was Manchester University professor Nicola Cullum, who was there to be made a Dame Commander of the Most Excellent Order of the British Empire for her services to nursing research. "My medal did fall off immediately," Dame Cullum laughed afterward. "I'm sure it was my fault. I think it was the way I curtsied."

Pomp and ceremony were, in fact, two of the most powerful public relations tools in the Windsor arsenal. After sitting out the State Opening of Parliament for seventeen years, Charles decided it was time to give the public a glimpse into the future. In May 2013 the king-to-be and his presumptive queen sat to Elizabeth II's right in the House of Lords—Charles in his full, medal-bedecked, gold-braided navy dress uniform and Camilla wearing a floor-length white gown, a pearl choker, the blue sash and brooch of a Dame Grand Cross of the Royal Victorian Order, and the Queen Mother's dazzling platinum-and-diamond Greville tiara. How significant was Charles's appearance after such a long absence? "Prince Charles," said the BBC's Luisa Baldini, "is clearly being positioned more as a 'king-in-waiting.'"

In truth, anything that happened in Great Britain in 2013—even an obvious ploy to make the British people sit up and take notice of their next monarch and his queen consort—was a mere distraction from the main event. On the afternoon of July 22, Charles and Camilla were on a long-planned tour of Yorkshire when they got the news that the rest of the world had been breathlessly anticipating: one full week past her expected due date and following twelve hours of labor, Kate had given birth to an eight-pound, six-ounce boy. Charles and Camilla boarded a helicopter for the 240-mile flight to London, then raced to St. Mary's Hospital in a royal limousine flanked by a full police escort.

Too late. In a breach of tradition that required senior royals to be the first extended family members to lay eyes on an heir to the throne, William welcomed Michael and Carole Middleton hours earlier. During the hour they spent with their infant grandson, both Middletons held him. "Amazing," Carole responded when asked how the first "cuddle" went. "It's all coming back." They also watched as William made his first fumbling attempt at changing the boy's diaper. "Not bad," commented Carole, who, unlike all the royals—who relied on nurses and nannies to take care of that sort of thing—was very familiar with the process. "He's a fast learner."

By contrast Charles and Camilla bolted out of their limousine and into the hospital, gazed at the as-yet-unnamed baby boy in Kate's arms, and, after expressing surprise that the Middletons had gotten there first, departed after only ten minutes. Neither Charles nor his wife, who was an unabashedly affectionate grandmother to her own five grandchildren, even asked to hold the baby. Once outside, Charles, meticulously attired in one of his double-breasted suits, pronounced the child "marvelous, thank you very much. Absolutely wonderful. You wait and see!"

Later, William and Kate brought "Baby Cambridge" outside to meet the small army of reporters who had been camped outside the hospital for days. Then, like any new parent, William struggled with securing his son in his car seat before climbing behind the wheel of his black Range Rover and driving off to Kensington Palace. Hours later, the Queen arrived to meet her great-grandson—and to be told his name before it was announced to the world: George Alexander Louis, His Royal Highness Prince George of Cambridge.

In the meantime, Charles and Camilla returned to Yorkshire, where they were met at every turn by cheering crowds. In the village of Bugthorpe, the Prince conceded that he had "cracked open some bubbly" to celebrate the night before, and that he was "thrilled and very excited—overjoyed" about becoming a grandfather for the first time. Camilla was no less effusive. "It's a wonderfully uplifting moment for the country," she said, adding that Charles would make a "wonderful grandfather. He's brilliant with children."

That remained to be seen. Certainly the Middletons left no doubt in anyone's mind that they intended to play a large role in the life of the future king. Carole Middleton had gone so far as to set up a nursery for little George at their house in Bucklebury. For the first six weeks of his life, Charles's grandson stayed with Kate and the Middletons while William commuted to his search-and-rescue base of operations in Wales. William, for one, had no illusions about which set of grandparents would be spending more time with Baby George. "My father will be a wonderful grandpa, I don't doubt that at all," he told a friend from St. Andrews. "It's just that he's so busy."

Busy, as it turned out, laying the groundwork for his reign. In November 2013, while the Middletons were enjoying their new grandson, Charles arrived in Sri Lanka to preside over the biennial Commonwealth summit. Although it was a common assumption that the role of Commonwealth chief was passed down automatically from monarch to monarch, the job would be up for grabs with Elizabeth's departure. Each member nation would actually be required to vote on whether it accepted Charles as its new leader once the time came.

It was the first time in her sixty-one-year reign that the Queen, who relished this part of the job in particular, was willing to step aside so that her son could take center stage. She had actively lobbied on her son's behalf in an effort to get each Commonwealth nation to commit to accepting Charles as the organization's leader and the Prince of Wales himself had essentially campaigned in thirty-three of the fifty-four Commonwealth nations.

Now he had a captive audience—and one shot at persuading them that he was a worthy successor to Elizabeth II. In what the *Daily Telegraph* described as "a pitch for himself as the Queen's eventual successor as head of the organization," Charles dropped the formalities and spoke of his personal attachment to the Commonwealth: "I feel very much part of the family. It's in my blood, I'm afraid," he told the assembled leaders, many of whom had previously hinted they would break away from the Common- wealth once Charles acceded to the throne. Eschewing anything so pedes- trian as a ballpoint, the Prince had jotted down his remarks using a special Parker fountain pen filled with organic ink. "I have been brought up in the family, and I think that what we are renewing here are those family ties—those family associations and family values. I feel proud and enor- mously privileged to be part of it all."

Camilla, who had watched anxiously as her husband of more than eight years delivered his speech, played a major part in the Prince's charm offensive. Gliding from one function to another with confidence and ease, she wheedled and cajoled prime ministers and ambassadors alike—"with- out ever making you feel that you were being put on the spot," marveled one diplomat. "She has a very light touch."

Even the press at the Sri Lanka summit warmed up to Camilla, espe- cially after she agreed to give her first on-the-record interview. The topic: Charles's sixty-fifth birthday, which he happened to be celebrating in the middle of the conference. "He never, ever stops working," the Duchess mock-complained as she met with reporters on a covered veranda in the middle of a Southeast Asian rainstorm. "He's exhausting. No matter what the day, he is always working. I am hopping up and down and saying, 'Darling. do you think we could have a bit of, you know, peace and quiet, enjoy ourselves together?' But he always has to finish something. He is so in the zone. You are outside, but he is always there in the zone, working, working, working."

The Duchess did manage to convince her workaholic husband to take a day off from their busy schedule and visit a luxurious seaside resort in nearby Kerala, India. But even then he was consumed with paperwork. After suggesting that she might just hold up a sign reading "Happy Birth- day" to get Charles's attention, Camilla vowed to spend the day "doing nothing. To be honest, I think I am just going to chill out, completely." Was it possible her Prince might join her, even for an hour or two? "I shall do my best. We see the sun all the time, but we never get the chance to just go and sit in it. So that would be bliss. But no, my husband is not one for chilling."

Camilla's savvy, backhanded tribute to the Prince's work ethic paid off. Not only were the Commonwealth leaders beginning to warm up to the idea of Charles replacing his mother as head of the organization, but back home he was being hailed as a skilled statesman. "Prince Charles was given a difficult and testing task," historian Andrew Roberts observed, "but there is no one in Britain better qualified to have taken it on. His handling of it suggests he will fulfill his role as king superbly."

Now that Charles was more than a year older than the oldest person ever to assume the throne—William IV, who succeeded George IV in 1830 at age sixty-four—speculation as to just what kind of king he might make reached a fever pitch. Adding to the hype was the premiere of Mike Bartlett's hit play *King Charles III* at London's Almeida Theatre in April 2014.

The play, written in blank verse, centers on a future King Charles refusing to give Royal Assent to legislation restricting press freedom after a tabloid phone hacking scandal—an unlikely scenario, given Charles's long history of antipathy toward the press. When the Prime Minister forces his hand, King Charles abruptly dissolves Parliament, triggering a constitutional crisis and riots in the streets. In the end, the fictional Duchess of Cambridge plots to undermine her father-in-law, ultimately forcing his abdication and replacing him with King William V. Along the way, the ghost of Diana visits both Charles and William, there is a sex scandal involving Prince Harry's antimonarchist girlfriend, and Harry winds up renouncing his titles and becoming a commoner.

The royal family would have plenty of time to see the critically acclaimed play. *King Charles III* enjoyed respectable runs on the West End and on Broadway, and garnered a number of awards before being adapted for a television production that aired on the BBC in England and PBS's *Masterpiece Theatre* in the United States. But for the time being, William and Kate were touring Australia and New Zealand with the crowd-pleasing one-year-old Prince George.

It was around this time that Camilla, who was unwinding with Charles at Birkhall in Scotland, picked up the phone to hear "an anguished voice on the end telling me that something terrible had happened to my indestructible brother." The news—that Mark Shand had died suddenly in New York City at the age of sixty-two—left Camilla "utterly devastated," Charles recalled. "She simply could not believe it."

A notoriously sybaritic lothario with a long list of conquests on both sides of the Atlantic, Shand was also an accomplished travel writer and passionate wildlife advocate. After raising $1.7 million at a Sotheby's auction to benefit his charity aimed at preserving the endangered Asian elephant, Shand knocked back five whiskies and a glass of champagne before joining friends at the Gramercy Park Hotel's trendy Rose Bar cocktail lounge. Around three in the morning, he walked outside for a cigarette, turned to go back in, but instead staggered backward and fell, smashing his head on the pavement. He was rushed to Bellevue Hospital with a fractured skull and died nine hours later. The coroner determined that Shand's blood alcohol level was twice the legal limit.

At her brother's funeral, Camilla leaned on Charles's arm and cried with her sister, Annabel, as the 1970s pop icon Cat Stevens (now Yusuf Islam) sang Mark's favorite song, "Wild World." Atop Shand's biodegradable wicker coffin were flowers and a handwritten note on lavender paper bearing the initial *C* and a crown. "Darling Mark," the note read, "With happy memories and all my love, Camilla."

———————

Less than three weeks later, Charles and Camilla were all smiles on the Prince's seventeenth visit to Canada. "You just keep going, that's all," Camilla told a well-wisher in Halifax, Nova Scotia, who expressed her condolences over Mark Shand's death. "Life goes on, you know," Camilla added, pointing to her husband, "and *he* never stops!"

During the Canadian tour, Charles continued to sound the alarm about global warming, now adding that his concerns had "come into even sharper focus now that I am a grandfather." He went on to warn that "all our grandchildren will pay the price . . . if we simply carry on with business as usual as if nothing has changed."

Ironically, Prince Charles paid little attention to the grandchild he credited for giving him a new world perspective. On July 22, 2014, everyone—including Prince Harry, several royal cousins, all the Middletons, and the Queen—showed up for Prince George's elaborate Peter Rabbit–themed first birthday party at Kensington Palace. Prince Charles opted instead to visit Glendelvine Estate, a conservation center for woodland creatures north of Balmoral, to speak on behalf of the "Saving Scotland's Red Squirrels" campaign. Charles was handed a giant stuffed red squirrel to give to Prince George but missed the party entirely. Rather than bring the squirrel to his grandson himself, he sent it to Kensington Palace via an equerry.

Charles had a standard line when asked what it was like to be a grandparent: "Spoil them, enjoy them, and give them back at the end of the day." But the Prince of Wales seemed to be doing very little spoiling and enjoying, opting instead to stick to his hectic schedule of conferences, ribbon cuttings, and walkabouts. As a result Charles and Camilla, on a tour of England's West Country, would also miss George's second birthday party—this one held at Anmer Hall in Norfolk, and again attended by the Queen and the rest of the royal family.

That Christmas, William and Kate broke with royal tradition by spending the bulk of the Christmas holiday not with the rest of the royal family but with the Middletons. The Duke and Duchess of Cambridge did attend church services at Sandringham on Christmas morning—just long enough to show the flag—but then dashed back to Bucklebury and their little Prince. It would be years before they brought George to Sandringham for Christmas, demurring on the grounds that the toddler was simply too rambunctious. While the Queen seemed to understand that the Cambridges might tilt toward Kate's parents at this stage in the life of their young family, Charles, despite his own inattention, felt slighted.

The arrival on May 2, 2015, of eight-pound, three-ounce Charlotte Elizabeth Diana—Her Royal Highness Princess Charlotte of Cambridge—was another cause for national celebration, and once again church bells tolled and artillery units fired off sixty-two-round salutes. There was a difference, of course: this time the fountains at Trafalgar Square ran pink, not blue.

No matter. Since the Queen had signed the letters patent abolishing primogeniture, Baby Charlotte was now fourth in line for the throne behind her big brother—the first Princess in British history to be on an equal footing with her male siblings. Just as before, Carole and Michael Middleton beat Charles and Camilla to the hospital, but this time Grandpa Wales seemed to take it in stride. Charles had hoped for a granddaughter, he said, and intended to "spoil her, absolutely." He added, wryly, that he was also "extremely thankful" for grandchildren who were going to "look after me when I'm tottering about."

While the Cambridges insisted that Charles was a doting grandfather to both George and Charlotte, William noted that he was "positively obsessed" with the little Princess. "As the father of sons, it was something he was missing. My mother," William added wistfully, "always said she would like to have a little girl." Indeed, Charles would soon be bragging to a reunion of nonagenarian World War II RAF pilots that Charlotte was not only sleeping through the night at the age of two months but also easier to handle than her fussy brother. "Charlotte is simply gorgeous, a beautiful child," he told a ninety-nine-year-old who flew Spitfires during the blitz of London. "She already sleeps through the night and is much easier on Mum than George."

Such tender observations aside, Charles began to complain that Kate's parents, the omnipresent Middletons, had effectively co-opted the royal grandchildren. "I'm sure they're very nice people," the Prince groused, "but they seem to be with George and Charlotte all the time, and I almost never see them." To be fair, Charles's breakneck schedule left little time for anything or anyone—a fact of life repeatedly bemoaned by Camilla. "Work, work, work," she protested to a visiting American friend. "There is simply no way to turn him off. I'd settle for a 'pause' button, if he had one. Which he doesn't."

As much as Kate was determined to be a hands-on, stay-at-home mom while William continued his dangerous work as an air ambulance pilot, George and Charlotte were largely left in the care of their Spanish nanny, Maria Teresa Borrallo. A graduate of Norland College, the prestigious three-year school for English nannies in Bath, Borrallo was trained in everything from tae kwon do to evasive driving to how to handle the paparazzi. The nanny, who occasionally wore the brown, short-sleeved Norland uniform with white gloves and a bowler hat, was described by an Anmer House staffer as "strict and firm with the children, but kind and soft as well."

What it meant to be a grandfather was on Charles's mind when, just a few weeks after Charlotte's birth, he paid an emotional and historic visit to Mullaghmore, the Irish fishing village where Lord Mountbatten had been assassinated by IRA terrorists. "At the time," Charles recalled of the bombing that also took the lives of three others, "I could not imagine how we would come to terms with the anguish of such a deep loss, since, for me, Lord Mountbatten represented the grandfather I never had."

In Mullaghmore, Charles was joined by his cousin Timothy Knatchbull. Timothy, who was fourteen at the time of the attack, had survived, but his identical twin brother Nicholas had not. The royal party met with villagers who'd pulled Timothy and other victims from the water, as well as with the parents of Paul Maxwell, the fifteen-year-old local boy who'd worked on the boat and was also killed in the blast. Charles went out of his way to praise locals who "showed the most extraordinary outpouring of compassion in the aftermath of the bombing."

With Camilla at his side, Charles explained that, now that he was a grandfather, his perspective was very different from that of the enraged young man who demanded revenge for his great-uncle's murder back in 1979. Now the Prince wanted only healing between Ireland and England, so that "all who have been so hurt and scarred by the troubles of the past . . . may leave our grandchildren a lasting legacy of peace, forgiveness, and friendship."

On the drive up to Classiebawn Castle, where the Mountbattens spent every summer, the Prince of Wales's motorcade slowed down beside a small, green wooden cross atop a cliff. From this vantage point, Charles had a perfect of view of the spot where the bomb went off in the harbor—and of the tiny red- and blue-hulled fishing boats that bobbed gently in the calm, gray waters below—just as they had when, as a youth, he used to visit his adored uncle. "Extraordinary," he murmured to Camilla as he gazed at the postcard-perfect scene. "All that hatred I felt—and I did hate the IRA as much as one can hate anything—gone."

That year's Trooping the Colour ceremonies in early June provided yet another image boost for the monarchy, if not necessarily for Charles. Both he and Camilla were seriously upstaged when William, still wearing the red-and-gold uniform signifying his rank as a colonel in the Irish Guards, stepped onto the Buckingham Palace balcony holding twenty-two-month-old George in his arms. The little Prince, who until now had essentially been kept under wraps while his parents tried to give him as "normal" a life as possible, wore the same powder-blue, lace-collared romper that William had worn when he took his first balcony nod in 1984.

"Prince George Steals the Show" trumpeted *People* magazine's headline, which added: "Princess Kate Looks Royally Perfect Six Weeks After Charlotte's Birth." Indeed, Charles's daughter-in-law got more than her fair share of kudos for looking "amazing" and "radiant" so soon after leaving the hospital. The newborn Princess Charlotte stayed at home in the care of Kate's parents and the nanny, but it scarcely mattered; even with one of their two adorable tots AWOL, the Cambridges outshone the Prince of Wales and his comparatively dowdy duchess. "The Queen still gets an enormous ovation," observed her former deputy private secretary, "but the crowds go wild for the younger royals. The Prince of Wales and Camilla are left hanging in the middle. You have to wonder if Prince Charles doesn't feel that, after waiting all this time, his chance has passed him by."

I wish you the most special and happiest of
birthdays, and long may you reign over us.
—Charles's toast to the Queen as she lit a ceremonial
beacon to celebrate her ninetieth birthday

I don't think she's wildly optimistic about life.
She's a genuine realist, a pragmatist.
—Princess Anne, on her mother

I'm discovering what it's like to be on your last legs.
—Prince Philip

TEN

THE NATION CAME TO A STANDSTILL

The distinction, she said, was "not one to which I have ever aspired." But on September 9, 2015, Elizabeth II nevertheless surpassed her great-great-grandmother Victoria's reign of 63 years, 216 days to become Britain's longest-reigning monarch. The Queen was standing on a train platform and in the process of opening the Borders Railway in Scotland when the milestone was passed. After she was congratulated by her Scottish hosts, Her Majesty politely and succinctly declined to make a fuss. "Inevitably, a long life can pass by many milestones," she told the crowd. "My own is no exception."

Still, had things gone differently just one year earlier, she might not have been queen at all—at least not the Queen of Scotland. In September 2014, after a bitter and divisive campaign, Scotland voted 55 percent to 45 percent against seeking independence from Great Britain. For the Queen and Prince Charles, who were at Balmoral and Birkhall when they learned of the Scottish people's decision not to bail out of the United Kingdom, it was cause for celebration. Direct descendants of Mary, Queen of Scots, James I (who was James VI of Scotland), and legendary fourteenth-century Scottish king Robert the Bruce, Charles and the Queen made no secret of their strong emotional ties to Scotland. Prime Minister David Cameron told former New York mayor Michael Bloomberg that the Queen "purred down the line" when he called her at Balmoral with the good news.

Still, throughout the yearlong debate, the Queen was careful not to take sides—at least not publicly. Behind the scenes Her Majesty, whose lifelong love affair with Scotland's history, traditions, countryside, and people was well documented, was distraught at the prospect of her kingdom breaking in two. "Have you ever seen her cheer people on at the Highland Games or dance a reel?" asked her cousin and confidante Margaret Rhodes. "Scotland is in the Queen's blood, so you can just imagine how she felt about Scottish independence."

Once the referendum was over and the Windsors could breathe a sigh of relief, the Queen applauded the 84.5 percent voter turnout as proof of Scotland's "robust democratic tradition." She added that, moving forward, "we have an enduring love of Scotland, which is one of the things that helps unite us all."

Charles had even more reason to be relieved than his mother. Even Scottish separatists insisted they would keep Elizabeth as their queen postindependence. The same offer, however, was not extended to the less popular Charles, who would eventually have to be approved by the Scottish Parliament and then go through a separate coronation process if he wanted to reign as both King of England and "King of Scots."

Barely two months after his mother broke Queen Victoria's record as the United Kingdom's longest-reigning monarch, Charles accompanied the Queen to another Commonwealth summit—only this time not as the headliner. After his star turn two years earlier in Sri Lanka, Charles settled back into a supporting role while the Queen opened the summit in Malta. Nostalgia played an important part in Mama's decision not to let her son take over as he had before; she'd longed to return to Malta, where she lived the simpler and arguably happier life as a naval officer's wife before becoming queen.

That did not mean, however, that Elizabeth was about to let up on her one-woman campaign on Charles's behalf. Working the room like any seasoned politician, the Queen schmoozed with old friends and inquired about their family members by name. Special care was taken to woo the new crop of leaders—most significantly Justin Trudeau, Canada's heart-throb new prime minister. The Queen had been particularly fond of Justin's father Pierre, Canada's charismatic, Kennedyesque prime minister from 1968 to 1979 and again from 1980 to 1984. At a time of political and cultural upheaval, when French-speaking separatists in Quebec threatened to tear Canada apart, the elder Trudeau remained a steadfast defender of the monarchy in general and Elizabeth II in particular.

Justin Trudeau had met the Queen when he was nine years old. "You seemed so tall to me then," said Trudeau, who at six foot two now towered over the five-foot-four-inch-tall sovereign. "So you can imagine how little I was then and how long ago that was." Later, when he toasted Her Majesty at the Commonwealth summit banquet in Malta's Corinthia Palace Hotel, Trudeau praised her as "Canada's indefatigable queen." He reminded his audience that in 1947 she had famously vowed to devote her whole life to serving the Commonwealth, and then told her directly, "You more than honored your vow."

When the young Canadian leader was through, the Queen rose to address the assembled leaders. "First, thank you to the Prime Minister of Canada," she deadpanned, "for making me feel so old."

Charles, who along with Camilla was strategically seated on the dais alongside the Queen, laughed with everyone else in the audience at his mother's wry remarks. In truth, he had every reason to be in a good mood. Soon to give the keynote address at the global climate change summit in Paris, he used his expertise to finagle an invitation to a closed-door executive session—the kind of nuts-and-bolts meeting that the Queen resolutely disdained. "Prince Charles is a real policy wonk, and those guys eat that up," commented a member of the Australian delegation. "He's also more of a charmer these days, much more loose and easygoing than he used to be." Indeed, the Canadian Prime Minister and the Prince of Wales hit it off instantly. "I have absolutely no idea what they could possibly be talking about," Camilla told one of her Maltese hosts as they looked across the room at Charles chatting up Trudeau, then doubling over with laughter.

"Something naughty, I suppose. Hmmm. My husband does seem to be enjoying himself, doesn't he?"

Nonetheless, it would take three more years of cajoling, sweet-talking, flattering, and royal arm-twisting to finally get Commonwealth leaders to unanimously endorse Charles as their future head—and only then after the Queen had summoned them to a closed-door summit at Windsor Castle. Once she had arranged a captive audience for her son, he stepped forward to make his own heartfelt pitch for the job.

"The Commonwealth has been a fundamental feature of my life for as long as I can remember," he told the assembled leaders, "beginning with my first visit to Malta when I was just five." When the verdict was finally announced, Charles issued a statement saying he was "deeply touched" by the show of confidence. He also breathed a sigh of relief. Anything less than a unanimous vote, one courtier said, "would have been deeply embarrassing for the Queen and a slap in the face for Prince Charles."

The gradual handoff of power continued at home, largely under the direction of Sir Christopher Geidt. After years of internecine warfare among various factions within the royal family—Charles's team at St. James's Palace and now Clarence House, Diana's at Kensington Palace, and the Queen's at Buckingham Palace—Geidt had pushed unsuccessfully for a consolidation of all power under one roof. Fearing a loss of autonomy, Charles had opposed the move—until William and Kate set up their own independent communications team at Kensington Palace. Finally convinced to go along with Geidt's scheme, Charles agreed that all three factions should be merged at Buckingham Palace—but with his people in the top spots. The Prince's own communications director, former BBC executive Sally Osman, was promptly put in charge of the consolidated operation, effectively handing over complete control of the monarchy's entire image-making apparatus to the Prince of Wales. The *Times* described the shift of media power as "another clear indication that major changes are afoot." The *Telegraph*'s Gordon Rayner concurred, noting that the merger gave "Prince Charles significantly more power. It's a major step in his journey toward becoming king."

Camilla, too, took another major step in her journey toward becoming queen. As part of Elizabeth's ninetieth birthday celebrations in the spring of 2016, the Queen appointed Camilla, along with William, to the powerful Privy Council. The appointments of her daughter-in-law and grandson to the body, routinely described by historians as a "cornerstone" of Britain's constitutional monarchy, were extraordinary. In her sixty-four years on the throne, the Queen had appointed only two other members of the royal family to the Privy Council: Prince Charles in 1977 and Sir Angus Ogilvy, the husband of her cousin Princess Alexandra, in 1997. Prince Philip is the longest-serving member, but he was not appointed by his wife; in 1947 Philip, then officially described as consort to the heiress presumptive, was appointed by his father-in-law, George VI.

The Queen was signaling more than just her respect for Camilla and William. When the monarch is replaced, either through death or abdication, within twenty-four hours the Prime Minister and his cabinet must convene an Accession Council made up of Privy Council members, high commissioners of Commonwealth countries, the Lord Mayor of the City of London, and other lords of the realm. In addition to hearing the new monarch take the requisite religious oath, the Accession Council formalizes the new sovereign's name. As part of the ongoing process of transition, the appointments of Camilla and William to the Privy Council made it clear the Queen wanted them to be there at the moment Charles was constitutionally certified as king.

It was just one of the many facets to "London Bridge"—or simply "the Bridge"—the code name used to describe not only the highly detailed funeral plans for the Queen but also the historic and monumentally fraught transition from one monarch to another. Realizing the enormous symbolic significance of a royal funeral, the Queen planned her own down to the finest detail—including which regimental units would participate and the color of their uniforms, as well as the guest list, flowers, and music.

Since the late 1970s, practice funeral processions for the Queen, Charles, Philip, and even William and Harry have been conducted once a year in the streets of London, and always secretly in the predawn darkness. Were Charles to die before his mother, his funeral—code-named "Menai Bridge," for the span between the mainland and the Welsh island of Anglesey—would have all the grandeur of a royal funeral. Since he was not the monarch, however, it would not technically be a state funeral.

Ceremony aside, the Queen's ninetieth birthday gave a new urgency to the issue of succession. While it was frequently reported that Elizabeth II had never considered abdicating, this was simply untrue. She discussed the issue on several occasions with her private secretary, Sir Christopher Geidt, and his predecessors Baron Fellowes and Lord Janvrin. Geidt, who broached the subject more directly than any of the Queen's other senior advisors, reminded her that if she remained on the throne and lived to be as old as her mother, Charles would be seventy-nine when he was crowned king. "It would not be a good thing for Prince Charles—or for the monarchy," he told her. "Or, Your Majesty, for the country."

With the passage of time, the Queen had clearly begun to soften on the issue of eventual abdication. Yet two obstacles remained: even after eighty years, the shock of Edward VIII's abdication and the toll it took on her father remained fresh in Her Majesty's mind. Even more important, Elizabeth II believed that God had anointed her queen and that she had a sacred duty, in the words of her cousin Margaret Rhodes, "to see it to the end."

In the short term, however, the Queen agreed privately to abdicate voluntarily were she to suffer a debilitating setback such as a stroke or dementia. The Regency Act 1937 would be invoked if she were no longer able to make that conscious decision. It took only a majority vote of five people—the Speaker of the House of Commons, the Lord Chief Justice of England, the Master of the Rolls, the Lord Chancellor, and the Monarch's Consort (Prince Philip)—to make Charles regent. As regent, he would become king in all but name—a situation that last occurred in Britain between 1811 and 1820, when the future George IV stepped in to rule after his father's mental illness made it impossible for him to govern.

Another Regency Period seemed unlikely for the foreseeable future, given Her Majesty's robust good health. As he had during the Diamond Jubilee celebrations four years earlier, Charles afforded the viewing public another heartwarming peek at life behind Palace walls in the television special *Elizabeth at 90: A Family Tribute*. "The most famous woman in the world," intoned the narrator, "through the eyes of the people who know her best." Yet it was Charles who provided the most trenchant commentary.

"When my mama was five years old, Britain's leading composer, Sir Edward Elgar, wrote some music in her honor," Charles says as the Queen is shown walking through the corridors of Buckingham Palace today. Elgar "called this piece *Dreaming*," Charles continued, "but at that point, he couldn't have dreamt that one day she would be queen." In praising his "mama," the Prince of Wales claimed that "in many ways," hers was "a life that has defined our age."

For much of the program Charles and his lavender-clad mother sit side by side in a cavernous Buckingham Palace salon, sharing memories as they watch another trove of Windsor home movies that he'd unearthed. As in previous BBC broadcasts, the films—shot by George VI, the Queen, Prince Philip, and other royals—show the Windsors cavorting in the countryside and at the beach, playing pranks (George VI in a fake beard), engaging in pillow fights, performing silly dance routines, zooming down a water slide on the royal yacht *Britannia*, and mugging outrageously.

Anne and several other members of the royal family make appearances as well, chortling as only British aristocrats can at their childhood games and royal tours gone awry—such as the time the royals, inappropriately dressed for summer on a tour of Canada's northern regions, were mercilessly buffeted by a helicopter in a driving rain. But it is the oddly muted relationship between Charles and his mother that is exceptionally revealing. While several reviewers wrote of the "obvious warmth" between mother and son, the affection displayed here is decidedly lopsided. Throughout, Charles widens his eyes with delight, laughs, jokes, and tries but invariably fails to elicit a similar response from the Queen. Instead, the

monarch seems intent on trying to recall the people, places, and circumstances surrounding each flickering image—and does so to an impressive
degree, even when the events took place eighty years earlier.

William and Harry, corralled by their father to participate, provide
their own brand of comic relief. At one point when the family is shown at
Harry's christening, William cracks, "It's hard to tell if you're a boy or a
girl in that." To which Harry replies with a smirk, "Thank you for that."
Watching his grandfather Prince Philip play with a four-year-old Charles,
Harry is surprised "how good-looking Grandpa is! He's an absolute stud!
Those glasses, slicked-back hair . . . presumably he was in the navy then?"

Watching their father as a toddler playing with a watering can, William comments, "Obviously, this is where his gardening interest started."
Harry adds that "Pa walks like George, or George walks like him." William agrees: "Yes, there's a purpose to the walk." In one particularly revealing scene, a two-year-old William scampers around the room at Windsor
while the Queen and everyone else try to intercept him without success—
at which point, Papa Charles suddenly appears to scoop the toddler up in
his arms. This fleeting glance at the bond between a young father (Charles
was thirty-five at the time) and son is forgotten quickly when the camera
cuts abruptly to the Queen's corgis romping in the snow at Sandringham.
"Nice, charming, friendly dogs," Her Majesty says as she watches the dogs
intently.

"*Endlessly* trying to bite," Charles replies with a laugh.

The Queen, flatly: "Yeah."

William appears to acknowledge what his father had said years earlier:
that the Queen is not much for warm hugs and smothering kisses. "It's a
very sort of subtle affection that she has," he explains in the film. "So she
keeps an eye on you without necessarily . . . She knows exactly what you're
up to and what's going on." He adds that "there is a look that the Queen
gives you if you've overstepped the mark or said something daft. You get a
glazed look, like she is thinking to herself, 'Who is this idiot?'"

Yet the brothers' respect for and devotion to Granny is unmistakable.
"She has led where others have faltered," William concludes. "She has just

been the most incredible grandmother to me. . . . I hope she realizes how dear and fond everyone is of her." Harry chimes in to praise Granny's "lifetime of dedication. Thank you, thank you so much for showing us the way."

In another ninetieth birthday documentary—this one broadcast by Sky News—William went out of his way to thank his grandmother for "being there for me" after Diana died. "Having lost my mother at a very young age, it's particularly important for me that I've had somebody like the Queen to look up to—who's understood some of the more complex issues. . . . She's been very supportive, and I'm very grateful."

William took advantage of all the hoopla surrounding the Queen's birthday to address another issue: the growing perception that he and Kate were lazy. While the Heir was still working as an air ambulance pilot in Norfolk and Kate was raising their two small children, they maintained the lightest schedule of any senior royals—by the end of 2016 a combined total of 328 appearances, compared with the 708 appearances Charles and Diana made when William and Harry were roughly the same ages as George and Charlotte. Even today, the Prince of Wales was racking up 530 royal appearances a year, with Anne a close second at 509. "It's all falling on the senior royals," observed veteran Palace watcher Phil Dampier. "It's time the younger generation stepped up."

To these persistent charges that he and Kate simply weren't pulling their weight, William told Sky News that both the Queen and Prince Charles were "very supportive of what I'm doing at the moment." Although the Queen was "very much at the helm . . . and her schedule's packed," William went on, she understood "that I'm a family man, and I want to be around for my children as much as I can." Describing his father as "very active, charitably and otherwise," William explained that there was "a time and place for taking on more responsibilities" once George and Charlotte were a little older and he felt he should quit the air ambulance service. For the time being, William let it be known that he considered what he was doing in the skies over Norfolk to be "important work, and I know my father and the Queen agree—very much so."

A year later, the young Prince would make good on his promise, leaving his day job as an ambulance pilot to become a full-time royal. The Duke and Duchess of Cambridge, who had already stood in for the Queen in Canada, the South Pacific, Australia, New Zealand, and India, soon added Germany, Poland, and Scandinavia to the list.

Orchestrated to a large extent by Charles, the Queen's ninetieth birthday celebrations stretched out over months, culminating in the ceremonial Trooping the Colour with another family tableau on the Buckingham Palace balcony—this time with Princess Charlotte as the royal family's newest and most darling addition. The message was clear: the monarchy was stronger than ever, and its survival all but assured even into the twenty-second century.

Yet 2016 was no ordinary year, and breaking through all the political noise was challenging even for the planet's most famous family. Just weeks after the Queen's birthday celebrations came to an end, Britons voted to exit the European Union—a seismic event that took the country's political establishment by surprise and forced the resignation of David Cameron as prime minister.

Brexit, as it was dubbed, had presented a unique set of problems for the Crown. As the debate intensified, there was even more pressure than usual for the royal family to take a stand—something the Queen resolutely refused to do. Privately, however, Elizabeth supported Brexit. Annoyed by what she saw as the European Union's meddling in the United Kingdom's domestic affairs, she welcomed what both she and Prince Philip viewed as an assertion of national sovereignty.

Charles, one of the great champions of international cooperation when it came to issues such as climate change and free trade, sided with his mother this time—and for reasons that had much to do with his own future as king. Brexit could be "a shot in the arm for the Commonwealth," observed one economist in the *Financial Times*, who argued that the organization—which Charles would someday head—might take up some of the slack left by a diminished EU.

Four months later, Charles and Camilla were winding up a tour of Bahrain, an island country in the Persian Gulf, when word reached them that Donald Trump had defeated heavily favored Hillary Clinton for the presidency of the United States. "What? Donald *Trump*?" he replied to the aide who relayed the news to him. "You're not serious. Shocking, absolutely shocking, isn't it?" Charles, who had met the Clintons on several occasions over the years, turned to Camilla. "I mean, we all thought Hillary was going to win, of course. . . . Donald Trump? Sometimes it seems the world has gone stark raving mad." Camilla, by contrast, seemed unfazed by news of the election upset. "Yes, well, darling," she said matter-of-factly. "It has."

The following month, Charles would take a less-than-subtle swipe at the president-elect in a BBC radio speech. "We are now seeing the rise of many populist groups across the world that are increasingly aggressive to those who adhere to a minority faith," he said in a clear reference to Trump's proposed Muslim ban and other perceived anti-immigrant policies. "All of this has deeply disturbing echoes of the dark days of the 1930s. My parents' generation fought and died in a battle against intolerance, monstrous extremism, and inhuman attempts to exterminate the Jewish population of Europe," he went on, concluding that the rise of such nationalist movements more than seventy years later "is to me, beyond all belief."

One person who did not mince words about Trump was Meghan Markle, Harry's new thirty-five-year-old American girlfriend and one of the stars of the USA Network TV series *Suits*. During the campaign, Markle, who filmed her series in Canada, went on British television to say that if Trump won the election, she intended to move there. Branding the new president a "misogynist," she insisted that "you don't really want that kind of world that he's painting—if that's the reality we're talking about, come on, that's a real game changer."

So was Meghan. Not only was the Los Angeles–born beauty an American and an actress, she was divorced, older than Harry, and biracial. The daughter of Black social worker Doria Ragland and white Emmy-winning lighting director Thomas Markle Sr., Meghan was—like her future sister-in-law Kate Middleton—college educated, with a degree from Northwestern University's School of Communication and a résumé that included an internship at the US embassy in Buenos Aires and a stint as one of the "briefcase girls" on the hit TV game show *Deal or No Deal*. After living with actor-producer Trevor Engelson for six years, she married him in 2011 and divorced Engelson two years later. Markle then moved in with celebrity TV chef Cory Vitiello—a relationship that lasted two years, ending in May 2016.

By the time they met on a blind date two months later, Harry had been through highly publicized, long-term affairs with Chelsy Davy and model and actress (and granddaughter of an earl) Cressida Bonas. Having scored a major triumph with the success of his annual Invictus Games for wounded veterans, the floundering Prince now felt he had found his true calling—and a new sense of calm that had eluded him in the past. "For the first time ever," he told British TV personality Denise van Outen at a birthday party just a few months before meeting Meghan, "I want to find a wife."

Meghan and Harry hit it off instantly ("I knew she was the one the very first time we met"), and within three weeks they were vacationing in Botswana. It was there, Harry would later say, that they told each other "We're going to change the world" and began planning their future together. For the next several months, the couple managed to dodge reporters while speculation about their relationship simmered online.

After returning from Botswana that fall, Harry introduced Meghan to his father and Camilla. The Prince of Wales found the young American actress—who bore a passing resemblance to Kate's sister, Pippa—"completely charming, absolutely delightful." At the time, Prince Charles had no idea that Harry's new girlfriend was biracial. "Not that it would have mattered at all, of course," Charles told an American friend. "But no, I didn't realize that until later."

Meghan's race certainly didn't escape the attention of Fleet Street. In the *Mail on Sunday*, columnist Rachel Johnson wrote that Meghan would "thicken" the Windsors' "watery, thin blue blood and Spencer pale skin and ginger hair with some rich and exotic DNA." On its website, the *Daily Mail* ran a headline saying "Harry's Girl Is (Almost) Straight Outta Compton," while on its front page, the *Sun* ran the headline "Harry's Girl's on Pornhub"—ignoring the fact that only intimate clips from *Suits* were posted on the salacious site, and not pornography. To make matters worse, reporters were now aggressively pursuing not only Meghan but also her family and friends.

Charles, who was traveling in the Middle East at the time, was forced to deal with the situation head-on when his younger son called him in Bahrain. Angry and choking back tears, Harry demanded that something be done. Charles agreed, green-lighting an unprecedented statement from Kensington Palace. In it, Prince Harry complained that "a line had been crossed," and that Meghan had been subjected to "a wave of abuse and harassment." Among many examples, he cited the "smear on the front page of a national newspaper, the racial undertones of comment pieces, and the outright sexism and racism of social media trolls and web article comments." Harry went on to say that he had never before witnessed such a "degree of pressure, scrutiny, and harassment from the media"—precisely the things that he believed ended his previous relationships and even resulted in his mother's death.

Many of the young couple's problems came from an unexpected quarter: Meghan's own family. Just days before Harry excoriated the press, Samantha Markle described her half sister as a "shallow social climber" whose behavior was "certainly not befitting of a royal family member." Samantha, who suffered from multiple sclerosis and was confined to a wheelchair, complained that Meghan had essentially turned her back on the Markle family—including their financially strapped father. "Being a Princess was something Meghan always dreamed of as a little girl," her sister recalled. "She always preferred Harry—she has a soft spot for gingers." The royal family, Samantha added, "would be appalled by what she's done to her own family. The truth would kill her relationship with Prince Harry."

There were other family-related obstacles to contend with, not the least of which was the aristocracy's long and storied history of racism. "The royal family's so tied in to the ideas of empire and colonialism, purity," said Kehinde Andrews, a sociology professor at Birmingham City University. The Windsors "are probably the primary symbol of whiteness that we have."

For her part, the Queen, who experienced countless up-close-and-personal encounters with people of all races, ethnicities, and religions during her record-breaking reign, appeared utterly devoid of prejudice. Not once had she ever been heard to make a racially insensitive comment. The same could not be said for Charles, although his gaffes were rare—like the time he told a writer of Guyanese descent that she didn't "look like" she was born in the British city of Manchester, presumably because she was black and wore dreadlocks.

Less infrequent were the disturbing remarks and curious actions of Princess Michael of Kent. The wife of Prince Michael of Kent, a grandson of George V and the Queen's first cousin, Princess Michael had once reportedly told a group of black diners in a New York restaurant to "go back to the colonies" because they were being too noisy. The Princess denied making the statement, but not the fact that she owned two black sheep at her Gloucestershire farm that she named Venus and Serena, after the tennis-playing Williams sisters. When she showed up at Meghan Markle's first Christmas lunch with the royal family wearing a large Blackamoor brooch—a style of jewelry that depicts exoticized images of servants and slaves of African descent—the Princess caused a furor. The next day, she officially apologized to Meghan, saying she was "very sorry and distressed" that she wore the brooch, but added that it was a gift she had worn "many times before, without controversy."

Prince Philip dismissed the Blackamoor brooch brouhaha as "complete nonsense," but then again, he was scarcely a paragon of political correctness. "If you stay here much longer," he told a group of British students during a royal visit to China, "you'll all be slitty eyed." On a trip Down Under, he turned to an aborigine and blurted, "Still throwing spears?" After looking at a messy fuse box while visiting an electronics factory in Scotland, Philip said it looked "as though it was put in by an Indian." Like others of his generation and his class, Philip had used the N-word with some frequency—although, said a retired member of the Balmoral household staff, "I haven't heard him use the word in a very long time—at least not since the 1970s."

Nonetheless, Philip, like Charles, warmed to Meghan immediately. So did the Queen, whose first meeting with her grandson's girlfriend occurred at Balmoral in September 2017, just weeks after William and Kate announced they were expecting their third child. Meghan was so nervous about meeting Queen Elizabeth that months earlier, while visiting her mother in California, she practiced drinking tea at the Rose Tree Cottage, a tea shop tucked away in nearby Pasadena. Markle needn't have worried; her love of dogs saved the day. "The corgis took to you straightaway," remembered Harry, who now lived with Meghan at Nottingham Cottage ("Nott Cott") on the grounds of Kensington Palace. "For the last thirty-three years, I've been barked at, and this one walks in, absolutely nothing, just wagging tails."

On a lazy Sunday night two months later, with a chicken roasting in the oven, Charles's younger son suddenly got down on one knee and proposed to Meghan. "I didn't even let him finish," she recalled, "before I said yes!" Harry had designed the ring himself: a three-carat cushion-cut solitaire diamond from Botswana, flanked by two brilliant-cut diamonds that had been left to Harry by his mother. (Although Harry had chosen Diana's famous sapphire-and-diamond engagement ring as a keepsake after she died, he willingly gave it to William when his older brother became engaged to Kate.)

While the younger generation promised a royal wedding and a royal birth, the Queen became the first sovereign in history to celebrate a Sapphire Jubilee marking sixty-five years on the throne. Yet, whether or not it was abundantly clear to his future subjects, the monarchy's day-to-day

affairs rested increasingly on Charles's sloped shoulders. In April 2017 he
traveled to Rome to meet for the first time with Pope Francis, who assumed the papal throne in 2013 after Benedict XVI became the first
pope in six hundred years to resign. That, and a string of abdications
around the same time (Queen Beatrix of the Netherlands, King Albert II
of Belgium, Spain's King Juan Carlos I), had prompted the Queen to at
least consider the question of abdication with Christopher Geidt and her
other top aides.

One royal who did not have to be convinced to retire was Prince
Philip. On August 1, 2017, Charles's ninety-six-year-old father performed
his 22,219th and last solo engagement as the Queen's consort. Standing in
a driving rain in the forecourt of Buckingham Palace, Philip reviewed a
parade of the Royal Marines, who had just completed a grueling series of
endurance feats. "You should all be locked up," he joked and then tipped
his bowler hat as they serenaded him with "For He's a Jolly Good Fellow."
As exits went, this was far preferable to the news that had been reported
erroneously earlier that day, when the *Daily Telegraph* website announced
Philip's death along with detailed plans for his funeral.

Philip's retirement was significant. Two years earlier, the Queen had let
it be known to her staff that after her husband's death, she intended to depart Buckingham Palace and make Balmoral her primary residence. If the
Queen was seriously considering abdication as an option—a historic move
that would make Charles King and her Dowager Queen—relocating to
Balmoral would have been a huge step in that direction.

The man chiefly responsible for making the Queen face up to her own
mortality, Christopher Geidt, would be duly rewarded for his efforts with
four knighthoods and a seat in the House of Lords. Most tellingly, the
Queen officially thanked Geidt, her eighth private secretary, for shaping "a
new approach to constitutional matters . . . and for the transition to a
change of reign."

Sadly for Geidt, that change was not coming about soon enough for
Charles. With the consolidation of all three royal households, Geidt had
continued to wield extraordinary power and influence over the monarchy.

"Day to day, Sir Christopher had the Queen's ear in a way that even Prince Charles didn't," a senior courtier said. "Prince Charles found that irksome." Irksome enough for the Prince of Wales to tell his mother that Geidt's position at the Palace was "untenable."

In an attempt to avoid a conflict with her son and heir, the Queen agreed. There was no doubt about who was behind Geidt's abrupt departure when he packed his bags and left in mid-September 2017. After ten years of loyal service to Her Majesty, the former British intelligence officer had been "forced out by Prince Charles," reported the *Times.* According to the BBC's royal correspondent, Peter Hunt, the "bloodless palace coup means Prince Charles can now exercise more control" over the direction of the monarchy. Just to underscore that control, Charles ordered that Buckingham Palace, Clarence House, and Kensington Palace take the unprecedented action of issuing a joint statement denying that a coup had taken place. It was, Hunt said, "a sign of how concerned the institution is about how this might look to the outside world."

The Charles-Camilla juggernaut continued through November, when the couple embarked on a two-week tour of India, Singapore, Brunei, and Malaysia as part of the Prince's ongoing efforts to romance the Commonwealth. Now old hands at traveling as a couple on behalf of the Crown, they handled the heat, the dust, and the crowds with ease. In New Delhi, the Cornwalls attended an elephant parade, and when asked by a nine-year-old if he would build a fort when he became king, Charles shot back, "I will!"

In Malaysia, Charles tried his hand at using a blowgun, while Camilla was greeted by hundreds of flag-waving students when she visited a school in Kuala Lumpur. At each stop, there were military parades, state dinners, and visits to zoos, parks, gardens, shrines, and monuments. The most telling moment may have come on the first day of their trip when they arrived in Singapore and spontaneously shared a rare public kiss. Hours later, both Charles and Camilla teared up when he placed a wreath on a war memorial honoring those who died defending the former British colony during World War II.

British diplomats viewed the Prince of Wales's tour of Southeast Asia as a resounding success. Nevertheless, he and Camilla returned home to blistering criticism for what the tour cost: more than $525,000, due largely to the fact that they traveled aboard the Voyager, an RAF aircraft usually reserved for international travel by the Prime Minister and his government staff. In contrast, journalists were eager to point out, William and Kate had traveled to India and neighboring Bhutan the year before on a commercial aircraft. The cost of that trip: a little less than $46,000.

Charles brushed aside such comparisons, along with complaints that he had spent a grand total of $1.4 million on travel in 2017 alone. But as he celebrated his sixty-ninth birthday, he told a major donor to one of his charities that he found "all the sniping so extremely frustrating. I'm trying to hold the whole damn thing—the Commonwealth—together. Doesn't anyone understand that?"

The Queen remained silent when it came to her son's spending. But she made clear her support for Charles on Remembrance Day, the day in November when Britain honors its war dead. In what the BBC called "an historic transfer of duties," the Queen stood on a Foreign Office balcony and watched as Charles placed a wreath at the cenotaph in Whitehall—a ceremony she had performed throughout her reign as head of state, head of the Armed Forces, and head of the Church of England.

In that moment, declared the *Sunday Express*, "the nation came to a standstill" in what was "widely seen as the clearest signal yet that the Queen is stepping back from her responsibilities and increasingly handing them over to her son and heir."

Perhaps, but Charles's solemn dedication to the job was no match for the vitality, glamour, romance, and fun embodied in Prince Harry and the Cambridges. The public's infatuation with a younger generation of royals intensified in 2018, beginning with the arrival of Charles's third grandchild on April 23. Once again artillery thundered, fountains were bathed in blue lights, and crowds waited outside the Lindo Wing of St. Mary's Hospital to catch a glimpse of Princess Catherine cradling Louis Arthur Charles—so named in part for Louis Mountbatten and, of course, the baby's grandfather. Louis (pronounced *Loo-ee*) was the name given to eighteen French kings but never to an English monarch. As soon as he was delivered, the littlest Prince occupied a unique place in history: he was the first royal heir born after the abolition of primogeniture and, therefore, pushed by big sister Charlotte from fourth to fifth in the line of succession.

"We are both so pleased at the news," Charles wrote to William and Kate that day. "It is a great joy to have another grandchild; the only trouble is, I don't know how I am going to keep up with them." He had certainly made the effort. After being cautioned by his friends that he would never get to know his grandchildren if he left everything in the hands of Carole and Michael Middleton, Charles installed a playscape with swings and slides at Highgrove and upgraded the treehouse originally built for William and Harry. Now both full-fledged, rambunctious preschoolers, Charlotte scampered about Highgrove's meticulously manicured grounds with George leading away. "My husband used to wince when he saw them run through the daffodils," Camilla told a visitor to the Gloucestershire estate. "Now he just thinks they're absolutely hysterical. He loves it!" Well, to a point. On a visit to Kew Gardens, he was presented with an oriental beech sapling for his beech tree collection. "I mustn't," he said, "let my grandchildren get hold of this."

In fact, away from public view, Charles was as tactile as any loving grandparent, picking them up in his arms, smothering them in hugs and kisses, and patiently showing them the flowers, plants, trees, and farm animals that made a place like Highgrove particularly fascinating to small children. To a great extent, Charles was motivated in his new, more hands-on approach to the grandchildren by his own memories of the Queen Mother. "It's a different part of your life," he mused. "The great thing is to encourage them. Show them things to take their interest. My grandmother did that; she was wonderful." It was "very important," he now believed, "to create a bond when they are very young."

Louis's arrival notwithstanding, the spring of 2018 belonged to Prince Harry and his American bride. In the weeks leading up to the May 19 wedding at Windsor Castle, there was the usual speculation about the guest list, the bridal gown, the vows, the reception, the honeymoon. Unfortunately, there was also family drama that played out on front pages around the world. After months of pummeling her half sister in the press, Samantha Markle was joined by her brother, Thomas Markle Jr. Like Samantha, Thomas Jr. claimed that the Markles had always been close knit, but that since finding fame as an actress and as Prince Harry's fiancée, their half sister, Meg, had turned her back on the family. "She is giving the greatest performance of her life," he said, claiming that Markle saw herself as "another Princess Diana. She is acting phony. Once she got into Hollywood, she turned into a different person. She's clearly forgotten her roots. . . . Maybe," he added, "we embarrass her. There's a whole different side of her that has started to surface, and it's ugly to see."

Things only got worse when neither sibling's name showed up on the list of six hundred invited guests. "I'm not bitter, just baffled," Thomas Jr. said. "It's hurtful given how close we once were. I'm confused and a little distraught. She's forgotten her own flesh and blood." Meghan's half-brother tried to contact her through the Palace but was "completely ignored." He pleaded with the royal family to intercede and force Meghan to mend the rift within her family—before the wedding. "Isn't this where Charles or the Queen step in and say, 'This is the way things are done. And your family needs to be involved'?"

Markle family members were involved, however. Doria Ragland flew in from California to help her daughter make final wedding preparations and, just days before the wedding, met Charles and Camilla over tea at Clarence House. Thomas Markle Sr. might have been there as well, had it not been for his decision to ignore Harry's advice and cooperate with the paparazzi weeks earlier. The supposedly candid images of him that circulated online showed Markle brushing up with books on Britain at a coffee shop, Googling the newlyweds, and even trying on his tuxedo for the big day. When it was disclosed that the photos had been staged, Thomas claimed he felt "stupid and hammy" and opted out of the wedding. Harry called his future father-in-law to say, "If you had listened to me, this would never have happened." Markle, who had suffered a heart attack, replied, "Maybe it would be better for you guys if I was dead. Then you could pretend to be sad." That said, Markle hung up on Harry.

All the Sturm und Drang was in sharp contrast to the kind words Meghan had for her father just two years earlier. "He taught me to write thank-you notes, to always arrive early," she recalled, thanking Markle for "the blood, sweat, and tears" he had invested in her future. "He put gas in my car when I went from audition to audition trying to make it as an actress. He is the person who believed in this grand dream of mine well before I could even see it as a possibility. I owe him so much."

Days after hanging up on Harry, Markle changed his mind and announced that he would give his daughter away. Unfortunately, a second heart attack forced him to bow out of the wedding altogether. It was assumed that Doria would step in—until Charles volunteered. The next day, Meghan broke tradition by walking down the first half of the St. George's Chapel aisle unescorted before being joined by Prince Charles. It was the bold, brave move of a young woman who was not afraid to challenge royal norms. Even Thomas Markle, watching at home in the United States while he recovered from heart surgery, was impressed. "Charles—how could I ask for a better replacement?" he said. "I was thrilled to tears that he was doing that for me. I just wish it had been my hand holding my daughter's, not his."

Waiting for them at the altar were Harry and his best man, Prince William. When Charles gave Meghan's hand to Harry, the groom said, "Thank you, Pa." Then he lifted the bride's veil. "You look amazing," Harry told her. "I'm so lucky." The Queen agreed. The day before the wedding, Her Majesty was photographed riding in the backseat alongside Meghan's rescue beagle, Guy, on her way to Windsor. The same day, the Queen bestowed the titles of Duke and Duchess of Sussex on the groom and bride.

Although the focus was obviously on the happy couple—a global audience of 1.9 billion tuned in to watch the ceremony—social media lit up over the warm relationship between Charles and Meghan's mother. The father of the groom and the mother of the bride were often lost in conversation, and at one particular point, Charles gallantly took Doria's hand as they went to sign the wedding registry—a moment that apparently brought many on the internet to tears. Later, Charles left the chapel with Camilla on his left arm and Doria on his right.

At the first of two receptions, Charles once again stirred emotions. He remembered changing Harry's nappy (diaper) and giving him a bottle, then got a laugh when he added "and look how well he turned out." Pa went on to praise Meghan, but his concluding words were what choked up many guests: "My darling old Harry, I'm so happy for you."

In another radical departure from tradition, Meghan gave a speech of her own proclaiming her love for Harry, thanking the royal family for being "so gracious and welcoming," and praising her mother "for always being there for me." In the course of all the speeches—by Charles, William, Harry, and Meghan—no one mentioned Diana. When the toasts were over, William took the microphone and asked, "Can anyone here play the piano?" It was then that Elton John performed a medley of "Your Song," "Tiny Dancer," "I'm Still Standing," and "Circle of Life" from *The Lion King*. Presumably, he thought it might be risky to sing another of his *Lion King* compositions: "I Just Can't Wait to Be King."

The official wedding photographs taken before the reception spoke volumes about changes going on within the royal family that would transform it forever. "When Diana left, I left," said Merle Mitchell, a fifty-seven-year-old nurse of African descent who admired the late Princess's activism. Pointing to Meghan's involvement in a wide range of charitable causes, Mitchell said Markle's activism might bring her back to the monarchist fold. Besides, she added, "we need a bit of color in the royal family. There hasn't been anyone in the palace that black women can point to and say, 'That person looks like me.'"

Being royal, as Charles knew too well, came at a cost. The Duchess of Sussex was no longer free to speak her mind on political matters, as she had done when she skewered then presidential candidate Donald Trump on British television. Yet Trump had no fans among the senior royals—

least of all the Prince of Wales. When Prime Minister Theresa May first invited the newly inaugurated president to pay a state visit to England in January 2017, outraged Britons took to the streets to protest. More than one and a half million signed a petition demanding that the invitation be withdrawn. When the Prime Minister stood her ground, Charles, according to a senior Clarence House advisor, did something he had never done before: he asked the Queen to instruct May to withdraw the invitation, or face the embarrassment of simply not having any member of the royal family there to greet Trump at Buckingham Palace.

The Queen refused. Not only did she have a curiously warm relationship with May, but she had also hosted state dinners for some of the world's most unsavory leaders, including Syrian president Bashar al-Assad, Zimbabwe's dictator Robert Mugabe, Republic of the Congo strongman Mobutu Sese Seko, Indonesia's notorious President Suharto—and Vladimir Putin of Russia. In the case of Romanian dictator Nicolae Ceausescu, French president Valery Giscard d'Estaing telephoned the Queen to warn her that Ceausescu and his wife Elena had pilfered valuables from their rooms at the Élysée Palace on a state visit to Paris. (The Ceausescus were overthrown, tried, and executed by firing squad in 1989.) "The Queen has dealt with dictators and despots," said William Hague, Britain's former secretary of state for foreign affairs. "She'll take a visit from Donald Trump in her stride."

Trump, however, was not interested in making the trip if it meant angry protestors would flood the streets. In June the White House put the President's visit on indefinite hold, although the issue would resurface several times throughout 2017. In stark contrast to his predecessor President Barack Obama, who generally saw eye to eye with the Prince of Wales, Trump pooh-poohed the notion of global warming. When Trump unilaterally pulled the United States out of the Paris Agreement on climate change in June, Charles made it clear through Foreign Office channels that he could not be expected to remain silent. "Donald Trump is engaged in an extraordinary diplomatic row with the Prince of Wales over climate change that threatens to disrupt his state visit to the UK," wrote Tim Shipman in the *Sunday Times*, pointing to their "violently divergent views on global warming." The White House warned officials that Trump would "erupt" if Prince Charles attempted to "lecture" the president on green issues. Instead, they asked that William and Harry greet Trump in their father's stead.

Public outrage rose up again on both sides of the pond that August when a white nationalist rally in Charlottesville, Virginia, resulted in the death of one protestor and injuries to dozens of others. In one of his most incendiary statements to date Trump, seeking to draw a moral equivalency between marching Nazis and the people who demonstrated against them, claimed there were "very fine people on both sides." Charles and his sons burned up the phone lines between Clarence House and Kensington Palace, with all three princes agreeing to work behind the scenes to discourage Trump's visit.

Throughout 2017 and into 2018, Britons seemed nearly as fascinated with the tweet-storming Trump as their American cousins. The royal family was no exception. At every opportunity, including Prince Harry's wedding reception, Charles took his wealthy and influential American friends aside and gently prodded them for information. It was important that he not push too hard or too far; some of the donors to his charities, including those with the deepest pockets, were Trump supporters. Still, when lent a receptive ear, Charles asked on several occasions how likely it was that President Trump would be impeached. "Trump seems to be detached from reality, doesn't he?" he asked a former Washington official who now headed up a major US conglomerate. "What a ghastly, awful man."

It didn't help that Trump had aggressively pursued Princess Diana after her divorce—overtures that were rebuffed—and claimed later on a radio program that he could have "nailed her if I wanted to," but only if she passed an HIV test. Trump used tweets to blast London's Muslim mayor, Sadiq Khan, for failing to stop terrorist attacks in his city ("He's done a terrible job, a very bad job, horrible") and seemed to defend the paparazzi for taking topless photos of Kate Middleton while she sunbathed in 2012. ("She shouldn't be sunbathing in the nude—only herself to blame.") Trump's criticism of Kate resulted in what one Clarence House butler referred to as "torrents of profanity" from both Prince Charles and his sons. (Even the Queen had a respect for colorful language. After veteran British actor Brian Blessed blurted out the F-word while telling an off-color story on BBC television, he was taken aside by the Queen during a reception at Buckingham Palace. "That was a funny story you told, Mr. Blessed," Her Majesty said. "What I would like to say to you is that the word *fuck* is an Anglo-Saxon word. It means 'spreading the seed.'")

By the time President Donald Trump finally made his way to the United Kingdom in early July, the trip had been scaled back and was no longer a full-blown state visit. On July 13, 2018, while thousands protested in London, the Queen stood patiently in the quadrangle of Windsor Castle waiting for the President and First Lady. They shook hands politely, and then Trump and the Queen reviewed the honor guard before going inside for tea. Forty-seven minutes later, they emerged. Trump called the Queen "very, very inspiring indeed," and then mistakenly claimed that it was "the first time in seventy years" that she had reviewed her honor guard. Not only had the Queen not been on the throne for seventy years, but reviewing the troops was one of the most routine aspects of the job—something she had done hundreds of times during her reign.

What was unusual, despite fervent Palace denials, was the total absence of any other royal during the Trump visit. Only two years earlier, William, Kate, and Harry had hosted a dinner for the Obamas at Kensington Palace, and millions were charmed by images of a chubby-cheeked Prince George greeting Barack and Michelle in his bathrobe. During the Obamas' first state visit to London in 2011, Charles and Camilla were in near-constant attendance, beginning with arrival ceremonies at Buckingham Palace. In 2003 Prince Charles greeted President George Bush and his wife Laura when they arrived at Heathrow Airport. This time Charles and William made a point of snubbing the American president. Refusing a request from Buckingham Palace to at the very least participate in the tea at Windsor, Charles and Camilla stayed at Highgrove while Prince William played in a charity polo match.

As Britain grappled with the complicated business of how to actually implement Brexit, the royal family once again made headlines. This time, the ninety-seven-year-old Duke of Edinburgh was driving on a public road near Sandringham in early January 2019 when his armor-plated Land Rover crashed into a minivan carrying two women and a nine-month-old boy. The Land Rover flipped on its side and Philip, bloodied but—amazingly—not seriously hurt, was pulled from his car by a passerby. Although the baby was not injured, the minivan driver was badly shaken and passenger Emma Fairweather suffered a broken wrist in the collision.

Police gave Breathalyzer tests to both Philip and the other driver on the scene, and both passed. But just two days later, having yet to offer an apology to Fairweather, Philip was photographed back behind the wheel—and not wearing a seat belt. The resulting public outrage not only prompted Philip to write a note of apology to Fairweather—in which he insisted that he knew the road well but that he had been temporarily blinded by the sun—but it also forced the Duke to surrender his driver's license in order to avoid criminal prosecution. "It was a shame he didn't make the decision to give up driving a bit sooner," Fairweather said, "but it's the right thing to do."

It was not the sort of decision the Queen would ever have to make. As the sovereign and titular head of state, she was the only person in Great Britain who required neither a passport nor a driver's license. "Mama loves driving too much," Charles told an American friend after his father's accident, "to give it up until she absolutely has to."

The same might have been said about her attitude toward giving up the throne—although there were still more surprise abdications taking place in other parts of the world. On April 30, 2019, Japanese Emperor Akihito stepped down thirty years after assuming the Chrysanthemum throne upon the death of his father, Emperor Hirohito. Becoming the first Japanese emperor to abdicate in two centuries, eighty-five-year-old Akihito—who now became Emperor Emeritus—was succeeded by his fifty-nine-year-old son Naruhito. The new emperor's wife, Masako, automatically became empress consort—as Camilla would automatically become queen consort if a similar scenario played out in the United Kingdom.

While St. James's Palace made sure that the Queen's senior advisors took note of the latest historic abdication, Charles focused on events closer to home—namely the birth of his fourth grandchild. On May 6, 2019, the Duchess of Sussex gave birth to a seven-pound, three-ounce boy at the Portland Hospital in London. Archie Harrison Mountbatten-Windsor, whose mere arrival was historic for a multitude of reasons, immediately took his place as seventh in line to the British throne.

Less than a month later, Meghan Markle would choose to stay at home when fellow American Donald Trump arrived in London for an official state visit. This time, amid concerns that the U.S. commitment to even its oldest allies was beginning to falter, senior members of the royal family pulled out the stops. Even as President Trump once again savaged London's Sadiq Khan (this time calling him a "stone-cold loser"), Charles and Camilla joined the Queen in welcoming Trump and First Lady Melania Trump to Buckingham Palace with an eighty-two-gun salute—half honoring the U.S. President and half honoring the sixty-sixth anniversary of Her Majesty's coronation. Then Charles, assuming another duty that would normally have fallen to the monarch, joined President Trump in reviewing the Grenadier Guards.

At a magnificent state banquet held in the Trumps' honor at Buckingham Palace, the President dined between Camilla and the Queen, while Charles, seated between his mother and Melania, chatted amiably with the American First Lady. Later, Charles and Camilla invited the Trumps to tea at Clarence House. The Prince of Wales and Trump were supposed to have had fifteen minutes put aside for a private conversation, but the President later said the meeting swelled to ninety minutes—during which the Prince "did most of the talking."

Charles was, Trump discovered for the first time, "really into climate change and I think that's great. What he really wants and what he really feels warmly about is the future. He wants to make sure future generations have climate that is good climate, as opposed to a disaster, and I agree."

Trump insisted he "totally listened" to Charles's arguments, but pushed back at any suggestion the U.S. should do more. "Well, the United States right now has among the cleanest climates there are based on all statistics," Trump told the Prince. "And it's even getting better because I agree with that. We want the best water, the cleanest water. It's crystal clean, has to be crystal clean, clear." Trump pointed to "China, India, Russia, many other nations" as the true culprits when it came to global warming. "They have not very good air, not very good water, and the sense of pollution. If you go to certain cities, you can't even breathe . . . They don't do the responsibility."

Their discussions continued during a reciprocal dinner hosted by the Trumps at Winfield House, official London residence of the U.S. Ambassador. If nothing else, the Prince impressed Trump with his earnestness. "I'll tell you what moved me is his passion for future generations," said Trump, who seemed genuinely impressed that the future King would have a deep concern for his subjects. "He's really not doing this for him; he's doing this for future generations. And this is real—he believes that. He wants to have a world that's good for future generations, and I do, too. You know, he's Prince Charles; he doesn't have to worry about future generations in theory unless he's a very good person who cares about people. That's what impressed maybe me the most, his love for this world."

Any hope on Charles's part that he may have gotten through to the President was dashed just a few days after Trump returned to the U.S. In defending his comment that he would listen if a foreign government gave damaging information about a political rival without reporting it to the FBI, Trump tweeted: "I just met with the Queen of England (U.K.), the Prince of Whales [sic], the P.M. of the United Kingdom, the P.M. of Ireland, the President of France and the President of Poland. We talked about 'Everything!' Should I immediately call the FBI about these calls and meetings? How ridiculous!"

Ridiculous was certainly one of the words that must have come to mind when Charles was informed that Trump had referred to him as the Prince of "Whales." Camilla told an American friend that she "couldn't stop laughing" when she heard of Trump's gaffe, but that her husband found it "more disappointing than funny. I think he just felt as if he'd been wasting all that time talking to the man."

What would have happened had King Charles III been on the throne when Donald Trump came to call? Perhaps he would have welcomed the American president only to scold him, or to sermonize on the environment, the dangers posed by technology, and the evils of intolerance. More likely, he would have short-circuited the process entirely by simply refusing to invite Trump in the first place. After all, as Prince of Wales, Charles had snubbed others for political reasons. To protest China's policies toward Tibet, he boycotted a 1999 Buckingham Palace banquet honoring Chinese president Jiang Zemin and did the same when Zemin's successor, Hu Jintao, visited six years later. In his diaries, Prince Charles described the "ridiculous rigmarole" involved in meeting the stiffly formal Chinese leaders, whom he described as "appalling old waxworks."

––––––––––

Charles and the rest of the royal family were soon forced to deal with a flamboyant, oddly coifed man-child populist of their own: New York City–born Boris Johnson, who took over the reins of the Conservative Party from an embattled Theresa May and became prime minister of Great Britain in July 2019. The first British prime minister born outside British territory, Johnson, like his counterpart across the Atlantic, had been widely accused of being a racist. When Barack Obama criticized Brexit, Johnson wrote an opinion piece noting "the part-Kenyan president's ancestral dislike of the British Empire." Astonishingly, Boris Johnson had also written columns calling black people "piccaninnies with watermelon smiles" and gay men "bumboys"—appalling comments for which, thankfully, he apologized during a mayoral debate in 2008.

Upon being elected party leader and then appointed prime minister by the Queen, Johnson immediately announced his intention to fulfill his campaign promise and go ahead with Brexit—with or without a deal spelling out the precise terms of Great Britain's departure from the European Union. Toward that end, the Queen met with her Privy Council and approved Johnson's request for a "prorogation" of Parliament—basically a temporary suspension of Parliament that would have short-circuited any chance for the new prime minister's critics to raise any objections to his Brexit plan on the floor of Commons. The courts nullified the prorogation request on the grounds that it was unconstitutional, but not before Johnson was forced to deny allegations that he had lied to the Queen, tricking her into granting his request for what was nothing more than a ham-fisted parliamentary maneuver.

As irritated as Charles was by Johnson's antics, this was far from the biggest crisis the Windsors faced. In August 2019 US financier Jeffrey Epstein was found hanged to death in a New York City jail cell while awaiting trial in federal court on sex trafficking charges. Epstein, who counted among his friends and frequent traveling companions Prince Andrew and former US president Bill Clinton, was a notorious abuser of underage girls and had already served prison time. The sixty-six-year-old bachelor's death was ruled a suicide, but the bizarre circumstances surrounding it—he had been on suicide watch only days before—sparked a number of conspiracy theories: Was Epstein murdered as an act of retribution or perhaps silenced by powerful friends who were afraid he knew too much?

The public at large was aware of Epstein's unsavory activities as far back as 2005, when the FBI compiled a list of "40 confirmed minors" he had abused and pursued charges against him. But even after he served thirteen months of an eighteen-month sentence, Epstein never stopped. In court documents filed in 2014, Epstein, who reportedly made dozens of out-of-court settlements with his victims, was accused of running a "sexual abuse ring" that lent underage girls to "prominent American politicians, powerful business executives, foreign presidents, a well-known prime minister, and other world leaders."

Prince Andrew was introduced to Epstein in 1999 by British socialite Ghislaine Maxwell, the financier's girlfriend at the time, and over the next twenty years was a frequent guest at various properties Epstein owned around the world. In the aftermath of Epstein's death, Buckingham Palace issued a series of statements in which Andrew admitted it was "a mistake" to spend time with Epstein after his release from prison in 2009 but also insisted that he "did not see, witness, or suspect any behaviors of the sort" that led to Epstein's conviction. When a 2010 video surfaced showing Prince Andrew standing inside the doorway of Epstein's New York mansion, waving to a young woman outside, the Palace issued yet another statement claiming the Duke of York was "appalled by the recent reports of Jeffrey Epstein's alleged crimes. His Royal Highness deplored the exploitation of any human being, and the suggestion he would condone, participate in, or encourage any such behavior is abhorrent."

Not so fast, said one of Epstein's alleged victims, Virginia Roberts Giuffre, who held a press conference to say that Prince Andrew "knows exactly what he's done, and I hope he comes clean about it." Later, Giuffre directly accused Andrew of sexually abusing her three times, saying that, while still underage, she was forced to have sex with the prince in London, New York, and on Epstein's private Caribbean island. Epstein kept her, Giuffre said, as his "sex slave."

With the evidence of his involvement with Epstein mounting, Prince Andrew decided to sit for a lengthy prime-time BBC-TV interview to refute Virginia Giuffre's allegations. The interview would prove to be an unmitigated disaster. Not only did Andrew repeatedly and unconvincingly state that he had no recollection of ever meeting Giuffre, but he flatly refused to say that he regretted his friendship with Epstein. The prince, who squirmed throughout the entire forty-five-minute broadcast as he searched for plausible ways to explain his relationship with Epstein, also neglected to express any sympathy for Epstein's victims. Prince Andrew did acknowledge, however, that by continuing his friendship with Epstein even after the convicted sex predator had been exposed and served prison time, he had "let the side down."

There was no doubt that by "the side," Andrew meant the Queen. While Elizabeth II was no longer surprised by much of anything her children did, Charles was another matter. The Prince of Wales was outraged that the younger brother whose earlier sexual exploits had earned him the sobriquet "Randy Andy" had behaved so recklessly, but he was also angry that Andrew thought he could talk his way out of his predicament in a no-holds-barred television interview.

Charles met with the Queen at Buckingham Palace and convinced her that drastic action was in order. Andrew was summoned to Sandringham for lunch with Charles and Prince Philip, both of whom informed Andrew that—for the sake of the monarchy—he would essentially be "retiring" as a senior member of the royal family. On November 19, 2019, Prince Andrew issued a statement acknowledging that his "association with Jeffrey Epstein has become a major disruption to my family's work" and that he had "asked Her Majesty if I may step back from public duties for the foreseeable future, and she has given her permission."

At Charles's urging, Andrew went on to say that he did "unequivocally regret" his "ill-judged association" with Epstein, that he "deeply sympathized" with Epstein's victims, and that he was willing to cooperate with law enforcement in its ongoing investigations of Epstein's alleged crimes. By the time his daughter Princess Beatrice married real estate developer Edoardo Mapelli Mozzi in July 2020, Andrew's banishment from royalty's inner circle was complete. Even though he walked the princess down the aisle, Andrew was omitted from all official wedding photographs released by Buckingham Palace.

It was another watershed moment in the history of the royal family, but one that at least meshed with the Prince of Wales's plans for the future. In his oft-expressed vision of a streamlined, "slimmed-down" monarchy, it was widely reported that Charles intended to essentially sideline not only Andrew but also Edward; Andrew's forced retirement was an important if awkward first step in that direction. What Charles had not anticipated, however, was the departure of another royal figure he had always seen as an integral part of his modern monarchy.

Over the Christmas holidays, Harry and Meghan sent minor shock waves through the Palace when they decided to spend Christmas with

Meghan's mother on Vancouver Island in British Columbia, skipping the Windsors' traditional holiday celebrations at Sandringham. Then, in early January 2020, they stunned the world by announcing on their official Instagram page that they also intended to "step back" in their roles as "senior members" of the royal family and "work to become financially independent, while continuing to fully support Her Majesty the Queen." As part of their desire to carve out "a progressive new role," the Sussexes also announced that they would no longer be living full-time in London, but would instead divide their time between the United Kingdom and North America—presumably Canada, where they intended to launch their new "charitable entity."

Although Harry and Meghan had been negotiating with Buckingham Palace for months, they had not cleared their statement with the Queen. Caught off guard, the Palace at first issued its own statement claiming that talks with the couple were "at an early stage." Once again Charles, who had not been consulted by his younger son, felt betrayed—a feeling shared by William, whose relationship with Harry had undergone major changes since Meghan's arrival on the scene. Although Harry had already acknowledged publicly that he and William were "on different paths" and that Diana's boys were no longer as close as they had once been, both brothers denied strongly the existence of a serious rift between them. And while it was true that Harry and Meghan had separated themselves from the Cambridges' charitable foundation to build one of their own, tensions between the two young princes were not the cause of the Sussexes' decision to reinvent their royal roles.

Within a matter of days, the Queen relented and gave her grandson and his American wife her blessing. "My family and I are entirely supportive of Harry and Meghan's desire to create a new life as a young family," Her Majesty said in a rare, highly personal statement. "Although we would have preferred them to remain full-time working members of the royal family, we respect and understand their wish to live a more independent life as a family while remaining a valued part of my family."

It was no secret that the Sussexes had long felt victimized by Britain's relentless tabloid press, which, in stories with obvious racial overtones, often portrayed Meghan as neurotic, scheming, and wantonly ambitious. In an ITV documentary on the Sussexes' charitable work in Africa, Harry said that the daily presence of the press in his life was a constant reminder of how his mother had been pursued by the paparazzi. "It's a wound that festers," he admitted. "I think being part of this family—in this role, in this job—every single time I see a camera, every single time I hear a click, every single time I see a flash, it takes me straight back."

In the same documentary, Meghan fought back tears when she was asked how she was holding up. "Thank you for asking," she replied. "Not many people have asked if I'm okay."

With press coverage ratcheting up exponentially following the birth of the couple's first child, Archie Harrison Mountbatten-Windsor, on May 6, 2019, Harry and Meghan fought back. "I lost my mother, and now I watch my wife falling victim to the same powerful forces," Harry said, explaining why he and Meghan were filing lawsuits against a number of tabloid publishers for intrusions on their privacy. At the same time, the royal couple felt more than comfortable cashing in on their global celebrity so that they could become "financially independent," applying to trademark hundreds of items, from T-shirts and socks, to hoodies and jeans, under the "Sussex Royal" logo.

Still, the Sussexes' unexpected declaration of independence ignited a firestorm of controversy and speculation. Even as the impeachment trial of an American president got under way for only the third time in history, "Megxit," as the royal brouhaha was soon called, landed on front pages across the world. For the most part, the Duke and Duchess of Sussex were roundly criticized on both sides of the Atlantic for their unilateral decision to go solo. As columnist Maureen Dowd wrote in the *New York Times*: "It wasn't cool for Meghan and Harry to pants the 93-year-old queen, defy her instructions, dump their Megxit plan on Instagram, and intensify the sad split between the brothers. . . . What's the rush to give up real influence to be an Instagram influencer? Besides, who unfollows their own grandmother?"

With up to 90 percent of their income coming from the Duchy of Cornwall, Harry and Meghan could not afford to anger the Prince of Wales; after all, as the Duke of Cornwall, he held the purse strings. But anger him they had. At one point, Charles suggested behind closed doors that if Harry and Meghan insisted on going it alone with a brand of their own, he would happily oblige the rebel royals and simply cut them off. "That is what they want, isn't it?" he asked in a fit of pique. "Not to be full-time members of this family?" Once William urged his father to consider the optics of such a move—Harry still ranked far higher than his father in popularity polls—Charles abandoned the idea.

Soon other, wholly unanticipated obstacles to the Sussexes' new plan arose: namely, the fact that Canada might bar them from migrating there. In a scathing editorial, Canada's largest and most influential newspaper, the *Globe and Mail,* argued that "the Trudeau government's response should be simple and succinct: No." The editorial went on to tell Harry and Meghan, "You are welcome to visit, but so long as you are senior royals, Canada cannot allow you to come to stay. . . . It breaks an unspoken constitutional taboo. . . . But though Canada borrowed from Britain, it isn't Britain and never was. And this country long ago took steps to make that unmistakably clear." So, despite the fact that England's monarch technically reigns over Canada, that nation maintains an arm's-length distance from the Crown to maintain its sovereignty. "[I]f you're a senior member of our royal family," the *Globe and Mail* declared, "this country cannot become your home." For Charles, the new controversy over whether or not his son and daughter-in-law would even be permitted to live abroad—and in a Commonwealth country, no less—was one more reminder of the tightrope he would have to walk as king.

As it turned out, the Sussexes didn't plan on staying in Canada for long. Scarcely two weeks after relocating there, they departed Vancouver for Los Angeles in the early morning hours of March 14, 2020, aboard Tyler Perry's $150 million Embraer E-190 private jet. Once they arrived in California, the royal couple and their infant son were spirited away to the actor and movie producer's $18 million, twenty-two-acre hilltop villa in tony Beverly Ridge Estates.

The top-secret mission to get the Sussexes south of the Canada-US border had been carried out in haste, but for a valid reason. For weeks now, health experts had been scrambling to stave off another global catastrophe like the 1918 flu epidemic that had infected one-third of the world's population and killed an estimated fifty million people around the world. The coronavirus, also known as Covid-19, had taken hold in Wuhan, China, but spread quickly to Europe and then to North America. To stop its transmission, Canada was about to restrict border crossings—a move that would conceivably make it difficult if not impossible for the Sussexes to visit Archie's grandmother Doria, now home in LA. It would also have forced Meghan to abandon plans to reconnect with her old Hollywood support network of friends and acting colleagues; she had just finished narrating the Disney documentary *Elephant* to benefit the wildlife charity Elephants Without Borders—a tentative first step toward resurrecting her career in front of the camera.

What neither Harry nor Meghan nor anyone else knew at the time was that the coronavirus had already struck close to home. On March 13, just one day before Harry and Meghan slipped stealthily into the United States, the Prince of Wales tested positive for the virus. A slew of engagements was abruptly canceled—including a trip to Jordan with Camilla—but no reason was given at the time. It seemed no small coincidence that Charles had lunched with Monaco's Prince Albert just three days before his diagnosis; Albert wound up testing positive for the virus the very same week.

Just three weeks after Charles's diagnosis, William also contracted the virus. Somehow he managed to keep that rather significant bit of news to himself for a full year.

———

At seventy-one, Charles certainly fell into the high-risk group for serious complications from the virus, but his immediate concern was for the

Queen. He had seen his ninety-three-year-old mother the day before his diagnosis, and they had shared two lingering hugs. While royal physicians examined the monarch, Charles and Camilla decamped Clarence House for a quick visit to Highgrove, where he communicated with his Clarence House staff via telephone and email. The prince had only begun to feel mild symptoms—headache, dry cough, slight fever—by the time he and Camilla boarded a royal jet bound for Scotland and Birkhall, their residence on the grounds of Balmoral. Within days, he had lost his sense of smell and his sense of taste, two additional symptoms of Covid-19.

Not surprisingly, Charles's arrival in their midst at a time when people were being discouraged or even barred from traveling did not exactly sit well with Scottish nationalists. "Presumably," sniped MP Joan McAlpine, "Charles thought those rules did not apply to him." Scottish first minister Nicola Sturgeon wished the prince well but noted that she didn't "want people to see the Highlands as a place where they can outrun the virus."

It was impossible to overstate the impact Charles's diagnosis had on his countrymen. "Within minutes of the news breaking," wrote Helen Lewis in the *Atlantic*, "I received the first of several texts from friends that all said essentially the same thing: 'Shit just got real.'" Lewis went on to explain that until this point, the coronavirus had been "an abstract idea for most Britons. This news brings it home. People you know—whether in real life or through the media—will get the virus. Some of them will become very ill. A few will die."

More than a few, as it turned out. Charles, who still watched his diet and exercised regularly, took some comfort in the knowledge that he had none of the underlying medical conditions that put many people his age at an increased risk of dying from the virus. The prince self-isolated at Birkhall, and both he and Camilla, who did not contract Covid-19, were careful to keep a safe distance from each other. All the remaining senior royals self-quarantined in an effort to stop the spread of the virus. While the Queen and Prince Philip holed up at Windsor Castle, the Cambridges remained sequestered at Anmer Hall on the grounds of Sandringham.

A world away in California, the Sussexes hunkered down in their lavish new digs, but—true to form—they would soon venture forth to distribute food to several hundred needy families hard-hit by the pandemic. Dressed in jeans and baseball caps and wearing protective masks, Harry and Meghan grabbed bags of groceries from the back of an SUV and carried them to the front doorsteps of people who were unable to leave their homes. It was all part of Project Angel Food, one of Doria Ragland's favorite charities.

Charles would soon be joined on the list of prominent Britons testing positive for Covid-19 by none other than Britain's controversial prime minister, who earlier told reporters he'd visited coronavirus patients in a London hospital and "shook hands with everybody, you'll be pleased to know." Charles, by his own admission, "got away very lightly" and was able to return to his duties a little more than a week after his initial diagnosis. Boris Johnson was not so lucky. With the number of cases rising sharply, Johnson finally decided it was time to curb the spread of the virus by ordering the nation to essentially lock down on March 23, 2020. Three days later, after appearing sweaty and ill at a press conference, the prime minister was diagnosed with Covid-19 and announced that he would be self-quarantining. Over the next ten days, his condition worsened, and he was hospitalized. It was not until he was admitted to intensive care that Johnson finally turned over the reins of government to his foreign secretary, Dominic Raab. By the time he was able to resume his post at the end of April, more than twenty-one thousand Britons had succumbed to the disease.

While the prime minister battled for his life in the ICU of St. Thomas's Hospital in London, the British government wheeled out the biggest gun in its public relations arsenal. On April 5, 2020, the Queen made a rare and historic televised "special address" to the nation—only the fifth in her reign—aimed at rallying the country behind efforts to curb the virus and thanking those health care workers on the front lines. The address was filmed in the White Drawing Room of Windsor Castle, chosen because it was large enough to maintain proper social distance between Her Majesty and the lone camera operator, who did wear a mask and gloves.

"I am speaking to you at what I know is an increasingly challenging time," the Queen said. "A time of disruption in the life of our country, a disruption that has brought grief to some, financial difficulties to many, and enormous changes to the daily lives of us all. . . . I hope in the years to come, everyone will be able to take pride in how they responded to this challenge. And those who come after us will say that the Britons of this generation were as strong as any." Evoking the same fighting spirit of Winston Churchill's speeches during World War II, the monarch promised her subjects that "better days will return. We will be with our friends again. We will be with our families again. We will meet again."

The Queen also cautioned patience and urged Britons to continue following rules outlined by infectious disease experts to defeat the virus. Still, despite the fact that he admitted his bout with the virus "could have gone either way," Boris Johnson went ahead in early May with his plan to loosen restrictions and gradually reopen the economy—a plan that was roundly criticized as premature in the face of the growing global pandemic.

Charles, as was so often the case, had a plan of his own. Speaking at the virtual opening of the World Economic Forum held each year in Davos, Switzerland, he argued that the pandemic offered a unique opportunity to reinvent the global economy. Covid-19's "unprecedented shock waves may well make people more receptive to big visions of change," suggested the prince, who then outlined his own five-point proposal stressing carbon pricing, sustainability, and more aggressive "green investments." Charles called his post-pandemic vision "the Great Reset."

The royal family, meanwhile, was undergoing a Great Reset of its own. Harry and Meghan, who suffered a miscarriage in July 2020, signaled their intention to put down roots in California by spending $14.65 million on a seven-acre Mediterranean-style estate north of Los Angeles in the exclusive Santa Barbara enclave of Montecito. Around the same time, according to Harry, Charles cut off his son financially and stopped returning his phone calls. Not that the Sussexes were in anything resembling financial distress. By this time, they had inked lucrative eight- and even nine-figure deals with several corporations, including a deal with Netflix to produce documentaries, docuseries, feature films, scripted shows, and children's programming.

One of the Sussexes' new deals was with Oprah Winfrey; the royal couple and the queen of American television announced that they would coproduce a docuseries on mental health. Before that happened, however, Harry and Meghan announced on Valentine's Day 2021 that they were expecting their second child. Then, as Buckingham Palace formally announced that the Sussexes had withdrawn permanently from royal duties, the two of them sat down with Oprah in their backyard for a three-hour-long, no-holds-barred interview.

When the Oprah interview aired on March 7, 2021, more than sixty million viewers tuned in to hear Meghan confess she had been driven to thoughts of suicide by pitiless palace officials and claim that her sister-in-law Kate had once reduced her to tears. Harry revealed that his father had not only stopped paying for his security but also had refused to speak to him for more than a year, saying, "There's a lot of hurt that's happened." Then there were accusations of racism, and the charge that before Archie's birth, someone within the royal family had raised "concerns" about what a child of theirs might look like—how dark the child's skin would be and "what that means" for the future of the monarchy.

Harry was quick to absolve the Queen and her gaffe-prone spouse, but that still left all the other senior royals in the crosshairs—especially Charles and William. Harry's additional claim that both his father and brother were "trapped" in their roles only made relations worse; both heirs took their duty to the country seriously, and William in particular felt especially protective toward the man who had willingly spent more than seven decades waiting to take on the job he was born to do. Soon William was no longer returning Harry's calls, either.

Not surprisingly, Charles was not exactly in a forgiving mood when it came to his younger son and his wife. Ever since Megxit started, he agreed with the measures the Queen had taken to make it clear that Harry could not function as a part-time royal—including Her Majesty's decision to

strip her grandson of his cherished ceremonial titles and the military regalia that went with them. Now Harry's hopes for breaking the deadlock
hinged on flying to London to celebrate the Duke of Edinburgh's hundredth birthday on June 10, which happened to be just a few days before
the Queen's official birthday. Even though the pandemic forced the cancel-
lation of Trooping the Colour and any large celebrations honoring Prince
Philip, Harry still planned to be there for the inevitable small family gathering at Sandringham.

Charles, however, was not at all convinced that his father would be
there for his milestone birthday. Philip, who had been in and out of hospitals in recent years, had been treated for an infection in February 2021 and
a month later underwent a heart procedure. Due to Covid restrictions, the
patient could see only a very limited number of visitors, which suited the
crusty, folderol-hating duke perfectly. Yet Charles was surprised that the
father he had once characterized publicly as bullying and aloof summoned
him to his hospital room. It was clear that Philip, not wanting to upset his
wife, trusted Charles to deliver any news of the duke's condition to the
Queen in a measured, unemotional manner. The Prince of Wales would
then remain in almost constant contact with his father, reporting back to
the Queen and other senior members of the family on a daily basis.

Princess Anne, Prince Andrew, and Prince Edward all called their father during his stay in the hospital and after he returned to recuperate at
Windsor—as did the Cambridges and the Sussexes. On April 8, Charles
was speaking with the Duke of Edinburgh on the phone and trying to get
him to discuss plans for his upcoming hundredth birthday. "We're talking
about your birthday," Charles said, waiting for a response. "We're talking
about your birthday! And whether there's going to be a reception."

"Well," Philip replied, "I've got to be alive for it, haven't I?"

"I knew you'd say that!" Charles shot back with a laugh.

The next day, with his wife of more than seven decades at his side,
Prince Philip died. Among other things, he was Britain's longest-serving
consort and the oldest male member of the royal family ever. "As you can
imagine," Charles said in an official statement, "my family and I miss my

father enormously. . . . My dear papa was a very special person who I think above all else would have been amazed by the reaction and the touching things that have been said about him."

Now all eyes were on Philip's funeral, and whether it would afford the opportunity for a reconciliation between the Sussexes and the rest of the royal family. Meghan was not expected to make the trip to London, and with good reason: her doctors believed it would be too risky at this late point in her pregnancy, especially during a pandemic. Even before Harry boarded the plane bound for London, it appeared that the Windsors were trying to accommodate him. Charles and William had originally planned to wear military uniforms to the small memorial service in St. George's Chapel at Windsor, but the Queen, aware that Harry had been banned from wearing military attire at royal functions, ordered that only civilian attire be worn by the mourners.

The funeral itself, like all others held during the pandemic, was a modest affair. As Charles led the procession of senior royals behind the Land Rover Defender TD 130 that carried his father's coffin to the chapel, he appeared genuinely stricken, his face etched with sadness. During the service, thirty masked family members were spaced ten feet apart in pews lining the sides of the chapel. Sitting closest to the standard-covered coffin was the Queen—a diminutive and solitary figure who seemed in that moment to be the focal point of a nation's grief. Charles and Camilla sat directly opposite Her Majesty on the far side of the nave, while the Queen's favorite child, Andrew, sat nearest the monarch, albeit ten feet away. From where he and the Duchess of Cornwall sat, Charles wanted to keep an eye on how his mother was doing but couldn't; Philip's coffin blocked his view.

Once the small but moving ceremony had ended, the Queen rode her state limousine up to the residence itself while mourners stripped off their masks and strolled up Castle Hill in the sunshine. William and Harry seemed to be getting along, chatting good-naturedly about how well the ceremony had gone. With all eyes on the possibility of reconciliation, Charles and William agreed to a brief meeting with Harry on the grounds of Windsor Castle—on the condition that they be the only three in attendance. But if Harry hoped that he would somehow bridge the chasm that separated him from the rest of the family, he was mistaken. Papa made no attempt to conceal his disappointment with his younger son and with actions by the Sussexes that cast one of the world's most enduring institutions, the British monarchy, in a wildly unflattering light. Harry did not even bother to stick around to wish Granny good wishes on her milestone ninety-fifth birthday, returning to California the day before.

It was only a matter of weeks before Harry was at it again, taking potshots at the Prince of Wales's parenting skills in a podcast and in another interview with Oprah, this one for their docuseries *The Me You Can't See*. "He's treated me the way he was treated," Harry said of his father, and went on to pledge that he would end the "genetic pain and suffering that gets passed on" by "breaking the cycle."

It now seemed increasingly unlikely that Charles would ever forgive his rebel son. Even the birth on June 4, 2021 of the Sussexes' second child, Lilibet "Lili" Diana Mountbatten-Windsor—so named in honor of the Queen, whose childhood nickname was Lilibet, and of course Harry's mother—did little to bridge the widening gap between Harry and his father and his brother. There were the usual pro forma statements welcoming the newest member of the family into the royal fold, but nothing more.

The next opportunity for rapprochement came on July 1, 2021, when Harry flew back to London to join his brother in dedicating a statue of their mother in the Sunken Garden at Kensington Palace—a place where they often played as children—on what would have been Diana's sixtieth birthday. Both the Queen and Charles pointedly chose not to attend. Nor did any other member of the royal family, which left only William and Harry on hand to greet their Spencer relatives and unveil the statue. In the end, it seemed clear that no progress had been made in the now ice-cold relationship between Charles's sons; once again they quickly went their separate ways.

Charles winced yet again when Harry announced he would be publishing a tell-all memoir in late 2022. In the future monarch's vision of a scaled-down, streamlined, more efficient monarchy, it became increasingly evident that there was little room for the Sussexes—at least not as long as they kept building their own "brand" on the other side of the Atlantic. Nor did it help that, in the process, Harry and Meghan seemed intent on sniping from the sidelines. "It is a very bitter pill for Prince Charles to swallow," said a former Clarence House staffer. "Harry has so much energy and so much charisma—he was one of the few people the Prince of Wales was counting on to play a key role once he took over as king." Now it appeared that most of that burden would fall squarely on the shoulders of William and Kate.

Harry's upcoming memoir wasn't the only potentially explosive book on Charles's radar. In late December 2021, several news organizations reported that Charles had been identified as the "royal racist" in my latest book, *Brothers and Wives: Inside the Private Lives of William, Kate, Harry, and Meghan*. As soon as the news broke, Buckingham Palace took the extraordinary step of immediately issuing a statement labeling the claim "fiction."

To be specific, *Brothers and Wives* relied on eyewitness accounts of an offhand and wholly innocent comment made by the Prince of Wales to Camilla during Harry and Meghan's engagement. At the time, Charles fondly speculated on what the famously attractive young couple's future offspring might look like—eye color, hair color—as any prospective grandparent would do.

Unfortunately, these benign musings had been overheard, repeated over time by palace operatives with their own agendas, and ultimately twisted into something more toxic by the time they reached Harry's ears. For their part, William and Harry remained curiously silent.

It remained to be seen if the Sussexes would ever find common ground with the rest of the royal family. So much hinged on whether Harry's grandmother would move unilaterally to bridge the gap. For a second year the traditional royal family Christmas at Sandringham was canceled due to a resurgence of the Covid-19 virus, and the press and public were eager to see if the Sussexes were once again included among the photographs displayed next to the Queen when she gave "Her Majesty's Most Gracious Speech." Those looking for some sign from the monarch were out of luck, however. For the first time in seventy-three years, Elizabeth was without a consort, and to mark the sad occasion there was only a single color photo of Elizabeth and her devoted husband on the desk beside her. "His sense of service, intellectual curiosity, and capacity to squeeze fun out of any situation were all irrepressible," said the Queen, who wore the striking Sapphire Chrysanthemum Brooch she had worn on their honeymoon. "That mischievous, enquiring twinkle was as bright at the end as when I first set eyes on him."

What the Queen had to say—or more to the point, what she didn't say—was most revealing. While complimenting the Prince of Wales and his eldest son—as well as their wives Camilla and Catherine—for carrying the torch on behalf of a cleaner environment, Her Majesty made no mention of Harry and Meghan for their efforts to combat climate change. Nor did the Queen mention any of the Sussexes by name at all.

The Queen's sin of omission did not go unnoticed by Charles, who, in the interest of fairness, trumpeted Harry's passionate dedication to the cause in an essay on the environment for *Newsweek*. Harry and Meghan read the article but were presumably unmoved, and there was apparently no attempt by either side to reach out to the other. Charles hoped that his younger son would make an attempt to attend a memorial service for Prince Philip at Westminster Abbey in late March—a first step toward attending the Queen's Platinum Jubilee festivities in early June and, hopefully, an important move in the direction of mending fences with the rest of the royal family. But Harry, now denied royal protection, worried about his family's safety when he was in England and took legal action to have it reinstated. Eager to pave the way for Harry's return, Charles, as I noted in the paperback edition of *Brothers and Wives*, privately invited the Sussexes to stay at Clarence House. There they would be afforded the same protection as the Prince of Wales and the Duchess of Cornwall. Sadly, Harry decided not to show up at the memorial service, which was nevertheless attended by no fewer than five kings and five queens.

While Charles contemplated ways to bridge the widening gap between Harry and his Windsor relatives, he actively lobbied to have his own brother virtually expelled from the royal family. After Ghislaine Maxwell was convicted in New York of helping to procure underage girls to be sexually abused by her friend Jeffrey Epstein, Prince Andrew tried and failed to have the civil case brought by the woman who accused him of rape, Virginia Giuffre, thrown out. The Queen, whose duty to the institution of the monarchy outweighed even the love she had for her adored favorite child, parceled out Andrew's patronages among other family members and revoked the honorary military titles that he, like all the other Windsors, held so dear. She also commanded Andrew not to use his HRH status in any official capacity.

Understandably, Charles worried—perhaps more than any other member of the royal family—that his younger brother's salacious behavior would leave the crown badly tarnished. Concurrently, the Prince of Wales pressed for other changes. At the top of his list was convincing his future subjects to accept Camilla as their Queen, and not merely his Princess Consort. Even after a November 2021 YouGov poll showed that only 14 percent of the country favored Camilla becoming Queen—and only 42 percent were willing even to accept her as "Princess Consort"—Charles remained undaunted. Rather than throw his hands up in defeat—after all, he had been trying to get the public to accept Camilla as his queen for nearly seventeen years— the Prince of Wales now pleaded with his mother to intervene. It was clear to Charles that nothing short of the Queen bestowing her heartfelt personal blessing on Camilla would create the sort of seismic shift in public opinion that was needed.

The Queen, still coming to terms with the death of her husband, demurred. But a confluence of events would soon occur that gave Charles unexpected leverage. With all of Andrew's legal maneuvers exhausted, it now appeared he would be forced to settle the case with Virginia Giuffre if there was hope of avoiding a civil trial and the explosively sleazy revelations it was bound to produce. For their part, the Queen and her Buckingham Palace advisors wanted nothing to mar the monarch's Platinum Jubilee celebrations in June.

Andrew's lawyers negotiated a reported settlement of $14 million, but who would pay for it? Andrew was in no position to—he had already shelled out more than $3 million in legal fees. With the clear understanding that not even one penny of taxpayer funds could be used, the Queen would have to dig into her own pocket to come up with the money. That meant either drawing on the roughly $33 million in excess funds generated by the Duchy of Lancaster estate each year—income paid directly to the Sovereign—or using some of the half-billion dollars in private savings and investments amassed by Her Majesty over the past seventy years.

Charles and William were among Andrew's harshest critics inside the family; they also felt Andrew should cooperate with the FBI. But they also knew that Favorite Son Andrew could count on the Queen to bail him out.

There was a catch, however. Since for all intents and purposes such funds would ultimately be coming out of Charles's inheritance—on becoming king he would inherit both access to the Duchy of Lancaster income and the bulk of his mother's vast holdings—Charles would have to, if not actually sign off on the deal, then at least not offer a public objection to it. As distasteful as it was to have a slice of his inheritance go for this purpose, Charles recognized a rare opportunity for some sort of informal quid pro quo. While the question of where the money would come from was still very much on the table, the Prince of Wales suggested privately that February 6, 2022—the seventieth anniversary of her father, George VI's, death—might be the ideal time to make some sort of statement in support of Camilla becoming queen.

The world was unaware of these maneuverings behind palace walls, and thus unprepared for the Queen's February 6 proclamation. In her statement, Elizabeth II thanked the British people for their support and praised Prince Philip for his contributions to the nation—all predictable enough. But she went on to say that it was her "sincere wish that, when the time comes, Camilla will be known as Queen Consort as she continues her own loyal service." The Queen's announcement seemed to have done the trick. Overnight, polls showed that fully half of Charles's future subjects were willing to accept Camilla as Queen Consort if that is what the Sovereign wished. However, that still left half the country opposed to seeing Camilla take the title that had once been intended for Diana.

One courtier observed that the "constant drumbeat" from Charles that Camilla had "earned" the title of Queen simply "wore Her Majesty down." Camilla and Charles issued a joint statement saying they were "touched and honored by Her Majesty's words"—and made no effort to stand in the way of using the Queen's funds to pay for Andrew's massive settlement in the Giuffre-Epstein case.

It was not long before impact of the pandemic once again took center stage as Charles tested positive for Covid a second time. Within a matter of days, the Queen and Camilla also tested positive. All suffered only mild symptoms, but images of the Queen released not long before her ninety-sixth birthday indicated that illness and her advanced years had taken their toll. Now that she was inevitably nearing the end of her reign, she would not be returning to Buckingham Palace except for the occasional brief ceremonial visit. From this point on, Windsor would be her official permanent home—interrupted by long stays at her even more-beloved Balmoral Castle.

Whichever castle they chose to call home, both the Queen and her son and heir continued to be fully apprised of what was going on in the world. The iconic red boxes of state that were delivered daily to the sovereign and the Prince of Wales now brimmed with classified dispatches warning that Russia was preparing to attack Ukraine. After the invasion was launched on February 24, Charles and Camilla used their Ash Wednesday visit to London's Ukrainian Catholic Cathedral to denounce Russia's "terrible aggression" and to praise "the extraordinary bravery, generosity, and fortitude" of the Ukrainian people. He would go on to decry Russian President Vladimir Putin's decision to pursue war against Ukraine as an "unconscionable" act of "brutal aggression." In truth, there was no love lost between Charles and Putin, whom the Prince of Wales had publicly compared to Adolf Hitler in 2017.

The war in Ukraine raged on into the summer of 2022, and every day brought new and increasingly chilling details of Russian atrocities aimed at civilians. Joining NATO and its other allies, Great Britain stood shoulder-to-shoulder with Ukraine's heroically defiant president, Volodymyr Zelenskyy.

Unprecedented sanctions were levied against Russia, and billions of dollars in military and humanitarian aid poured into the beleaguered nation that had once been part of the Soviet Union.

Both the Queen and her successor, willing captives to the Red Leather Boxes of State, eagerly pored over the top secret dispatches detailing what was going on in Ukraine and other hot spots, making mother and son two of the most well-briefed people in the world.

At this point, Charles had taken on so many of the monarch's duties—presiding at investitures, accepting diplomatic credentials, and much more—that it was less jarring than it might otherwise have been when, on May 10, 2022, he filled in for his mother at the ceremonial State Opening of Parliament.

It was only the third time in seventy years that the Queen, who was coping with "mobility issues," missed the ceremony; the other two times she was pregnant with her two youngest children, Andrew and Edward, in the 1960s.

The historic moment offered a glimpse into a future with Charles as king, but reminded everyone that he was not there yet. He did not sit on the gilded Sovereign's Throne, but instead on the Consort's Throne, which is nearly identical but a significant inch shorter. The speech he delivered, which is actually written by the government and outlines its priorities for the year, had to be altered to accommodate the Queen's absence; instead of saying "my government," Charles had to repeatedly refer in the speech to "Her government." If that weren't enough, the Imperial State Crown sat on a red velvet cushion to Charles's immediate right—just to remind.

Flanking Charles but one step down were a future king and a queen consort—William and Camilla—there to round out the face of the monarchy well into the twenty-first century. Such symbolism aside, Charles was unhappy that, in his first speech at the State Opening of Parliament, there was not a single mention of the environment.

It was difficult to imagine that any single event could distract from the blood-soaked horrors being visited upon Ukrainians on a daily basis. But on May 24, 2022, all eyes turned to the U.S. when a lone eighteen-year-old gunman armed with an assault rifle murdered nineteen children and two adults at Robb Elementary School in the small South Texas town of Uvalde. It was the deadliest school shooting in the U.S. since 2012, when twenty children and six adults were killed at Sandy Hook Elementary School in Newtown, Connecticut.

Charles joined the Queen and the rest of the royal family in expressing their condolences, but Meghan went a step further and made an unannounced visit to Uvalde itself just two days after the massacre to pay her respects "as a mother." As it happened, her estranged father, Thomas Markle, had suffered a stroke on the same day as the Uvalde shootings and was recovering in the hospital. Critics wasted no time suggesting that Meghan should have visited her seriously ill father rather than travel to Uvalde to stage what Meghan's half-brother Thomas Jr. slammed as a "PR stunt."

As strained as relations may have been between the Sussexes and the rest of the family, none of the senior royals stepped forward to criticize Meghan's decision to visit Uvalde. Charles and the Cambridges in particular were shaken by what had happened—a stark reminder that thousands of Americans were losing their lives to senseless gun violence every year. At one point Kate told a friend that she understood why Meghan, as an American and the mother of two young children, would feel compelled to show up in person. It was, in fact, something Kate herself had done when she showed up unannounced the previous year at a candlelight vigil in London for a young woman who had been murdered by a police officer. The glaring difference was that Kate had not been subjected to the sort of blistering criticism now aimed at her American sister-in-law.

In a welcome break from mayhem and madness, the unprecedented Platinum Jubilee of a British monarch kicked off on June 2 with Trooping the Color, followed by the traditional Royal Air Force flypast over

Buckingham Palace. This time, the scene on the palace balcony reflected Charles's efforts to streamline the thousand-year-old institution he was poised to inherit.

Only "working royals" were invited to appear, which meant for the first time in his life Harry, once a member in good standing of the "Magnificent Seven," was not allowed to wave at the adoring multitudes alongside his father, brother, and the Queen.

While the monarch was the undisputed star of the events that week, four-year-old Prince Louis stole the limelight more than once by making faces and covering his ears as British warplanes screamed overhead. As for the Queen, she now walked with a cane—a "stick" in British parlance—but seemed energized by the crowds. Apparently it took all her stamina merely to show up. The next day, Her Majesty bowed out of a memorial service at St. Paul's, once again leaving Charles to carry the ball as senior royal.

The Queen skipped a number of high-profile Jubilee events, including the star-studded "Party at the Palace" pop concert. With the Sussexes effectively sidelined—they returned home to California after the Queen agreed to give them only fifteen minutes for a perfunctory private audience—Charles, William, and their wives now had center stage to themselves.

Behind the scenes, the Cambridges were quietly making plans to relocate to Windsor so that they could be closer to the Queen and to Prince Charles. Now that William was turning forty and the children were getting older, Charles had suggested that it was perhaps time to leave Anmer Hall in Norfolk and move closer to the center of power.

The property William and Kate had their eye on was Adelaide Cottage, a modest four-bedroom house built by the last King William—William IV, for his consort, Queen Adelaide. This way, since Kensington Palace would continue to be their in-town residence, William and Kate would never be far from George, Charlotte, and Louis as they headed off to schools in the London area.

For Charles, who along with others in the royal court was once concerned about William's preference for flying rescue helicopters over his ceremonial duties, the Cambridges' move to Windsor was yet another sign of family solidarity. With Harry not only out of the picture but presumably poised to reveal more family secrets in his forthcoming memoir, the future kings would need to lean on each other more than ever.

As he entered his mid-seventies, Charles bore scant physical resemblance to the lean and callow youth who pledged to become the Queen's "liege man of life and limb" during his 1969 investiture as Prince of Wales. Gray haired and thicker beneath his immaculately tailored double-breasted suits, he looked every inch the grandfatherly country squire. Yet unlike most other men who came of age in the late 1960s, Charles in old age still retains the essential qualities of his youth. Never a rebel but always curious and questioning, the overly formal young man who was derided for being more a creature of the nineteenth century than the twentieth now seemed to have fully grown into himself. Words such as *seasoned, polished, mellowed, mature, wise*—qualities one would hope to find in a sovereign—were now routinely used to describe Elizabeth II's son and heir.

Constitutional monarchy is an oxymoron. There is nothing democratic about the concept of a king—a point made by increasingly vocal antimonarchist republicans in the United Kingdom and several Commonwealth countries. Yet by separating politics from its titular head of state, Britain has sustained a strong representative democracy and a national character that is unique. Indeed, its very existence requires that a delicate balance be maintained between pomp, ceremony, and symbolism on one hand and true political power and influence on the other. Nor should the global allure of Britain's monarchy be underestimated. By some estimates, the royal family brings more than one billion tourist dollars into the United Kingdom annually.

Years ago Charles hinted that he intends to streamline the monarchy, starting with a somewhat pared-down but still awe-inspiring coronation (for the first time, there are plans for social media to play a part). Now that Charles is getting everything he wanted, Camilla is to be seated next to him in her own coronation chair, nervously waiting to be crowned Queen Consort. In the months following, the King will pursue his plans for a leaner, more efficient Buckingham Palace: staff will be reduced, responsibilities reassigned, and tasks delegated to others so that Charles has the time to plow through the red boxes of state that consume so much of a sovereign's time.

No one understands the constraints of his new position better than Charles, whose entire life has been guided, controlled—and to a large extent constrained—by Palace operatives. Although not obligated to take the advice of government officials, Charles always submits his writings to them for comment. As monarch, he will essentially be required to make official pronouncements only on the advice of ministers—although, like his mother, he will speak without interference when delivering his annual Christmas and Commonwealth Day broadcasts.

Unlike his mother, Charles will almost certainly not Keep Calm and Carry On. He lacks the Queen's self-discipline, quiet confidence, and patience—all qualities that served Elizabeth II and her realm well. As a result, Charles is destined to lock horns not only with government officials but also Palace operatives. The Men in Gray who had so vexed Diana and intimidated even the Queen ("There are powers at work . . .") will no longer be obeyed without question by a compliant, duty-bound-to-the-bitter-end monarch. If the last seventy years are any indication, the new monarch will be a much noisier one: prodding, needling, and debating with his prime minister during their weekly sessions, dashing off more Black Spider memos to bureaucrats, speaking out on the issues that have always intrigued him while somehow managing to remain above the political fray.

Charles knows better than anyone that his reign will not be a long one. Bookended by the most admired and longest-reigning monarch in history and a dashing young Prince who is heir to the mystique of a martyred Princess, Charles can hope only to win the people's affection with his particular brand of quiet dignity, old-world charm, and new-world activism.

A neglected, bullied, and abused child. An awkward, jug-eared, largely friendless young man more attuned to the nineteenth century than his own. A scorned adulterer. An embattled husband caught up in a power struggle with the world's most adored woman. A loving father and doting grandfather. A visionary, an iconoclast, a self-pitying whiner. A world-class, yet largely unheralded, philanthropist. A dutiful son, and a patient yet restless heir. Charles has been all these things, and now, finally: King.

When a shy twenty-year-old nursery school teacher married the heir to the British throne on July 29, 1981, more than 750 million people tuned in—including millions of bleary-eyed Americans who rose before dawn to watch the joyous event as it happened. Sixteen years later a worldwide audience of two billion people was both mesmerized and saddened by the sight of young Princes William and Harry walking, eyes downcast, behind the coffin of their mother Princess Diana as it made its way through London streets lined with more than a million heartbroken mourners. The world would wait until 2011 for Britain's royal family to deliver another record-shattering global spectacle. This time it was the long-anticipated wedding of William to Kate Middleton at Westminster Abbey, which was watched by a jaw-dropping two-and-a-half billion people from Boston to Beijing.

As planet-rattling events go, the departure of one monarch and the coronation of another is one of history's most well rehearsed. Yet as we moved closer to the inevitable, it became increasingly clear that nothing could really prepare us for the end of the second Elizabethan era and the dawn of the age of King Charles III. By the end of her millennium-spanning reign, the woman known to billions simply as the Queen could lay claim to being the most celebrated figure of the modern age—a central actor on the world stage for longer than anyone in all of recorded history.

It is no small irony that Elizabeth's heir apparent, no less an object of curiosity and speculation for more than seven decades, remains largely unknown to us. For forty years, I have covered the royal family, writing several *New York Times* bestsellers about the star-crossed, scandal-plagued Windsor dynasty. Yet in writing the definitive biography of Charles, I discovered that, as Winston Churchill once said famously of the Soviet Union, the new monarch is nothing less than a riddle wrapped in a mystery inside an enigma.

Equally daunting was the task of keeping up with a family that, having been transformed by the life and death of the remarkable Diana, now not only allowed change but fervently, even passionately, embraced it. Harry's marriage to the divorced, biracial American actress Meghan Markle and the birth of their son Archie Harrison Mountbatten-Windsor would have seemed unimaginable scarcely a decade earlier. That the new king would approve of his younger son's choice of a bride—unprecedented on so many levels—seemed astounding in itself. That Charles would walk his new daughter-in-law down the aisle and publicly shower her with otherwise rarely seen public displays of affection bordered on the surreal.

My wife and I first encountered the entire royal family up close and personal in 1977, when the Queen was a mere fifty-one years old and celebrating her Silver Jubilee. Charles was only twenty-eight, and Diana, a fifteen-year-old schoolgirl, was not yet on anyone's radar. Over the next forty-two-plus years, I would write six books on the Windsors, covering every unexpected twist and hairpin turn in their remarkable family saga. Now, at this start of yet another exciting chapter in the thousand-year history of the world's oldest monarchy, I find Charles to be as unfathomable—and unpredictable—as ever.

Once again I find myself working with some of the finest talents the publishing world has to offer. I am particularly grateful to my editor, Gallery's editorial director, Aimée Bell, for her passionate commitment to the project and our shared fascination with all things royal. My thanks, as well, to the entire Gallery/Simon & Schuster team—especially Jennifer Bergstrom, Jonathan Karp, the late Carolyn Reidy, Jennifer Long, Jennifer Robinson, Max Meltzer, Lisa Litwack, John Vairo, Caroline Pallotta, Natasha Simons, Paul O'Halloran, Davina Mock-Maniscalco, Celeste Phillips,

Chelsea Cohen, Michael Kwan, Samantha Hoback, Brigid Black, Felice Javit, Karyn Marcus, Molly Gregory, and Lisa Rivlin.

After thirty-five books together, I hope that my great friend and agent for life, Ellen Levine, hasn't tired of my effusive expressions of gratitude. They are as heartfelt as they were when I first began including them in my acknowledgments back in 1983. My thanks to Ellen's consummately professional colleagues at Trident Media Group, including Claire Roberts, Martha Wydysh, Nicole Robson, Caitlin O'Beirne, Diana Rodon, Alicia Granstein, Meredith Miller, Alexander Slater, and Alexa Stark.

Ever since we met as undergraduates at the University of California at Berkeley more than a half century ago, my amazing and witty wife Valerie has been, as Elizabeth said of Philip, "my strength and stay." While pursuing her own career in international banking and being an active member of our community, Valerie also played an integral part in the publishing process. Our elder daughter, the journalist and historian Kate Andersen Brower, has learned how valuable an editorial advisor, brainstormer, and all-around literary guru her mother can be. Like her dad, Kate (who has written three major nonfiction bestsellers of her own while doing a phenomenal job raising three small children) makes certain that Valerie gets that all-important first look at every manuscript. We are eternally grateful for the important role she plays in shaping the direction and tone of our work—not to mention the patience, support, encouragement, and inspiration she has always lavished not just on us but on her larger circle of family and friends. To which Valerie would reply, "Yes, I'm a living saint." People think she's kidding. She's not. And just maybe she's right.

We are fortunate to have not one but two remarkable daughters. Kate's younger sister Kelly, the only one in the family to show real talent as an artist, is seeking to apply her master's degree in contemporary art from the University of Manchester/Sotheby's Institute of Art in London to a museum career. Kate's husband, meanwhile, has thus far acquitted himself well, at least as far as sons-in-law go. Seriously, it's hard to find anything remotely critical to say about him—which makes my assigned role as the curmudgeonly father-in-law extremely hard to play. Brooke Brower is a highly regarded executive at CNN in Washington, a devoted dad to Graham, Charlotte, and Teddy—and an all-around great guy.

My late parents remain a profound if unseen force in all our lives. As time goes on, it seems all the more astounding to me that my father, Cdr. Edward Andersen, flew bombers off aircraft carriers in the Pacific and was shot down in Manilla Bay—one of many wartime experiences (he also went on to serve in Korea and Vietnam) this career naval officer seldom discussed. My mother, Jeanette, a voracious reader and simply one of the smartest women I've ever known, would have loved to pursue a career as a newspaper reporter—think Rosalind Russell in *His Girl Friday*—but as an officer's wife, it was enough that she watched after her young family as we moved from one military base to another at the height of the Cold War. She is the reason that, at the age of sixteen, I became a working journalist.

Additional thanks to Alan Hamilton, Lady Margaret Rhodes, Peter Archer, Aileen Mehle, Richard Kay, Countess Mountbatten, Lord Mishcon, Andrew Gailey, Janet Jenkins, Lady Elsa Bowker, Vivian Parry, Lady Yolanda Joseph, Mark Shand, Penny Walker, Guy Pelly, Dr. Frederic Mailliez, Lord Carnarvon, Harold Brooks-Baker, Jules Knight, Tara Palmer-Tomkinson, Joan Rivers, Geoffrey Bignell, Alexandra ("Tiggy") Legge-Bourke Pettifer, Beatrice Hubert, Vivienne Parry, Lucia Flecha de Lima, Philip Higgs, Hamish Barne, Mimi Massy-Birch, the Countess of Romanones, James Whitaker, Richard Greene, Norman Parkinson, Lord Bathurst, Raine Spencer, Natalie Symonds, Lynn Redgrave, Gered Mankowitz, Richard Grant, Andy Radford, Pierre Trudeau, Cecile Zilkha, Winston Spencer-Churchill, Hugh Massy-Birch, Emma Sayle, Max Clifford, Jules de Rosee, the Duchess of Alba, Thierry Meresse, Muriel Hartwick, Janet Lizop, the Earl of Powis, Penny Russell-Smith, Sharman Douglas, Patrick Demarchelier, Tom Sykes, Ezra Zilkha, Kitty Carlisle Hart, Elizabeth d'Erlanger, Lord Olivier, Adrian Munsey, Miriam Lefort, Claude Garrick, Peter Allen, Delissa Needham, Jeanne Lecorcher, Lady Elizabeth Longman, Laura Watts, Mark Butt, Pierre Suu, Jessica Hogan, Alfred Eisenstaedt, Alain-Phillipe Feutre, Mary Robertson, Malcolm

Forbes, Rosemary McClure, Dee Ennifer, Rachel Witburn, John Kaufman, Remi Gaston-Dreyfus, John Marion, Regina Feiler, Fred Hauptfuhrer, Debbie Goodsite, Dudley Freeman, Daniel Taylor, Ian Walde, Mel Lyons, Tom Wolfe, Yvette Reyes, Larry King, Matthew Lutts, Rhoda Prelic, Jeanette Peterson, Tom Corby, Bill Diehl, Simone Dibley, Scott Burkhead, Kevin Lemarque, David McGough, Hilary Hard, Mary Beth Whelan, Hazel Southam, Marc Halpern, Andy Rouvalis, Steve Stylandoudis, Wolfgang Ratay, Tasha Hannah, Paula Dranov, Betty Kelly Sargent, Charles Furneaux, Lord Glenconner, Connie Erickson, Marcel Turgot, Everett Raymond Kinstler, Julie Cammer, John Stillwell, Michael Cantlebury, Amber Weitz, Vincent Martin, Michelle Lapautre, David Bergeron, Stuart Scheinman, Alla Diment, Tucker DiEdwardo, Mick Magsino, Lindsay Sutton, Art Kaligos, Ron Galella, Elizabeth Loth, Tiffany Miller, Francis Specker, Jane Clucas, Tim Graham, Tom Freeman, Tom McShane, Ray Whelan Jr., Lindsay Potenza, Kyle Cowser, Barry Schenck, Agnieszka Mejri, Gary Gunderson, the Press Association, Buckingham Palace, Clarence House, Kensington Palace, Windsor Castle, St. James's Palace, Cheam School, Gordonstoun School, Trinity College, Cambridge University, Timbertop, Geelong Grammar School, University of St. Andrews, Eton College, Ludgrove School, the Royal Military Academy Sandhurst, the BBC, Channel Four Television Ltd, Sky News, *Times* of London, *Guardian, Daily Mail, Daily Telegraph, Mail on Sunday, Sunday Times, Daily Express, New York Times, Financial Times, London Evening Standard,* the New York Public Library, the Bodleian Library Oxford, the Reading Room at the British Museum, Bancroft Library of the University of California at Berkeley, the Yale University Beinecke Rare Book and Manuscript Library, the Gunn Memorial Library, the Silas Bronson Library, the Litchfield Library, the Reform Club, the Lansdowne Club, the Athenaeum, the Savile Club, the Garrick Club, the East India Club, the Lotos Club, Bloomberg News, Associated Press, Reuters, Rex USA, Globe Photos, Getty Images, Capital Art, and Shutterstock.

SOURCES AND CHAPTER NOTES

The following chapter notes are designed to provide an overall view of sources accessed for the research and writing of *The King*, but are not to be considered all-inclusive. Important sources at Buckingham Palace, Windsor Castle, St. James's Palace, Clarence House, Balmoral, Sandringham, Highgrove, Kensington Palace, Lambeth Palace, Cheam School, Gordonstoun, Ludgrove, Cambridge University, Marlborough College, Eton, Scotland Yard, Sandhurst, and the University of St. Andrews—as well as relatives, close friends and acquaintances, former teachers and classmates, advisors, government officials, employees, and colleagues—agreed to cooperate only if they were permitted to remain anonymous. These are, in many cases, the same impeccable inside sources who have provided accurate and remarkably detailed information to me over the decades for my five previous books on the royal family. Out of respect for their wishes and in gratitude for their continuing cooperation, the author has not named these sources either here or elsewhere in the text. It is worth noting that the vast majority of information contained in *The King* is on the record.

It goes without saying that millions of words have been written about Charles, the Queen, Prince Philip, Princess Diana, Camilla, Prince Andrew and his ex-wife Sarah Ferguson, the Queen Mother, and Princess Margaret—not to mention princes William and Harry, their spouses Kate and Meghan, and their adorable offspring. Indeed, since the tragic and shocking death of Princess Diana in 1997, the royal family has been afforded a degree of news coverage that can be described only as unprecedented—such is the public's fascination with the House of Windsor. Among those publications in which relevant articles appeared are the *New York Times*, the *Times* (London), the *Guardian* (UK edition), the *Sunday Times* (London), the *Wall Street Journal*, the *Daily Mail* (UK), the *Washington Post*, the *Daily Telegraph* (UK), the *Boston Globe*, the *Los Angeles Times*, *Vanity Fair*, *Time*, *People*, *Newsweek*, the *New Yorker*, *Life*, *Le Monde* (France), *Paris Match*, and the *Economist*, and carried over the Associated Press, Reuters, and Bloomberg wires.

CHAPTERS 1 AND 2

Interview subjects included Lady Margaret Rhodes, Countess Mountbatten, Norman Parkinson, Lord Mishcon, Alan Hamilton, Mark Shand, Dr. Frederic Mailliez, the late Lady Elsa Bowker, Sharman Douglas, Jeanne Lecorcher, Beatrice Humbert, Richard Kay, Thierry Meresse, Harold Brooks-Baker, Lady Yolanda Joseph, Mark Butt, Richard Greene, Peter Archer, Andy Radford, Ezra Zilkha, Tess Rock, Claude Garreck, Josy Duclos, Malcolm Forbes, Remi Gaston-Dreyfus, Barry Schenck, Miriam Lefort, Janet Lizop, Pierre Suu, Steve Stylandoudis, and Peter Allen. Published sources included Philip Eade, *Prince Philip: The Turbulent Early Life of the Man Who Married Queen Elizabeth II* (New York: Henry Holt, 2011); Hannah Lazatin, "How Prince Philip's Tragic Childhood Affected His Relationship with His Son, Prince Charles," *Town & Country*, December 11, 2017; John Parker, *Prince Philip: His Secret Life* (New York: St. Martin's Press, 1991); *The Coronation*, BBC One, January 14, 2018; A. P. Herbert, "Here Comes the Queen," *Life*, April 27, 1953; John Brooke-Little, *Royal Ceremonies of State* (London: Littlehampton, 1980); "The Ceremonial of the Coronation of Her Majesty Queen Elizabeth II," Supplement to the *London Gazette*, November 17, 1952; "The Form and Order of Service That Is to Be Performed and the Ceremonies That Are to Be Observed in the Coronation of Her Majesty Queen Elizabeth II in the Abbey Church of St. Peter, Westminster, on Tuesday, the Second Day of June 1953," Church of England/Anglican Liturgical Library; Tom Sykes, "What Will Happen When the Queen Dies?," *Daily Beast*, last modified June 2, 2015; *Inaugurating a New Reign: Planning for Accession and Coro-*

nation (London: University College, 2018); Rob Price, "This Is What Happens When the Queen Dies: The Death of Queen Elizabeth Will Be the Most Disruptive Event in Britain in the Last 70 Years," *Business Insider*, last modified May 6, 2015; Matthew Weaver, "UK Republicans Debate How to React When the Queen Dies," *Guardian*, July 12, 2015; Robert Lacey, *Majesty* (New York: Harcourt Brace Jovanovich, 1977); Adrian Higgins, "How Britain Came to Revere Elizabeth II," *Washington Post*, September 8, 2015; Duncan Hill et al., *The Royal Family: A Year by Year Chronicle of the House of Windsor* (New York: Parragon, 2012); Charles Moore, "An Act of National Communion—But What Will Happen at the Next Coronation?," *Daily Telegraph*, May 31, 2013; "The Nation Unites Against Tradition," *Observer* (UK), September 7, 1997; Lord Stevens of Kirkwhelpington, *The Operation Paget Inquiry Report into the Allegation of Conspiracy to Murder Diana, Princess of Wales, and Emad El-Din Mohamed Abdel Moneim Fayed*, December 14, 2006; Emily Nash, "Diana: The Verdict," *Daily Mirror* (UK), December 11, 2006; "Farewell, Diana," *Newsweek*, September 15, 1997; "Charles Escorts Diana Back to a Grieving Britain," *New York Times*, September 1, 1997; Anthony Holden, "Why Royals Must Express Remorse," *Daily Express* (UK), September 3, 1997; "The Princes' Final Farewell," *Sunday Times*, September 7, 1997; Alan Hamilton, Andrew Pierce, and Philip Webster, "Royal Family Is 'Deeply Touched' by Public Support," *Times*, September 4, 1997; "Diana, Princess of Wales 1961–1997," *Week*, September 6, 1997; John Simpson, "Goodbye England's Rose: A Nation Says Farewell," *Sunday Telegraph* (UK), September 7, 1997; "Driver Was Drunk," *Le Monde*, September 3, 1997; Andrew Morton, *Diana: Her True Story* (New York: Simon & Schuster, 1997); Christopher Andersen, *The Day Diana Died* (New York: William Morrow, 1998); Christopher Wilson, *A Greater Love: Prince Charles's Twenty-Year Affair with Camilla Parker Bowles* (New York: William Morrow, 1994); "Boys to Men," *New York Daily News*, December 21, 1997; Robert Jobson and Greg Swift, "Look After William and Harry," *Daily Express*, December 22, 1997; Tess Rock and Natalie Symonds, "Our Diana Diaries," *Sunday Mirror*, November 16, 1997; Simone Simmons, *Diana:*

The Last Word (New York: St. Martin's Press, 2005); "Flashback to the Accident," *Liberation*, September 2, 1997; Robert Hardman, "Princes' Last Minutes with Mother," *Daily Telegraph*, September 3, 1997; Howard Chua-Eoan et al., "A Death in Paris: The Passing of Diana," *Time*, September 8, 1997; "Diana: Investigation of the Investigation," *Le Point*, September 13, 1997; Rosa Monckton, "Time to End False Rumors," *Newsweek*, March 2, 1998; Jerome Dupuis, "Diana: The Unpublished Report of Witnesses at the Ritz," *L'Express*, March 2, 1998; Thomas Sancton and Scott MacLeod, *Death of a Princess: The Investigation* (New York: St. Martin's Press, 1998); Angela Levin, "Exclusive: Prince Harry on Chaos After Diana's Death and Why the World Needs 'the Magic' of the Royal Family," *Newsweek*, June 21, 2017; Earl Spencer, "I Was Lied to Over Princes' Wish to Follow Diana's Coffin," BBC Radio 4 Today, July 26, 2017; "Diana: 7 Days That Shook the World," BBC One, September 13, 2017; Marianne Macdonald, "A Rift Death Can't Heal," *Observer*, September 14, 1997; Jonathan Dimbleby, *The Prince of Wales: A Biography* (London: Little, Brown UK, 1994); "Princess Diana's Brother Says He Was Lied to Over Princes Following Coffin," *Guardian*, July 26, 2017; Abe Hawken, "Diana's Brother Says Royal Officials Lied to Him," *Daily Mail*, July 26, 2017; Sarah Bradford, *The Reluctant King: The Life and Reign of George VI, 1895–1952* (New York: St. Martin's Press, 1990); "The Day the King Died," BBC One, February 6, 2002; William Shawcross, *Queen Elizabeth the Queen Mother: The Official Biography* (London: Macmillan, 2009); "1952: King George VI Dies in His Sleep," BBC One, February 6, 1952; H. C. Matthew, "George VI (1895–1952)," *Oxford Dictionary of National Biography* (Oxford: Oxford University, 2004); Sir John Wheeler-Bennett, *King George VI: His Life and Reign* (New York: St. Martin's Press, 1958); Ben Pimlott, *The Queen: A Biography of Elizabeth II* (New York: John Wiley & Sons, 1996); Sally Bedell Smith, *Elizabeth the Queen* (New York: Random House, 2012); Sarah Lyall, "Peter Townsend Dies at 80: Princess Margaret's Love," *New York Times*, June 21, 1995; Peter Townsend, *The Last Emperor* (London: Weidenfeld and Nicolson, 1975); "Princess Margaret and a Love Affair Denied," *Daily Mail*,

February 9, 2002; Theo Aronson, *Royal Family: Years of Transition* (London: Thistle, 2014); Noreen Taylor, "Saying What Everyone Thinks: Private Secretary Lord Charteris, Still with a Keen Finger on the Royal Pulse," *Spectator*, January 7, 1995; Hayley Mick, "The Special Role of Britain's Royal Nannies," *Globe and Mail* (Can.), June 17, 2013; Kathryn Hughes, "Royal Nannies, Past and Present," *Daily Telegraph*, July 19, 2014; Anthony Holden, *Prince Charles* (London: Atheneum, 1979); Alex Renton, "Abuse in Britain's Boarding Schools: Why I Decided to Confront My Demons," *Guardian*, May 4, 2014; Joanna Scutts, "Britain's Boarding School Problem: How the Country's Elite Institutions Have Shaped Colonialism, Brexit, and Today's Global Superrich," *New Republic*, September 14, 2018; Robert Verkaik, *Posh Boys: How the English Public Schools Ruin Britain* (London: One World Publications, 2018).

CHAPTERS 3–5

Interviews and conversations for these chapters included Janet Jenkins, Alan Hamilton, the Duchess of Alba, Peter Archer, Lady Yolanda Joseph, Emma Sayle, Lord Bathurst, Lord Mishcon, Patricia Knatchbull, the late Lady Elsa Bowker, Hamish Barne, the Duchess of Alba, Hugh Massy-Birch, Prince Rupert Loewenstein, Charles Furneaux, Jules Knight, Tom Sykes, Mimi Massy-Birch, Delissa Needham, Alice Tomlinson, Pat Charman, Earl McGrath, Richard Greene, Guy Pelly, Geoffrey Bignell, Penny Walker, Tess Rock, Jules de Rosee, Richard Kay, Farris Rookstool, Fred Hauptfuhrer, Colin St. John Wilson, Evelyn Phillips, Susan Crimp, Kitty Carlisle Hart, Elizabeth Widdett, the late Joan Rivers, Janet Allison, and Mary Robertson. Published sources include Claire Carter, "Prince Charles's School Hit by Claims of Child Sex Abuse," *Daily Mail*, April 12, 2015; Alex Renton, "Rape, Child Abuse, and Prince Charles's Former School," *Guardian*, April 12, 2015; Magnus Linklater, "Gordonstoun School Asks Former Pupils If They Were Abused," *Times*, June 24, 2017; Marc Horn, "Miranda Doyle Tells of 'Abuse' at Gordonstoun," *Times*, June 4, 2018; Christopher Wilson, "Charles Punched as He Slept, Friends Tortured with Pliers," *Daily Mail*, February 1, 2013; Sarah Lyall, "British

Boarding School Walls Hid Abuse," *New York Times*, October 11, 2004; A. N. Wilson, "Scarred for Life by the Boarding School Sadists," *Daily Mail*, May 16, 2014; "Prince Charles, Cambridge B.A. (with Honors)," *New York Times*, June 24, 1970; "Prince Charles at Trinity College, Cambridge University," Pathé News, October 12, 1967; "Prince of Wales Forgets His Lines," *Times*, February 23, 1970; Zoe Heller, "Where Prince Charles Went Wrong," *New Yorker*, April 10, 2017; Peter Gordon and Denis Lawton, *Royal Education: Past, Present, and Future* (London: Psychology Press, 2003); "Education," Royal Household, the official website of the Prince of Wales, https://www.princeofwales.gov.uk; Tim Heald and Mayor Mohrs, *The Man Who Will Be King* (New York: Arbor House, 1979); "Investiture of the Prince of Wales," British Pathé, July 1, 1969; "Buckingham Palace Event Marks Prince of Wales's 50 Years," BBC, March 5, 2019; Royal Household, Prince of Wales website, "Honours of the Principality of Wales"; Dermot Morrah, *To Be a King* (Arrow Books, 1969); Leonard Downie Jr., "Lord 'Rab' Butler, Tory Leader, Is Dead," *Washington Post*, March 10, 1982; "The Man Who Will Be King," *Time*, May 15, 1978; Crispin Gill, *The Duchy of Cornwall* (London: David and Charles, 1987); Duchy of Cornwall website, https://duchyofcornwall.org; *Prince Charles at 50: A Life in Waiting*, *Panorama*, BBC, November 9, 1998; Mollie Butler, *August and RAB: A Memoir* (London: Robin Clark, 1992); Jonathan Dimbleby, *The Prince of Wales: A Biography* (London: Little, Brown, 1994); "The New Boy at Timbertop," *Australian Women's Weekly*, February 9, 1966; "Prince Had Happy Time at Timbertop," *Canberra (Austral.) Times*, January 31, 1973; Caroline Davies, "I Loved It All, Says Prince on Return to Geelong, the School That Gave Him Hell," *Daily Telegraph*, March 4, 2005; Prince Charles, "150th Anniversary Dinner of the Royal Institute of British Architects, Hampton Court Palace, London, May 30, 1984," *Speeches and Articles*, the Official Website of HRH the Prince of Wales; Katy Winter, " 'William and Harry Get Their Moves from Me,' " *Daily Mail*, September 23, 2013; "Royal Residences: Balmoral Castle," Home of the Royal Family, accessed May 19, 2019, https://www.royal.uk/royal-residences-balmoral-castle; "The Final Interview," *Le Monde*, August 27, 1997; Stephen Barry, *Royal Service: My Twelve Years as Valet to Prince Charles* (New York: Macmillan, 1983); James Hewitt, *Love and War* (London: Blake, 1999); Delia Millar, *Queen Victoria's Life in the Scottish Highlands* (London: Philip Wilson, 1985); Annick Cojean, "Balmoral: The History of the Scottish Holiday Home to the Royal Family," Balmoral: Scottish Home to the Royal Family, accessed May 20, 2019, www.balmoralcastle.com; Ronald Clark, *Balmoral: Queen Victoria's Highland Home* (London: Bloomsbury, 2012); Richenda Miers, *Scotland's Highlands and Islands* (London: Cadogan Books, 1994); HRH Prince Charles, *The Old Man of Lochnagar* (London: Royal Collection Trust, 1980); "Balmoral: Why the Royals Love Spending Time There," *Hello!*, September 7, 2016; Katie Frost, "Balmoral: Everything You Need to Know About the Queen's Scottish Retreat," *Harper's Bazaar*, August 7, 2018; Patrick Sawer, "Why the Queen Loves Balmoral," *Daily Telegraph*, December 26, 2015; Philip Ziegler, *Mountbatten* (London: Smithmark, 1986); "A Man Should Sow His Wild Oats," correspondence from Mountbatten to Charles, Mountbatten Archives, February 14, 1974; "Charles Begins Naval Career, 1971," *Prince of Wales: The Man Who Would Be King*, BBC, November 14, 2018; Christopher Lydon, "Prince Charles Talks with Nixon for over an Hour," *New York Times*, July 19, 1970; Christopher Andersen, *George and Laura: Portrait of an American Marriage* (New York: William Morrow, 2002); Christopher Ogden, *Legacy: A Biography of Moses and Walter Annenberg* (New York: Little, Brown, 1999); Alvin Shuster, "Prince Charles Speaks in Lords," *New York Times*, June 14, 1974; Anna Quindlen, "Barbra Streisand, Superstar," *New York Post*, March 15, 1975; "Prince Charles Reflects on 40 Years of the Prince's Trust," BBC, April 15, 2016, www.princes-trust.org.uk; Tom Quinn, "What a Naughty Girl! Camilla's Great-Granny Alice Keppel Who Famously Seduced Edward VII Also Bedded Men for Money," *Daily Mail*, September 9, 2016; Christopher Wilson, "Prince Charles and His Relationships," *Sunday Telegraph*, November 10, 2013; Annette Witheridge, "I Helped Charles Bed Dozens of Girls," *Sunday Mirror*, January 20, 2002; Warren Hoge, "Queen Breaks the Ice: Camilla's out of the Fridge," *New*

York Times, June 5, 2000; Rita Delfiner, "Camilla Finally Comes in from the Cold," *New York Post*, June 6, 2000; Richard Kay, "William Stalked by His Uncle's TV Crew," *Daily Mail*, September 27, 2001; Bob Colacello, "A Court of His Own," *Vanity Fair*, October 2001; Alan Cowell, "Charles's Leaked Letters Land Him in Hot Water," *New York Times*, September 26, 2002; Roxanne Roberts, "Fairy Tale for Grown-Ups: Charles and Camilla Once Upon a Time," *Washington Post*, February 11, 2005; "A Love Lived in Public and in Private," *Guardian*, February 10, 2005; Caroline Graham, *Camilla and Charles: The Love Story* (London: Blake, 2005); Heather Timmons, "The Once and Future Camilla," *New York Times*, April 3, 2005; Peter Foster, "Has the Puppet-Master of St. James's Palace Finally Pulled One String Too Many?" *Daily Telegraph*, December 1, 2001; Penny Junor, *The Duchess: The Untold Story* (London: William Collins, 2017); Sarah Ferguson, *Finding Sarah: A Duchess's Journey to Find Herself* (New York: Atria Books, 2011); P. D. Jephson, *Shadows of a Princess* (New York: HarperCollins, 2000); Robert Hardman, "Just (Call Me) William," *Daily Telegraph*, June 9, 2000; David Leppard and Christopher Morgan, "Police Fears over William's Friends," *Sunday Times*, February 27, 2000; Reiss Smith, "The Royal House of Windsor: Prince Charles's Girlfriends from Diana's Sister to Camilla," *Daily Express*, March 16, 2017; Annette Witheridge, "Exclusive: The Friend Who 'Fixed' Young Prince's Love Life," *Sunday Mirror*, January 20, 2002; Vanessa Thorpe, "Secret Life of Royal Guru Revealed," *Guardian*, February 3, 2001; Christopher Booker, "Small Lies and the Greater Truth," *Spectator*, October 20, 2001; Dinitia Smith, "Master Storyteller or Master Deceiver?," *New York Times*, August 3, 2002; J. D. F. Jones, *Teller of Many Tales: The Lives of Laurens van der Post* (London: Carroll & Graf, 2002); "A Prophet Out of Africa," *Times*, September 7, 2006; Stephen Cook and Joe Joyce, "IRA Bombs Kill Mountbatten and 17 Soldiers," *Guardian*, August 28, 1979; "Britain: A Nation Mourns Its Loss," *Time*, September 10, 1979; Richard Hough, *Mountbatten: A Biography* (New York: Random House, 1981); Timothy Knatchbull, *From a Clear Blue Sky: Surviving the Mountbatten Bomb* (London: Hutchinson, 2009); Fred Barbash, "The Case of the Telltale Valet," *Washington Post*, January 17, 1995; "Rejoice! A Prince Is Born!," *Time*, July 5, 1982; "His Name Is Prince William of Wales," *Times*, June 29, 1982; "They'll Never Call Him Bill," UPI, August 15, 1982; Jo Thomas, "The Early Education of a Future King," *New York Times*, April 13, 1986; Fred Bernstein, "William the Terrible," *People*, July 7, 1986; Wendy Berry, *The Housekeeper's Diary* (New York: Barricade Books, 1995); Graham Jones and Jenny Shields, "Champagne Flows and Charles Hits a Polo Hat Trick," *Daily Telegraph*, September 17, 1984; Sue Ryan, "Here's Harry!," *Mail on Sunday*, October 14, 1984; Tony Frost, "Hello Bright Eyes," *Sunday Mirror*, October 14, 1984; Nicholas Davies, *William: The Inside Story of the Man Who Will Be King* (New York: St. Martin's Press, 1998); "Di's Son Injured," Associated Press, June 4, 1991; Ken Wharfe, with Robert Jobson, *Diana: Closely Guarded Secret* (London: Michael O'Mara Books, 2003); Paul Harris and Tom Kelly, "Queen's Fury at 'Squidgygate' Tape," *Daily Mail*, January 10, 2008; Prince Charles, "A speech by HRH the Prince of Wales at the 150th Anniversary of the Royal Institute of British Architects (RIBA), Royal Gala Evening at Hampton Court Palace, 30 May 1984," the Official Website of the Prince of Wales, https://www.princeof wales.gov.uk; Terry Trucco, "2 New Fronts in Charles's Architecture War," *New York Times*, September 9, 1989; Stephen Bayley, "I'll Show You a Real Carbuncle, Charles," *Guardian*, December 6, 2008; HRH the Prince of Wales, *A Vision of Britain: A Personal View of Architecture* (New York: Doubleday, 1989); Sally Bedell Smith, *Diana in Search of Herself* (New York: Signet, 2000); Matilda Battersby, "A Day That Shook The World: Windsor Castle Fire," *Independent*, November 18, 2010; Richard W. Stevenson, "Big Fire in Windsor Castle Raises Fear About Artwork," *New York Times*, November 21, 1992; "A Speech by the Queen on the Fortieth Anniversary of Her Succession (Annus Horribilis Speech)," November 24, 1992, the Home of the Royal Family, accessed May 19, 2019, www.royal.uk/annus -horribilis-speech; William E. Schmidt, "Charles and Diana Are Separating 'Amicably,'" *New York Times*, December 9, 1992; Paul Harris, "Christmas Sadness," *Daily Mail*, December 24, 1992; Oliver Morgan and Alexander Hitchen, "Diana's Chilly Royal Christmas," *Sunday Express*, November 28, 1993.

CHAPTERS 6–8

Information for these chapters was based in part on conversations with Richard Kay, Mark Shand, Martin Bashir, Ezra Zilkha, Richard Greene, Mimi Massy-Birch, Peter Archer, Lord Mishcon, Winston Spencer-Churchill, Alan Hamilton, the Countess of Romanones, the late Joan Rivers, Hugh Massy-Birch, Guy Pelly, the late Lady Elsa Bowker, Grigori Rassinier, Oonagh Toffolo, Emma Sayle, Lucia Flecha de Lima, Cecile Zilkha, Philip Higgs, Geoffrey Bignell, Aileen Mehle, Muriel Hartwick, Alex Shirley-Smith, Sioned Compton, Robin Leach, Gared Mankowitz, Natalie Symonds, and Janet Lizop. Published sources include "Prince Charles Keeps His Cool Under Fire," *Sun Journal* (Lewiston, ME), January 27, 1994; "Student Fires 2 Blanks at Prince Charles," *Los Angeles Times*, January 27, 1994; Dickie Arbiter, *On Duty with the Queen: My Time as a Buckingham Palace Press Secretary* (London: Blink, 2014); "An Interview with HRH the Princess of Wales," *Panorama*, BBC One, November 20, 1995; Anna Pasternak, *Princess in Love* (New York: Dutton, 1994); Richard Alleyne, "Princess Diana 'Deeply Regretted' *Panorama* Interview," *Daily Telegraph*, December 15, 2007; Rebecca Flood, "'I Understand': Prince William Opens Up over Princess Diana's Bombshell *Panorama* Interview," *Daily Express*, August 23, 2017; Tony Blair, *A Journey: My Political Life* (New York: Knopf, 2010); Sean O'Neill, "Lady 'Kanga' Tryon Is Detained Under Mental Health Act," *Daily Telegraph*, June 18, 1997; Christopher Wilson, "The Lonely Death of Charles's Other Mistress," *Daily Mail*, October l0, 2008; "Diana: The Man She Really Loved," *Point de Vue, Images du Monde*, November 5–11, 1997; Kate Snell, *Diana: Her Last Love* (London: Granada Media, 2000); David Ward, "Prince's Pride in His Sons," *Guardian*, September 20, 1997; "Royal First as Queen Goes to the Pub," *Independent*, March 28, 1998; Richard Kay and Geoffrey Levy, "A Son to Be Proud Of," *Daily Mail*, May 23, 1998; Warren Hoge, "William, a Shy

Conqueror, Pursued by Groupies," *New York Times*, June 22, 1998; Charles Rae, "Wills and Harry Do Full Monty," *Sun* (UK), August 1, 1998; "Charles's Mistress Joins His Sons for 50th Birthday Party," *Chicago Tribune*, August 2, 1998; "Charles, A Life in Waiting," *Panorama*, BBC One, November 9, 1998; Judy Wade, "Marking a Milestone in Charles's and Camilla's Relationship," *Hello!*, August 15, 1998; Alan Hamilton, "The Pariah Prince Wins Back the Hearts of His Public," *Times*, October 24, 1998; Rachel Donnelly, "Charles Tries to Shield Camilla After Her Son Admits Using Cocaine," *Irish Times*, May 20, 1999; Christopher Mason, "Orchestrating the Camilla Parker Bowles Visit," *New York Times*, September 26, 1999; Samuel Maull, "Friend: Astor Disparaged Parker Bowles, Zeta-Jones," Associated Press, May 18, 2009; Melissa Grace and Corky Siemaszko, "Brooke Astor's Prince Charles 'Mistress' Crack to Camilla Parker Bowles in 1999," *New York Daily News*, May 19, 2009; Christopher Andersen, *After Diana* (New York: Hyperion, 2007); *Prince Charles at 50: A Life in Waiting*, *Panorama*, BBC; Sally Bedell Smith, *Prince Charles: The Passions and Paradoxes of an Improbable Life* (New York: Random House, 2017); HRH the Prince of Wales, "Broadcast for BBC Radio 4's 'Thought for the Day,'" January 1, 2000; *Speeches and Articles*, Official Website of the Prince of Wales, https://www.princeofwales.gov.uk; Christopher Morgan and David Leppard, "Party Girl in William's Circle Snorted Cocaine," *Sunday Times*, February 26, 2000; David Leppard and Christopher Morgan, "Police Fears over William's Friends," *Sunday Times*, February 27, 2000; Barbara Kantrowitz, "William: The Making of a Modern King," *Newsweek*, June 26, 2000; Andrew Pierce and Simon de Bruxelles, "Our Mother Was Betrayed," *Times*, September 30, 2000; Michelle Tauber, "Speaking His Mind," *People*, October 16, 2000; Sarah Goodall and Nicholas Monson, *The Palace Diaries: The True Story of Life at the Palace by Prince Charles's Secretary* (London: Dynasty Press, 2008); "Diana's Butler Is Charged in Theft of Family Personal Items," Associated Press, August 17, 2001; Earl Spencer Interview with Simon Mayo, "Charles Has Yet to Visit Diana's Grave," Radio 5 Live, August 2001; Ben Summerskill, "The Trouble with Harry," *Observer* (UK), January 13, 2002; Antony Barnett, "Prince Taken to Drink and Drugs Rehab Clinic," *Observer*, January 13, 2002; Warren Hoge, "Charles's Response to Use of Drugs by Son Is Praised," *New York Times*, January 14, 2002; J. F. O. McAllister, "Once upon a Time, There Was a Pot-Smoking Prince," *Time*, January 28, 2002; "The Queen Mother Dies Peacefully, Aged 101," *Guardian*, March 30, 2002; "A Tribute by HRH the Prince of Wales Following the Death of Her Late Majesty Queen Elizabeth the Queen Mother on Saturday 30th March, 2002, London," April 4, 2002; "Queen's Evidence Clears Butler," *Guardian*, November 1, 2002; "Diana Butler Theft Case Thrown Out," CNN, November 1, 2002; "Chronology of the Queen's Involvement in the Paul Burrell Case," statement issued by the press secretary to the Queen, Buckingham Palace, November 14, 2002; Paul Henderson, "I Was Raped by Charles's Servant," *Mail on Sunday*, November 10, 2002; Warren Hoge, "As Royal Rumors Swirl in Britain, Charles Orders a Palace Inquiry," *New York Times*, November 13, 2002; Dominick Dunne, "Diana's Secrets," *Vanity Fair*, January 2003; Ben Glaze and Nicola Bartlett, "Prince Charles Claimed Fox-Hunting Was 'Romantic' in a 2002 Letter to Tony Blair," *Sunday Mirror*, October 8, 2017; Caroline Davies, "'Blackadder' Keeps Close Ties to Camilla," *Daily Telegraph*, January 6, 2003; Joan Smith, "Prince Charles: What a Guy! What a Boss! What?," *Independent*, March 12, 2003; Peter Archer, "My Normal Life as a Student Prince: William's 21st Birthday Interview," Press Association, May 30, 2003; Tom Rawstorne, "William: In His Own Words," *Daily Mail*, May 30, 2003; Matthew Bayley, "William the Young Yob: Charles Forced to Apologize for His Son's Road-Rage," *Daily Mail*, June 16, 2003; "Partying Prince Turns Windsor Wild," BBC News, June 22, 2003; Owen Bowcott and Brian Logan, "Comedy Terrorist Inquiry Exposes Royal Security Farce," *Guardian*, August 14, 2003; Christopher Andersen, "The Divided Prince," *Vanity Fair*, September 2003; Peter Archer and Tim Graham, *William* (New York: Simon & Schuster, 2003); Richard Kay and Michael Seamark, "Charles on the Rack," *Daily Mail*, November 8, 2003; John Arlidge, "Why Palace Is Under Siege over Sex Rumor Frenzy," *Guardian*, November 8, 2003; Stephen Glove, "The Royals Must Change . . . or Die," *Daily*

Mail, November 11, 2003; Mary Riddell, "Blackadder Bites Back," *British Journalism Review* 15 (2004); Michael Dynes and Alan Hamilton, "Harry's Sobering Stay in the AIDS Kingdom," *Times*, March 4, 2004; Andrew Pierce, " 'I'm Sorry for Wearing Nazi Swastika,' Says Prince Harry," *Times*, January 13, 2005; Neil Tweedie and Michael Kallenbach, "Prince Harry Faces Outcry at Nazi Outfit," *Daily Telegraph*, January 14, 2005; Mark Bolland, "Secret Meeting I Hosted for Charles, Camilla, and Peter Mandelson That Cleared the Way for Saturday's Wedding," *London Evening Standard*, April 6, 2005; "After Star-Crossed Romance, Prince Charles Will Get Married," *New York Times*, February 10, 2005; Josh Tyrangiel, "The Prince Proposes," *Time*, February 21, 2005; Thomas Fields-Mayer and Pam Lambert, "Royal Stepmum," *People*, February 28, 2005; Sholto Byrnes, "Mark Bolland: Marital Aide," *Independent*, March 30, 2005; Patrick Jephson, "Everybody Loves a Royal Wedding . . . Usually," *Sunday Telegraph*, March 27, 2005; Hamish Bowles, "At Long Last Love," *Vogue*, April 2005; Heather Timmons, "The Once and Future Camilla," *New York Times*, April 3, 2005; Alan Cowell, "Wedding Put Off One Day for Funeral," *New York Times*, April 5, 2005; Live coverage of the wedding of Charles and Camilla by the BBC, MSNBC, CNN, Fox News (for which the author provided live commentary), April 9, 2005; Simon Freeman, "The Royal Wedding Day, Minute by Minute," *Times*, April 9, 2005; Andrew Alderson, "Husband and Wife—At Last," *Sunday Telegraph*, April 10, 2005; Jasper Gerard, "Wed at Last After 34 Years," *Sunday Times*, April 10, 2005; Anne-Marie O'Neill, "Finally, Husband and Wife," *People*, April 25, 2005; Barbara Kantrowitz, "Legal at Last," *Newsweek*, April 18, 2005; Susan Schindehette and Allison Adato, "Princes in Love," *People*, August 8, 2005; Nicola Methven, "Hypno-Di-Sed: Hewitt Put in a Trance," *Daily Mirror*, September 19, 2005; Michelle Green, "Is She the One?," *People*, October 17, 2005; Joyce Wadler and Christopher Mason, "Charles and Camilla in Low-Key U.S. Debut," *New York Times*, November 2, 2005; Victoria Warden Washington, "U.S. Media Dubs Camilla 'New York's Frump Tower,' " *Independent*, November 3, 2005; Caroline Davies, "First Royal Sandringham Christmas for Camilla," *Daily Tele-*

graph, December 24, 2005; Paul Cheston, "Charles's Dicey Court Drama," *Evening Standard*, March 17, 2006; Caroline Davies, "Duchess Gets a Glimpse of Life Behind the Veil in Saudi Arabia," *Daily Telegraph*, March 30, 2006; Robert Jobson, *William's Princess* (London: Blake Publishing, 2006); "Key Aides Move to Windsor Ahead of Queen's Retirement," *Evening Standard*, November 18, 2006; Alex Tresniowski and Ashley Williams, "Will & Kate: The Perfect Match," *People*, December 11, 2006; "Prince William Graduates as an Officer," *Guardian*, December 15, 2006; John Elliott, "Charles Plans a Mansion Fit for Lovebirds," *Sunday Times*, December 17, 2006; Christopher Wilson, "Kate, the Coal Miner's Girl," *Daily Mail*, December 22, 2006; Deirdre Fernand, "The Girl Who Would Be Queen," *Sunday Times*, December 31, 2006; HRH the Prince of Wales with Stephanie Donaldson, *The Elements of Organic Gardening* (Carlsbad, CA: Kales Press, 2007); Kira Cochrane, "In Diana's Footsteps," *Guardian*, January 9, 2007; "Lawyers Planning Test Case to Stop Paparazzi Hounding Kate Middleton," *Times*, January 9, 2007; "*News of the World* Journalist Jailed," Reuters, January 26, 2007; Oliver Marre, "Girl, Interrupted," *Observer*, March 18, 2007; Zoe Griffin and Grant Hodgson, "Wills & Kate 2002–2007: The Fairytale's Over," *Sunday Mirror*, April 15, 2007; Laura Collins, Katie Nicholl, and Ian Gallagher, "Kate Was Too Middle Class," *Mail on Sunday*, April 15, 2007; Rajeev Syal, "Tony Blair: Let Them Be, They Are Young," *Times*, April 16, 2007; Laura Collins and Louise Hannah, "As Kate Re-Emerges More Tanned and Confident, a New Middleton Girl Takes a Bow," *Daily Mail*, May 27, 2007; Karen Rockett, "It's Back On," *Sunday Mirror*, June 24, 2007; Richard Woods, "Leave Us Alone," *Sunday Times*, October 7, 2007; Andrew Alderson, "Prince Eyes Legal Action," *Sunday Telegraph*, October 7, 2007; Andrew Alderson, "The Queen and I, by Her Majesty's PA," *Sunday Telegraph*, December 9, 2007; Robert Jobson and Keith Dovkants, "Kate, the 'New Royal,' Gets Her Own Bodyguards," *Evening Standard*, January 9, 2008; Andrew Pierce, "Prince's Lawyers Warn Paparazzi Off Stalking Middleton," *Daily Telegraph*, February 23, 2008; Rebecca English, "William Landed His Air Force Helicopter in Kate's Garden," *Daily Mail*, April 21,

2008; "William and RAF Sorry for Prince's *Five* Chinook Joyrides," BBC News, April 23, 2008; Richard Kay and Geoffrey Levy, "Camilla and the Blonde Private Secretary Who's Paid the Price for Being Too Close to Prince Charles," *Daily Mail*, June 13, 2008; Lucy Cockcroft, "Prince William's Chinook Flight to Stag Party Costs 8,716 Pounds," *Daily Telegraph*, June 30, 2008; Alan Hamilton, "A Feather in His Cap: Young Prince Is New Recruit to the World's Oldest Order of Chivalry," *Times*, June 17, 2008; Richard Kay, Geoffrey Levy, and Katie Glass, "Wild Side of Kate's Family," *Daily Mail*, August 9, 2008; Vicky Ward, "Will's Cup of Tea," *Vanity Fair*, November 2008; Geoffrey Levy and Richard Kay, "How Many *More* Skeletons in Kate's Closet?," *Daily Mail*, July 22, 2009; James Whitaker and David Collins, "One's Been Frozen Out: Queen Tells Kate It's Family *Only* at Sandringham This Christmas," *People*, December 20, 2009; Liz Hoggard, "Let Them Eat Cake," *Evening Standard*, February 18, 2010; Alex Tresniowski, "A Royal Love," *People*, May 3, 2010; "Duchess of York Scandal," ABC News, May 24, 2010; David Stringer, "Prince William Makes First Royal Rescue for RAF," Associated Press, October 5, 2010.

CHAPTERS 9–10

For these chapters, the author drew in part on conversations with Lady Margaret Rhodes, Countess Mountbatten, the late Joan Rivers, Lord Bathurst, Lady Yolanda Joseph, James Whitaker, Shana Alexander, Tom Sykes, Wendi Rothman, Cecile Thibaud, Mark Shand, Liz Smith, Richard Kay, Wendy Leigh, Elizabeth d'Erlanger, Alex Kidson, Robin Leach, David McGough, Janet Allison, Lucia Flecha de Lima, and John Marion. Published and other sources include live coverage of the wedding of William and Kate by the BBC, CBS, NBC, ABC, CNN, HLN, Fox News (for which the author provided live commentary), April 29, 2011; Sarah Lyall, "A Traditional Royal Wedding, but for the 3 Billion Witnesses," *New York Times*, April 29, 2011; Victoria Murphy, "You Look Like You Need a Drink," *Daily Mirror*, February 20, 2012; Rachel Cooke, "What the Royals Eat at Home," *Guardian*, May 19, 2012; "A Speech by HRH the

Prince of Wales Paying Tribute to Her Majesty the Queen on Her Diamond Jubilee, Buckingham Palace," June 4, 2012, the Prince of Wales and the Duchess of Cornwall, accessed May 20, 2019, www.princeofwales.gov .uk/speech/speech-hrh-Prince-wales-paying-tribute-her-majesty-queen -her-diamond-jubilee-buckingham; Robert Hardman, *Her Majesty: Queen Elizabeth II and Her Court* (New York: Pegasus Books, 2012); "Queen Camilla? How Once Sidelined Duchess Is Now Center-Stage . . . and Could Take Title When Charles Is King," *Daily Mirror*, June 6, 2012; Penny Junor, *The Firm: The Troubled Life of the House of Windsor* (New York: Thomas Dunne Books, 2008); Luisa Kroll, "Queen Elizabeth Lives Like a Billionaire but Is Herself Not Quite as Rich," *Forbes*, June 7, 2012; Doug Saunders, "Britain's Crisis of Succession," *Globe and Mail*, August 23, 2012; "Prince Harry—Partying Completely Naked in Vegas!," TMZ online, last modified August 21, 2012, www.tmz.com/videos/0_412ff1b5; Rebecca English, "Palace Fury at Harry Naked Photos," *Daily Mail*, August 22, 2012; Laura Butler, "Not Even the Heir to the Throne Can Protect the Playboy Prince in Fallout over Naked Vegas Pictures," *Irish Herald*, August 23, 2012; Andrew Marr, *The Real Elizabeth* (New York: St. Martin's Press, 2012); Catherine Mayer, "The Queen's Era Is Drawing to an End as Prince Charles Assumes New Royal Duties," *Time*, May 7, 2013; Robert Booth and Julian Borger, "Christopher Geidt: The Suave, Shrewd and Mysterious Royal Insider," *Guardian*, May 31, 2013; Alice Philipson, "Queen and Prince Charles Using Power of Veto over New Laws, Whitehall Documents Reveal," *Daily Telegraph*, January 15, 2013; Robert Booth, "Secret Papers Show Extent of Senior Royals' Veto Over Bills," *Guardian*, January 14, 2013; Paul Owen et al., "Royal Baby: Duchess of Cambridge Gives Birth to a Boy—As It Happened," *Guardian*, July 22, 2013; Gordon Rayner and Victoria Ward, "The Middletons Have Become the Future King's First Visitors," *Daily Telegraph*, July 23, 2013; "Royal Baby: Kate and William Visited by Prince Charles," BBC News, July 23, 2013; "The Christening of Prince George of Cambridge," News and Diary, the Prince of Wales and the Duchess of Cornwall, September 27, 2013, accessed May 20, 2019, https://www.princeofwales.gov.uk.;

Christopher Andersen, *William and Kate and Baby George: Royal Baby Edition* (New York, Gallery Books, 2013); Jessica Derschowitz, "Prince Charles 'Overjoyed' at Being a Grandfather," CBS News, July 22, 2013; Richard Palmer, "It's Fun to Be a Grandfather, Says Prince Charles," *Daily Express*, July 26, 2013; "Prince George Makes Friends on Royal Tour of New Zealand," Reuters, April 9, 2014; Nicholas Witchell, "Royal Tour: Prince George Steals the Show as Support for Monarchy Rises," BBC News, April 25, 2014; Catherine Mayer, *Charles: The Heart of a King* (London: W. H. Allen, 2015); Ingrid Seward, "Duchess of Dazzle: How Camilla Amassed a Treasure Trove of Jewels, Thanks to Charles and the Saudis," *Daily Mail*, February 21, 2015; Emma Green, "Why It's Now Easier for a Princess to Become Queen," *Atlantic*, May 2, 2015; "Royal Baby: London Gun Salutes Mark Birth of Princess," BBC News, May 4, 2015; "Royal Princess Named Charlotte Elizabeth Diana," BBC News, May 4, 2015; Tom Sykes, "William and Kate Should Stop Hiding Prince George and Princess Charlotte Away," *Daily Beast*, last modified October 11, 2015; Vanessa Friedman, "The Duchess of Cambridge and Sartorial Diplomacy," *New York Times*, October 21, 2015; Minyvonne Burke, "Prince William Reveals Christmas Plans for Prince George, Princess Charlotte," *International Business Times*, December 6, 2015; Antony Barnett, "The Prince of Property and His 460 Million Pound Business Empire," *Guardian*, January 29, 2005; Anna Pukas, "Revealed: Positive Impact of Camilla on Prince Charles After a Decade of Marriage," *Daily Express*, April 8, 2015; Penny Junor, "Camilla Has Won Us Over and Deserves to Become Queen," *Daily Telegraph*, April 8, 2015; James Tapper, "Prince George Makes First Appearance on Buckingham Palace Balcony," *Guardian*, June 13, 2015; Maria Puente, "Prince George Makes Palace Balcony Debut," *USA Today*, June 13, 2015; Chris Pleasance, "All Eyes on Gorgeous George!," *Daily Mail*, June 13, 2015; Angela Levin, "Will Charles Risk Making Camilla, Duchess of Cornwall, His Queen?," *Newsweek*, December 9, 2015; *Elizabeth at 90: A Family Tribute*, narrated by HRH the Prince of Wales, BBC One, April 20, 2016; Erik Sherman, "Queen Elizabeth: A Look at 90 Years of Vast Wealth and Perks," *Fortune*,

April 21, 2016; Peter Hunt, "Queen Lobbies for Prince Charles to Be Commonwealth Head," BBC News, October 10, 2016; Hannah Furness, "Prince Harry Rumored to Be Dating American Actress Meghan Markle," *Daily Telegraph*, October 31, 2016; Robert Booth and Lisa O'Carroll, "Prince Harry Attacks Press over 'Wave of Abuse' of Girlfriend Meghan Markle," *Guardian*, November 8, 2016; Siobhan Fenton, "Donald Trump and Prince Charles in Diplomacy Row over Climate Change Ahead of President's First UK Visit," *Independent*, January 29, 2017; Katie Mettler, "'All of This Grief': Prince Harry Opens Up About His Mental Health," *Washington Post*, April 17, 2017; Angela Levin, "Exclusive: Prince Harry on Chaos After Diana's Death and Why the World Needs 'the Magic' of the Royal Family," *Newsweek*, June 21, 2017; Graham Norwood, "Poundbury: A Look at Prince Charles' Sustainable Village in Dorset, on Its 30th Birthday," *Daily Telegraph*, April 26, 2017; Fleur Netley, "Meghan Markle's Pre-Prince Dating History," *Marie Claire*, September 29, 2017; Elise Taylor, "Prince Harry and Meghan Markle's Love Story: A Timeline," *Vogue*, November 27, 2017; "Harry and Meghan: How the Prince Proposed," BBC News Joint Interview, November 27, 2017; "Leaders Approve Prince Charles to Succeed Queen as Commonwealth Head," Reuters, April 20, 2018; Karla Adam, "Commonwealth Backs Prince Charles as Its Next Leader," *Washington Post*, April 20, 2018; Hannah Furness, "Prince Charles 'Deeply Touched' to Be Confirmed as Queen's Head of the Commonwealth Successor," *Daily Telegraph*, April 20, 2018; "Financial Statements of the Duchy of Cornwall, 2012–2018," Duchy of Cornwall website, accessed May 20, 2019, https://duchyofcornwall.org /financial; Margo Jefferson, "No Cinderella: Margo Jefferson on the Real Meghan Markle," *Guardian*, May 5, 2018; Jane Onyanga-Omara and Maria Puente, "Meghan Markle Says Her Father Won't Attend Her Wedding to Prince Harry," *USA Today*, May 17, 2018; Live coverage of the wedding of Harry and Meghan Markle by the BBC, CBS, NBC, ABC, CNN, Fox News, and other major media outlets, May 19, 2018; "Royal Wedding 2018: Who Is Meghan Markle?," BBC News, May 18, 2018; Doreen St. Felix, "The Profound Presence of Doria Ragland," *New Yorker*,

May 21, 2018; Paul Withers, "Meghan Markle Urged to 'Do the Right Thing' and Fly Father to London in Wake of Royal Wedding," *Daily Express*, May 22, 2018; Joy Basu, "Charles' Budding Bond with Meghan's Mum Doria," *Daily Star* (UK), May 23, 2018; Carolyn Durand, "Prince Harry Makes Emotional, 'Private Visit' to Sentebale Charity in Lesotho," ABC News, June 24, 2018; Tim Shipman and Roya Nikkhah, "Royal Family 'Snub' Donald Trump During UK Visit," *Sunday Times*, July 15, 2018; Caroline Hallemann, "Prince Charles and Prince William Reportedly Refused to Meet with Donald Trump," *Town & Country*, July 16, 2018; Aine Cain, "What Is Prince Charles Worth?," *Business Insider*, last modified August 22, 2018; Alix Langone and Jennifer Calfas, "All the Members of the Royal Family, Ranked by Net Worth," *Money*, May 14, 2018; Jessica Contrera, "The Making of Meghan Markle," *Washington Post*, May 16, 2018; Rob Picheta, "Prince William Launches Mental Health Website," CNN, September 11, 2018; Robert Hardman, "Charles on His Fears for George's World," *Daily Mail*, November 2, 2018; Abbie Llewelyn, "Peas in a Pod: Meghan Markle and Prince Charles Bonded over Their Dysfunctional Families," *Express*, November 4, 2018; "The Man Who Would Be King, Eventually: Prince Charles Turns 70," Reuters, November 5, 2018; Meaghan Wray, "Prince Harry Reveals Prince Charles's Excited Reaction to Walking Meghan Down the Aisle," *Hello!*, November 8, 2018; Cecelia Rodriguez, "At 70, Is Prince Charles Ready to be King?," *Forbes*, November 14, 2018; "The Queen Gives a Toast at The Prince of Wales' 70th Birthday Party," official website of Buckingham Palace, November 14, 2018; Rebecca Mead, "A Birthday Celebration for Prince Charles Amid the Chaos of BREXIT," *New Yorker*, November 19, 2018; Vanessa Grigoriadis, "Inside the Meghan Markle Family Breakdown," *Vanity Fair*, December 19, 2018; "'Fab Four' Prince William, Prince Harry, Duchess Kate and Duchess Meghan Join Queen Elizabeth to Celebrate Prince Charles' Anniversary," ABC News, March 5, 2019; "Prince Charles Cuddles with Grandson Prince Louis," NBC News, November 19, 2018; Katie Kindelan, "Will Prince Charles Ever Be Crowned King?," *Week*, March 6, 2019; Robert Booth, "What Kind of King Will Charles III Be?," *Guardian*.

Allison, Ronald, and Sarah Riddell, eds. *The Royal Encyclopedia*. London: Macmillan, 1991.

Andersen, Christopher. *After Diana: William, Harry, Charles and the Royal House of Windsor*. New York: Hyperion, 2007.

———. *The Day Diana Died*. New York: William Morrow, 1998.

———. *The Day John Died*. New York: William Morrow, 2000.

———. *Diana's Boys*. New York: William Morrow, 2001.

———. *Game of Crowns: Elizabeth, Camilla, Kate, and the Throne*. New York: Gallery Books, 2016.

———. *William and Kate: Royal Baby Edition*. New York: Gallery Books, 2013.

———. *William and Kate: A Royal Love Story*. New York: Gallery Books, 2011.

———. *William and Kate: Special Wedding Edition*. New York: Gallery Books, 2011.

Anne, H.R.H., the Princess Royal, with Ivor Herbert. *Riding Through My Life*. London: Pelham, 1991.

Arbiter, Dickie. *On Duty with the Queen: My Time as a Buckingham Palace Press Secretary*. London: Blink, 2014.

Aronson, Theo. *Royal Family: Years of Transition*. London: Thistle, 2014.

Barry, Stephen P. *Royal Service: My Twelve Years as Valet to Prince Charles*. New York: Macmillan, 1983.

Beaton, Cecil. *Beaton in the Sixties: More Unexpurgated Diaries*. London: Weidenfeld & Nicolson, 2003.

Berry, Wendy. *The Housekeeper's Diary*. New York: Barricade Books, 1995.

Blair, Tony. *A Journey: My Political Life*. New York: Alfred A. Knopf, 2010.

Boca, Geoffrey. *Elizabeth and Philip*. New York: Henry Holt, 1953.

Botham, Noel. *The Murder of Princess Diana*. New York: Pinnacle Books, 2004.

Bradford, Sarah. *Diana*. New York: Viking, 2006.

———. *Elizabeth*. New York: Riverhead Books, 1996.

Brander, Michael. *The Making of the Highlands*. London: Constable, 1980.

Bryan, J., III, and Charles J. V. Murphy. *The Windsor Story*. New York: William Morrow, 1979.

Burrell, Paul. *A Royal Duty*. New York: New American Library, 2004.

———. *The Way We Were: Remembering Diana*. New York: William Morrow, 2006.

Campbell, Lady Colin. *Diana in Private*. London: Smith Gryphon, 1993.

Cannadine, David. *The Decline and Fall of the British Aristocracy*. New Haven, CT: Yale University Press, 1990.

Cannon, John, and Ralph Griffiths. *The Oxford Illustrated History of the British Monarchy*. Oxford and New York: Oxford University Press, 1992.

Cathcart, Helen. *The Queen and Prince Philip: Forty Years of Happiness*. London: Hodder and Stoughton, 1987.

———. *The Queen Herself*. London: W. H. Allen, 1983.

Clarke, Mary. *Diana Once Upon a Time*. London: Sidgwick & Jackson, 1994.

Clifford, Max, and Angela Levin. *Max Clifford: Read All About It*. London: Virgin, 2005.

Davies, Nicholas. *Diana: The Lonely Princess*. New York: Birch Lane, 1996.

———. *Queen Elizabeth II*. New York: Carol, 1996.

———. *William: The Inside Story of the Man Who Will Be King*. New York: St. Martin's Press, 1998.

Delderfield, Eric R. *Kings and Queen of England and Great Britain*. London: David & Charles, 1990.

Delorm, Rene. *Diana and Dodi: A Love Story*. Los Angeles: Tallfellow Press, 1998.

Dempster, Nigel, and Peter Evans. *Behind Palace Doors*. New York: Putnam, 1993.

Dimbleby, Jonathan. *The Prince of Wales: A Biography.* New York: William Morrow, 1994.

Dolby, Karen. *The Wicked Wit of Queen Elizabeth II*. London: Michael O'Mara Books, 2015.

Edwards, Anne. *Diana and the Rise of the House of Spencer*. London: Hodder and Stoughton, 1999.

Ferguson, Ronald. *The Galloping Major: My Life and Singular Times*. London: Macmillan, 1994.

Fisher, Graham and Heather. *Elizabeth: Queen & Mother*. New York: Hawthorn Books, 1964.

Foreman, J. B., ed. *Scotland's Splendour*. Glasgow: William Collins Sons, 1961.

Fox, Mary Virginia. *Princess Diana*. Hillside, NJ: Enslow, 1986.

Goldsmith, Lady Annabel. *Annabel: An Unconventional Life*. London: Phoenix, 2004.

Goodall, Sarah, and Nicholas Monson. *The Palace Diaries: A Story Inspired by Twelve Years of Life Behind Palace Gates*. London: Mainstream, 2006.

Graham, Caroline. *Camilla: The King's Mistress*. London: John Blake, 1994.

———. *Camilla and Charles: The Love Story.* London: John Blake, 2005.

Graham, Tim. *Diana: HRH the Princess of Wales*. New York: Summit, 1988.

———. *The Royal Year 1993*. London: Michael O'Mara, 1993.

Gregory, Martyn. *The Diana Conspiracy Exposed*. London: Virgin, 1999.

Hardman, Robert. *Her Majesty: Queen Elizabeth II and Her Court*. New York: Pegasus Books, 2012.

Hewitt, James. *Love and War*. London: John Blake, 1999.

Hill, Duncan, Alison Guantlett, Sarah Rickayzen, and Gareth Thomas. *The Royal Family: A Year by Year Chronicle of the House of Windsor*. London: Parragon, 2012.

Hoey, Brian. *All the King's Men*. London: HarperCollins, 1992.

Holden, Anthony. *Charles*. London: Weidenfeld and Nicolson, 1988.

————. *The Tarnished Crown*. New York: Random House, 1993.

Hough, Richard. *Born Royal: The Lives and Loves of the Young Windsors*. New York: Bantam, 1988.

HRH the Prince of Wales. *The Old Man of Lochnagar*. London: Hamish Hamilton Children's Books, 1980.

————. *A Vision of Britain: A Personal View of Architecture*. London: Doubleday, 1989.

————. *Watercolours*. London: Little, Brown (UK), 1991.

HRH the Prince of Wales and Charles Clover. *Highgrove: Portrait of an Estate*. London: Chapmans, 1993.

HRH the Prince of Wales, with Tony Juniper and Ian Skelly. *Harmony: A New Way of Looking at Our World*. New York: HarperCollins, 2010.

HRH the Prince of Wales and Candida Lycett Green. *The Garden at Highgrove*. London: Weidenfeld & Nicholson, 2000.

Hutchins, Chris, and Peter Thompson. *Sarah's Story: The Duchess Who Defied the Royal House of Windsor*. London: Smith Gryphon, 1992.

Jephson, P. D. *Shadows of a Princess*. New York: HarperCollins, 2000.

Jobson, Robert. *Harry's War*. London: John Blake, 2008.

————. *The New Royal Family: Prince George, William and Kate, the Next Generation*. London: John Blake, 2013.

————. *William's Princess: The Love Story That Will Change the Royal Family Forever*. London: John Blake, 2006.

Joseph, Claudia. *Kate*. New York: Avon, 2009.

Junor, Penny. *Charles*. New York: St. Martin's Press, 1987.

————. *The Firm*. New York: Thomas Dunne Books, 2005.

————. *Prince William: The Man Who Will Be King*. New York: Pegasus Books, 2012.

Knatchbull, Timothy. *From a Clear Blue Sky: Surviving the Mountbatten Bomb*. London: Hutchinson, 2009.

Lacey, Robert. *Majesty*. New York: Harcourt Brace Jovanovich, 1977.

————. *Queen Mother*. Boston: Little, Brown, 1986.

Lathan, Caroline, and Jeannie Sakol. *The Royals*. New York: Congdon & Weed, 1987.

Lloyd, Ian. *William & Catherine's New Royal Family: Celebrating the Arrival of Princess Charlotte.* London: Carlton Books, 2015.

Lord Stevens of Kirkwhelpington. *The Operation Paget Inquiry Report into the Allegation of Conspiracy to Murder Diana, Princess of Wales, and Emad El-Din Mohamed Abdel Moneim Fayed.* London, December 14, 2006.

Lorimer, David. *Radical Prince.* Edinburgh: Floris Books, 2003.

Maclean, Veronica. *Crowned Heads.* London: Hodder & Stoughton, 1993.

Marr, Andrew. *The Real Elizabeth: An Intimate Portrait of Queen Elizabeth II.* New York: St. Martin's Press, 2012.

Martin, Ralph G. *Charles & Diana.* New York: Putnam, 1985.

Mayer, Catherine. *Born to Be King: Prince Charles on Planet Windsor.* New York: Henry Holt, 2015.

———. *Charles: The Heart of a King.* London: W. H. Allen, 2015.

Montgomery-Massingberd, Hugh. *Burke's Guide to the British Monarchy.* London: Burke's Peerage, 1977.

Morrah, Dermot. *To Be a King: A Privileged Account of the Early Life and Education of H.R.H. the Prince of Wales, Written with the Approval of H.M. the Queen.* London: Hutchinson, 1968.

Morrow, Ann. *The Queen.* London: Granada, 1983.

Morton, Andrew. *Diana: Her True Story.* New York: Simon & Schuster, 1997.

———. *Diana: In Pursuit of Love.* London: Michael O'Mara, 2004.

———. *Inside Buckingham Palace.* London: Michael O'Mara, 1991.

Pasternak, Anna. *Princess in Love.* London: Bloomsbury, 1994.

Pimlott, Ben. *The Queen: A Biography of Elizabeth II.* New York: John Wiley & Sons, 1996.

Reese-Jones, Trevor, with Moira Johnston. *The Bodyguard's Story.* New York: Warner Books, 2000.

Rhodes, Margaret. *The Final Curtsey.* London: Umbria, 2011.

Sancton, Thomas, and Scott Macleod. *Death of a Princess: The Investigation.* New York: St. Martin's Press, 1998.

Sarah, the Duchess of York, with Jeff Coplon. *My Story.* New York: Simon & Schuster, 1996.

Seward, Ingrid. *The Queen and Di.* New York: HarperCollins, 2000.

———. *William & Harry: The People's Princes.* London: Carlton Books, 2009.

Simmons, Simone, with Susan Hill. *Diana: The Secret Years.* London: Michael O'Mara, 1998.

———. *The Last Word.* New York: St. Martin's Press, 2005.

Smith, Sally Bedell. *Diana in Search of Herself.* New York: Times Books, 1999.

———. *Elizabeth the Queen: The Life of a Modern Monarch.* New York: Random House, 2012.

———. *Prince Charles: The Passions and Paradoxes of an Improbable Life.* New York: Random House, 2017.

Snell, Kate. *Diana: Her Last Love.* London: Granada Media, 2000.

Spencer, Charles. *The Spencers: A Personal History of an English Family.* New York: St. Martin's Press, 2000.

Spoto, Donald. *The Decline and Fall of the House of Windsor.* New York: Simon & Schuster, 1995.

———. *Diana: The Last Year.* New York: Harmony Books, 1997.

Thornton, Michael. *Royal Feud.* London: Michael Joseph, 1985.

Thornton, Penny. *With Love from Diana.* New York: Pocket Books, 1995.

Vickers, Hugo. *Alice: Princess Andrew of Greece.* New York: St. Martin's, 2002.

———. *Elizabeth the Queen Mother.* London: Arrow, 2006.

Wade, Judy. *The Truth: The Friends of Diana, Princess of Wales, Tell Their Stories.* London: John Blake, 2001.

Warwick, Christopher. *Princess Margaret: A Life of Contrasts.* London: Andre Deutsch, 2000.

Wharfe, Ken, with Robert Jobson. *Diana: Closely Guarded Secret.* London: Michael O'Mara Books, 2003.

Whitaker, James. *Diana v. Charles.* London: Signet, 1993.

Wilson, Christopher. *A Greater Love: Prince Charles's Twenty-Year Affair with Camilla Parker Bowles.* New York: William Morrow, 1994.

———. *The Windsor Knot.* New York: Citadel Press, 2002.

York, Rosemary, ed. *Charles in His Own Words.* London: W. H. Allen, 1981.

Ziegler, Philip. *Queen Elizabeth II.* London: Thames & Hudson, 2010.

INDEX